Teach Yourself®
Microsoft®
Office 97

Teach Yourself®
Microsoft®
Office 97

Brian Underdahl

with Keith Underdahl and Faithe Wempen

IDG Books Worldwide, Inc.
An International Data Group Company

Foster City, CA • Chicago, IL • Indianapolis, IN • New York, NY

Teach Yourself® Microsoft® Office 97

Published by
IDG Books Worldwide, Inc.
An International Data Group Company
919 E. Hillsdale Blvd., Suite 400
Foster City, CA 94404
www.idgbooks.com (IDG Books Worldwide Web site)

Library of Congress Catalog Card Number: 98-88719

ISBN: 0-7645-7511-2

Printed in the United States of America

10 9 8 7 6 5 4 3

1B/RS/QT/ZZ/IN

Distributed in the United States by IDG Books Worldwide, Inc.

Distributed by Macmillan Canada for Canada; by Transworld Publishers Limited in the United Kingdom; by IDG Norge Books for Norway; by IDG Sweden Books for Sweden; by Woodslane Pty. Ltd. for Australia; by Woodslane (NZ) Ltd. for New Zealand; by Addison Wesley Longman Singapore Pte Ltd. for Singapore, Malaysia, Thailand, Indonesia, and Korea; by Norma Comunicaciones S.A. for Colombia; by Intersoft for South Africa; by International Thomson Publishing for Germany, Austria, and Switzerland; by Toppan Company Ltd. for Japan; by Distribuidora Cuspide for Argentina; by Livraria Cultura for Brazil; by Ediciencia S.A. for Ecuador; by Ediciones ZETA S.C.R. Ltda. for Peru; by WS Computer Publishing Corporation, Inc., for the Philippines; by Unalis Corporation for Taiwan; by Contemporanea de Ediciones for Venezuela; by Computer Book & Magazine Store for Puerto Rico; by Express Computer Distributors for the Caribbean and West Indies. Authorized Sales Agent: Anthony Rudkin Associates for the Middle East and North Africa.

For general information on IDG Books Worldwide's books in the U.S., please call our Consumer Customer Service department at 800-762-2974. For reseller information, including discounts and premium sales, please call our Reseller Customer Service department at 800-434-3422.

For information on where to purchase IDG Books Worldwide's books outside the U.S., please contact our International Sales department at 317-596-5530 or fax 317-596-5692.

For consumer information on foreign language translations, please contact our Customer Service department at 800-434-3422, fax 317-596-5692, or e-mail rights@idgbooks.com.

For information on licensing foreign or domestic rights, please phone +1-650-655-3109.

For sales inquiries and special prices for bulk quantities, please contact our Sales department at 650-655-3200 or write to the address above.

For information on using IDG Books Worldwide's books in the classroom or for ordering examination copies, please contact our Educational Sales department at 800-434-2086 or fax 317-596-5499.

For press review copies, author interviews, or other publicity information, please contact our Public Relations department at 650-655-3000 or fax 650-655-3299.

For authorization to photocopy items for corporate, personal, or educational use, please contact Copyright Clearance Center, 222 Rosewood Drive, Danvers, MA 01923, or fax 978-750-4470.

is a trademark under exclusive license to IDG Books Worldwide, Inc., from International Data Group, Inc.

IDG BOOKS WORLDWIDE

ABOUT IDG BOOKS WORLDWIDE

Welcome to the world of IDG Books Worldwide.

IDG Books Worldwide, Inc., is a subsidiary of International Data Group, the world's largest publisher of computer-related information and the leading global provider of information services on information technology. IDG was founded more than 30 years ago by Patrick J. McGovern and now employs more than 9,000 people worldwide. IDG publishes more than 290 computer publications in over 75 countries. More than 90 million people read one or more IDG publications each month.

Launched in 1990, IDG Books Worldwide is today the #1 publisher of best-selling computer books in the United States. We are proud to have received eight awards from the Computer Press Association in recognition of editorial excellence and three from Computer Currents' First Annual Readers' Choice Awards. Our best-selling *...For Dummies*® series has more than 50 million copies in print with translations in 31 languages. IDG Books Worldwide, through a joint venture with IDG's Hi-Tech Beijing, became the first U.S. publisher to publish a computer book in the People's Republic of China. In record time, IDG Books Worldwide has become the first choice for millions of readers around the world who want to learn how to better manage their businesses.

Our mission is simple: Every one of our books is designed to bring extra value and skill-building instructions to the reader. Our books are written by experts who understand and care about our readers. The knowledge base of our editorial staff comes from years of experience in publishing, education, and journalism — experience we use to produce books to carry us into the new millennium. In short, we care about books, so we attract the best people. We devote special attention to details such as audience, interior design, use of icons, and illustrations. And because we use an efficient process of authoring, editing, and desktop publishing our books electronically, we can spend more time ensuring superior content and less time on the technicalities of making books.

You can count on our commitment to deliver high-quality books at competitive prices on topics you want to read about. At IDG Books Worldwide, we continue in the IDG tradition of delivering quality for more than 30 years. You'll find no better book on a subject than one from IDG Books Worldwide.

John Kilcullen
Chairman and CEO
IDG Books Worldwide, Inc.

Steven Berkowitz
President and Publisher
IDG Books Worldwide, Inc.

*Eighth Annual
Computer Press
Awards ≥1992*

*Ninth Annual
Computer Press
Awards ≥1993*

*Tenth Annual
Computer Press
Awards ≥1994*

*Eleventh Annual
Computer Press
Awards ≥1995*

IDG is the world's leading IT media, research and exposition company. Founded in 1964, IDG had 1997 revenues of $2.05 billion and has more than 9,000 employees worldwide. IDG offers the widest range of media options that reach IT buyers in 75 countries representing 95% of worldwide IT spending. IDG's diverse product and services portfolio spans six key areas including print publishing, online publishing, expositions and conferences, market research, education and training, and global marketing services. More than 90 million people read one or more of IDG's 290 magazines and newspapers, including IDG's leading global brands — Computerworld, PC World, Network World, Macworld and the Channel World family of publications. IDG Books Worldwide is one of the fastest-growing computer book publishers in the world, with more than 700 titles in 36 languages. The "...For Dummies®" series alone has more than 50 million copies in print. IDG offers online users the largest network of technology-specific Web sites around the world through IDG.net (http://www.idg.net), which comprises more than 225 targeted Web sites in 55 countries worldwide. International Data Corporation (IDC) is the world's largest provider of information technology data, analysis and consulting, with research centers in over 41 countries and more than 400 research analysts worldwide. IDG World Expo is a leading producer of more than 168 globally branded conferences and expositions in 35 countries including E3 (Electronic Entertainment Expo), Macworld Expo, ComNet, Windows World Expo, ICE (Internet Commerce Expo), Agenda, DEMO, and Spotlight. IDG's training subsidiary, ExecuTrain, is the world's largest computer training company, with more than 230 locations worldwide and 785 training courses. IDG Marketing Services helps industry-leading IT companies build international brand recognition by developing global integrated marketing programs via IDG's print, online and exposition products worldwide. Further information about the company can be found at www.idg.com. 1/24/99

Credits

Acquisitions Editor
Andy Cummings

Development Editors
Ellen Dendy
Valerie Perry

Technical Editor
Edward Hanley

Copy Editor
Zoe Brymer

Associate Project Coordinator
Tom Missler

Book Designers
Daniel Ziegler Design
Cátálin Dulfu
Kurt Krames

Layout and Graphics
Lou Boudreau
Angie Hunckler
Brent Savage
Janet Seib
Kate Snell

Proofreaders
Kelli Botta
Nancy Price
Rebecca Senninger
Ethel M. Winslow
Janet M. Withers

Indexer
York Graphical Services, Inc.

About the Authors

Brian Underdahl has authored over 30 computer-related titles on a broad range of topics, including Windows 95, Microsoft Office, and the Internet. His recent efforts include *Presenting Windows 98 One Step at a Time*, *Windows 98 One Step at a Time*, *Internet Bible*, and *Small Business Computing For Dummies* for IDG Books Worldwide.

Keith Underdahl is an author and expert on electronic publishing, specializing in the publication of books on CD-ROM for a variety of computer platforms. He has served as author or technical editor on dozens of computer titles from IDG Books Worldwide, on topics ranging from Internet software and Web publishing to PC hardware, word processing, and productivity software. He is also the Pacific Northwest Editor for *Street Bike Magazine*, a motorcycle magazine serving the western United States.

Faithe Wempen, M.A., is the author of over 20 books on hardware and software, including *The Essential Excel 97 Book*, *The Microsoft Office Professional 6-in-1*, *Learn Word 97 in a Weekend*, and *The 10 Minute Guide to PowerPoint*. She is also A+ Certified and operates Your Computer Friend, an Indianapolis-based computer training and troubleshooting business.

Welcome to
Teach Yourself

Welcome to Teach Yourself, a series read and trusted by millions for nearly a decade. Although you may have seen the Teach Yourself name on other books, ours is the original. In addition, no Teach Yourself series has ever delivered more on the promise of its name than this series. That's because IDG Books Worldwide recently transformed Teach Yourself into a new cutting-edge format that gives you all the information you need to learn quickly and easily.

Readers told us that they want to learn by *doing* and that they want to learn as much as they can in as short a time as possible. We listened to you and believe that our new task-by-task format and suite of learning tools deliver the book you need to successfully teach yourself any technology topic. Features such as our Personal Workbook, which helps you practice and reinforce the skills you've just learned, ensure that you get full value out of the time you invest in your learning. Handy cross-references to related topics and online sites broaden your knowledge and give you control over the kind of information you want, when you want it.

More Answers . . .

In designing the latest incarnation of this series, we started with the premise that people like you, who are beginning to intermediate computer users, want to take control of their own learning. To do this, you need the proper tools to help you answer questions so you can solve problems now.

In designing a series of books that provide such tools, we have created a unique and concise visual format. The added bonus: Teach Yourself books actually pack more information into their pages than other books written on the same subjects. Skill for skill, you typically get much more information in a Teach Yourself book. In fact, on average, Teach Yourself books cover twice as many skills as other computer books — as many as 125 skills per book — so they're more likely to address your specific needs.

...In Less Time

We know you don't want to spend twice the time to get all this great information, so we provide lots of time-saving features:

- ▶ A modular task-by-task organization of information: Any task you want to perform is easy to find and includes simple-to-follow steps.
- ▶ A larger than standard size makes the book easy to read and convenient to use at a computer workstation. The large format also enables us to include many more illustrations — 500 screen illustrations show you how to get everything done!
- ▶ A Personal Workbook at the end of each chapter reinforces learning with extra practice, real-world applications for your learning, and questions and answers to test your knowledge.
- ▶ Cross-references appearing at the bottom of each task page refer you to related information, providing a path through the book for learning particular aspects of the software thoroughly.

- ▶ A Find It Online feature offers valuable ideas on where to go on the Internet to get more information or to download useful files.
- ▶ Take Note sidebars provide added-value information from our expert authors for more in-depth learning.
- ▶ An attractive, consistent organization of information helps you quickly find and learn the skills you need.

These Teach Yourself features are designed to help you learn the essential skills about a technology in the least amount of time, with the most benefit. We've placed these features consistently throughout the book, so you quickly learn where to go to find just the information you need — whether you work through the book from cover to cover or use it later to solve a new problem.

You will find a Teach Yourself book on almost any technology subject — from the Internet to Windows to Microsoft Office. Take control of your learning today, with IDG Books Worldwide's Teach Yourself series.

Teach Yourself
More Answers in Less Time

Go to this area if you want special tips, cautions, and notes that provide added insight into the current task.

Search through the task headings to find the topic you want right away. To learn a new skill, search the Contents, chapter opener, or the extensive index to find what you need. Then find — at a glance — the clear task heading that matches it.

Creating Reports

You may be both surprised and pleased to learn that creating Access reports is quite similar to creating Access forms. If you consider that both forms and reports are alternative methods of viewing database information, it's easier to understand how the two tasks might be similar.

In spite of the fact that creating forms and creating reports are similar tasks, there are some important differences between forms and reports. It is most likely that you will create forms for viewing on your screen, and lay them out with data entry as a top priority. Reports, on the other hand, work well if you intend to produce printed copies, laying them out with data analysis as the priority. These differences aside, what you've learned about forms will help you learn about reports.

When you're designing a report, it's good to think about the purpose of your report. If you want a short report that provides basic information, there's probably no reason to include all of the fields in the database. Just create a short summary report that includes only the necessary information. Not only will you use less paper, your short report will be much easier to use because you won't have to wade through information you don't need.

As you add fields to your new report, you can greatly improve the appearance by using the Format ⇨ Align options just as you did when you created a new form. Nothing spoils the appearance of

a report more than fields that don't line up — especially fields that are in the same row. To select several fields and field labels at the same time, drag a selection box across all of them using the mouse. Once you've selected two or more fields you can choose the alignment options that look the best for your report. Be careful not to select fields that are in different rows when you specify vertical alignment options, or in different columns when you specify horizontal alignment options. If you make a mistake, select Edit⇨Undo immediately to return the objects to their previous positions.

Continued

Learn the concepts behind the task at hand and, more important, learn how the task is relevant in the real world. Time-saving suggestions and advice show you how to make the most of each skill.

TAKE NOTE

▶ **USE LESS PAPER**

When you're designing a report, remember that each record uses the amount of space you've allocated in the detail area of the report. To reduce wasted paper, keep the fields near the top of the detail area, and drag the separator between the detail and page footer areas up to reduce the size of the detail area.

▶ **USE THE RIGHT ORIENTATION**

If you need to include quite a bit of information about each record, you may want to consider using landscape rather than portrait orientation. Select File ⇨ Page Setup and click the Page tab to select the page orientation.

After you learn the task at hand, you may have more questions, or you may want to read about other tasks related to that topic. Use the cross-references to find different tasks to make your learning more efficient.

CROSS-REFERENCE	FIND IT ONLINE
See "Sorting Reports" later in this chapter.	For a complete listing of Access reports and examples of their uses, check out the Total Access SourceBook Procedure Reference at http://www.fmsinc.com.

374

Use the Find It Online element to locate Internet resources that provide more background, take you on interesting side trips, and offer additional tools for mastering and using the skills you need. (Occasionally you'll find a handy shortcut here.)

WELCOME TO TEACH YOURSELF

The current chapter name and number appear in the top right-hand corner of every task page, so you always know exactly where you are in the book.

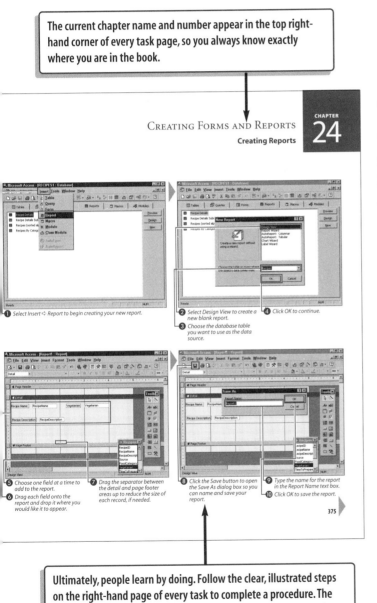

CREATING FORMS AND REPORTS

Creating Reports

CHAPTER **24**

① Select Insert ⬩ Report to begin creating your new report.

② Select Design View to create a new blank report.

③ Choose the database table you want to use as the data source.

④ Click OK to continue.

⑤ Choose one field at a time to add to the report.

⑥ Drag each field onto the report and drop it where you would like it to appear.

⑦ Drag the separator between the detail and page footer areas up to reduce the size of each record, if needed.

⑧ Click the Save button to open the Save As dialog box so you can name and save your report.

⑨ Type the name for the report in the Report Name text box.

⑩ Click OK to save the report.

375

Ultimately, people learn by doing. Follow the clear, illustrated steps on the right-hand page of every task to complete a procedure. The detailed callouts for each step show you exactly where to go and what to do to complete the task.

Who This Book Is For

This book is written for you, a beginning to intermediate PC user who isn't afraid to take charge of his or her own learning experience. You don't want a lot of technical jargon; you *do* want to learn as much about PC technology as you can in a limited amount of time. You need a book that is straightforward, easy to follow, and logically organized, so you can find answers to your questions easily. And you appreciate simple-to-use tools such as handy cross-references and visual step-by-step procedures that help you make the most of your learning. We have created the unique Teach Yourself format specifically to meet your needs.

Personal Workbook

It's a well-known fact that much of what we learn is lost soon after we learn it if we don't reinforce our newly acquired skills with practice and repetition. That's why each Teach Yourself chapter ends with your own Personal Workbook. Here's where you can get extra practice, test your knowledge, and discover ideas for using what you've learned in the real world. There's even a visual quiz to help you remember your way around the topic's software environment.

Feedback

Please let us know what you think about this book, and whether you have any suggestions for improvements. You can send questions and comments to the Teach Yourself editors on the IDG Books Worldwide Web site at **www.idgbooks.com**.

Personal Workbook

Q&A

❶ How is the view of your data different in a form than in a table?

❷ Is it possible for a form to show multiple records?

❸ What important step is necessary before Access will show you a list of fields you can use on a form?

❹ How many of a table's fields must you include on a form?

❺ What can you do if your report won't fit the width of your paper?

❻ What happens if you don't specify a sort order for your reports?

❼ What happens if you specify a sort on a field where some records are blank?

❽ What property do you have to set to prevent a record from starting on one page and finishing on the next?

ANSWERS: PAGE 41

382

After working through the tasks in each chapter, you can test your progress and reinforce your learning by answering the questions in the Q&A section. Then check your answers in the Personal Workbook Answers appendix at the back of the book.

Welcome to Teach Yourself

Another practical way to reinforce your skills is to do additional exercises on the same skills you just learned without the benefit of the chapter's visual steps. If you struggle with any of these exercises, it's a good idea to refer to the chapter's tasks to be sure you've mastered them.

CREATING FORMS AND REPORTS

Creating Reports

CHAPTER
24

Read the list of Real-World Applications to get ideas on how you can use the skills you've just learned in your everyday life. Understanding a process can be simple; knowing how to use that process to make you more productive is the key to successful learning.

EXTRA PRACTICE

❶ Create a new form for the recipes database that is based on the recipe ingredients table.

❷ Create a new report based on the recipe ingredients table.

❸ Sort your new report using the IngredientID field.

❹ Add a report title to the new report.

❺ Add page numbers to the bottom of each page of the report.

❻ Add the date to the bottom of the last page of the report.

REAL-WORLD APPLICATIONS

✔ If you volunteer to maintain the membership database for an organization, you might need to prepare a form to make it easy to sign in the members at an annual dinner meeting.

✔ If you become the organization's treasurer, you might need to produce a report that shows when each club member's dues are due.

✔ If you are asked to produce a report on your company's sales, you might need to be able to sort the report in several different ways to please each of the company directors.

Visual Quiz

What is the purpose of the dialog box titled Toolbox? How can you display this dialog box? What do you need to do to make the associated report area appear in the design window?

_____

_____

_____

_____

383

Take the Visual Quiz to see how well you're learning your way around the technology. Learning about computers is often as much about how to find a button or menu as it is about memorizing definitions. Our Visual Quiz helps you find your way.

Acknowledgments

I have many people to thank for all of the help they provided with this project. Among them are: Andy Cummings, acquisitions editor, for providing yet another great opportunity as well as support. Ellen Dendy and Valerie Perry, development editors, for keeping this project on course and doing a great editing job. Faithe Wempen and Keith Underdahl, authors, for helping me get this book written on time and for adding expertise that made this an even better book. Ed Hanley, technical editor, for ensuring technical accuracy. Zoe Brymer for her detail to copy edit, and finally Tom Missler, project coordinator, for ushering the book through the production cycle.

Contents

CONTENTS

CONTENTS

CONTENTS

PART

I

Learning Common Office Tasks

More than just a single program, Office 97 is actually a *suite* of software. Its programs enable you to perform the most common computing tasks. Using Office 97 programs you can communicate with others, type memos, chart profits, keep records, plan your day, and even present information to a group.

Word is probably the most versatile program that comes with Office 97. It's a word processor that lets you type letters and other printed documents. You can even use Word to publish a Web page on the Internet. Office 97 also includes Excel, a spreadsheet program that helps you keep track of important numbers and data. Excel can be used as a simple expense ledger, or it can perform complicated calculations and graph data.

Another useful tool that comes with the Standard Edition of Office 97 is PowerPoint. PowerPoint helps you prepare presentations for meetings, forums, and other gatherings where professionalism is paramount. Outlook, another Office program, serves as a communication center, calendar, address book, and more. Finally, Access serves as a database where you can keep track of important records and information.

The chapters in Part I of this book help you get started with Office 97 programs, and introduce you to some basic concepts that are common to every Office program. Understanding these basic skills will get you started on the right track and improve the quality of your work.

CHAPTER 1

Understanding Office 97 Basics

Once upon a time, using a computer involved a great deal of effort and expertise on the part of the user. Even a task as simple as starting a new program required complicated and often confusing text based commands, "switches," and various other aggravations.

Since then things have got a lot easier. The Graphical User Interface (GUI) arranges your computer's resources graphically on the screen, in a way that is simple to understand and intuitive to use. You can open programs and perform tasks by simply moving a mouse pointer and clicking the items you want.

Windows is one such interface. Programs that run in Windows — such as Office 97 — open up in virtual windows on your screen (called the "desktop"), and each window contains some standard controls. You can also run two or more programs simultaneously, because each time you launch a program it opens in its own individual window. In this book we assume that you are already familiar with the most basic elements of the interface for whichever version of Windows you are using.

You can open Office 97 applications in windows on your desktop. Within these windows are menus and other controls that enable you to perform the many tasks that are described in this book. Programs that come with Office 97 have a lot in common with other Windows applications, but they also have some special elements of their own. Some of the most basic tasks such as opening and closing programs, using menus and toolbars, or changing the view, are performed the same way no matter which Office application you happen to be using. This helps you familiarize yourself with the applications without having to relearn the basic techniques every time you start using a different Office program.

This chapter describes how to perform some of these basics. Most of the tasks described in this book require you to do one or more of the things listed above, so take this opportunity to get familiar with all the subtle nuances of the Office 97 interface. Once you've mastered the basics, you can use some of these techniques to tailor Office 97 programs to your own specific needs and preferences.

Opening and Closing Programs

It goes without saying that the first thing you need to do to complete most of the tasks described in *Teach Yourself Office 97* is open a program. For instance, if you plan to type a memo using Word, you must first open the Word program before you can begin typing. Likewise, if you want to copy some text from that memo into an e-mail message in Outlook, you need to launch the Outlook program before doing so.

In the interest of accommodating a wide variety of needs and wants, Office 97 programs can be opened using a number of different methods. Back in the days before Windows, opening a program like Word involved typing an executable filename at a DOS prompt, but today it is much simpler thanks to the Windows interface.

Inevitably, the time will come for you to close your program. Just as with opening a program, Office 97 programs can be shut down in a variety of ways. Usually, when you choose to close a program you will be prompted to save your work first. Follow the onscreen commands to save your document to ensure that all those hours of work are not wasted.

The first two figures on the facing page show the most common methods used to open programs. The last two figures show two different methods for closing a program.

Spend some time experimenting with each method for opening and closing a program. You may discover that you really like using the Windows Start menu, for instance, or you may prefer using shortcuts on the desktop. Whichever one you use will depend entirely on your preferences and the situation you find yourself in at the time.

TAKE NOTE

OPENING DOCUMENTS

If you are going to edit a document that you created earlier, you may not need to go to the trouble of opening the Office 97 program first. Simply locate the file using My Computer or Windows Explorer and click the document icon. The correct program should open automatically.

CLOSE UNNEEDED PROGRAMS

Although Windows makes it possible to have multiple programs open simultaneously, it's a good idea to close programs you don't plan to use for a while. This will free up your computer's memory so that the programs you *do* need run more efficiently.

HOW MANY CLICKS?

In the past the technique for opening shortcuts on the desktop was to double-click the icon. However, if you have Windows 98 and the icon names are underlined, all you need to do is click once on the icon.

CROSS-REFERENCE
See "Opening and Closing Office Files" in Chapter 3 for more information on opening and closing files within programs.

FIND IT ONLINE
Check out the University of Georgia "How to" Word page: **http://www.uga.edu/~ucns/helpdesk/ information/howto/Windows**.

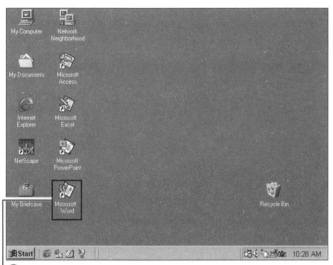

1 *Single- or double-click a shortcut icon on your desktop to open a program.*

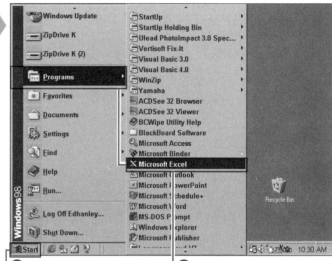

2 *Click the Windows Start button to open the Start menu.*

3 *Click Programs and select the program you want to open.*

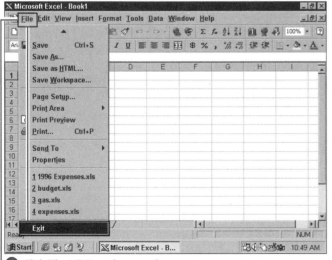

4 *Click File ➪ Exit on the menu bar.*

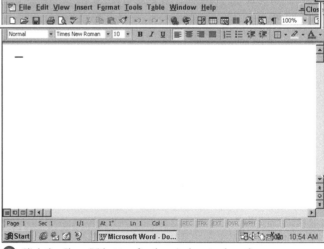

5 *Click the Close (X) button for the window to close the program.*

Using the Menus

The programs that come with Office 97 are powerful tools that can help you get the job done to your satisfaction. The power of each program comes from the many special features that are available. For instance, Word contains tools to help you improve your spelling, create a table, insert graphics, change the way your text looks, and much more.

Other Office programs such as Excel contain very different tools to accomplish the tasks they were designed for. Most Excel features focus on manipulating spreadsheets, crafting formulas, and graphing data, rather than text editing. Of course, Excel shares a few similarities with Word, Access, and Outlook, primarily when performing the most basic functions such as opening or saving a file. But it contains many unique features that can only be accessed from within the program itself.

So the features are there, but *where* exactly? Most program functions reside in menus. Menus open up in various places in Office 97 programs, and each one provides a list of tools and functions for you to choose from. In this respect, it is similar to a menu you might see in a restaurant with many different choices on it. And just like being in a restaurant, once you've made your choice the menu disappears.

Menus appear in a variety of locations. All Office 97 programs have a Menu bar at the top of their respective windows to provide quick access to that program's most important functions. Some of these menus contain submenus, indicated by an arrow next to the item. You may also encounter drop-down menus that enable you to pick an item from a list, such as a font for your text. Finally, in the case of the menu bar at the top of the window, you may have the freedom to move menus around to suit your own needs. See the section titled "Using the Toolbars" later in this chapter to learn more.

The four figures on the facing page demonstrate how to access several different menus. Each one contains a different kind of menu that you are likely to encounter while using Office 97 programs. Simply click an item to select it from the menu.

TAKE NOTE

BUTTONS IN MENUS

Some menu items in Office 97 applications have buttons next to them that resemble toolbar buttons. These buttons help your eyes pick out certain items more quickly.

SOME MENUS LEAD TO DIALOG BOXES

Many menu items lead to dialog boxes rather than actually doing something themselves. These items have an ellipsis (...) after them to denote this.

OOPS, WRONG MENU...

If you don't like any of the choices in a menu you just opened, click a blank space outside of the menu or press Esc to close it.

CROSS-REFERENCE

See "Using Dialog Boxes" later in this chapter for more on what to do when you see one.

FIND IT ONLINE

Get help with Word menus and toolbars at Penn State's tutorial site: **http://www.psu.edu/dept/cac/ets/ archive/projects.1997/modules/Word.**

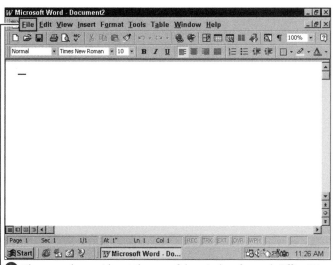

① *The menu bar resides at the top of the window for each Office 97 program. Click the menu's name to open it.*

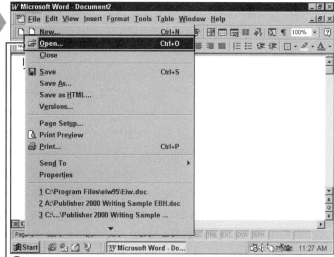

② *Click this item to open a dialog box.*

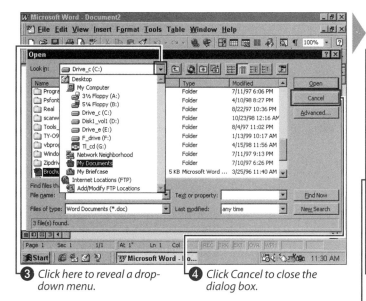

③ *Click here to reveal a drop-down menu.*

④ *Click Cancel to close the dialog box.*

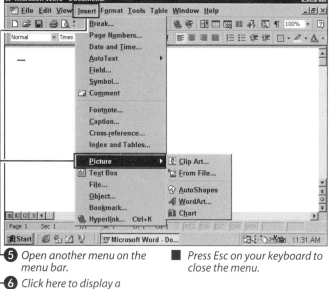

⑤ *Open another menu on the menu bar.*

⑥ *Click here to display a submenu.*

■ *Press Esc on your keyboard to close the menu.*

Using Context Menus

In the previous task, you learned how to use the many different kinds of menus that accompany Office 97 programs. Most program features and tools can be accessed through these menus, no matter which program you are in or what you are working on.

In addition to these basic menus, Office 97 applications also utilize some handy items called *context menus*. Clicking an item with the right mouse button accesses a context menu. No matter where you are in any program you can right-click some text, data, or even blank space in the window to bring up a context menu. Context menus typically pop up to the right of the item you clicked.

Every context menu is different. As with other menus — such as those that pop down from the menu bar — context menus can be almost any size. But what makes the context menu different is that it only contains menu commands that apply specifically to whatever item the pointer was pointing at when you clicked the right mouse button. Context menus are specifically tailored to each individual circumstance, hence the name.

Context menus offer a great way to speed up many repetitive tasks. For instance, if you find that you need to change the font used in various parts of a Word document, you can highlight a block of text with the mouse and right-click it. One of the options in the context menu opens the Font dialog box, which may be a lot quicker than finding it in the menu bar.

More common commands such as Cut, Copy, and Paste can also be found in many context menus. These commands are also available only a short distance away on the program's toolbar, so for just one occurrence it may not seem as if the context menu is saving you very much time. However, if you are doing numerous Cut-and-Paste or Copy-and-Paste tasks you may find that those few seconds saved here and there turn into many minutes in the long run. Furthermore, context menus may reduce the amount of mouse movement you are required to do, helping to reduce painful hand and wrist injuries that plague many computer users.

The figures on the following page show several context menus being used in most Office 97 programs. Each one is different, so you should practice on your own to become familiar with context menus that help you work more efficiently.

> **TAKE NOTE**
>
> ### CONTEXT MENUS IN OTHER PROGRAMS
>
> Office 97 programs aren't the only programs that use context menus. In fact, you can usually pop open a context menu almost anywhere within the Windows environment. Context menus in other programs may have some of the same options as those in Office 97, but without the visual buttons next to some items.

CROSS-REFERENCE

Learn how to select areas of text in "Selecting Words and Paragraphs" in Chapter 5.

FIND IT ONLINE

Learn to use Word shortcut keys at: http://www.als.uiuc.edu/infotechaccess/win-sc-Word.

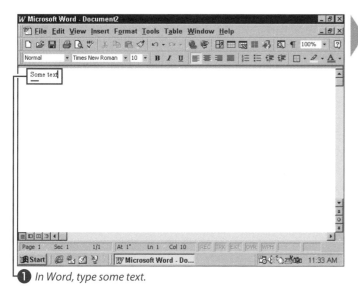

① In Word, type some text.

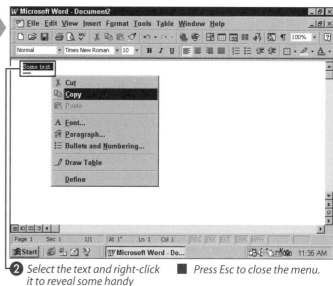

② Select the text and right-click it to reveal some handy options.

■ Press Esc to close the menu.

③ Right-click a toolbar to display this list of view options.

④ Click an item in the list to display that toolbar.

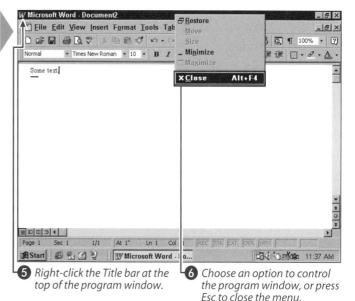

⑤ Right-click the Title bar at the top of the program window.

⑥ Choose an option to control the program window, or press Esc to close the menu.

Using the Toolbars

As we have already seen, you can access virtually all features of the Office 97 applications via the numerous menus offered within these programs. Menus simplify the use of these programs by enabling you to use the mouse to navigate through an intuitive series of choices to complete various tasks.

In addition to menus, Office 97 applications offer toolbars to further simplify the use of these programs. A *toolbar* is a bar that resides somewhere in a program's window and contains buttons to complete certain tasks. To perform a function, just click a button with the mouse pointer. This can often speed things up by eliminating the need to first open a menu and then make a choice.

All Office 97 programs already have at least one toolbar that resides near the top of the window, directly under the menu bar. Some buttons are common to all programs, while others perform more specialized tasks. In addition to the basic toolbars that each program provides, there are usually other toolbars that you can display if you wish. Furthermore, you can often customize toolbars and add your own buttons to new toolbars. This may be useful if you find yourself regularly using a program feature that was too obscure to be included on any of the default toolbars. You can also create toolbar buttons to activate such things as Word macros that you might have created. The possibilities are limitless, but be careful

not to take up all your workspace with gimmicky toolbars and buttons!

Besides being able to add and customize toolbars and buttons, you can also move toolbars to better fit your window. You can even drag toolbars away from the top of the window so that they float free around your desktop. Free-floating toolbars will stay on top of any work you might be performing in the program window.

The first figure on the facing page demonstrates where toolbars are normally located. The second and third figures refer to the Customize toolbar dialog box where you can choose which toolbars to display. The last figure shows how to add a button to a toolbar.

TAKE NOTE

▶ WHAT DOES THAT BUTTON DO?

If you're unsure about a button's purpose, hold the mouse pointer over it but don't click it. After about one second a small help bubble appears next to the pointer that tells you what that button is for.

▶ AVOID TOO MANY TOOLBARS

Although toolbars can be quite handy, take a look at your programs from time to time and get rid of toolbars or buttons you never use. This cleans up the program window and gives you more room for your work.

CROSS-REFERENCE

See "Using the Menus" earlier in this chapter to learn more about how the menu bar works.

FIND IT ONLINE

Interested in a cool custom toolbar for Windows? Check out Toolbar Pro at **http://www.toolbar.com/**.

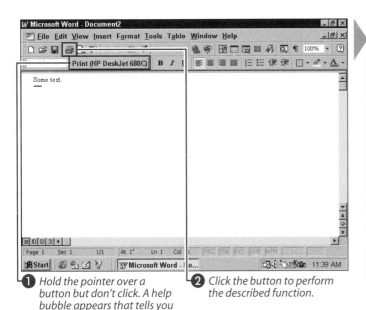

① *Hold the pointer over a button but don't click. A help bubble appears that tells you what the button is for.*

② *Click the button to perform the described function.*

③ *Choose View ⇨ Toolbars ⇨ Customize to open the Customize dialog box.*

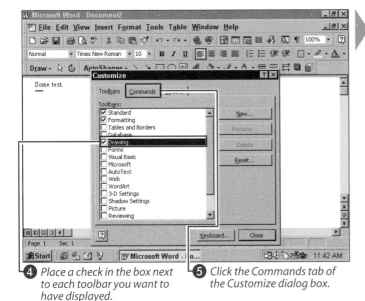

④ *Place a check in the box next to each toolbar you want to have displayed.*

⑤ *Click the Commands tab of the Customize dialog box.*

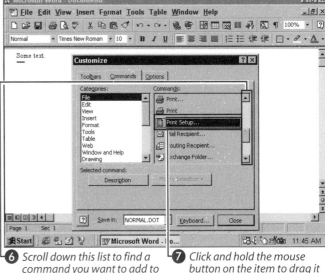

⑥ *Scroll down this list to find a command you want to add to the toolbar.*

⑦ *Click and hold the mouse button on the item to drag it to a toolbar. Release it at the location for the new button.*

13

Using Dialog Boxes

As described in the last three tasks, you use menus and toolbar buttons to perform most operations in Office 97 programs. You make selections from a menu or click a button to accomplish both simple and more complex tasks through the course of your work.

For many tasks, your selection leads to a dialog box where you can make additional choices. As mentioned earlier, menu items that lead to dialog boxes have an ellipsis (...) after them to indicate this. Clicking one of these menu items opens a dialog box where you can adjust settings, manipulate data, or perform many other tasks.

Dialog boxes exist for both simple and complex tasks. For instance, when you choose to open a document or save a file, a dialog box that is virtually identical in all Windows-based applications appears. Other dialog boxes are more complex. If you want to edit entries in your Contacts list in Outlook, a relatively large dialog box that helps you do that appears. Editing data in dialog boxes may involve typing text into text boxes, selecting options with check-boxes or radio buttons, or choosing something from a drop-down menu.

Another type of box called a *message box* may warn you of a problem or provide a simple reminder. Often you won't have any choice except to click OK after reading a warning in one of these small boxes. In this case, Office 97 programs use message boxes just to get your attention rather than to perform any real task.

Dialog boxes share some common controls. The first figure on the facing page shows how to open one of the most common dialog boxes in Office 97 applications. The second and third figures describe some of the options you can select in a dialog box. The last figure shows a typical message box.

TAKE NOTE

▶ CHANGING YOUR MIND

You may decide that you don't want to keep some or all of the changes you make in a dialog box. In this case, click Cancel to close the dialog box without incorporating any of the choices you made.

▶ COPY DATA INTO DIALOG BOXES

You may find that it is easier to copy certain types of data into dialog boxes, rather than type it in. For instance, you can copy an e-mail address from an e-mail message into your Outlook Contacts list to ensure that a simple typo doesn't cause problems later on.

▶ SEEK HELP

Help is available for most items in a dialog box. Just right-click an item you are curious about and choose "What's This?" from the small shortcut menu that appears.

CROSS-REFERENCE

See "Using the Office Help System" in Chapter 2 to learn more about getting help on items in dialog boxes.

FIND IT ONLINE

For Word processing help: **http://duff-5. ucs.ualberta.ca/HELP/wordpro**.

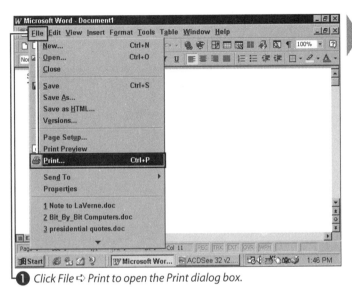

1 Click File ➪ Print to open the Print dialog box.

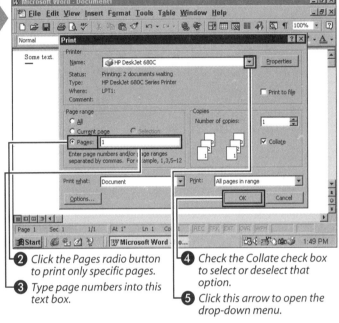

2 Click the Pages radio button to print only specific pages.

3 Type page numbers into this text box.

4 Check the Collate check box to select or deselect that option.

5 Click this arrow to open the drop-down menu.

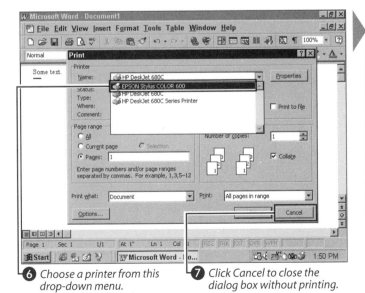

6 Choose a printer from this drop-down menu.

7 Click Cancel to close the dialog box without printing.

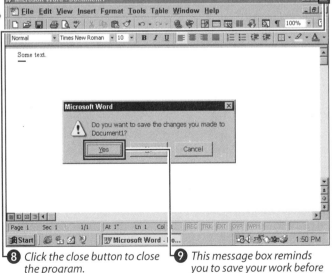

8 Click the close button to close the program.

9 This message box reminds you to save your work before closing the program. Choose Yes to save before quitting.

Controlling the View

When you first install Office 97 programs, they have some default settings that cause them to look a certain way. Fortunately, you have a number of options to tailor the way these programs look and feel to better suit your needs. These programs are delivered in a sort of "one size fits all" format, but of course this is never the case.

The options you have for changing the view depend on which program you are using at the time. Perhaps the most basic things you will want to change are the toolbars. All applications that come with Office 97 have toolbars, and you can change and manipulate how and where they are displayed. There are usually many additional toolbars that can be displayed, or you can hide the toolbars altogether.

Of course, you have many other view options that can be changed. Every Office 97 application has a View menu on the menu bar, and this menu contains most of the options you need. In addition to displaying information about showing and hiding some toolbars, you should have some options to change the way your documents are displayed. Some programs give you the option of changing the view so that the onscreen document more closely resembles what the actual printed product will look like. Other options enable you to view different pieces of document information. Programs that have multiple windows onscreen — such as Outlook — also let you hide windows that you don't need to see.

The figures on the facing page demonstrate how to use some of the view options in Word. The first two figures show some of the options that change which toolbars and other onscreen elements are displayed. The last two figures demonstrate how to change the view of your actual document. Although these tasks apply specifically to Word, most other Office 97 programs contain similar options. Just look in the View menu of whichever program you are using and see what changes are available.

TAKE NOTE

SEE MORE OF YOUR WORK IN EXCEL

One of the view options available in Excel is the Full Screen option. This option hides all of the toolbars, as well as the Windows taskbar. This enables you to see more of your spreadsheet, and can be especially useful if you are using Excel as part of a presentation.

REDUCE ONSCREEN CLUTTER

It can be easy to get carried away with manipulating the way your programs look onscreen, but don't forget to save room for your actual work. A program window cluttered by too many toolbars and whatnot can be a strain on the eyes, and may not let enough of your documents be shown onscreen at any given time.

CROSS-REFERENCE
Learn more about how menus work in the section called "Using the Menus" earlier in this chapter.

FIND IT ONLINE
Download Word plug-ins and other shareware from DaveCentral at **http://www.davecentral.com/**.

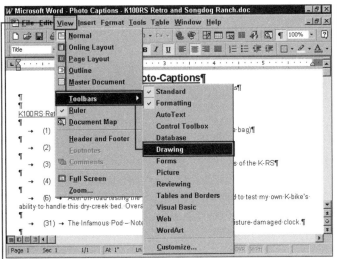

1 In Word, click View ➪ Toolbars ➪ Drawing to display the Drawing toolbar.

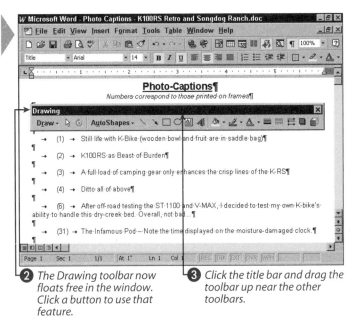

2 The Drawing toolbar now floats free in the window. Click a button to use that feature.

3 Click the title bar and drag the toolbar up near the other toolbars.

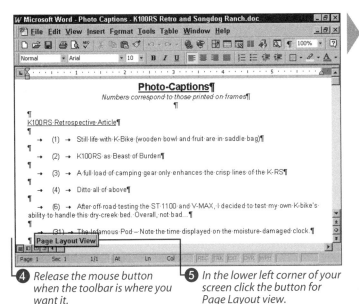

4 Release the mouse button when the toolbar is where you want it.

5 In the lower left corner of your screen click the button for Page Layout view.

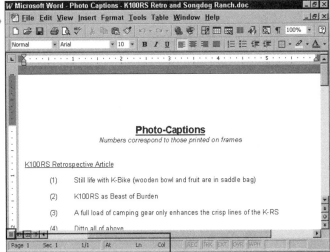

■ The document is displayed in Page Layout view. Your document will look like this when it is actually printed.

6 Click the Normal view button to return to the Normal view.

Personal Workbook

Q&A

1 What are two different ways to open an Office 97 program?

_____

_____

_____

2 How can you close a program without using the window's close (X) button?

_____

_____

_____

3 What is the quickest way to reject changes you make in a dialog box?

_____

_____

_____

4 What does an ellipses (...) next to a menu item mean?

_____

_____

_____

5 How do you know if a menu item contains a submenu?

_____

_____

_____

6 How do you open a context menu?

_____

_____

7 Which Office 97 programs have toolbars?

_____

_____

8 Where can you find the dialog box that enables you to customize your toolbars?

_____

_____

9 What does the Page Layout view represent?

_____

_____

ANSWERS: PAGE 401

EXTRA PRACTICE

1 Open Word using the Start Menu.

2 Use the View menu to open the Customize Toolbars dialog box.

3 Add the Word Count tool to your toolbar.

4 Use the context menu on the toolbar to display the Control toolbox.

5 Change the document window to Outline view.

6 Set the view in Excel to Full Screen.

7 Right-click an Excel cell to view its content menu.

REAL-WORLD APPLICATIONS

✔ If you frequently need to use drawing objects such as lines and boxes in a word processing document, you may want to add the Drawing toolbar to the top of your screen.

✔ If you receive a lot of important e-mail messages, you may want to create a folder in Outlook where you can save those messages. You can then use context menus to quickly move read messages to that folder for future reference.

✔ Knowing how to open Office 97 programs using both the Windows Start menu and desktop shortcuts is critical. While you may often prefer to use the desktop shortcuts, there will eventually come a time when you will have one program open and need to open another. In this case, the Start menu is usually easier to use.

Visual Quiz

How do you open the program shown here? How do you show the Drawing toolbar as displayed here? How can you display the dialog box needed to make these changes? How can you switch to Page Layout view?

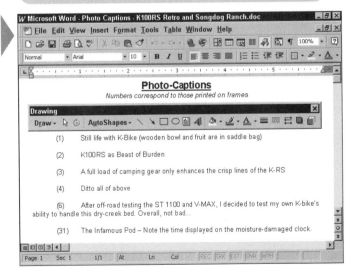

_____

_____

_____

_____

CHAPTER 2

MASTER THESE SKILLS

▶ Using the Office Assistant

▶ Using the Office Wizards

▶ Using the Office Help System

▶ Searching the Help System

▶ Using Online Help Resources

Getting Some Help

Strange though it may seem, no one is born knowing everything. And when it comes to using computer software, many of us feel lost as often as not. Even jaded experts occasionally find themselves struggling for the answer, unable to remember that certain procedure that will help get the job done.

Thankfully, Office 97 programs are ready to offer a helping hand in these times when the answer seems just beyond our grasp. All Office 97 programs have useful help systems that provide solutions to almost every problem you are likely to encounter. Can't remember how to filter your e-mail? What were those steps for selecting a range of cells again? Not to worry; quick solutions are a mouse click away.

Help systems within programs are nothing new. As in many other Windows-based applications, Office 97 programs offer a Help program that provides a searchable index of topics. You can browse through the topics or search for a keyword to find specific instructions to help you complete your task.

In addition to the basic Help program, Office 97 offers a number of other innovative elements to help you get your job done quickly and efficiently. The most obvious one, and probably one of the first things to catch your eye when you first started to use a program, is the Office Assistant. The Office Assistant is the wacky little guy who lives in a small dialog box on your screen and bears more than a passing resemblance to a paper clip. The Office Assistant reviews what you are doing and provides timely advice and tips to help you speed up your work.

There are also tools called wizards. A wizard is basically a glorified dialog box that asks you a series of questions as you begin a new document or task. The questions ask you for some basic information about what you plan to do. Office wizards automatically create a document or perform a task based on the information you provid. Finally, Microsoft provides online help for Office 97 users. If you have Internet access you can use online help to receive up-to-the-minute product news, tips, free software plug-ins, or even technical support.

This chapter describes how to use the many help tools offered by Office 97 programs. Each one can prove helpful in different situations, and the following practice will help you get familiar with each.

Using the Office Assistant

The idea of providing help for software users is nothing new. Perhaps the most basic type of help is that which you get from technical manuals and books such as this. Another basic help tool is the help system which virtually every Windows-based application comes with today. These are useful tools that are always there when you need them.

In addition to books and a help system, Office 97 programs offer another innovative tool called the Office Assistant. The Office Assistant is represented as a cartoon-like paper clip figure that lives in a small dialog box on your screen. From time to time it blinks its eyes, wiggles, makes noises, or unfolds itself just to remind you it's still there.

The Office Assistant differs from other forms of help in that it doesn't wait for you to go looking for help; help comes to you. Whether you ask for it or not, the Office Assistant continually monitors your progress and offers timely advice as you work. You will probably also encounter the Office Assistant every time you open an Office 97 program. By default, the Office Assistant provides a *Tip of the Day* every time you open a program. You can turn this feature off by clicking the Options button in the Office Assistant dialog bubble. Most of the time, the Office Assistant remains discrete but close at hand for you to call on as needed. Furthermore, if you do not use the Office Assistant for several minutes, its window actually gets smaller so that it takes up less of your screen.

Help comes in many different forms from the Office assistant. The first figure on the next page shows a typical Tip of the Day from the Office Assistant that appears when a program is first opened. The second figure shows how to open the Office Assistant if it has been closed, and the last two figures demonstrate ways of using tips and help that the Office Assistant can provide.

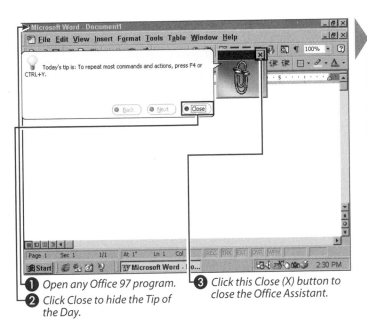

1 Open any Office 97 program.

2 Click Close to hide the Tip of the Day.

3 Click this Close (X) button to close the Office Assistant.

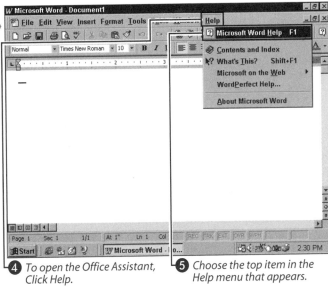

4 To open the Office Assistant, Click Help.

5 Choose the top item in the Help menu that appears.

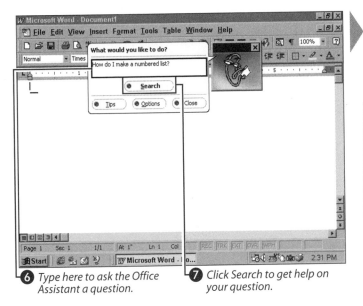

6 Type here to ask the Office Assistant a question.

7 Click Search to get help on your question.

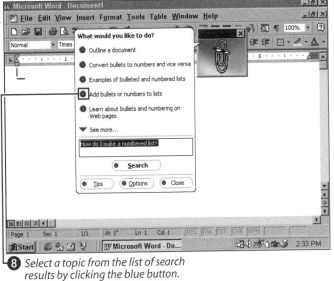

8 Select a topic from the list of search results by clicking the blue button.

Using the Office Wizards

Creating a new document with a certain look and feel can be a complicated task. For instance, suppose you want to create a fax cover sheet in Word. Professionals expect a cover sheet to conform to a certain appearance, and it should contain specific bits of information. Above all, it should be easy to read so that the recipient can glean pertinent information from it quickly.

Creating a good fax cover letter in Word could take a fair amount of time. First you have to figure out exactly which information to include, such as a page count for the fax, phone numbers, addresses, and other contact information. Then there are layout issues, such as where to set margins, graphical elements, and the like. Before you know it, you've just blown thirty minutes on a simple cover letter that the recipient is probably going to look at for five seconds and then throw away. Wouldn't it be nice if there was a way to speed up these monotonous yet crucial tasks?

With Office 97, help is just a mouse click away, so to speak. Most Office programs provide tools called wizards to guide you through otherwise time-consuming and complicated tasks. These wizards offer step-by-step procedures to simplify the creation of new documents without many of the headaches. The wizards ask you simple questions about what you want the document to look like and what information you want it to contain. Wizards take your information

and automatically create a document, preformatted with much of your information already filled in. In the following example, once the wizard has done its work there is little more to do than print it out!

The figures on the facing page demonstrate how to use the Fax Wizard in Word to create exactly what we've been talking about: a fax cover letter. This particular wizard demonstrates how Word makes the task of creating a cover letter like this a matter of only a minute or two, and the finished product is professional-looking as well as attractive.

Continued

TAKE NOTE

▶ MORE THAN TEMPLATES

Although you open wizards the same way you begin a new document using a template, they are not the same. A template offers more of a "no-frills" approach to creating a document, where more manual creation is required on your part.

▶ CUSTOMIZE THE DOCUMENT FURTHER

Although wizards provide an attractive and easy format to use, you may want to make some minor changes to customize the cover letter to your own tastes. Once you have completed the wizard steps the document can be edited just like any other, and you can change anything you want.

CROSS-REFERENCE

Learn how to create a new Word document with a template instead of a wizard in "Getting Started and Entering Text" in Chapter 7.

FIND IT ONLINE

Microsoft offers extra wizards and templates on its Web site. Click Help ⇨ Microsoft on the Web ⇨ Product News.

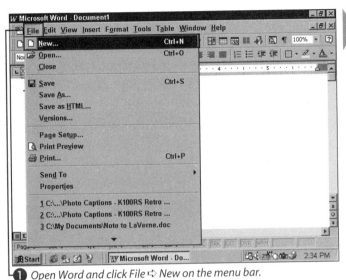

1 Open Word and click File ⇨ New on the menu bar.

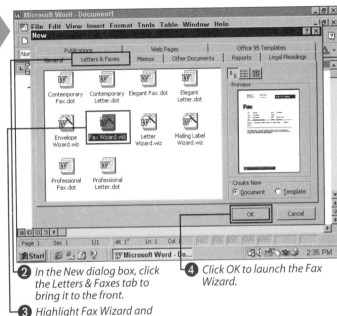

2 In the New dialog box, click the Letters & Faxes tab to bring it to the front.

3 Highlight Fax Wizard and view a preview of the document you will create.

4 Click OK to launch the Fax Wizard.

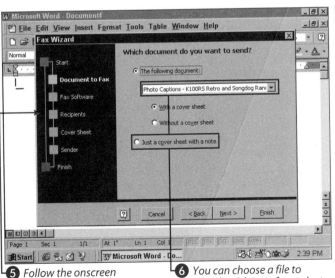

5 Follow the onscreen instructions to enter required data. You are also asked for contact information both for yourself and the recipient.

6 You can choose a file to include with your fax, or just fax a cover sheet with a note on it.

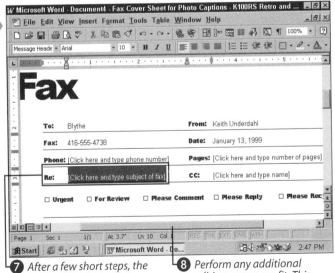

7 After a few short steps, the finished product will appear in Word. Type a subject for the fax here.

8 Perform any additional editing as you see fit. This space allows you to type a note to the recipient.

Using the Office Wizards
Continued

As you saw on the previous page, wizards can be used to create new documents right from the start, eliminating the need to spend a lot of time setting up the document and formatting it. This is especially useful when you are creating the most common types of documents, because in many cases, the people who created the program anticipated your needs.

Office 97 programs provide other wizards to help you complete your work. In some cases, a wizard might help you complete a task within a program; for instance, some of the formula wizards in Excel guide you through complex calculations. The wizards ask you some basic questions to quickly and easily create a formula, and take care of some important steps that you might have otherwise forgotten.

Another one of these "in document" wizards is the Word Letter Wizard demonstrated opposite. The Letter Wizard helps you accomplish one of the most common tasks in business and personal communication, writing a letter. We don't usually think about it, but every time we compose a letter to a friend or colleague we spend a lot of time just setting up the letter in the proper format. People expect a letter to look and feel a certain way, so proper formatting is important. But setting up the letter can take some time. What information should be included? What should that information look like? Where should it be positioned on the page? These are all important questions to ask if you want your letter to look just write, uh, right.

The Word Letter Wizard considers all of this, and creates a letter based on some simple questions that you answer and options you select. It asks you how formal the letter should be, whom the letter is going to, and for any other pertinent information that you might want to include. When it's done, a letter is quickly produced that is ready for you to print and send. The figures on the facing page take you through the steps for creating a letter with the Letter Wizard.

TAKE NOTE

TYPE YOUR TEXT FIRST

The Letter Wizard works within an existing document, which means you can go ahead and type the text that will make up the body of the letter first. That's right; you still have to type the main body of the letter yourself!

FURTHER MODIFICATIONS

Although you may be perfectly satisfied with what the Letter Wizard creates, you may want to change some of the information that the wizard included in the letter. Once the wizard is done and the information has been placed on the page, you can edit, move, or delete it just like any other text.

CROSS-REFERENCE

Learn more about entering text to begin your letter in "Getting Started and Entering Text" in Chapter 7.

FIND IT ONLINE

Find an "alternative" type of letter wizard at Scott Pakin's Automatic Complaint Letter Generator: http://www-csag.cs.uiuc.edu/individual/pakin/complaint.

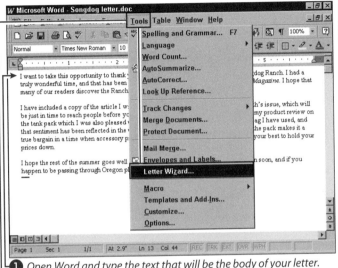

① Open Word and type the text that will be the body of your letter.

② On the menu bar click Tools ⇨ Letter Wizard.

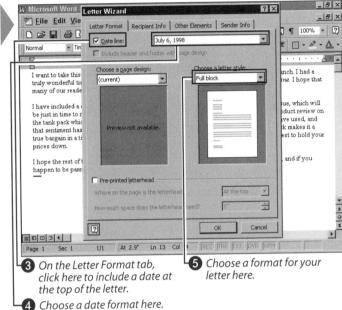

③ On the Letter Format tab, click here to include a date at the top of the letter.

④ Choose a date format here.

⑤ Choose a format for your letter here.

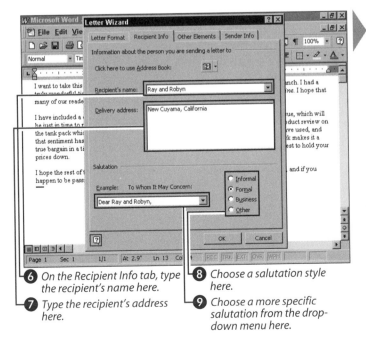

⑥ On the Recipient Info tab, type the recipient's name here.

⑦ Type the recipient's address here.

⑧ Choose a salutation style here.

⑨ Choose a more specific salutation from the drop-down menu here.

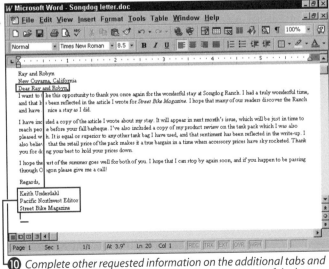

⑩ Complete other requested information on the additional tabs and click OK to finish the Wizard. Review the appearance of the letter.

Using the Office Help System

If you've been following along up to now, you already know that Office 97 offers a number of innovative features to help you complete your work. The Office Assistant serves as a friendly and intuitive sidekick to help you when you need it most, and the Office wizards guide you through otherwise complicated tasks with relative ease.

But as useful as the Office Assistant and wizards are, they still rest on the backbone of the Office Help System. The Office Help System serves as a virtual treasure trove of descriptions, tips, and detailed steps to perform almost any task you can imagine, and probably a few that you can't. Microsoft engineers have spent years perfecting the Office Help system, and there are few questions it can't answer.

You can take advantage of the Office Help System in a number of different ways. If you seek help from the Office Assistant, you ultimately end up linking directly to some topic or list of topics in the Help System. Likewise, if you look for help in one of the wizards or any dialog box, a topic from the Help System should appear.

In addition to these methods, you can also access the Office Help System directly. These will be the times where you have a no-frills question and need a no-frills answer. You can access the Help System easily, and once there, you may find that it is arranged in much the same way as this book.

A Contents list provides an outline of the major topic areas covered by Office Help, and there is also an alphabetical index of all topic areas. The Help System can also be searched, but we cover that in the next task.

The first figure on the facing page shows you how to open the Office Help System from within any Office 97 application. The next figure demonstrates how to use the Contents tab of the Help System, and the third figure uses the Index tab. The last figure shows you how to open and read help topics.

TAKE NOTE

PRINTING A HARD COPY OF HELP

You can print a hard copy of a help topic that you expect to refer back to again in the future. To print the topic, click the Options button near the top of the window and choose Print Topic.

MAKE YOUR OWN HELP NOTES

You may want to make notes for yourself to help you remember certain procedures in the future. Rather than plaster your office wall with Post-It notes, annotate help topics by clicking the Options button in the topic and choosing Annotate. A paperclip will appear next to the topic heading which links to the notes you make.

CROSS-REFERENCE

See the next task in this chapter, "Searching the Help System," to learn how to perform searches in Help.

FIND IT ONLINE

Get more great Office 97 add-ins from Office Toys at http://www.officetoys.com/.

GETTING SOME HELP

Using the Office Help System

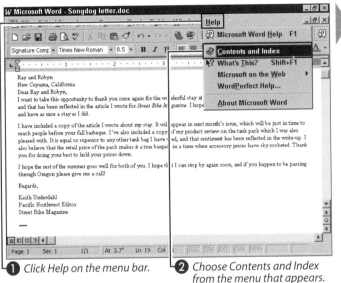

1 Click Help on the menu bar.

2 Choose Contents and Index from the menu that appears.

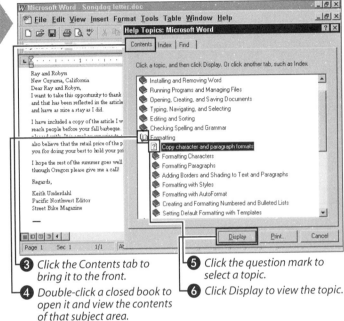

3 Click the Contents tab to bring it to the front.

4 Double-click a closed book to open it and view the contents of that subject area.

5 Click the question mark to select a topic.

6 Click Display to view the topic.

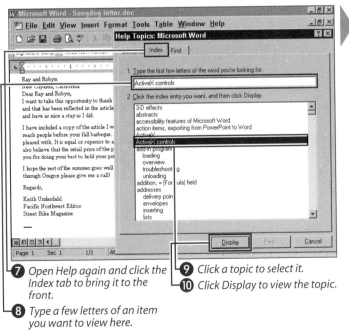

7 Open Help again and click the Index tab to bring it to the front.

8 Type a few letters of an item you want to view here.

9 Click a topic to select it.

10 Click Display to view the topic.

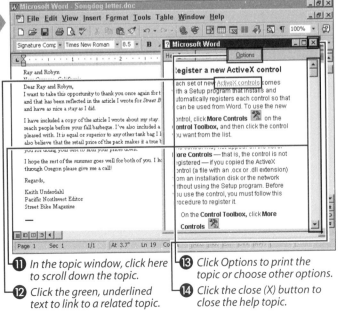

11 In the topic window, click here to scroll down the topic.

12 Click the green, underlined text to link to a related topic.

13 Click Options to print the topic or choose other options.

14 Click the close (X) button to close the help topic.

Searching the Help System

When Microsoft developed the Help System for Office 97, they spent a great deal of time cataloging and organizing topics into what seemed at the time to be a logical order. And for the most part, they did a good job. Most help topics are relatively easy to find using either the Contents or Index tab of the Help System, and tools such as the Office Assistant lead you right to them.

However, there will come a time when you simply can't find an answer to your problem, an answer you know must be there somewhere. Rest assured, it probably is. Inevitably, on a few occasions your mind reading skills will fail, and you will not be able to figure out what category your help topic might be filed under. Don't feel bad; it happens to everyone from time to time. In fact, you may encounter a similar problem when you try to search for something in your phone company's yellow pages: You know you're looking for a record store, but what does the phone company call it?

Fortunately, the Office Help System has something that the yellow pages do not: a search engine. It enables you to search the entire help system using a single word or phrase, meaning you don't have to try guessing what the topic was called by someone else. Search results will be displayed, and you can choose topics from a list.

The Office Help search engine does its job by first building a database of words used in all the help topics. It then searches for any occurrence of the word (or phrase) you type in the Help program's Find tab. So, if you are working in Outlook and need to find information on image attachments to e-mail messages, you could simply search using the word *image*. A list of topics would appear at the bottom of the Help dialog box and you could choose one that fits your needs.

TAKE NOTE

► SETTING UP FIND

The first time you use Find, a Setup Wizard appears. The program needs to create a database of every word in your Help files, a process that takes several minutes. Choose one of the three choices in the text box and click Next to finish the wizard. If you're not sure which option to select, go with the one that says *Recommended*.

► USE THE CONTENTS TAB

If you'd like a lot more information about Office, click the Contents tab. You'll find in-depth details on a variety of topics in using Office — it's a built-in, onscreen manual. Main topics are divided into subtopics which you can print, copy, or bookmark for future reference

CROSS-REFERENCE

You can also perform searches using the Office Assistant. See "Using the Office Assistants" earlier in this chapter.

FIND IT ONLINE

For information and lots of helpful tips see:
http://www.dialspace.dial.
pipex.com/town/avenue/xjs41

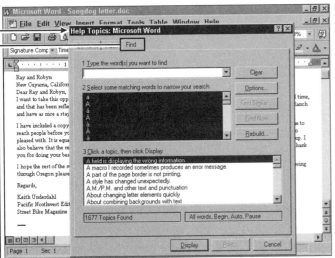

1 Open the Office Help Topics and click the Find tab to bring it to the front.

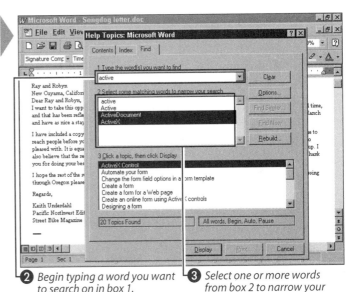

2 Begin typing a word you want to search on in box 1.

3 Select one or more words from box 2 to narrow your search.

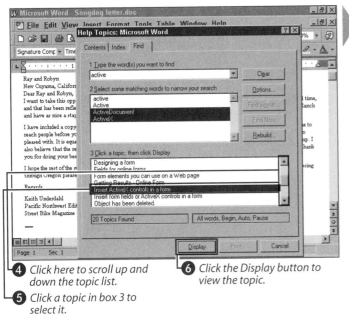

4 Click here to scroll up and down the topic list.

5 Click a topic in box 3 to select it.

6 Click the Display button to view the topic.

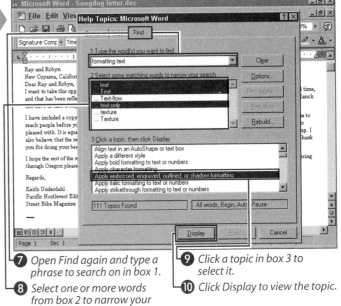

7 Open Find again and type a phrase to search on in box 1.

8 Select one or more words from box 2 to narrow your search.

9 Click a topic in box 3 to select it.

10 Click Display to view the topic.

Using Online Help Resources

In this chapter, you've learned that Office 97 programs have a plethora of help features for you to choose from. Each resource fits a specific need and you may find each one useful at different times and in different applications.

But the resources covered up to this point – the Office Assistant, Office wizards, and Office Help System – have one key limitation. Namely, the information available is limited to what was originally included with the Office 97 programs suite when Microsoft created it. Any tips, tricks, or fixes that Microsoft engineers might have come up with since the software was published, will not be included on the CD that you purchased.

Software development is always an ongoing process and the people who created the Office 97 programs want to be able to offer you the most up-to-date assistance they can. To make this possible, Office 97 incorporates an innovative Online Help system, whereby you can use your Internet connection to get up-to-the-minute help and support directly from Microsoft. All you need is a modem and an account with an Internet Service Provider (ISP) to get online.

When you access online resources for Office 97 programs, you are taken to Microsoft's Web site. Many services are available, including online technical support, a forum for providing Microsoft with user feedback, and general product information. But perhaps the most important resource available to you is the free software add-ins and updates that can be downloaded from the Web site. This software may simply fix or improve the way Office programs perform certain tasks, or they might provide enhancements that change the look and feel of your Office 97 programs.

The figures on the facing page demonstrate how to find and download an important patch program that fixes a bug in Word 97. This particular bug affects the capability of computers using older versions of Word to read documents you created in Word 97. The patch allows you to save files in the proper format so that they can be read on other computers. It is typical of software add-ins developed by Microsoft, in that it is simple to download and takes only a few seconds to install. The first figure on the facing page shows you how to check the Microsoft Product News for all your Office 97 programs. You should do this on a regular basis to ensure that you have the most up-to-date software available.

TAKE NOTE

A NEW LOOK FOR THE OFFICE ASSISTANT

If you're tired of the paper clip Office Assistant, Microsoft has other Office Assistants that you can download, such as a dolphin, puppies, robots, and more. Click Help ➪ Microsoft On the Web ➪ Free Stuff and look for the link for new Office Assistants.

CROSS-REFERENCE

For an overview of how to use Web pages, see "Opening Web Documents" in Chapter 6.

FIND IT ONLINE

If you have trouble using the online help links, check the Microsoft Web site at **http://www.microsoft.com/** and look for Products information.

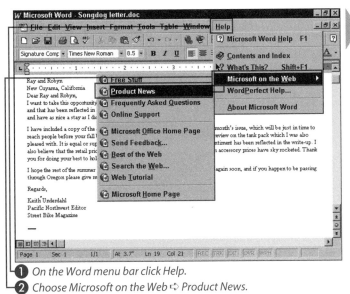

1 On the Word menu bar click Help.

2 Choose Microsoft on the Web ⇨ Product News.

3 Your Web browser should open. Connect to the Internet if you are prompted to do so.

4 Click the link for the Word Binary Converter for Microsoft Word 97.

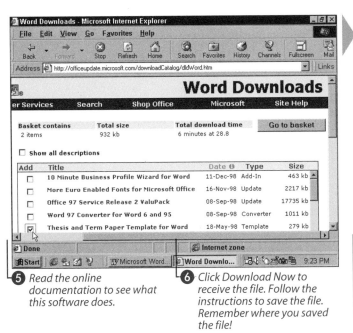

5 Read the online documentation to see what this software does.

6 Click Download Now to receive the file. Follow the instructions to save the file. Remember where you saved the file!

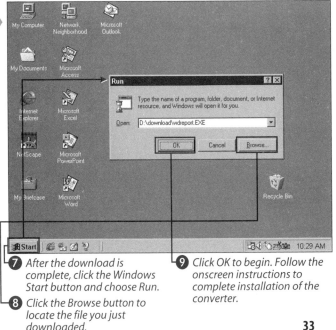

7 After the download is complete, click the Windows Start button and choose Run.

8 Click the Browse button to locate the file you just downloaded.

9 Click OK to begin. Follow the onscreen instructions to complete installation of the converter.

Personal Workbook

Q&A

1 What does the Office Assistant usually show when you start an Office 97 program?

_____

_____

_____

2 How can you search for help using the Office Assistant?

_____

_____

_____

3 What key can you press to quickly open the Office Assistant?

_____

_____

_____

4 What's the quickest way to create a professional-looking fax cover sheet?

_____

_____

_____

5 How do you open the Office Help System?

_____

_____

_____

6 Which tab in the Office Help System lets you search for a keyword or phrase?

_____

_____

_____

7 How do you print a help topic?

_____

_____

_____

8 Give two examples of software you can download from Microsoft to augment Office programs.

_____

_____

_____

ANSWERS: PAGE 402

EXTRA PRACTICE

1 Open Word and close the Tip of the Day.

2 Create a resume using the Resume Wizard.

3 Search for help on International Features in Word.

4 Print the help topic.

5 Download a new Office Assistant from the Microsoft Web site.

6 Explore the subtopics under Printing from the Contents tab of Office's Help System.

REAL-WORLD APPLICATIONS

✔ If you need to try a new feature of an Office application, the help system often provides quick answers.

✔ If you and your coworkers often perform similar tasks, you can print a help topic on that task and share copies of it with your colleagues.

✔ Microsoft sometimes creates new wizards and add-ins for Office programs. You can download them from the Microsoft Web site. Using the Help menu to access this information eliminates the need for spending a lot of time searching around Microsoft's rather large Web site for the exact information that you need.

Visual Quiz

How do you find the help topic shown here? How do you print a copy of it? What part of this topic links to another help topic?

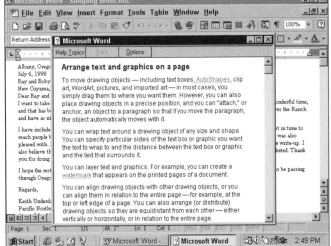

_____

_____

_____

_____

CHAPTER 3

MASTER THESE SKILLS

▶ Saving Office Files

▶ Opening and Closing Office Files

▶ Changing Filenames

▶ Deleting Old Files

▶ Creating New Folders

▶ Inserting a File into a Document

▶ Working with Text Files

Managing Your Files

All of the Office 97 programs you use run from program files that are recorded on the hard drive of your computer. Most of these files were copied there from a CD-ROM when the programs were originally installed on the computer. For the most part, these files do not change once installation is complete.

When you actually open a program and begin working with it, the program files are loaded into the Random Access Memory (RAM) of your computer for actual use. Likewise, any work you do — such as typing text, entering data, and so forth — also exists in RAM while you use it. Data that exists in RAM is of a very transitory nature; it is always changing. If you close a program, it will no longer be loaded in RAM. Or, if the computer is physically turned off, anything in RAM will forever disappear into the electronic ether.

This means that anything you're working on that only exists in RAM can disappear at the flip of a power switch. This is why it is very important to save your work on the computer's hard drive, in the form of document files. This way, there will always be a copy of what you do, even if the power is shut off or if you close a program.

An important aspect of working on your computer is knowing how to create and manage document files. You must know how to open and close files, save files, name and rename files, and so on. It is also important to know how files should be organized on your computer so that you will be able to find them again at a later time. As simple as these skills may sound, they are often missing among new computer users, resulting in lost productivity and poor organization.

This chapter describes how to perform some basic file management tasks. You learn how to save a file once you've created a document, open and close files, rename files, delete old files, and organize files on your hard drive. We also discuss how you can insert files into documents, and show you how to use text files, which often include important program information about Office 97 and other programs.

Saving Office Files

We could probably write an encyclopedia of reasons why a computer is superior to a typewriter. One of the most important advantages is that a computer enables you to save files on disk so they can be worked on again on another day. Without this capability, all of your hours spent slaving over a hot keyboard would blink out of existence every time you flipped off the power switch.

In addition to being able to work on your files at a later date, the ability to save files on disc enables you to use them on other computers as well. For instance, suppose that you are creating a presentation using PowerPoint. You might create the presentation on the desktop computer in your office, even though it is something that you plan to use on the road. If you also have PowerPoint installed on a laptop computer, you could use a 3.5" floppy disk to transfer the file from your desktop computer to the laptop. Connect the laptop to a projector, start PowerPoint, open the file, and you're ready to go!

Saving files has many other advantages. It enables you to keep a running record of your work, a bit like keeping a photocopy of every memo you send out. Or you may simply want to create an archive of past projects. That way, if you begin a similar project sometime in the future, you can refer back to the old files to see what you did back then. A saved file can be reused after lunch or ten years from now. One handy tool that Office 97 programs use is a dialog box that reminds you to save your work before closing a program. This helps to ensure that your valuable work is not lost simply because you clicked the Close (X) button when you didn't really mean to.

The first three figures on the facing page demonstrate how to save a file in any Office 97 program. In addition to the basic saving procedure, also demonstrated are other options that you might want to use, depending on the kind of file you are working with. The last figure shows you how to save your file periodically while you work.

TAKE NOTE

USE SAVE AS TO MAKE A NEW FILE COPY

After you've saved your work, you can use the Save As command in the File menu to make a new copy of the file. This command may be handy if you are creating similar memos but need to save a separate copy of each.

SAVE YOUR WORK FREQUENTLY

It's a good idea to save your files often; every ten minutes is a good rule of thumb. This habit will help to ensure that something like a locked up computer or power outage doesn't result in many hours of lost labor.

CROSS-REFERENCE
See "Creating New Folders" later in this chapter to learn more about organizing your saved files.

FIND IT ONLINE
Visit PC World's onine Word tip site:
http://www.pcworld.com/software/word-processing/articles/nov97/1511tips.

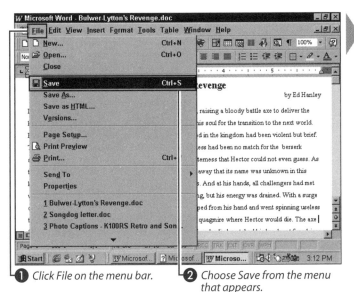

① Click File on the menu bar.

② Choose Save from the menu that appears.

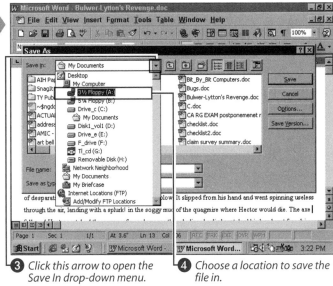

③ Click this arrow to open the Save In drop-down menu.

④ Choose a location to save the file in.

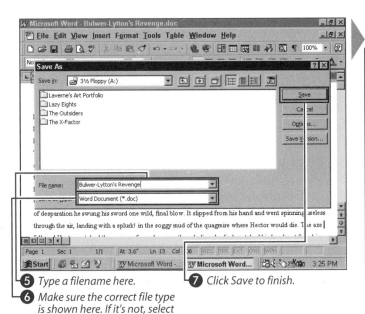

⑤ Type a filename here.

⑥ Make sure the correct file type is shown here. If it's not, select the correct one from the drop-down menu.

⑦ Click Save to finish.

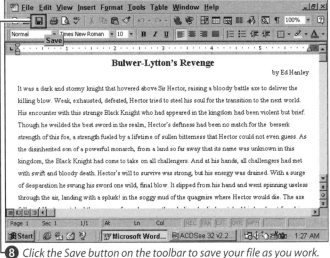

⑧ Click the Save button on the toolbar to save your file as you work.

Opening and Closing Office Files

You may remember that the very first task in Chapter 1 described how to open and close Office 97 programs. Obviously, this is a critical first step towards completing your work, but it is only one step you must take before you can edit your files and documents.

When you perform work in an Office program, you almost always save your work before exiting the program. As you saw in the previous task, this file is separate from program files and should have its own, descriptive name. You can create an infinite number of files within a single program; each one can be opened or closed as needed, independently of each other.

The files you create are generally small enough to fit on a removable diskette, making it possible to share the file among computers. For example, if you create a PowerPoint presentation on the desktop computer in your office, you can then transfer it to a laptop via a floppy disk. This means that you won't have to haul your desktop around whenever you need to make that presentation.

Of course, saving a file is only one small part of the picture. Since you probably saved the file so that it can be used again later, being able to open and close files is an important skill for any Office 97 program. You can use one of several techniques for opening a file, whether the program that goes with that file is already open or not. You should also know how to close an individual file without also closing the program, because sometimes you may want to continue using the program.

The first figure on the following page demonstrates how to open a file before you have even opened a program. The second and third figures show how to open a file from within a program. The last figure demonstrates how to close a file without also closing the program you are currently using.

TAKE NOTE

USING WINDOWS EXPLORER OR MY COMPUTER

You can also open a file directly from Windows Explorer or My Computer even if you haven't opened the right program yet. Simply locate the file you want and double-click (single-click in Windows 98) it to open the file and the program it belongs to.

CONVERTING FILES FROM OTHER PROGRAMS

Some Office programs are able to convert files that were created with other programs to the correct format. For instance, Word is capable of converting WordPerfect files. However, if you see a dialog box warning you of such a conversion, keep a close eye out to make sure the file converts properly. Close the file *without* saving it if things don't look right.

CROSS-REFERENCE
See "Opening and Closing the Programs" in Chapter 1 to learn more about working with the actual programs.

FIND IT ONLINE
Free and downloadables:
http://www.passthoneshareware.com.

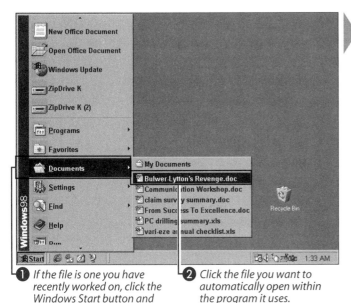

1 If the file is one you have recently worked on, click the Windows Start button and choose Documents.

2 Click the file you want to automatically open within the program it uses.

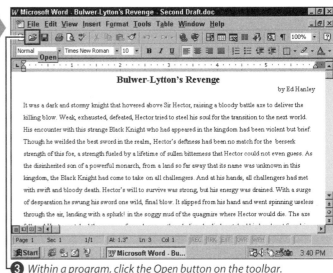

3 Within a program, click the Open button on the toolbar.

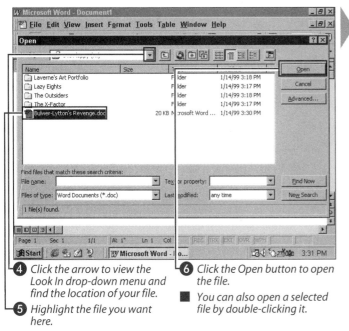

4 Click the arrow to view the Look In drop-down menu and find the location of your file.

5 Highlight the file you want here.

6 Click the Open button to open the file.

■ You can also open a selected file by double-clicking it.

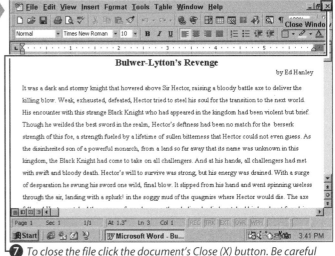

7 To close the file click the document's Close (X) button. Be careful not to confuse it with the program's Close button!

Changing Filenames

You have learned that giving a file a name is an important part of the file saving process. Ideally, a filename should be descriptive enough that you can easily remember what it is the next time you need to find it.

Fortunately, giving a file a descriptive name is much easier now than it used to be. Modern operating systems permit filenames that are as long as 256 characters, whereas in the past you could only use eight characters. An old-style filename might have looked something like this: geormem2.

But with long filename support, you can give the file a somewhat less cryptic name, such as: Memo to George on 4 July 1998.

Which file would you have an easier time identifying, especially if you're not exactly sure what you are looking for?

Descriptive names or not, there will come a time when you will find the need to rename a file. Sometimes you simply need to rename an existing file, which is very simple. At other times you may need to make a new copy of a file using a different name. This is common when you might need to make a second draft of a document, or if you are creating a new document based on one you made previously. In this respect, you would be using the old document as you would a template.

Renaming a file is straightforward. It can be done from within Office 97 programs, or it can be done using one of the operating system tools such as Windows Explorer or My Computer. In these Windows applications, the easiest way to rename a file is to right-click it and choose Rename from the context menu.

The figures on the facing page demonstrate ways to rename a file from within Office 97 programs. The first two figures demonstrate how to save a copy of a file under a new name, and the last two figures show how to rename an existing file.

TAKE NOTE

▶ TROUBLES WITH LONG FILENAMES

Older operating systems such as DOS and Windows 3.1 do not support long filenames, nor does the Internet. If you plan to use any of your documents on these systems, you will have to resort back to using only eight characters in a filename.

▶ ILLEGAL CHARACTERS FOR FILENAMES

Windows lets you use a variety of characters, spaces, and punctuation in your filenames. However, you are not able to use any of the following characters when naming your files: / \ : < > | " * or ?. If you get an error message when you try to save a file, check to see if you accidentally used one of these illegal characters.

CROSS-REFERENCE

Learn how to create and name Web documents in "Creating Web Pages" in Chapter 6.

FIND IT ONLINE

See a list of filename extensions and what they mean at **http://stekt.oulu.fi/~jon/jouninfo/extension.html**.

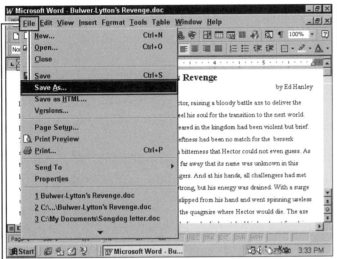

1 On the menu bar, click File ➪ Save As.

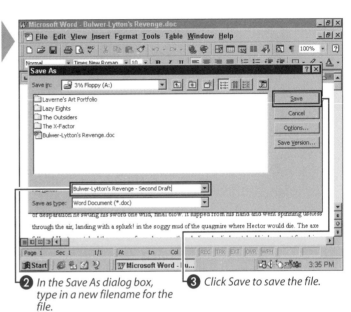

2 In the Save As dialog box, type in a new filename for the file.

3 Click Save to save the file.

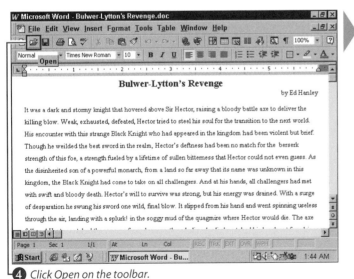

4 Click Open on the toolbar.

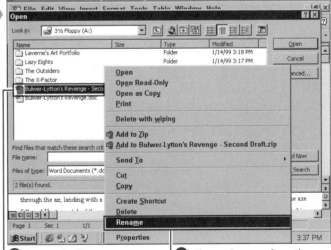

5 Locate the file you want to rename and right-click it.

■ Click Cancel if you want to close the dialog box without opening a file.

6 Choose Rename from the context menu that appears. Type a new name in the filename box, and press Enter when you are done.

Deleting Old Files

As you have learned, you will constantly be creating new files throughout the course of your work. Since these files may be created on an almost daily basis, the hard drive on your computer (where most of your files are probably stored) might begin to fill up. Eventually, you will find that your hard drive is cluttered with many files that never get used anymore.

To save space on your hard drive, you may want to delete some of the older, unused files. Even if you have a large hard drive with what seems like plenty of free space, cleaning up older files makes finding the files you actually need much easier. This is not to say that you should start indiscriminately deleting any file that hasn't been opened in more than a week. You might want to retain some files for record keeping or archival purposes, or you may want to use some older files as reference examples when you create new documents. Of course, you need to decide for yourself what is worth saving and what can be thrown away, but choose wisely.

Once you have decided to delete files, and which files to delete, you have several options available to you. You can get rid of unwanted files from within Office 97 programs, or you can use one of the Windows tools such as Windows Explorer or My Computer. In either program, simply highlight the files you don't need and click the Delete button on the toolbar. You can also click File ⇨ Delete on each program's menu bar.

The figures on the facing page demonstrate how to delete files from within any Office 97 application. You may find managing your files from one place to be easier, or you may prefer to use the Windows tools designed specifically for this process. One advantage of using the Open dialog box in Office 97 programs is that only document files for that program are displayed, so you are less likely to inadvertently delete the wrong file.

TAKE NOTE

▶ BE CAREFUL WHAT YOU DELETE

When you are viewing files on your hard drive, it may be difficult to determine exactly what some of them are. Windows Explorer and My Computer display files of all types, including system files. Deleting system files is dangerous and could make your computer cease to function, so if you don't know what it is, don't delete it!

▶ SAVE FILE ARCHIVES ON DISKETTES

Another great alternative to deleting old files is to save copies of them on a removable disk. A 3.5" floppy works well, as do larger media such as ZIP disks. This way, you always have copies of important files, just in case.

CROSS-REFERENCE

See the next task, "Creating New Folders", to learn how to save old files in a new folder.

FIND IT ONLINE

Subscribe to WOW, Woody's Office Watch, a free, weekly newsletter, for updates, MSOffice humor, and insider tips.

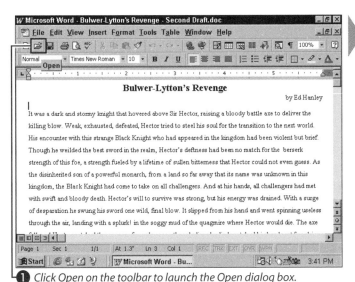

1 Click Open on the toolbar to launch the Open dialog box.

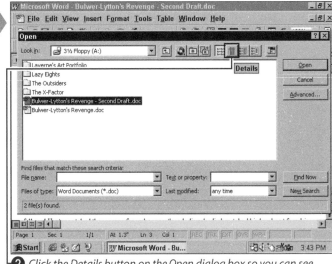

2 Click the Details button on the Open dialog box so you can see how long it has been since each file was edited.

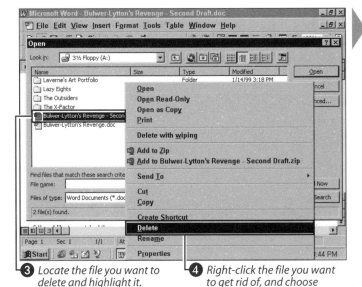

3 Locate the file you want to delete and highlight it.

4 Right-click the file you want to get rid of, and choose Delete from the context menu that appears.

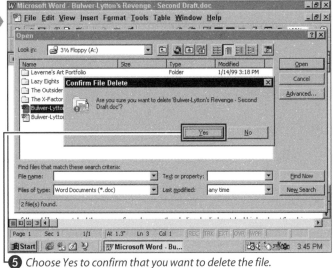

5 Choose Yes to confirm that you want to delete the file.

Creating New Folders

The hard drive of your computer is capable of holding many, many files. In fact, it already does. Because you have so many files on your hard drive, they must be organized in a way that enables you to find and use the ones you actually need.

A good way to think of your hard drive is as a drawer in a file cabinet. Each file you work with is a piece of paper that must be stored in that drawer. If you simply throw each piece of paper into the drawer, you will soon have a hard time finding anything that you need. You will simply have a large drawer filled with a large, chaotic pile of papers. Since you have better organizational skills than that, you know that it would be more effective to organize the papers by putting them in labeled folders within the drawer.

This is, in essence, the system that is used to organize files on your hard drive. Files reside in virtual folders on the drive, and each folder has a descriptive name. In many cases, folders exist within folders to further catalog and organize the files on the drive. These folders-within-folders are called subfolders, and are a key piece of the organizational puzzle on your computer. This system also works on removable disks, by the way, so you can organize your files there in a similar manner.

To provide your own custom touch to this process, you have the ability to create your own folders and subfolders as you see fit. For instance, if you save most of your work in a folder on your hard drive called *My Documents*, you may want to create subfolders within the My Documents folder for different projects, clients, and so on.

As with most other file management procedures, you can create folders either within Office 97 programs, or in Windows Explorer and My Computer. In the Windows programs, click File ➪ New ➪ Folder on the menu bar to create a new folder inside whatever folder you happen to be in. Be sure to type a new name for the new folder.

The figures on the opposite page demonstrate a technique for creating new folders from within Office 97 programs. Follow along to create new folders in which to store your own work.

TAKE NOTE

I SAY FOLDERS, YOU SAY DIRECTORIES

If you have spent any time working on a computer with an older operating system such as DOS or Windows 3.1, you may remember the term *Directories*. Folders are exactly the same as Directories, but with a new and improved name.

NAMING FOLDERS

Folders can have long, descriptive names, just like files. Remember that subfolders within a single folder must each have a unique name.

CROSS-REFERENCE

Folder names can be changed just like filenames. See how in "Changing Filenames" earlier in this chapter.

FIND IT ONLINE

Learn more than you ever cared to know about folders and directories from the PCGuide at http://www.pcguide.com/ref/hdd/file/index.htm.

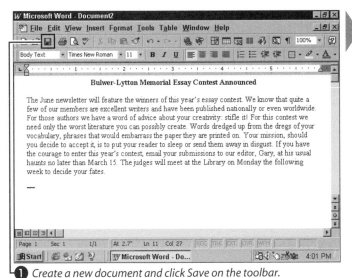

❶ Create a new document and click Save on the toolbar.

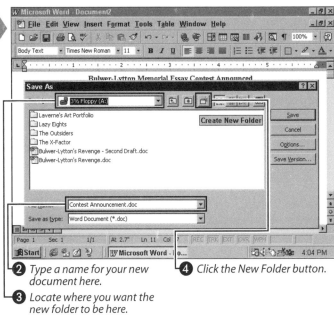

❷ Type a name for your new document here.

❸ Locate where you want the new folder to be here.

❹ Click the New Folder button.

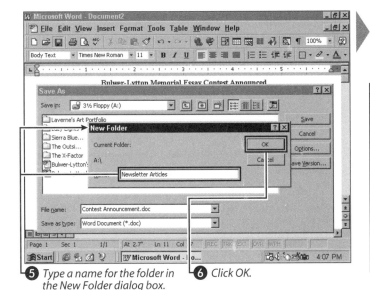

❺ Type a name for the folder in the New Folder dialog box.

❻ Click OK.

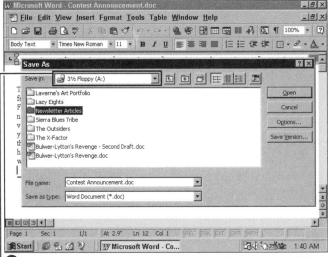

❼ To be sure the document is saved in the new folder, double-click it to display it in the Save In box.

47

Inserting a File into a Document

Now that you have mastered some of the more basic file management techniques, let's try moving on to something a little more advanced. Understanding the basic structure of files on your computer is paramount to performing many of the most important tasks involved with your work.

One of the more interesting things you can do with files is to combine them. This task can be as simple as inserting one Word file into another, which is little more than a cut-and-paste affair. This is relatively simple, since the files are of the same type (word-processing documents) in the first place. A more complex use of this concept would be to embed an Excel worksheet into a PowerPoint presentation.

Office 97 programs give you a number of other options to spice up your documents by the use of file insertions. For instance, you can insert sound and picture files into documents, thus adding a multimedia element to otherwise bland documents. This type of operation serves as your first introduction to a software concept called Object Linking and Embedding (OLE). Inserting files is only one part of OLE, which allows for much more complex program linking capabilities. You can insert objects and files from nearly any type of program that is supported by Windows into an Office 97 program. The possibilities are limited only by your imagination. Learning how

to insert files is your first step towards accomplishing even more complicated linking tasks.

The figures on the facing page demonstrate how to perform some very basic file insertions. The first two figures show how to insert one word processing file into another, which is the simplest form of file insertion. The last two figures show how to insert a sound file called a MIDI sequence into a word processing file, a task that from a software standpoint is just a bit more complex. Of course, the magic of OLE is that it won't be any more complex for you to do; it only sounds that way!

TAKE NOTE

▶ INSERT OBJECTS INSTEAD OF FILES

An object is a single element from a program, such as a block of text from Word or a chart from Excel. You can insert an object instead of a whole file by selecting Insert ⇨ Object from the menu bar. A dialog box appears where you can select what kind of object you want to enter.

▶ INSERTING FILES V. COPY-AND-PASTE

When you are inserting an entire file into another one, you may find it easier to use the technique described here instead of a copy-and-paste procedure. Not only does this require fewer steps, but it also ensures that the file you insert retains all of its original formatting.

CROSS-REFERENCE

Learn about copying and pasting portions of a document in "Copying and Moving Objects" in Chapter 5.

FIND IT ONLINE

Find an excellent online primer for OLE concepts at **http://www.microsoft.com/oledev/olecom/ aboutole.htm.**

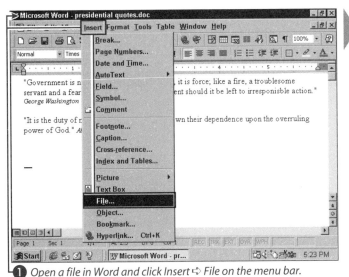

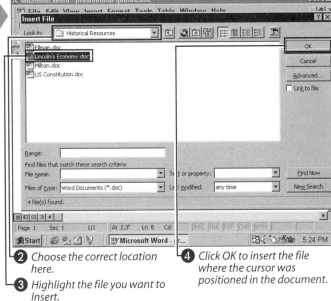

1 Open a file in Word and click Insert ➪ File on the menu bar.

2 Choose the correct location here.

3 Highlight the file you want to Insert.

4 Click OK to insert the file where the cursor was positioned in the document.

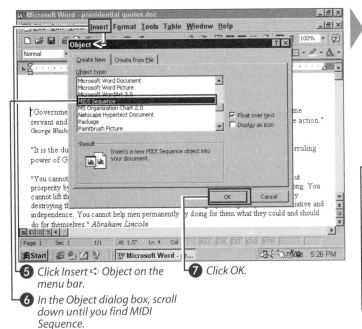

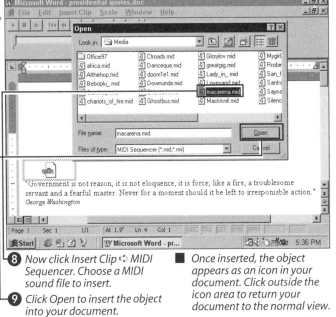

5 Click Insert ➪ Object on the menu bar.

6 In the Object dialog box, scroll down until you find MIDI Sequence.

7 Click OK.

8 Now click Insert Clip ➪ MIDI Sequencer. Choose a MIDI sound file to insert.

9 Click Open to insert the object into your document.

■ Once inserted, the object appears as an icon in your document. Click outside the icon area to return your document to the normal view.

Working with Text Files

The personal computer revolution has been driven by the relative uniformity of computers. However, when the industry had its start back in the late 1970s, it was populated by many different computers from a variety of manufacturers, none of which was compatible with another. In other words, a program that worked just fine on your TRS-80 would not work on an Apple II, and vice versa.

IBM introduced its revolutionary PC in 1981, and around that modest machine today's crop of PC-compatibles grew. By following a basic standard and running the same operating system (in this case, Windows), PC "clones" from other manufacturers can all run the same software. That's why you can install the same Office 97 programs on computers built by Micron, Toshiba, Gateway, Hewlett Packard, or even the nerd down the hall.

As miraculous as this may seem, things don't always work out exactly as planned. Subtle differences create serious conflicts, not only with certain pieces of hardware but with other bits of software as well. Product vendors are no more capable of resolving all hardware and software conflicts than automobile manufacturers are capable of preventing all traffic accidents.

The best solution is to test the software, resolve as many problems as possible, and then warn the users of potential problems they might encounter in the course of their work. Almost all programs distributed today — including Office 97 — provide these warnings to customers in the form of text files that accompany the program files. A text file is just about the most basic kind of file you can use on a PC, and is readable on virtually any computer. The files can also be edited easily using simple editing tools supplied with the operating system. They can also be read and edited using a word processing program like Word.

The first figure on the facing page shows you how to find important text files that accompany Office 97. The remaining figures show how to view, edit, and save text files for your own use.

TAKE NOTE

▶ CREATE YOUR OWN TEXT FILES

You can use Word to create your own text files, which should then be readable on virtually any computer. For example, if you need to send a text document to someone with a PC running UNIX, or Linux, or a Macintosh, a text file is the most fool-proof method for doing that.

▶ WHAT'S YOUR EXTENSION?

Text files can usually be identified by the .TXT extension that is attached to the end of the file-name. To ensure they can be used on other computers, text files should not have names that are longer than eight characters.

▶ PLEASE READ ME

Most programs come with a file called README.TXT. Open and read it first before you begin installing new software.

CROSS-REFERENCE
See "Getting Started and Entering Text" in Chapter 7 to learn more about typing text into a document.

FIND IT ONLINE
Learn more about text files and ASCII text from Jim Price's ASCII Chart at **http://www.jimprice.com/jim-asc.htm**.

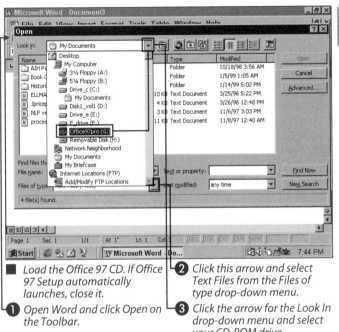

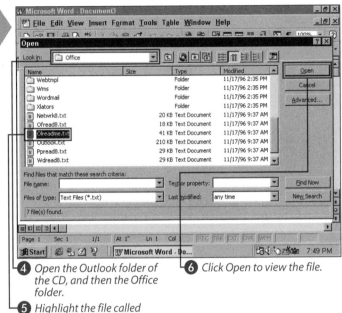

■ Load the Office 97 CD. If Office 97 Setup automatically launches, close it.

① Open Word and click Open on the Toolbar.

② Click this arrow and select Text Files from the Files of type drop-down menu.

③ Click the arrow for the Look In drop-down menu and select your CD-ROM drive.

④ Open the Outlook folder of the CD, and then the Office folder.

⑤ Highlight the file called olreadme.

⑥ Click Open to view the file.

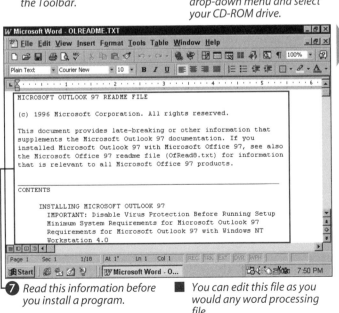

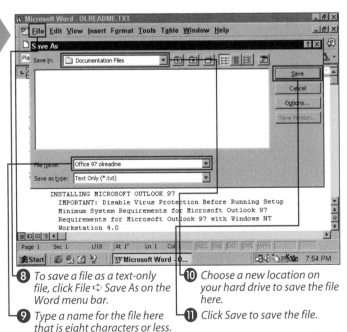

⑦ Read this information before you install a program.

■ You can edit this file as you would any word processing file.

⑧ To save a file as a text-only file, click File ▷ Save As on the Word menu bar.

⑨ Type a name for the file here that is eight characters or less.

⑩ Choose a new location on your hard drive to save the file here.

⑪ Click Save to save the file.

Personal Workbook

Q&A

1 How can you save an Office document?

_____

_____

_____

2 How can you save a copy of an Office document with a new name?

_____

_____

3 Should you always wait until you are finished to save your work?

_____

_____

_____

4 How do you open an Office document without first opening an Office program?

_____

_____

_____

5 What dialog box should you open if you want to rename an existing file from within an Office program?

_____

_____

6 How long can a filename be?

_____

_____

7 What are two ways to delete a file?

_____

_____

8 How do you create a new folder from within an Office program?

_____

_____

9 What is the quickest way to combine the text of two separate documents?

_____

_____

_____

ANSWERS: PAGE 402

EXTRA PRACTICE

1. Create a short document using Word and save it with the name Letter 1.

2. Save a copy of the letter as Letter 2.

3. Close Word and then reopen Letter 2 using the Start menu.

4. Save Letter 2 in a new folder called Letters to Mom.

5. Change the name of Letter 2 to Letter to Mom.

6. Insert Letter 1 into Letter to Mom.

7. Save Letter to Mom as a text file.

REAL-WORLD APPLICATIONS

✔ If you are frequently sending out similar memos or letters to various people, you can simplify your tasks by copying the old letter as you see fit.

✔ You may want to create a separate folder on your hard drive for each client you deal with. If you save all documents that pertain to a given client in the correct folder, you can use the folder as a record of your business dealings with that person.

✔ Insert an Excel pie chart into a Word document to enhance your memo to sales.

Visual Quiz

How do you create the Articles folder that this file is saved in? How do you change the name of one of the other files in this folder? How do you save the article as a text-only file? What does the icon which reads "In the Hall of the Mountain King" represent? How did it get there?

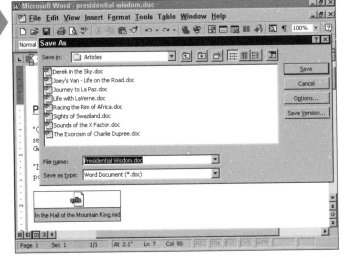

CHAPTER 4

MASTER THESE SKILLS

▶ **Choosing What to Print**

▶ **Previewing Before Printing**

▶ **Controlling Your Printer**

▶ **Printing to Files**

Printing Documents

For the better part of the last three decades, futurists have been predicting the advent of the "paperless office." Obviously, reaching that goal is still quite a ways off, and in the meantime, you have a lot of documents to print.

As you have begun the process of working with Office 97 programs, you may or may not have noticed that printing a document can be extremely simple. All Office 97 programs — along with many of the windows that open within these programs — have Print buttons on the toolbar that enable you to print your work quickly and easily. Indeed, printing a document could be the simplest thing you ever do. It would be all too easy to just mention that Print button and move on.

But wait: There is much more to printing a document than meets the eye. It is not always prudent or desirable to click the toolbar button because the printed product is not always what you have in mind. Often, when you click the Print button, the result is that the program prints more than you need, less than you need, or the printed product doesn't appear on paper the way you hoped it would. The end result of wanton use of the toolbar Print button is wasted time, paper, and printer toner, and none of these things will be getting cheaper any time soon.

Office 97 programs give you a number of options to help make your printed work more productive and efficient. Various options make it possible to print only a portion of a document, print multiple copies of a document, or preview the finished item before you actually print it. You can even change which printer it prints on if you are lucky enough to have multiple printers. A plethora of options awaits you.

This chapter discusses these options, and tells you how to make the best use of your final printed products. We also discuss ways to get files ready for printing even though a printer might not currently be available to your computer. These techniques can be used in virtually any Office 97 program, as well as many other Windows-based applications. Also, the Print dialog box is shared by all programs in Windows that use your printer, so these skills are very important to have.

Choosing What to Print

Every Office 97 program has a Print button on the toolbar. This makes many printing tasks extremely simple because it turns the whole process into a single-click affair. Just click that little button (it even looks like a little printer) and your entire document begins to spew forth from the printer's mouth.

Easy though it may sound, you should know a few things about it before you start using it. For one thing, it begins printing your document immediately, which means you won't be able to change printers or change any other print options. Furthermore, it prints your *entire* document, no matter how much of the document you actually want or need. This can be an especially major problem with things like a large Excel worksheet, where printing the entire document would be impractical.

Office 97 programs give you a number of options for printing portions of data, text, and other file elements. The simplest way to print portions of a document involves printing only specified pages. Options in the Print dialog box for Office programs enables you to select the entire document, the current page — that is, the page that the cursor is currently on — or a specific page or range of pages.

Another method of printing portions of a document involves selecting parts of text or data and using options in the Print dialog box to print the selection. Using this method may be useful if you only need small pieces of information from a document. For instance, suppose your friend sends you a rather lengthy e-mail message that contains both his political manifesto and directions to a movie theater where you plan to meet. In the Outlook Message window, you can select only the directions to the theater for printing, and save the manifesto for later.

The first two figures on the following page demonstrate how to open the Print dialog box and select some basic options. The last two figures demonstrate how to select text for printing, open the Print dialog box, and only print the selection.

TAKE NOTE

► USE CARE WHEN PRINTING REPLACEMENT PAGES

Users often only reprint one or two pages after they have done some touch-up editing to a document, which is a good idea. However, you should be careful to ensure that the seemingly minor changes you made did not also in some way affect the other pages that you are not going to reprint.

► PRINTING A SELECTION

If you opened the Print dialog box after selecting an area of data or text, you can probably see the Selection option available in the Page Range box. Make sure it is selected before trying to print that document piece.

CROSS-REFERENCE
Learn how to select an area of text or data in "Selecting Words and Paragraphs" in Chapter 5.

FIND IT ONLINE
Check out the Word tutorial for editing and adding graphics and text: **http://www.caut.ac.uk/title/word**.

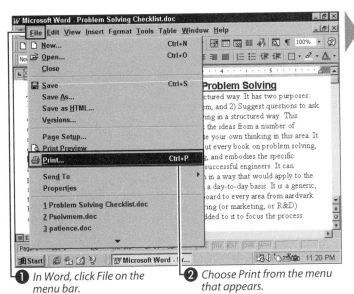

① In Word, click File on the menu bar.

② Choose Print from the menu that appears.

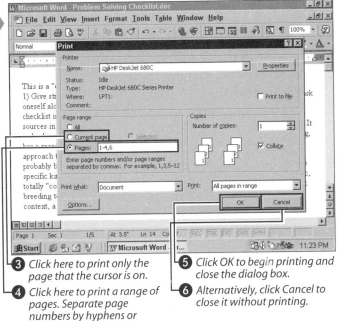

③ Click here to print only the page that the cursor is on.

④ Click here to print a range of pages. Separate page numbers by hyphens or commas.

⑤ Click OK to begin printing and close the dialog box.

⑥ Alternatively, click Cancel to close it without printing.

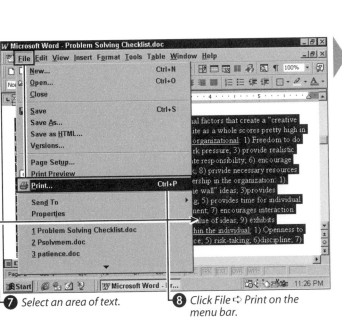

⑦ Select an area of text.

⑧ Click File ⇨ Print on the menu bar.

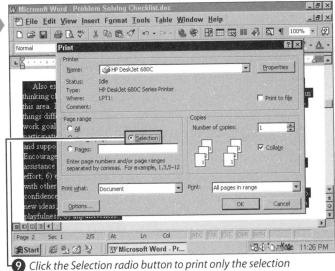

⑨ Click the Selection radio button to print only the selection you made.

Previewing Before Printing

When you view a document on your computer's screen, it may or may not resemble the final, printed product. Documents on your screen often display important information — such as paragraph breaks — that is not intended to appear on the printed copy. This information is important for you to see while you work on a document, but it would have no value printed on paper. Furthermore, the actual layout of the document on your screen may differ drastically from the printed copy; Excel worksheets are infamous for this. Word documents that use columns may be just as confusing.

Office 97 programs offer a useful tool to help you alleviate much of this confusion as you develop your documents and get them ready for printing. The Print Preview option gives you a fairly accurate representation of what your document is going to look like when it is printed out on paper. You have a number of view options, depending on the program, that enable you to change the view and even the document itself. In most Print Previews you can zoom in or out, and in Word and PowerPoint you are able to view multiple pages at once. This is a useful feature, because it gives you a better idea what facing or adjacent pages look like when they are actually together. You may have additional options, depending on which program you are using at the time.

The most important result of Page Preview is that it reduces or even eliminates the need to print draft copies of a document. It is entirely possible that you will not need to print any pages until the final draft is ready. This saves a great deal of time, not to mention paper and printer toner.

The first two figures on the facing page show you how to preview a Word document. They also illustrate some of the options that are available to you. The last two figures show you how to preview a document in Excel. Excel has a very different Print Preview, so it's worth getting familiar with while you're here.

TAKE NOTE

ONLY AS GOOD AS YOUR PRINTER...

As wonderful as a document may look in Print Preview, you may still be limited by your printer. For instance, if you only have a black-ink printer, don't expect multicolored items in the document to come out very well. Print Preview always assumes you have the latest and greatest in Printer technology.

SAVE ONE TREE IN WORD'S PRINT PREVIEW

Word's Print Preview offers a unique feature that automatically reduces the amount of paper your document requires by one sheet. Click the Shrink to Fit button on the Preview toolbar to see the result. If you don't like it, click Edit ⇨ Undo to undo the change.

CROSS-REFERENCE
You can also get a rough idea of the printed page using Page Layout View. See "Controlling the View" in Chapter 1 to learn more about this.

SHORTCUT
Press Esc to quickly close the Print Preview window and return to the main program.

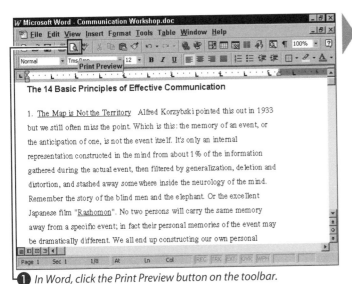

1. In Word, click the Print Preview button on the toolbar.

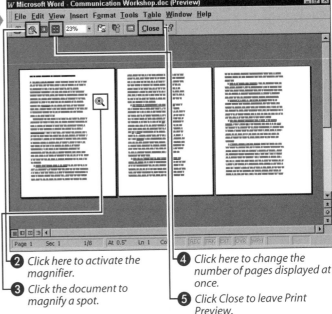

2. Click here to activate the magnifier.

3. Click the document to magnify a spot.

4. Click here to change the number of pages displayed at once.

5. Click Close to leave Print Preview.

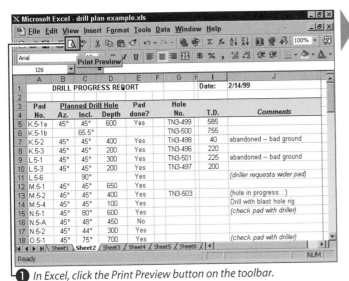

1. In Excel, click the Print Preview button on the toolbar.

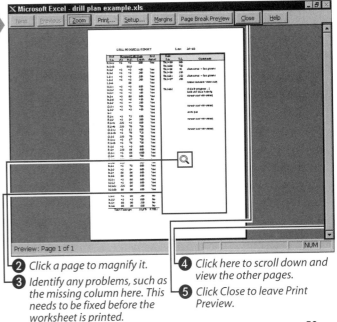

2. Click a page to magnify it.

3. Identify any problems, such as the missing column here. This needs to be fixed before the worksheet is printed.

4. Click here to scroll down and view the other pages.

5. Click Close to leave Print Preview.

Controlling Your Printer

As previously mentioned, the quickest and easiest way to print a document is to simply click the Print button on the toolbar. It is quick and effective, but doesn't give you a whole lot of control over the printing process. This is just fine in many printing situations, but for others it isn't.

Being able to control the printing process is important to ensure that you get the most efficient use out of your computer. You have already learned how to select portions of a document to print, and how to preview a print job before you send it to the printer. Now we need to learn about some of the other, more advanced options that you can set when you start a printing job.

Initially, you need to tell the printer what to print. Once you've done that, it's time set other options. Office 97 programs enable you to print multiple copies of a document, and you can choose to have your documents collated as well. For example, if you are producing a six-page newsletter with Word and need to print 20 copies, you should probably select the Collate option. With the Collate option set, the printer prints one copy of each page of the newsletter, and then starts over and prints another copy of each page. This way, when all 20 copies are done, all you have to do is staple them together! With the Collate option turned off, it would print 20 copies of page one, then 20 copies of page two, and so on. If you were producing the newsletter, this would be considerably more time-consuming because you would have to manually collate the pages before you could staple them. However, you should turn the Collate option off if each page is a form that you use at work and you need 20 copies of each form. In this case, you don't necessarily want the forms collated.

A final option you may want to exercise is to choose a different printer. If you have multiple printers, you can use Office 97 programs to switch between them. For example, you may have a dot matrix printer in the office just for printing mailing labels, not for printing important documents that must look professional.

The figures on the facing page demonstrate how to change some of these options before you print.

TAKE NOTE

START A PRINT JOB BEFORE LUNCH

Having printing options you can set, enables you to start fairly big printing jobs on the computer that may take many minutes or even an hour or two to complete. Start your big print jobs right before lunch, so that the computer can keep working while you take a break!

CROSS-REFERENCE

Learn more about using dialog boxes in "Using Dialog Boxes" in Chapter 1.

SHORTCUT

Press Ctrl+P to open the Print dialog box.

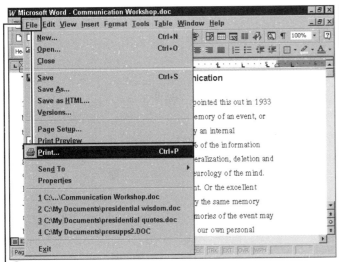

❶ On the menu bar, click File ➪ Print.

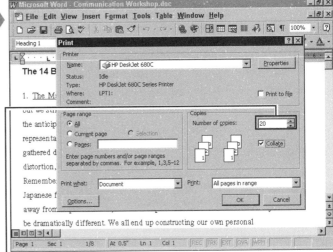

❷ In the Print dialog box, change the number of copies you want to print by clicking the arrows.

■ You can also type the desired number over the currently displayed number.

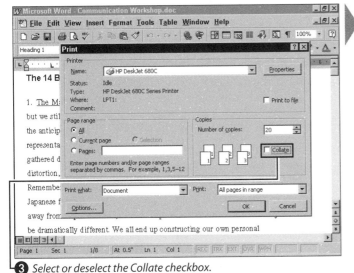

❸ Select or deselect the Collate checkbox.

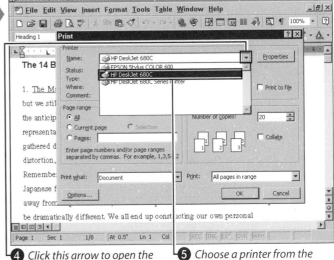

❹ Click this arrow to open the Printer Name drop-down menu.

❺ Choose a printer from the menu that appears.

Printing to Files

Generally speaking, when we think of a document being printed, we assume that means printed onto a piece of paper. And, for the most part, when you use the term *print* around computers, that is exactly what it means.

But this can cause a slight problem for some users. What if a printer isn't currently hooked up to the computer you are working on? What if you want to use a printer that is connected to a non-Windows computer? Sometimes, when you need to print a document, you simply don't have the hardware available to make it happen.

One possible solution to this problem is to print the document to a file. You can do this with any printable document, and for the most part you even follow the same printing procedures. The only difference is that instead of being sent to the printer, it is saved as a *print file*. This file will be saved in the language format for whatever printer you select. Because of this, the printer driver for whatever printer you will ultimately use must be installed on the computer that you are working on, even if the printer is not physically connected to it.

Once you have created the print file, it must be copied to the printer from a DOS prompt. This adds a certain level of complication for many people, but it also has its advantages. For instance, it means that the print file can be transferred to any computer, regardless of the operating system. If you want to print the file using a printer connected to a Macintosh, a Linux machine, or even an ancient IBM PC running DOS, you won't have any trouble doing so.

This method of "remote" printing may not suit your day-to-day needs very well. Nonetheless, it gives you added capability and can enable you to take better advantage of the resources that may be around you. The figures on the facing page demonstrate how to print a document to a file, and then print it using the MS-DOS prompt available in Windows 95 and 98.

TAKE NOTE

USING OTHER TYPES OF COMPUTERS

You can use a printer that is connected to virtually any kind of computer running almost any operating system. Just make sure that the printer driver for the printer itself is installed on the computer you create the print file with. Contact your network administrator or tech support specialist to learn the specific commands to use on other computers.

DON'T USE LONG FILENAMES

Because you will be printing this file in DOS, you may have a problem if you give the print file a long name. To ensure that you are able to access it later, do not use more than eight characters (including spaces) in the print file's name.

CROSS-REFERENCE

Learn more about using the MS-DOS prompt, in one of IDG's operating system titles such as 1998's *Windows 98 Bible* by Alan Simpson.

FIND IT ONLINE

Find out where to download printer drivers online at **http://www.printgrc.com/template/pdrivers.cfm**.

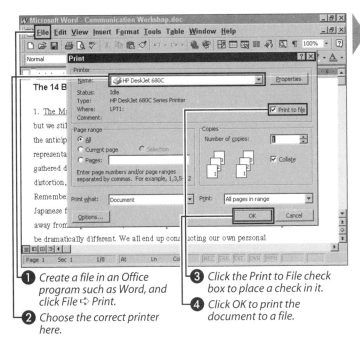

1 Create a file in an Office program such as Word, and click File ➪ Print.

2 Choose the correct printer here.

3 Click the Print to File check box to place a check in it.

4 Click OK to print the document to a file.

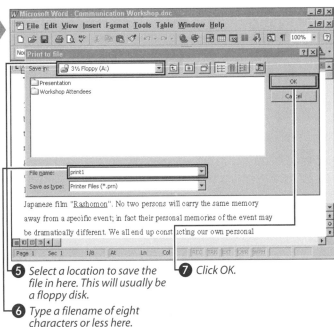

5 Select a location to save the file in here. This will usually be a floppy disk.

6 Type a filename of eight characters or less here.

7 Click OK.

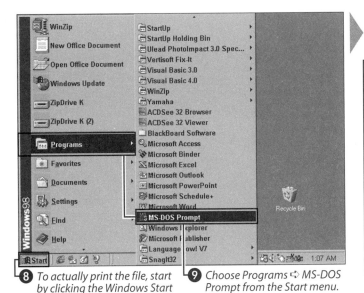

8 To actually print the file, start by clicking the Windows Start button.

9 Choose Programs ➪ MS-DOS Prompt from the Start menu.

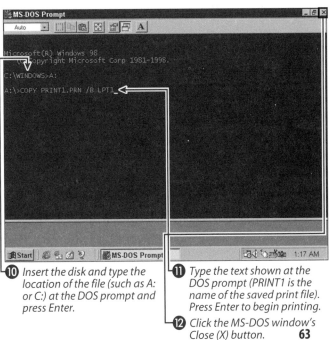

10 Insert the disk and type the location of the file (such as A: or C:) at the DOS prompt and press Enter.

11 Type the text shown at the DOS prompt (PRINT1 is the name of the saved print file). Press Enter to begin printing.

12 Click the MS-DOS window's Close (X) button.

63

Personal Workbook

Q&A

1 What is the quickest way to print a document?

_____

_____

2 How do you select a range of pages to print?

_____

_____

3 What are two ways of opening the Print dialog box?

_____

_____

4 Why is it a good idea to use Print Preview before printing your work?

_____

_____

_____

5 What are two ways of closing Print Preview without printing?

_____

_____

6 How do you print multiple copies of a document?

_____

_____

_____

7 Can you print to a printer that is not connected to your computer?

_____

_____

_____

8 Can you print to a printer if its driver is not installed on your computer?

_____

_____

_____

9 How long should the filename of a print file be?

_____

_____

_____

ANSWERS: PAGE 403

EXTRA PRACTICE

1. Create a two-page document and preview what the printed product will look like.

2. Print two copies of the second page of your document.

3. Print two copies of the first page to a file.

4. Print the entire document to a file.

5. Open the MS-DOS prompt and print using the print file.

REAL-WORLD APPLICATIONS

✔ You are constantly printing documents throughout the course of your work. Mastering the techniques for previewing and printing will save time and waste for you and your company.

✔ Not all documents need to be printed out on a fancy printer. For example, you might use Word's advanced layout abilities to create mailing labels, and want to print them on an older dot matrix printer with a tractor feed that is connected to a computer running UNIX elsewhere in your office. If you print your mailing label document to a file, you can easily print it using that tractor-fed dot matrix printer.

Visual Quiz

How do you open this dialog box? Where do you click to select a different printer? How do you select only certain pages to print? Where can you increase the number of copies to be printed? What does the Collate option do?

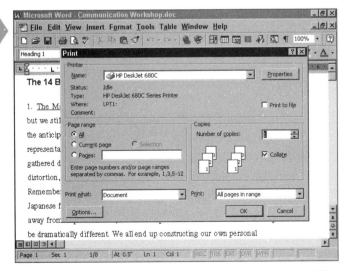

CHAPTER 5

**MASTER
THESE
SKILLS**

▶ **Selecting Words and Paragraphs**

▶ **Selecting Cells**

▶ **Selecting Objects and Graphics**

▶ **Using Drag and Drop**

▶ **Copying and Moving Objects**

Making Selections

As you spend time working with the Office 97 programs on your computer, you begin to learn a lot about working with various kinds of data. If you've been following along since the beginning of this book, you have learned a lot of useful skills to help you control and use the information on your computer. You've learned how to open and manipulate Office 97 programs, get help on tasks as you go, manage files you create with Office 97, and print documents.

For the most part, all of the topics preceding this one had one thing in common: they all involved files and program features. But to create those files and take advantage of the many features that Office programs can offer, you also need to know how to enter and manipulate *data*. Data in this case refers to the letters, words, and numbers you type into the programs as you work. It can also refer to other kinds of input, including sound files and pictures.

Typing in data is pretty easy; no doubt you've done quite a bit of it already. But for many of the tasks you perform in Office 97 programs, simply typing on the keyboard is not the only way to work with data. For instance, suppose you need to copy a paragraph of text from a Word document into an e-mail message in Outlook. How would you tell the computer which paragraph you want copied? How would you actually copy it? Or, what if you need to copy data from one cell on an Excel worksheet into another? What if you need to copy a group of cells?

The tasks in this chapter address these questions. Here you learn how to select different kinds of data, one of the most important skills you must master to work efficiently and effectively. Selecting data is the first step toward accomplishing many Office 97 program procedures, from simple copy-and-paste operations to more advanced tasks such as creating formulas.

In this chapter, we show you how to select words and paragraphs, and cells like those used in Excel. In addition we demonstrate techniques for selecting graphics and other miscellaneous objects. We go on to demonstrate some of the things you can do with your selections.

Selecting Words and Paragraphs

It won't take you long to learn that one of the most commonly used skills in any Office 97 program — or virtually any program on your computer for that matter — is the ability to select words and paragraphs of text. The term *select* is often interchanged with *highlight* because selected text looks as if it has been marked over by an onscreen highlighter. Of course, the highlighting might actually be dark, but that is beside the point.

You can do a lot with selected text. It can be copied to another part of the document, or it can be copied into a new document altogether. Text itself is ubiquitous on a computer, so much so that you can actually copy it almost anywhere you want. For instance, text from the body of a Word document can be copied into a text box in a dialog box and vice versa. You can copy a name from an e-mail message into a cell in Excel or a record in Access, and you can cut a paragraph from a Word document and make it a slide caption in a PowerPoint presentation.

As with anything, limitations exist that you should know about. When you copy text, some formatting may not be copied with it. Many programs and dialog boxes only use text in its purest form, with no italics, underlining, or even special fonts. So if you copy a word that is bold in a Word document and then try to paste it into a dialog box where formatting is not used, the bold formatting will be lost. This isn't normally a problem; as in the example given, you don't need bold text in a dialog box.

You can select words and paragraphs in several different ways. The easiest way is to use the mouse by dragging the cursor over the text you want to select while holding down the left mouse button. You can also use double- and triple-click combinations of the mouse button to select whole words or paragraphs.

The figures on the facing page demonstrate several techniques for selecting text. The first three figures show various methods using the mouse, and the last figure shows how to select text using the keyboard.

TAKE NOTE

SELECTING WITHOUT THE MOUSE

You can select text without a mouse by holding down the Shift key on your keyboard and moving the cursor over the text with arrow keys. Hold down Shift+Ctrl and the left or right arrow key to select whole words, or Shift+Ctrl and the up or down arrows to select whole paragraphs.

DELETE A SELECTION

You can select a large area of text to delete it as well as copy it. Just select the text you want to get rid of and press Del on the keyboard.

CROSS-REFERENCE
Learn how to print a selection in "Choosing What You Want to Print" in Chapter 4.

FIND IT ONLINE
Learn simple editing options in N. Dakota State University's tutorial: **http://www.agu.ndsu.nodak.edu/ lessons/word/margins.**

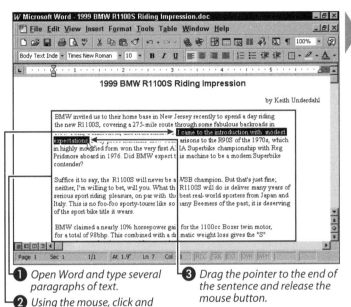

1 *Open Word and type several paragraphs of text.*

2 *Using the mouse, click and hold the left mouse button at the beginning of a sentence.*

3 *Drag the pointer to the end of the sentence and release the mouse button.*

■ *Click outside the selection to cancel it.*

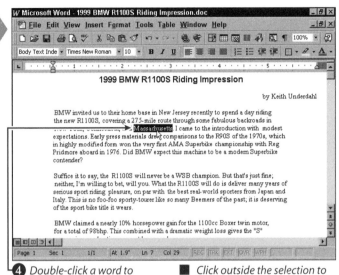

4 *Double-click a word to select it.*

■ *Click outside the selection to cancel it.*

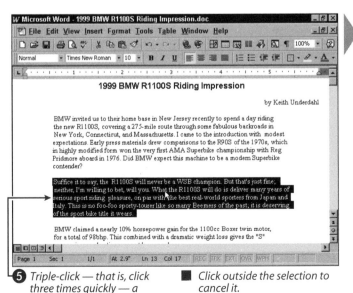

5 *Triple-click — that is, click three times quickly — a paragraph to select it.*

■ *Click outside the selection to cancel it.*

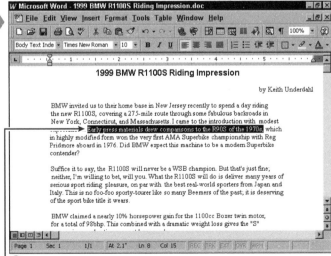

6 *Hold down the Shift key and move the cursor using the right arrow key. Hold down Ctrl and Shift and do the same thing.*

■ *Click outside the selection to cancel it.*

Selecting Cells

In the previous task, you learned how to select words and paragraphs. Words and paragraphs fall into the realm of text-based data and are relatively easy to select. But easy or not, it is an important skill to master because it can be, and frequently is, used in any Office 97 program.

Another kind of data you might have to select is a *cell*. Usually, the term cell refers to a cell of data in an Excel worksheet. Pieces of data in a worksheet are arranged into cells that are positioned next to each other in a grid-like pattern. A given cell may only have a single digit in it, or it could hold an entire paragraph of text. In fact, a cell might not have anything in it at all. Whatever it contains, each cell acts like a single entity on the worksheet.

If you are working with Excel, you need to select cells on a regular basis. Obviously, it is a quick way to copy cells and move them around, but selecting a cell or a range of cells is also central to performing many of the most basic worksheet tasks. If you need to format a cell or enter a formula in it, or even just enter data, you need to select it first. If you want Excel to calculate the sum (or any value) of a range of cells, you need to know how to select a range. It is a simple task and can be done using either the mouse or the keyboard.

The figures on the facing page demonstrate several ways to select cells. The first figure shows you how to select one cell using the mouse, and the second figure shows you how to select a range of cells. The last two figures show you how to select cells using the keyboard.

TAKE NOTE

CELLS IN TABLES

If you have created a table in a word document, the areas of the table are also known as cells. You can select cells in a table using the same techniques as you would for selecting cells in a worksheet.

WHICH CELL DISPLAYS IN THE FORMULA BAR?

By its very nature, the Formula bar can only show the contents of one cell at a time. If you select a range of cells, the Formula bar only displays whichever cell you clicked the mouse pointer on first. The Name box next to the Formula bar tells you which cell is currently being viewed. Also, the cell that is being displayed in the formula bar is a different color from those selected cells that are *not* displayed.

CROSS-REFERENCE

Learn more about selecting a range of cells for use in formulas in "Selecting a Range" in Chapter 14.

SHORTCUT

Click outside the selected text to cancel the selection.

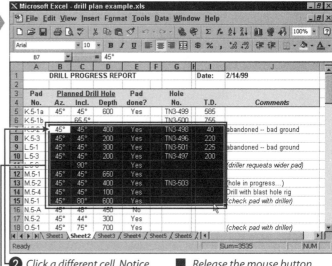

1 In Excel, click a cell on a worksheet to select it.

2 Click a different cell. Notice that the first cell you clicked is no longer selected.

3 Click and hold the left mouse button on the cell. Move the pointer down and to the right.

■ Release the mouse button. Notice that a group of cells has been selected.

■ Click anywhere else on the worksheet to deselect the group of cells.

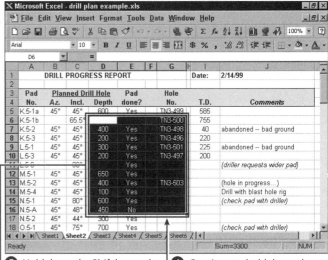

4 Using only the arrow keys on the keyboard, move the cursor to a different cell on the worksheet. As you press the arrow keys, different cells are selected.

5 Hold down the Shift key and press the down arrow to select a column of cells.

6 Continue to hold down the Shift key and press the left arrow key.

Selecting Objects and Graphics

So far, you've learned how to select two different kinds of data used by Office 97 programs: text and cells. As you may have noticed, the techniques used for selecting text and cells are quite similar, whether you are using the mouse or the keyboard to do it.

Many other kinds of data are used in Office 97 programs. One of the more common types of data that can be used is a *graphic*. Graphics can be pictures, artwork, or other elements that help enhance the look and feel of the documents you create. A graphic may even contain text that you can edit, as in the case of WordArt. You will often find the need to select graphics, whether it be to move the graphic, copy it, change it, or delete it.

Other types of data that can appear in your Office 97 documents include sound files, video files, attached files, and more. These things are usually referred to as *objects*. Technically, graphics can also be called objects, but the menu options in Office programs usually just refer to them as "graphics." When working with graphics and other objects, you will find that many of the commands that worked well with text and cells also work here.

If you want to create truly versatile, professional-looking documents, you need to learn how to select and manage these data types. The figures on the facing page show you how to select two different data types. The first two figures show you how to select a graphic, and the third figure shows you how to select more than one graphic at a time. The last figure demonstrates how to select a sound file, which is similar to many other object types.

TAKE NOTE

CHECK THE DOCUMENT VIEW

In Word documents, graphics and other such elements are best viewed in Page Layout View. Word usually switches to Page Layout View automatically when you insert a graphic, but if for some reason it doesn't, click View ⇨ Page Layout on the menu bar.

LINKS IN WEB DOCUMENTS

If you are working on a Web document, some images may actually serve as hyperlinks. If this is the case, you should use the keyboard method for selecting the graphic.

USE HANDLES TO RESIZE GRAPHICS

When you select a graphic, look for the little squares all around the border of the graphic. These are called handles, and enable you to change the size and shape of the graphic quickly. To do this, simply hold the mouse pointer over a handle until a two-way arrow appears. Then click and hold the left mouse button while you drag the handle back and forth. Release the mouse button when the object is the size you want it.

CROSS-REFERENCE

See "Adding Graphics" in Chapter 6 to learn about using graphics in Web documents.

FIND IT ONLINE

Start looking for free clip art graphics at the Clipart Directory at **http://www.clipart.com/**.

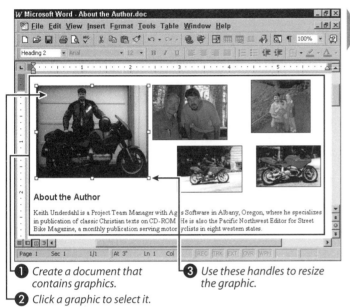

1 Create a document that contains graphics.

2 Click a graphic to select it.

3 Use these handles to resize the graphic.

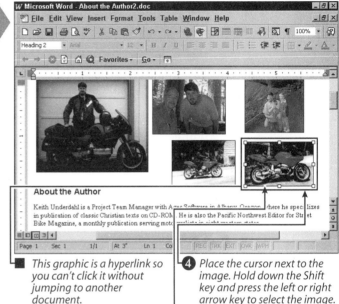

■ This graphic is a hyperlink so you can't click it without jumping to another document.

4 Place the cursor next to the image. Hold down the Shift key and press the left or right arrow key to select the image.

5 Use these handles to resize the graphic.

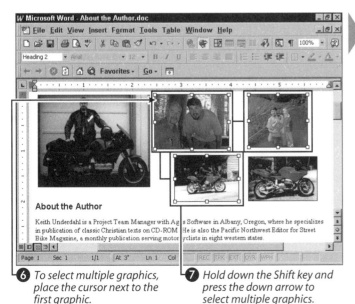

6 To select multiple graphics, place the cursor next to the first graphic.

7 Hold down the Shift key and press the down arrow to select multiple graphics.

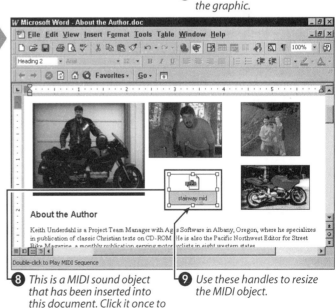

8 This is a MIDI sound object that has been inserted into this document. Click it once to select it.

9 Use these handles to resize the MIDI object.

Using Drag and Drop

You now know how to select almost any type of data you are likely to encounter. Once again, this is an extremely important skill because you need to know how to select items before you can do anything to them. Now you know how to select words, paragraphs, worksheet cells, graphics, and more.

So you know how to select these things; now what? Obviously, the purpose of selecting an object is ultimately to do something with it. One of the most common things to do with the objects you have selected is move them around. Here is a good rule of thumb: If you can select it, you can move it. Of the many different ways to do this, which method you use will depend on your preferences and the situation at hand.

You are no doubt going to want to move many things around in your Office documents. For example, suppose you are writing a letter in Word. Before you print the letter you change your mind about the order of the paragraphs and decide to move them around a bit. Moving objects around that are inside the same document is very simple to do. However, you may decide that one of the paragraphs from your letter would actually look better in a worksheet you're working on and want to move it there. This is a little more complex because it involves moving

something not only into another document but also to another program entirely.

Thankfully, Office 97 makes this easy. Using a technique called *drag and drop* you can literally drag a selected item and drop it in a new location. It is a straightforward procedure that is simple to use.

The figures on the following page demonstrate how to use drag and drop on several kinds of objects. The first two figures demonstrate how to move a piece of text from one place to another within the same document. The last two figures show you how to move a piece of text to another program entirely, in this case an Outlook e-mail message.

TAKE NOTE

▶ **USE DRAG AND DROP ON FILES TOO**

You can use the same drag and drop techniques to manage your files as well. In Windows Explorer or My Computer you can drag and drop files to new locations, the Recycle Bin, or even the Windows Desktop.

▶ **DRAG AND DROP SCRAPS TO THE DESKTOP**

If you want to continue using a piece of data from a document, drag and drop it to the Windows Desktop. It appears as a *Document Scrap*, and can be pasted into other documents as you see fit.

CROSS-REFERENCE

You must select an object before you can drag and drop it. See "Selecting Words and Paragraphs" earlier in this chapter.

SHORTCUT

To get rid of an object quickly, click it and press the Delete key on your keyboard.

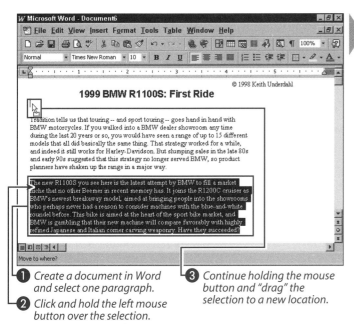

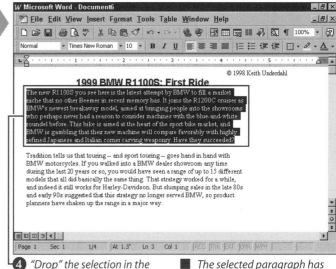

1 Create a document in Word and select one paragraph.

2 Click and hold the left mouse button over the selection.

3 Continue holding the mouse button and "drag" the selection to a new location.

4 "Drop" the selection in the new location by releasing the mouse button.

■ The selected paragraph has been moved to a new location. Click outside the selection to deselect it.

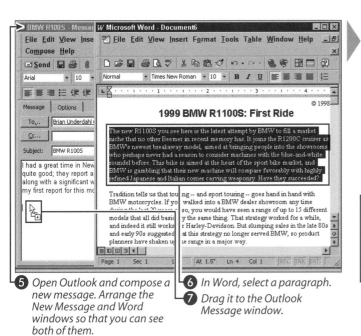

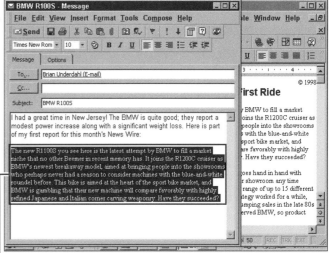

5 Open Outlook and compose a new message. Arrange the New Message and Word windows so that you can see both of them.

6 In Word, select a paragraph.

7 Drag it to the Outlook Message window.

8 Drop the paragraph in the message window. It now appears as part of the message.

■ Click outside of the selection to deselect it.

Copying and Moving Objects

In the previous task, you learned one very simple way to move objects around in Office 97 programs. Drag and drop is versatile yet simple and can be a true timesaver when you need to do some heavy-duty editing.

In addition to drag and drop, you can move data and objects around in your documents many other ways. In fact, you might be surprised to learn that many experienced users almost never use drag and drop. Everyone has different tastes when it comes to how they use a computer, and Office 97 programs give you many, many options. Differences between these options boil down to how the computer is controlled. Generally speaking, you control your computer using the keyboard and a mouse. For increased versatility, most mouse operations have keyboard equivalents, and vice versa. Some users shun the mouse and use the keyboard almost exclusively, while others prefer the user-friendliness that the mouse provides.

Drag and drop appeals more to users who prefer to use the mouse more heavily. Those who prefer the keyboard tend to use a few keyboard shortcuts and hotkeys to perform their copying and moving operations. Even if you prefer drag and drop, it is important to have a basic understanding of what these operations involve and how to perform them. Sometimes you won't be able to use the mouse, so knowing other techniques will help you in the long run.

When you select an object or piece of data, Office gives you a couple of options for what you can do with it. The two most common options are *cut* and *copy*. Cutting an item means it will no longer exist where you originally selected it. If you want to move something to a new location, this is the technique to use. Copying simply makes a copy of the selected object, but the original stays put. Regardless of whether you cut or copy an object, you can paste it from the clipboard to any place you wish.

The figures on the facing page demonstrate how to do this. The first two figures show you how to cut and paste an object from one place to another. The last two figures demonstrate how to copy and paste an object.

TAKE NOTE

PASTING FROM THE CLIPBOARD

Whenever you select cut or copy for an object, that object is copied to a component of Windows called the Clipboard. When you paste the item, it is copied there from the Clipboard. You can continue to paste the same item from the Clipboard as many times as you want until you send something else to the clipboard by another cut or copy command.

SHORTCUT

On the keyboard use Ctrl+X to cut an object or Ctrl+C to copy an object.

FIND IT ONLINE

Learn about Clipboard Magic, a clipboard archiving tool for Windows, at **http://www.cyber-matrix.com/clipmag.htm**.

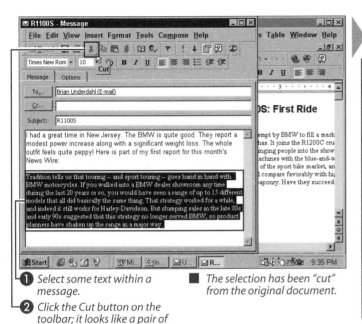

1 Select some text within a message.

2 Click the Cut button on the toolbar; it looks like a pair of scissors.

■ The selection has been "cut" from the original document.

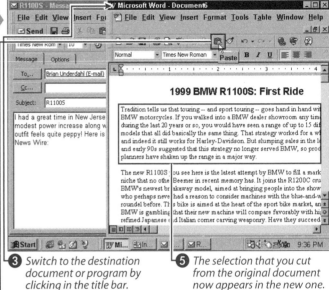

3 Switch to the destination document or program by clicking in the title bar.

4 Place the cursor where you want it and click the Paste button.

5 The selection that you cut from the original document now appears in the new one.

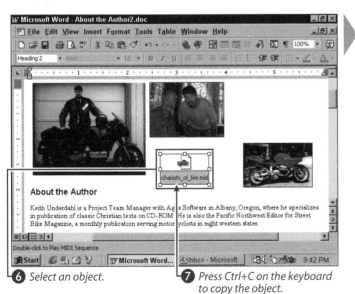

6 Select an object.

7 Press Ctrl+C on the keyboard to copy the object.

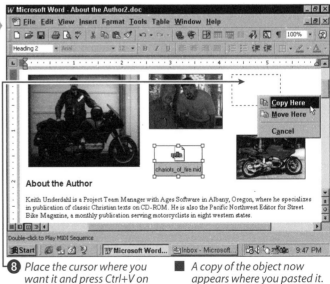

8 Place the cursor where you want it and press Ctrl+V on the keyboard.

■ A copy of the object now appears where you pasted it. Note that this technique works on many kinds of objects, including text and MIDI objects.

Personal Workbook

Q&A

1 How can you select a whole paragraph without dragging the mouse pointer over the whole thing?

_____

_____

_____

2 How do you select an object using only the keyboard?

_____

_____

_____

3 How do you select a graphic?

_____

_____

_____

4 How do you select a graphic that is also a hyperlink?

_____

_____

_____

_____

5 How do you know if something like a MIDI sound object is selected?

_____

_____

_____

_____

6 What is the difference between *cut* and *copy*?

_____

_____

_____

7 When you cut or copy an object, where does it go?

_____

_____

_____

8 How do you paste an object using only the keyboard?

_____

_____

_____

ANSWERS: PAGE 404

EXTRA PRACTICE

1 Create a Word document with several paragraphs of text and a picture.

2 Place a copy of the first paragraph at the end of the document.

3 Move the picture to the end of the document.

4 Put another copy of the picture at the beginning of the document.

5 Cut some text from one document and paste it into another.

REAL-WORLD APPLICATIONS

✔ Being able to move and copy information saves you time by enabling you to make better use of the resources on your computer. Rather than typing something twice in a memo and an e-mail message, you can simply use *copy and paste* to share the text.

✔ You or someone else around your office might have spent a lot of time putting together a monthly report in a certain way. If you don't have time to create a whole new document from scratch, you can copy some elements from the old monthly report into the new one.

Visual Quiz

How can you move the picture of the motorcycle to the bottom of the screen? Can it be moved to a different program altogether? How? Why do you suppose the same MIDI sound object appears at both the top and bottom of the page? Can you reproduce that action without the mouse? How?

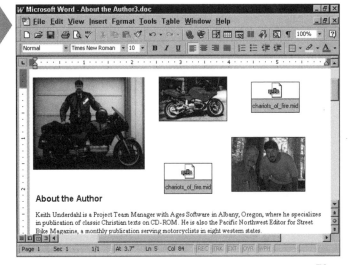

CHAPTER 6

MASTER THESE SKILLS

▶ Creating Web Pages

▶ Linking Pages Together

▶ Adding Graphics

▶ Opening Web Documents

Putting Documents on the Web

Of all the kinds of documents you can create on a computer, none has flourished quite so much in the last couple of years as documents for the World Wide Web. The World Wide Web came into widespread use in 1994 as an offshoot of the Internet. At this time, the Internet was primarily used by schools, various U.S. Government agencies, and a nerd or two.

With the incarnation of the World Wide Web came a new flurry of interest in the online world. The Web provided a simpler and more entertaining way to access information on the Internet and is now a powerful source of information that literally spans the globe. Use of the Web is widespread for entertainment, education, and business.

Chances are, you'll eventually have a need or desire to produce your own Web documents. Web documents can be used for a wide variety of applications, limited — to wear out an old cliché — only by your imagination. Even if your company hires a professional Web developer to create a Web site, you may still need to create some Web documents yourself. You can even use Web documents on a company *Intranet*, which is in essence, a miniature version of the Internet right inside your own company. You might use Web documents to share commonly used information between departments, such as a worksheet of monthly production or sales figures.

Perhaps you will never need to produce a Web document in your profession. You can still use this technology for your personal use by creating a personal Web page from your home. Many people produce Web pages dedicated to their hobby or other personal interests. Families often use Web pages to share photographs that would otherwise be expensive and time-consuming to duplicate. Again, let your imagination guide you.

This chapter introduces you to Web documents and guides you through the relatively simple process of producing them. You start by creating a very basic Web site with two pages and then learn how to link those pages together. We teach you how to add some graphics to your Web pages to spice them up and make them more interesting for the viewer. Finally, we show you how to actually open and view your Web documents.

Creating Web Pages

Many of the terms used to describe the online world can be somewhat confusing. We often hear the terms "Internet," "World Wide Web," "Cyberspace," etc., and wonder exactly what it is that is being talked about. Generally speaking, Internet refers to everything online, including e-mail, Web pages, newsgroups, Gopherspace, and virtually anything else you can think of that requires a modem to access.

The Internet has actually been around in one form or another since the late 1960s. But it wasn't until 1994 when it really captured the public's attention with the creation of the World Wide Web. The Web is made up of documents called *Web pages,* published by anybody and everybody. Web page documents are stored in *Web servers* that are permanently connected to the Internet, so anyone with an Internet connection can download and view the page. Web pages are interactive, easy to use documents that can contain text, graphics, links to other pages, and a variety of other elements.

You can create your own Web pages using Office 97. Word has the built-in capability to create, view, and edit Web pages, which are also sometimes called *HTML documents.* HTML stands for *HyperText Markup Language,* which is the programming language used on the Web. Although Word is not the most advanced Web page editor around, it is quite sufficient for most needs. Besides, you've already paid for it! You can use this capability to create your own page for the World Wide Web, your company's local Intranet, or even just on your own computer.

The figures on the facing page show you how to create a Web page. Start by creating a basic Web page with some headings and text. The last figure shows you how to save the document as an HTML document so that it can actually be used on the Web. After completing this, move on to the next page where we demonstrate how to create a second, more sophisticated Web page.

Continued

Continued

TAKE NOTE

FILENAMES FOR WEB PAGES

You need to be careful when naming a Web page. Long filenames are not supported on the Internet, so you have to use eight characters or less. Also, you should name the main page of your Web site "Index" or "Home" to ensure that most Internet software can find it quickly.

PUBLISH YOUR PAGE

Before anyone on the Internet can actually view your Web page, it must be published to a Web server. Many Internet Service Providers (ISPs) provide free disk space on their servers for your Web pages; check with your ISP to see what you can put there, and also ask them how to transfer your Web page files over to their server.

CROSS-REFERENCE

Learn how to create a folder for your Web pages in "Creating New Folders" in Chapter 3.

FIND IT ONLINE

See where the World Wide Web got its start at **http://www.cern.ch/**.

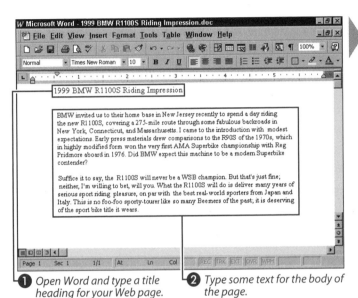

1 Open Word and type a title heading for your Web page.

2 Type some text for the body of the page.

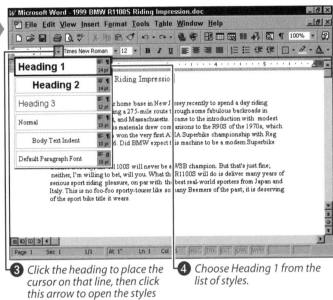

3 Click the heading to place the cursor on that line, then click this arrow to open the styles drop-down menu.

4 Choose Heading 1 from the list of styles.

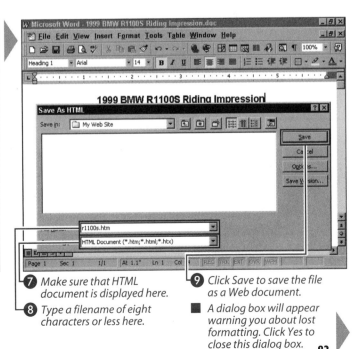

5 Click here to center the heading.

6 Choose File ⇨ Save as HTML to open the Save as HTML dialog box.

7 Make sure that HTML document is displayed here.

8 Type a filename of eight characters or less here.

9 Click Save to save the file as a Web document.

■ A dialog box will appear warning you about lost formatting. Click Yes to close this dialog box.

Creating Web Pages
Continued

Congratulations! You have just taken the first step of that proverbial thousand-mile journey towards becoming an honest-to-goodness Web publisher. However, you have many steps ahead before your journey is complete. Obviously, you could transfer the file you created on the last page over to a Web server right now and you would be an official publisher, but you probably want to do more with your Web page than simply produce a single page of text. You can do so many things, including adding pictures and linking to other pages.

A mistake that many new Web publishers make is to heap everything they have onto one single page. This causes a number of problems, all of which serve to keep surfers from visiting your Web page more than once. For one thing, even with relatively fast modems, downloading these files over the Internet can be time-consuming. If your page takes several minutes to download, potential readers get frustrated and just go somewhere else. A popular solution is to create multiple Web pages, all of which are collectively known as your Web site. This way, viewers can choose to download only the information they want to look at. Each page can be linked together; this is discussed in the next task.

You should also work to arrange the information on your pages in a logical and attractive format. You can use a number of basic tools to improve the look and feel of your Web pages, enhancing the readability for your viewers. Some information can be inserted into numbered or bulleted lists, and you can use tables to arrange various items side-by-side on the page. This avoids the dreaded "single-page-syndrome" where the reader must scroll endlessly down a single, ugly page.

The figures on the following page show you how to utilize some of these elements. Begin by creating another Web page and incorporating both a bulleted list and a table. The table will come in handy if you plan to insert a graphic; we show you how to do this later in the chapter.

TAKE NOTE

► CHECK YOUR BANDWIDTH

When publishing a Web site, try to avoid making it a *bandwidth hog*. Bandwidth is a term generally applied to how much time it takes your Web site to download. If you are blessed with an excellent Internet connection, test your Web site with a slower modem to make sure it doesn't load too slowly.

► SAVE YOUR FILES IN ONE FOLDER

For simplicity, save all of the files you plan to use with your Web pages — including graphics — in one folder. Copy graphics files and suchlike to that folder before you insert them.

CROSS-REFERENCE
Learn more about using tables in "Creating Tables" in Chapter 10.

FIND IT ONLINE
Check out Sun Microsystem's guide to Web design at http://wwwseast2.usec.sun.com/styleguide.

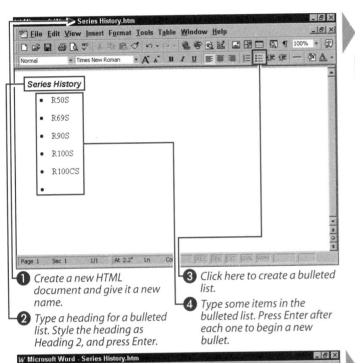

1 Create a new HTML document and give it a new name.

2 Type a heading for a bulleted list. Style the heading as Heading 2, and press Enter.

3 Click here to create a bulleted list.

4 Type some items in the bulleted list. Press Enter after each one to begin a new bullet.

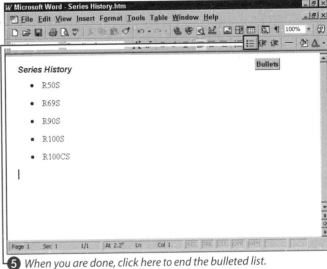

5 When you are done, click here to end the bulleted list.

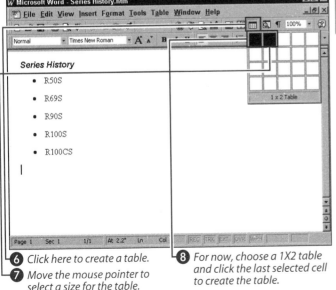

6 Click here to create a table.

7 Move the mouse pointer to select a size for the table.

8 For now, choose a 1X2 table and click the last selected cell to create the table.

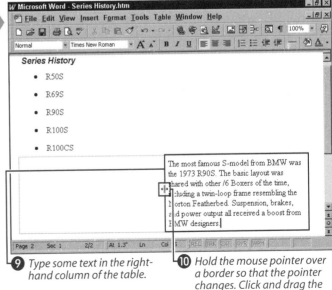

9 Type some text in the right-hand column of the table.

10 Hold the mouse pointer over a border so that the pointer changes. Click and drag the borders to resize the table and cells.

Linking Pages Together

A Web page derives its name from the larger entity that it is a part of: the World Wide Web. Basically the Web is millions and millions of documents that are linked together in a giant network that conceptually resembles a spider's web. These documents are linked together by what are called *hyperlinks*. When a viewer clicks a hyperlink with a mouse pointer, the file the hyperlink leads to is immediately opened. The file that is being linked to is often called a *target* because the link has to be aimed at something before it can work.

In the first task of this chapter you created two Web pages. It stands to reason that if a person reads one of those pages they also want to read the other. Thus, you should create a hyperlink that connects the two pages to each other. This is easy to do, and brings a more dynamic element to the pages that is the touchstone of the World Wide Web.

Creating hyperlinks between your pages turns your entire Web site into a single entity. In addition to creating links between your own pages, you probably want to link to other Web sites as well. For instance, suppose you have created a Web page that provides information about your company to potential investors. You may want to provide them with a link to the Web site of the New York Stock Exchange (http://www.nyse.com/) so they can get up-to-the-minute stock pricing for your company. Links help your Web pages really come alive by linking them to the rest of the world.

The figures on the following page show you how to create several kinds of hyperlinks. The first and second figures show you how to link the pages you created in the previous task. The third figure demonstrates how to create a link to a different Web site, and the last figure shows how to create an e-mail link.

TAKE NOTE

CREATING E-MAIL LINKS

If you want some feedback from your Web site viewers, you can make it easy by providing an e-mail link on each of your pages. Create the e-mail link just as you would any other, but in the Insert Hyperlink dialog box type "mailto:" and then your e-mail address. For example: mailto:kcunderdahl@proaxis.com.

CHECK HYPERLINKS REGULARLY

The Internet is ever changing. While that is certainly one of its main strengths, it can also present a few problems. If you create hyperlinks to other Web sites, check them on a regular basis to ensure they still work. Broken links frustrate your viewers and gives the impression that you haven't updated your information for a while.

CROSS-REFERENCE
See "Selecting Words and Paragraphs" in Chapter 5 to learn how to select text when you create a link.

SHORTCUT
Instead of typing the URL, select it in your Web browser and press Ctrl+C. Then use Ctrl+V to paste it in the Create Hyperlink dialog box.

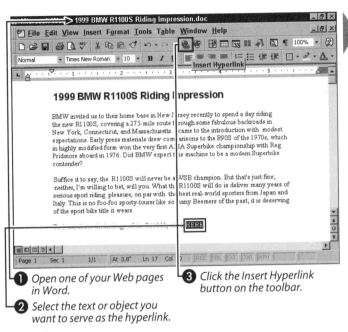

❶ Open one of your Web pages in Word.

❷ Select the text or object you want to serve as the hyperlink.

❸ Click the Insert Hyperlink button on the toolbar.

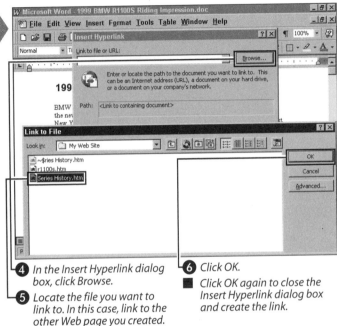

❹ In the Insert Hyperlink dialog box, click Browse.

❺ Locate the file you want to link to. In this case, link to the other Web page you created.

❻ Click OK.

■ Click OK again to close the Insert Hyperlink dialog box and create the link.

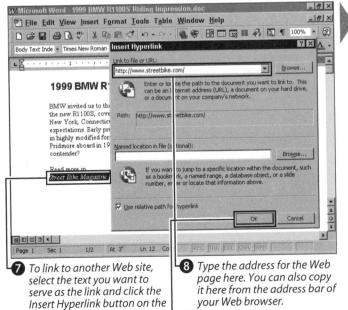

❼ To link to another Web site, select the text you want to serve as the link and click the Insert Hyperlink button on the toolbar.

❽ Type the address for the Web page here. You can also copy it here from the address bar of your Web browser.

❾ Click OK to create the link.

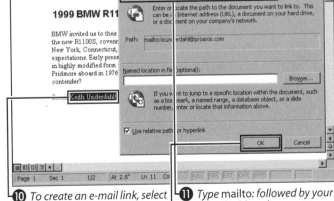

❿ To create an e-mail link, select the text for the link and click the Insert Hyperlink button on the toolbar.

⓫ Type mailto: followed by your e-mail address here.

⓬ Click OK to create the link.

Adding Graphics

The Internet has been around for quite a while now, but it hasn't always had the broad ranging appeal that it now enjoys. Credit this to the fact that back in the dark ages before the World Wide Web (that would be prior to 1994), almost everything on the Internet was text. That's right; there were no compromising photos, spy cams, "Under Construction" banners, interactive Mr. Potato Heads, or even so much as little green buttons next to every link. It was geek heaven for sure, but not very interesting to most people with an actual life.

Enter the miracle of the World Wide Web, where Web sites are not only capable of containing pictures and graphics, but these days are expected to. The text-only pages you have already created may be filled with great information, but chances are you want to spice them up a bit with some graphics. Not only can graphics give your Web pages broader visual appeal, they can also convey additional information that would be difficult to communicate in print. In the case of the Web page we have been creating here for the introduction of a new motorcycle, it's a good bet that readers want to see what the machine looks like as much as they want to read about it. To publish a Web page like this without a picture would very nearly be sacrilege. Sometimes a picture truly is worth a thousand words.

In terms of bandwidth, a picture may actually be worth *many* thousands of words. Graphics take up a lot more disk space than the HTML file for your Web page, so you need to be careful about how many graphics you include. If the graphics are too large, few viewers will hang around for several minutes while they download.

The figures on the following page show you how to insert graphics into your Web documents. Use the Web page you created earlier with a table in it to learn how to align text and pictures side by side. The last figure shows how to turn one of those graphics into a hyperlink.

TAKE NOTE

► CHECK YOUR FILE FORMATS

Generally speaking, only two kinds of graphic file formats are allowed on the Internet: GIF and JPEG. If you have another kind of graphic such as a Bitmap (BMP) image, you will not be able to use it. Consider buying some sort of image editing software such as Adobe Photoshop so you can convert graphics to the proper format.

► LINKS TO BIGGER PICTURES

To conserve bandwidth, try using relatively small images on your main pages. These smaller pictures are often called thumbnails and you can link a thumbnail to a larger version of the same picture. Then viewers can choose whether or not to download the larger pictures.

CROSS-REFERENCE

Learn about selecting graphics in "Selecting Objects and Graphics" in Chapter 5.

FIND IT ONLINE

Visit Barry's Clip Art Server at **http://www.barrysclipart.com/** for more great free graphics.

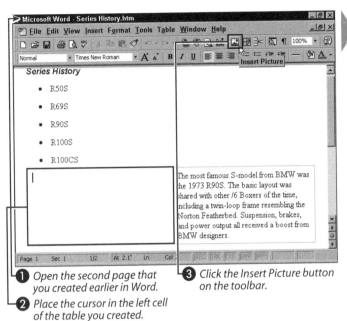

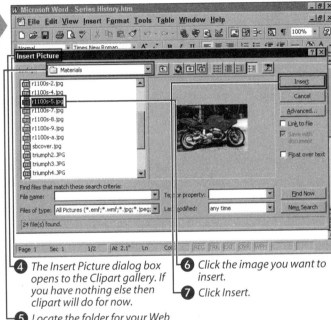

❶ *Open the second page that you created earlier in Word.*

❷ *Place the cursor in the left cell of the table you created.*

❸ *Click the Insert Picture button on the toolbar.*

❹ *The Insert Picture dialog box opens to the Clipart gallery. If you have nothing else then clipart will do for now.*

❺ *Locate the folder for your Web page stuff here.*

❻ *Click the image you want to insert.*

❼ *Click Insert.*

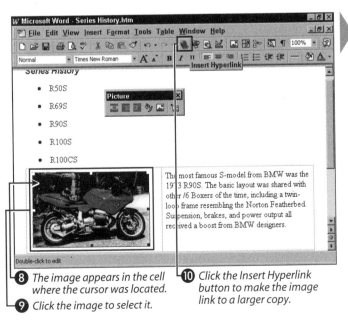

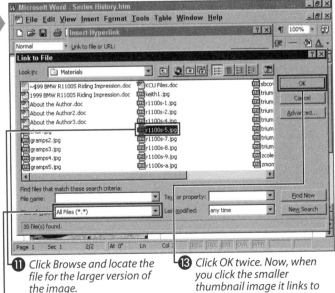

❽ *The image appears in the cell where the cursor was located.*

❾ *Click the image to select it.*

❿ *Click the Insert Hyperlink button to make the image link to a larger copy.*

⓫ *Click Browse and locate the file for the larger version of the image.*

⓬ *Select All Files in the Files of Type drop-down list.*

⓭ *Click OK twice. Now, when you click the smaller thumbnail image it links to the larger copy of the same image.*

Opening Web Documents

Although we have spent time describing how to publish some basic Web documents in this chapter, some of you may not need to actually create any Web pages of your own. Many companies now hire professional Web publishers to produce their Web sites, or the task may be accomplished in-house by someone else. However, even if you never have to create a Web page, there is a very good chance that you will need to open a Web page made by someone else. The World Wide Web has worked its way into almost every aspect of daily life around the globe, so knowing how to open and use documents used on the Web is an important skill.

If you *have* created your own Web pages, knowing how to open these documents is doubly important. One of the first things you should do after publishing a Web page is to test it. You need to test all of the hyperlinks, view all of the graphics, proofread text, and visit each and every page. This helps you identify potential problems that didn't appear when you created the pages in the first place.

Opening Web documents is simple. The best way to open a Web document is usually with a Web browser, such as Netscape Communicator, Internet Explorer, or NeoPlanet. It is very likely that you already have at least one of these programs on your computer, and if you are using Windows 98 then Internet Explorer is built right in. But in addition to these Web-specific programs, you can also open Web documents using Word with Office 97. Word lacks some of the features of a true Web browser, but some users may prefer to stick with a program that they are already familiar with.

The figures on the facing page show you how to open a Web document in Word. Depending on which version of Windows you have, the Web documents may or may not actually open in Word. If you have a real Web browser installed — such as Internet Explorer, Netscape, or NeoPlanet — it will probably launch when you display the selected page.

TAKE NOTE

GET CONNECTED

You can access Web documents on your hard drive any time you want, but to access documents over the Web you need an Internet account. Check in your phone company's yellow pages under "Internet Service Providers" to find one in your area.

INTERNET ADDRESSES

The proper name for an Internet address is *Uniform Resource Locator* (URL). URLs usually begin with *http://* or something to that effect. You can type a URL into the address box of the Word Web toolbar to visit that page.

CROSS-REFERENCE
See "Opening and Closing Office Files" in Chapter 3 for more information about opening files in general.

SHORTCUT
You can quickly refresh a Web page with Internet Explorer or NeoPlanet by pressing F5.

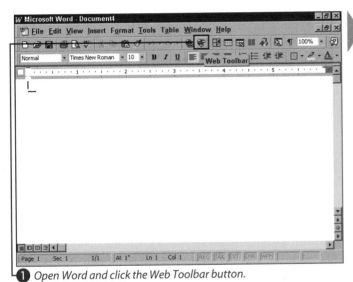

1 Open Word and click the Web Toolbar button.

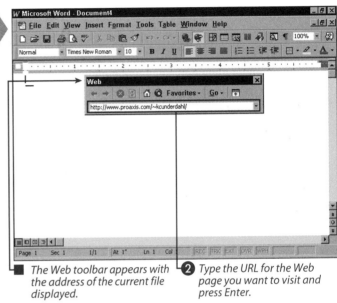

■ The Web toolbar appears with the address of the current file displayed.

2 Type the URL for the Web page you want to visit and press Enter.

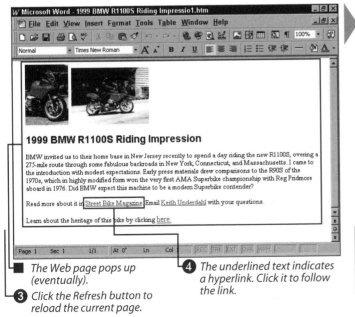

■ The Web page pops up (eventually).

3 Click the Refresh button to reload the current page.

4 The underlined text indicates a hyperlink. Click it to follow the link.

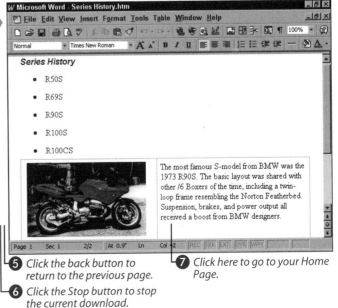

5 Click the back button to return to the previous page.

6 Click the Stop button to stop the current download.

7 Click here to go to your Home Page.

Personal Workbook

Q&A

1 How do you create a Web document using Word?

_____

_____

_____

2 Can you publish documents you create in Word on the Internet?

_____

_____

_____

3 How should you name files to be used on the Internet?

_____

_____

_____

4 What is the easiest way to align text alongside an image rather than under it?

_____

_____

_____

5 What is a hyperlink?

_____

_____

_____

6 How do you create a hyperlink?

_____

_____

7 What kind of graphic files may be used on the Internet?

_____

_____

8 What is a thumbnail?

_____

_____

9 Do you have to have a Web browser program to view Web documents?

_____

_____

ANSWERS: PAGE 405

EXTRA PRACTICE

1 Create a Web page using Word.

2 Insert an image into your Web page so that it is aligned alongside a paragraph of text.

3 Create a hyperlink from the image to the IDG Books Web site located at http://www.idgbooks.com/.

4 Save and close your Web page.

5 Reopen Word and visit your Web site. Follow the link to the IDG Web site on the Internet.

6 Explore the IDG Books Web site by clicking several hyperlinks.

7 Click the browser's Back button to return to the previous page.

REAL-WORLD APPLICATIONS

✓ You can use a simple Web page to post schedules of important events such as meetings on your company's Intranet. Make sure that this page is set as the Start Page on all computers and attendees will have one less excuse for being late!

✓ A Web page can be a great way to share family pictures with distant relatives. Use thumbnails so that they can link to high quality copies of your cute kids. Toner cartridges make great stocking stuffers!

✓ Many companies publish technical documents using Word. If you want to share these documents on a Web page, all you have to do is save them as HTML files and upload them to your Web site.

Visual Quiz

How was this Word document turned into a Web document? Can it be published on the Internet? How could the image be aligned alongside the text rather than above it? What does the underlined text mean?

_____

_____

_____

_____

_____

PART

II

Learning Important Word Tasks

Word is the top-selling word processing program in the world, and it's little wonder. This program is both easy to use and feature-rich, and is suitable for almost any text-creation task from creating a company newsletter to writing a book report.

Part II of this book teaches you how to get around in Word, and how to type and format text. Formatting includes things such as setting margins, choosing a typeface, and adjusting spacing between lines and paragraphs. You also learn how to dress up a document by adding graphics to it. You can use a scanner to import your own pictures into Word, or you can make use of Word's extensive supply of predrawn clip art.

Also in this part, you learn how to make professional-looking documents with tables and multicolumn lists, and how to avoid embarrassment by carefully checking your spelling and grammar. You can find out how to mail-merge a form letter with a list of names and addresses, producing personalized letters in record time.

CHAPTER 7

Creating Documents

No matter what type of document you ultimately wish to create, you need to begin with some basic steps. Every document, whether a single-page letter or a thousand-page manuscript, really begins when you start entering your text. Oh sure, it helps to have an idea about the information you want to include in the document, but that's a part of your planning. What we're talking about here is getting down to the real meat and potatoes of creating your document — typing in the words.

As important as this first step is, making certain your document doesn't contain embarrassing mistakes is just as vital. Nothing distracts readers as much as careless spelling or grammatical errors. No matter how important your message may be, it won't make a very good impression if the document looks sloppy and unprofessional.

Creating a good-looking document may sound like a lot of work, but fortunately you've got some very good help installed in your computer. Your word processor can find and help you correct your typing mistakes so you can concentrate on what you want to say — not just on your typing skills. In fact, Word even corrects many common typing errors automatically! If you have a habit of typing "teh" when you mean to type "the" (or any of quite a few other common typing errors), Word fixes the mistake without even asking. You may think you've suddenly become a great typist!

Word can help you create documents in plenty of other ways. Did you ever finish typing a long letter only to discover you misspelled someone's name or mentioned the wrong city in several places? Let Word find every instance and replace them for you. Do you have certain long or complicated phrases such as a legal description you need to include quite often, but you'd rather not have to worry about making a typing error? Let Word come to the rescue. You can even tell Word to expand a short abbreviation into a complete phrase — boosting your typing speed immensely.

The one thing Word can't do for you is create the document all on its own. You have to do *some* of the work for yourself. So turn the page, and see how to begin.

Getting Started and Entering Text

Word processors have made a big change in the way most people look at ordinary documents. Back in the days of the typewriter, everyone pretty much expected most documents to consist of plain, unadorned text. These days, most people have come to expect documents to look more lively. Documents need a little style if they're going to be noticed. Fortunately, Word makes it easy for you to create documents that have lots of style.

Every document you create in Word begins with a *document template*, which is just a fancy way of saying you don't have to start from scratch, defining all the styles you may want to use in a document. If you want to use certain fonts, type sizes, and different combinations of attributes for headings and normal text, the predefined styles contained in each template provide a fast and easy way to apply them. You aren't forced to use defined styles but they're there when you want a little extra help creating a good-looking document. Just click the down-arrow at the right edge of the Style list box to see what's available.

The first two figures on the facing page show you how to choose a template. (Templates have the extension .dot.) As you try out different Word templates, you'll find they often include more than just styles you can apply to your text. Some include sample text to show you where you should place certain types of text, such as headings and footnotes, and others include automated assistance to help you perform such tasks as creating mailing labels or envelopes.

Once you've selected the basis for your document, you're ready to begin typing. As shown in the third figure on the facing page, just keep typing when you reach the end of a line — Word automatically moves the insertion point to the beginning of the next line. You only need to press the Enter key when you wish to begin a new paragraph or leave a blank line in your document.

TAKE NOTE

IGNORING TEMPLATES

Even if you start a new Word document without choosing a template, you're still using a template as the basis for your document. If you don't specifically select a template, Word uses Normal.dot, the "Blank Document" template. Word also uses Normal.dot if you click the New button at the left edge of the Word toolbar.

VIEWING MORE TEMPLATES

If you don't see the template you want when you choose File ➪ New, try the other tabs on the New dialog box. Word organizes the templates into several categories to help you choose the one you want.

USING EXISTING DOCUMENTS

You can work on an existing document rather than creating a new one by selecting File ➪ Open and choosing the document you wish to use.

CROSS-REFERENCE

See Chapter 8 for more information on formatting your text.

FIND IT ONLINE

You can find additional Word templates at
http://www.microsoft.com/office/enhword.asp.

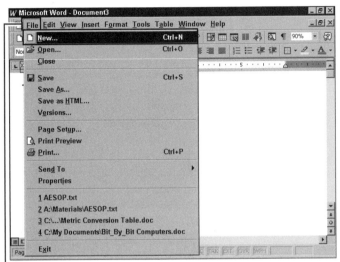

1 Select File ➪ New from Word's menu to choose a document template.

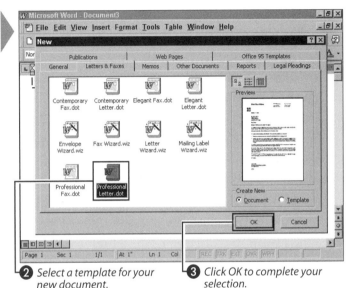

2 Select a template for your new document.

3 Click OK to complete your selection.

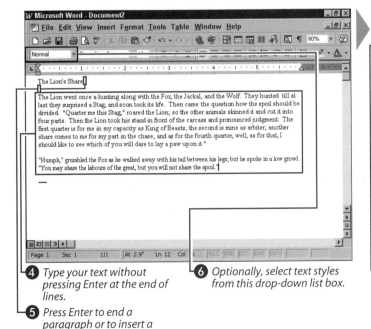

4 Type your text without pressing Enter at the end of lines.

5 Press Enter to end a paragraph or to insert a blank line.

6 Optionally, select text styles from this drop-down list box.

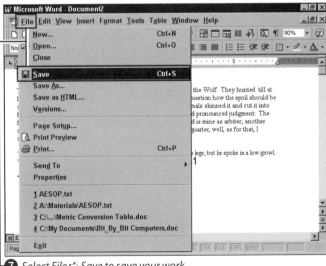

7 Select File ➪ Save to save your work.

Editing Typed Text

Very few people are superb typists, or plan every document perfectly from the start. You will probably find that you need to add or remove some text, or that you need to change the way something is phrased.

For small errors, such as the misspelling of a word, the easiest method of correction is to reposition the insertion point in the document and then press Backspace or Delete. Backspace removes a character to the left of the insertion point; Delete removes a character to the right of it. After you have removed the errant letters, you can then retype the text correctly.

To replace entire words or sentences, it is easiest to select (highlight) the word or sentence first and then type. When you type with some text selected, the new typing automatically replaces the entire selected block. This eliminates the need to delete the old text before typing the new.

To insert a new word or phrase, you can simply position the insertion point where you want it to go and then type. Word automatically moves the existing text over to make room for the new.

As you type, you may notice some red or green wavy underlines beneath some words or phrases. This is Word's automatic spelling (red) and grammar (green) checker kicking in.

TAKE NOTE

▶ INSERT V. OVERTYPE

If, when trying to insert new text the existing text does not move over, you may have inadvertently placed Word in Overtype mode. To return to Insert mode (the default), press the Insert key on the keyboard.

▶ QUICK SELECTION

As a shortcut to dragging the mouse pointer over words and sentences to select them, you can double-click a word to select it or triple-click a paragraph to select it. To quickly select a single line in a paragraph, position the mouse pointer to the left of the line, so that the pointer arrow points to the right (toward the paragraph). Then click to select that line.

▶ MOVING THE INSERTION POINT

Instead of clicking to move the insertion point, you can use the arrow keys. You can also use shortcut key combinations to move the insertion point. Pressing the Ctrl+left or right arrow moves one word to the left or right; the combination of Ctrl+up- or down-arrow moves one paragraph up or down; hitting the End button moves to the end of the line, and Home moves the cursor to the beginning of the line.

CROSS-REFERENCE

See Chapter 13 for more information on spelling and grammar checking.

FIND IT ONLINE

You can find additional help on Word at http://www.microsoft.com/office/astword.asp.

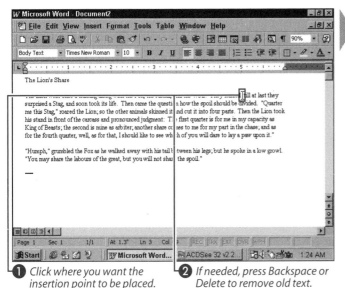

1 *Click where you want the insertion point to be placed.*

2 *If needed, press Backspace or Delete to remove old text.*

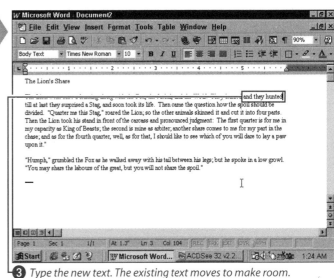

3 *Type the new text. The existing text moves to make room.*

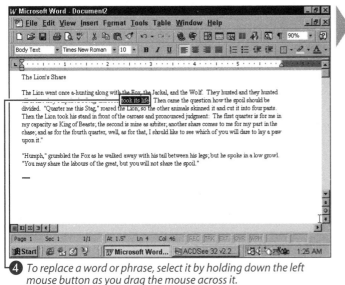

4 *To replace a word or phrase, select it by holding down the left mouse button as you drag the mouse across it.*

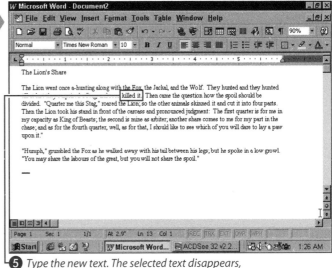

5 *Type the new text. The selected text disappears, replaced by the new.*

Finding and Replacing Text

Finding and replacing text is often a vital step in making certain a document is correct. You might, for example, discover that throughout a letter to an important client you've misspelled his/her last name, or that you used an incorrect amount in discussing a business proposal. Rather than taking the chance of missing an instance of the error, you can ask Word to search for and, if necessary, replace the incorrect text, as shown on the next page.

Although most people think of finding and replacing text in terms of a single word at a time, there's no reason that you can't search for, and replace, complete phrases. Some people even use a sort of shorthand by typing a short but unusual combination of characters to later replace with a hard-to-spell word or long phrase. You might, for example, choose to type your document with the characters "ibw" and later replace all instances of these characters with a longer phrase such as "IDG Books Worldwide" to save yourself some extra typing. This technique is pretty useful if you're going to use the same phrase many times in a single document, but as you learn later in this chapter, Word offers a couple of other ways to automatically enter text you use often in a number of documents. Before you click that Replace All button, be sure that's what you really want to do — especially if you're replacing a word that may actually be used correctly somewhere in the document.

It's better to verify the replacements individually if you're not sure of the results. You wouldn't want to automatically replace all instances of "meet" with "meat" only to find that your letter told someone you intended to "meat with them," would you?

TAKE NOTE

CHOOSING BETWEEN FIND AND REPLACE

You may notice that both the Edit ⇨ Find and Edit ⇨ Replace commands display the Find and Replace dialog box — although they do display different tabs of the dialog box. So why would you want to choose Edit ⇨ Find when Edit ⇨ Replace also finds specified phrases? To safeguard you from accidentally replacing a phrase you were only trying to locate.

REUSING FIND AND REPLACE TERMS

If you need to find or replace the same words or phrases in more than one document, open those additional documents and do the find or replace before you close Word. The Find and Replace dialog box retains a list of all the words or phrases used in the Find what and Replace with list boxes during the current session. Click the down-arrow at the right side of each list box to select one of the previously used words or phrases — even if they were used in a different document.

CROSS-REFERENCE

See the next section "Advanced Find and Replace Techniques" for more information on searching for specific styles or special characters.

FIND IT ONLINE

Go to **http://support.microsoft.com/support/ kb/articles/q120/7/75.asp** for more information on using Find and Replace.

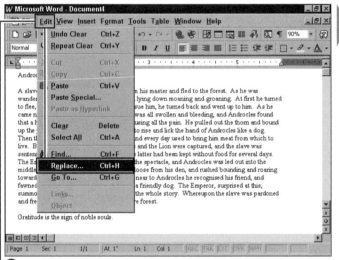

❶ *Select Edit ⇨ Replace (or Edit ⇨ Find) to display the Find and Replace dialog box.*

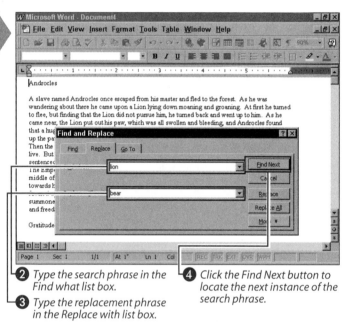

❷ *Type the search phrase in the Find what list box.*

❸ *Type the replacement phrase in the Replace with list box.*

❹ *Click the Find Next button to locate the next instance of the search phrase.*

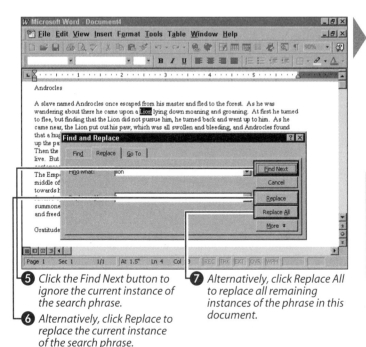

❺ *Click the Find Next button to ignore the current instance of the search phrase.*

❻ *Alternatively, click Replace to replace the current instance of the search phrase.*

❼ *Alternatively, click Replace All to replace all remaining instances of the phrase in this document.*

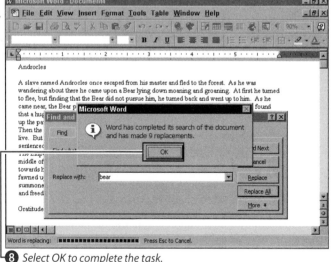

❽ *Select OK to complete the task.*

Advanced Find and Replace Techniques

W hen you think about using Find and Replace, you probably automatically associate it with finding or replacing words or phrases. While you'll probably use Find and Replace for this purpose most often, you should know that Word has many more powerful tricks hidden in these commands.

In addition to searching for words or phrases, Word can easily locate other pieces of your document, as you see in the following steps. Consider an example: If you've ever imported an e-mail message into a document, you've probably noticed that the lines of text look kind of funny on your screen. They probably alternate between long and short lines, and they don't flow from one line to the next the way normal text usually does. That's because the imported e-mail message has what Word calls paragraph marks at the end of each of the short lines. If you want to make the imported message look normal, you have to replace those paragraph marks with spaces. But there's no reason to go through the document manually — let Word's Find and Replace do the work for you!

You can also use find and replace techniques to search for things like styles or text attributes. In fact, you can search for anything you can place in a Word document. If you discover you've used the wrong style for a number of elements in your document, just search for the named style and replace it with the correct style. If you decide you don't like a particular font you used in several dozen headings, simply search for that style and replace it with one you do like.

TAKE NOTE

▶ USING SPECIAL CHARACTERS

Special characters, such as paragraph marks and white space (pretty much anything other than a printable character), may hold a few surprises for you. If, for example, you decide to replace every paragraph mark with a space, you'll reduce your entire document to a single paragraph — probably not quite what you intended. To remove extra paragraph marks without this undesired consequence you first need to replace double paragraph marks with an unusual character sequence, such as X#X, then replace the remaining paragraph marks with a space, and finally replace the X#X with a single paragraph mark. It may help to first click the Show/Hide paragraph marks button so you can see what is happening.

▶ USE COPY AND PASTE

If you're not certain how Word refers to certain special characters or attributes, copy a sample to the Clipboard before you open the Find and Replace dialog box. Then use Ctrl+V to paste the sample into the Find what or Replace with list box.

CROSS-REFERENCE

See Chapter 8 for more information on using named styles in your documents.

FIND IT ONLINE

To find more than one word, use Pattern Matching. See **http://support.microsoft.com/support/kb/articles/ q106/6/22.asp** for details.

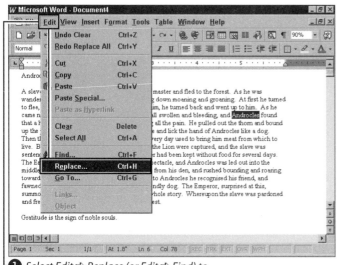

1 Select Edit ➪ Replace (or Edit ➪ Find) to display the Find and Replace dialog box.

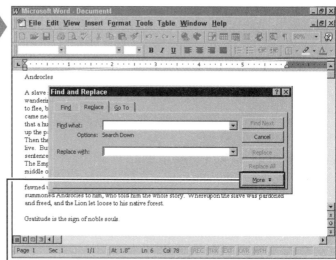

2 Click the More button to display the advanced Find and Replace options.

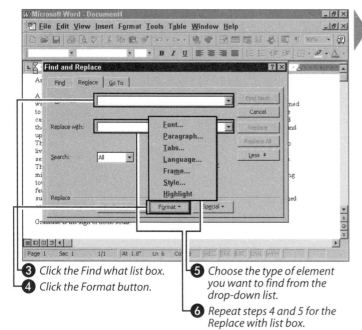

3 Click the Find what list box.

4 Click the Format button.

5 Choose the type of element you want to find from the drop-down list.

6 Repeat steps 4 and 5 for the Replace with list box.

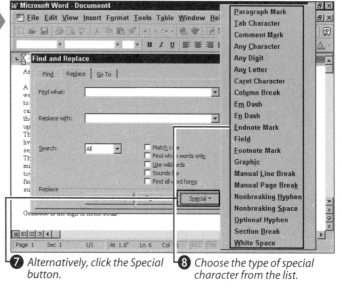

7 Alternatively, click the Special button.

8 Choose the type of special character from the list.

Using AutoCorrect

s handy as the Find and Replace feature is for replacing one text entry with a different entry, Word offers easier ways to automatically enter text that you need to use often. AutoCorrect is a Word feature that helps you create documents by automatically entering words or phrases as you type. You might, for example, have Word insert your full name when you type your initials, or perhaps your company name when you enter a short abbreviation. The following steps teach you how to set up an AutoCorrect entry.

You're not limited to simple AutoCorrect entries such as your name. You might want to think of AutoCorrect as your own personal typing assistant. Whenever you have a word or phrase you use often, you may want to consider creating your own abbreviation that Word will automatically expand for you. Simply create an easy-to-type shortcut abbreviation using a unique combination of characters that you aren't likely to encounter in other words. When you type the shortcut, Word replaces it with your designated replacement text.

If you need to control when Word expands your shortcut entry into a complete phrase, you may want to consider using the AutoText variation on the AutoCorrect theme. See the Take Note section for more details on AutoText. If you find that Word is incorrectly changing things as you type, you may also want to check out the four options at the top of the AutoCorrect dialog box. Most of the time you'll appreciate Word's help, but you may not always want changes made automatically.

TAKE NOTE

USING AUTOTEXT

AutoText is a special variation of AutoCorrect that enables you to approve automatic text entries before they're added to your documents. Unlike normal AutoCorrect entries which always replace the specified text, AutoText entries only replace the text if you confirm the substitution. You can use the AutoText tab of the AutoCorrect dialog box to set up AutoText entries. You can also use this tab to remove AutoText entries that Word has added automatically. This is especially handy if Word has created AutoText entries that slow you down by always offering to automatically enter words you don't want to use.

CREATING AUTOCORRECT ENTRIES

As handy as the AutoCorrect feature is, you need to be aware of one important thing — whenever Word encounters your AutoCorrect shortcut it expands the characters into the designated replacement phrase. As a result, you need to use some caution in creating AutoCorrect shortcuts. Never use a set of characters that may occur in another word. For example, if you were to set "cha" as a shortcut for character, you wouldn't be able to type the name Charles in a document without Word changing the name to Characterrles. One handy trick is to include a numeral in the shortcut because real words never combine letters and numbers.

CROSS-REFERENCE
See Chapter 13 for more information on using AutoCorrect to correct spelling errors.

FIND IT ONLINE
You can find Word tutorials at
http://www.microsoft.com/office/astword.asp.

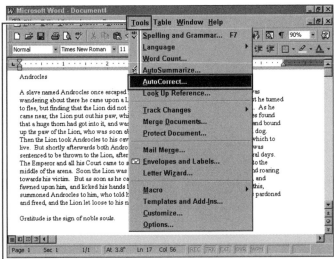

1 Select Tools ⇨ AutoCorrect to display the AutoCorrect dialog box.

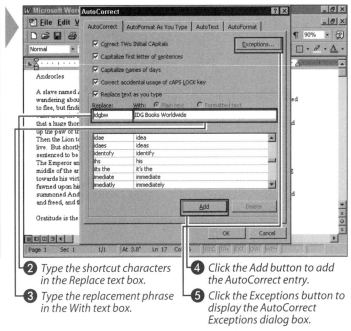

2 Type the shortcut characters in the Replace text box.

3 Type the replacement phrase in the With text box.

4 Click the Add button to add the AutoCorrect entry.

5 Click the Exceptions button to display the AutoCorrect Exceptions dialog box.

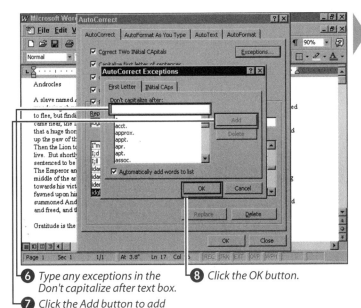

6 Type any exceptions in the Don't capitalize after text box.

7 Click the Add button to add the exception.

8 Click the OK button.

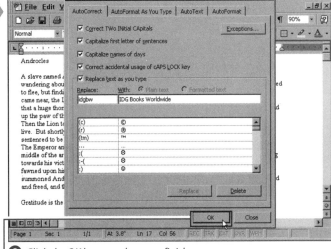

9 Click the OK button when you finish entering your AutoCorrect entries.

Creating Headers and Footers

Headers and footers are a special type of text that appears at the top (headers) or the bottom (footers) of each page of a document. Headers and footers can be as simple as a page number, or they can include a lot of additional information such as the author's name, the filename, the date, the total number of pages in the document, and so on. In certain instances, you may also wish to include things like copyright notices or even warnings about the confidential nature of the document. However, don't use too much space in your headers and footers — you are taking away space from the body of the document.

As the last figure on the facing page demonstrates, you can use *fields* in your headers and footers — information Word knows about the document. Fields offer a major advantage over static text because Word automatically updates field information before printing a document. If you insert the PrintDate field, for example, Word automatically inserts the current date whenever you print a document. The Field dialog box contains a lot of useful fields.

Documents often require a different appearance for the first page from that of the remaining pages. Often no header or footer is used on the first page, but one is required on the other pages. In some cases, you may also need different odd and even page headers and footers. To do this, select View ➪ Header and Footer, click the Page Setup button on the Header and Footer toolbar, click the Layout tab, and use the Different odd and even and Different first page checkboxes to control these settings. This creates sections in your document so different formatting options can be used.

TAKE NOTE

▶ UPDATING FIELDS

It's possible to lock a field to prevent automatic updates. If you've added fields to your document, you can update a field by selecting the field and pressing the F9 key. If this doesn't work, try selecting the field and pressing Ctrl+Shift+F11 to unlock the field, and then press F9 again to update the field.

▶ FORMATTING HEADERS AND FOOTERS

Headers and footers have their own named styles, so formatting changes you make to the rest of the document generally don't modify the appearance of your headers and footers. To see how your headers and footers will appear in the final document, select View ➪ Page Layout. In page layout view, you can click within a header or footer to make the header or footer active and available for editing. Remember that any formatting you use in a header or footer applies to all headers or footers within the document section.

CROSS-REFERENCE

See Chapter 8 for more information on using formatting.

FIND IT ONLINE

The Office home page is at
http://www.microsoft.com/office/default.asp.

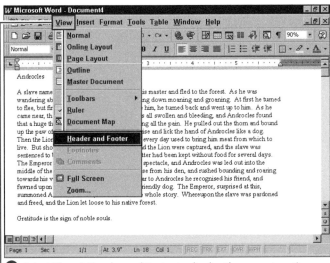

① Select View ⇨ Header and Footer to display the current section header and the Header and Footer toolbar.

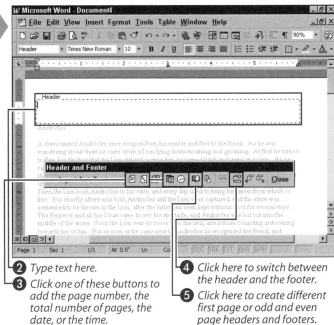

② Type text here.

③ Click one of these buttons to add the page number, the total number of pages, the date, or the time.

④ Click here to switch between the header and the footer.

⑤ Click here to create different first page or odd and even page headers and footers.

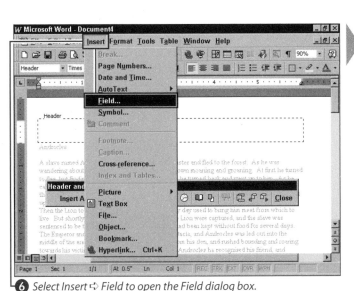

⑥ Select Insert ⇨ Field to open the Field dialog box.

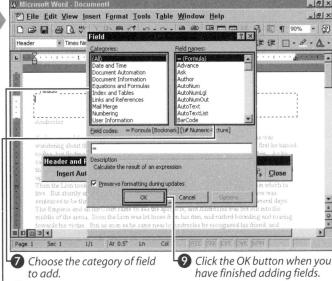

⑦ Choose the category of field to add.

⑧ Choose the specific field from the Field names list box.

⑨ Click the OK button when you have finished adding fields.

Personal Workbook

Q&A

1 What are document templates?

_____

_____

2 If you don't select a template, which template does Word use?

_____

_____

3 What does a wavy red underline under a word mean?

_____

_____

4 What does a wavy green underline under a phrase mean?

_____

_____

5 When using Find and Replace, when should you use the Find Next button rather than the Replace all button?

_____

_____

_____

6 How can you replace the same words in more than one document without retyping the Find what and Replace with phrases?

_____

_____

_____

7 What is likely to happen if you replace all the paragraph marks in your document with spaces?

_____

_____

_____

8 How can you see the paragraph marks in a document?

_____

_____

_____

9 How can you create a different first page footer?

_____

_____

_____

ANSWERS: PAGE 406

EXTRA PRACTICE

① Start a new document by selecting a template.

② Use the spelling and grammar checker to verify that you don't have mistakes in your new document.

③ Find and replace a word throughout your document.

④ Replace all the paragraph marks in your document with tabs.

⑤ Create a footer with your name, the date, and the page number.

⑥ Explore the AutoCorrect dialog box and its list of corrections.

REAL-WORLD APPLICATIONS

✔ If you are creating a report for work and one of the people on the project is replaced, use Find and Replace to replace all references to that person with the new person's name.

✔ If you enter a short story contest and the rules call for a listing of the total number of words in the story on the first page, you might consider creating a first-page footer that includes the NumWords field.

✔ If you are writing a research paper that references a number of long, difficult names, you can create AutoCorrect entries to make certain each reference is correctly entered.

Visual Quiz

How do you display the dialog box shown here? What do you need to do to display the advanced options shown at the bottom of the dialog box? How can you reuse a search phrase you used earlier?

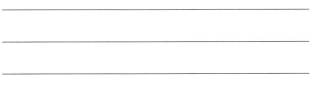

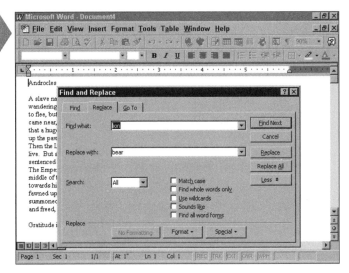

CHAPTER 8

MASTER THESE SKILLS

▶ Formatting Text

▶ Setting Paragraph Alignment and Spacing

▶ Setting Tabs

▶ Setting Margins and Paper Size

▶ Using AutoFormat

▶ Using Styles

Formatting Documents

Formatting can make a big difference to how your message is perceived. Suppose, for example, you presented your coworkers with several pages of small, plain type. Few of them would probably take the time to read it. But if you improve such a document by adding headings, using a large, easy-to-read font, and adding space between paragraphs, the document becomes a much more appealing read.

The most basic way to format a document is to change its text. This is called *character formatting*, and it can include selecting a different font (typeface), altering the type size, and making letters bold, italic, and underlined.

Moving up to the paragraph level, you can format by setting tab stops. Tab stops work just like on a typewriter; you set the stops where you want them, and then press the Tab key to move the insertion point to the next stop. You can also specify how a paragraph's text aligns. The default is left alignment, which means that each line starts neatly at the left side of the page, but you can choose right, center, or full alignment instead if you prefer. You learn more about these alignment options later in this chapter.

At the whole-page level, you can specify the paper size you're working with. Most people work with letter-size (8.5" x 11") sheets, but occasionally you may need to print on legal-size paper or odd-sized stationery. You can also choose a page orientation, which means the direction that the text runs on the page (across the wide or narrow edge). You can also set margins in Word to specify the amount of white space on each edge of the paper where the text doesn't go.

Word has several formatting shortcuts to help you produce attractive documents more easily. For example, Autoformat automatically applies formatting to your work. Another example is Styles, named formatting conventions that you can apply for consistency. For instance, you might apply a style called Heading 1 to all the major headings in your document to ensure that they are all formatted the same way.

Formatting Text

Character formatting includes any formatting that you can apply to individual letters. The three main changes you can make are font, font size, and attributes.

Font is another word for typeface, a style of lettering. This book, for example, is printed in the font named Minion. Font sizes are measured in *points*. One point is ½ of an inch. A 10-point font size means that the tallest letters in the font (for example, a capital T) are 10 points high on the printed page. You select the font and the font size independently, as shown on the opposite page; any font can be used in any size.

The default font for new blank documents that you create (that is, documents not based on a special template) is 10-point Times New Roman. To change the font and/or font size, you select the text you want to change and then choose from the Font and Font Size drop-down lists on the Formatting toolbar, as shown in the first two figures on the next page.

Attributes are special qualities you can apply to your lettering. They include bold, italic, underline, strikethrough, superscript, subscript, and several others. Each of these is a separate on/off toggle, so you can apply as many or as few of them to your text as you wish. You can also make your text any color you want. (For example, you might make the headings a different color to make them stand out.) Some attributes can be applied from the toolbar; others require you to use the Font dialog box, as shown in the last figure on the facing page.

TAKE NOTE

SYMBOL FONTS

Some fonts, like Wingdings, consist only of symbols. If you apply such a font to your text, the result is gibberish. If you accidentally do this, just reselect the text and reapply a more ordinary font such as Times New Roman or Arial. To insert symbols in your document from these symbol fonts, use the Insert ⇨ Symbol command.

GETTING MORE FONTS

You can buy disks that contain hundreds of different fonts at your local computer software retailer. You then install these fonts using an installation program or the Windows Control Panel, making them available to all your Windows-based programs (including Word).

CHANGING THE DEFAULT FONT

If you want the default font for new blank documents to be different, start a new document by clicking the New button on the Standard toolbar. Then choose Format ⇨ Font and make your font changes in the Font dialog box. Then click the Default button and then click Yes to make your new selections the default settings.

CROSS-REFERENCE

See "Using Templates" in Chapter 10 to learn about Templates, another shortcut to formatting.

FIND IT ONLINE

To send a document with fonts that any recipient can view, see **http://support.micorsoft.com/support/kb/articles/q113/8/22asp.**

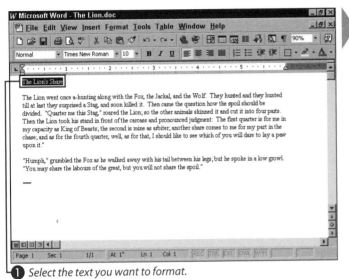

1 Select the text you want to format.

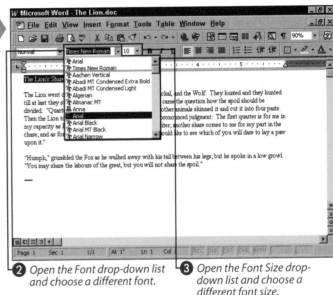

2 Open the Font drop-down list and choose a different font.

3 Open the Font Size drop-down list and choose a different font size.

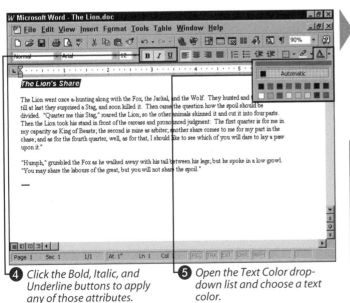

4 Click the Bold, Italic, and Underline buttons to apply any of those attributes.

5 Open the Text Color drop-down list and choose a text color.

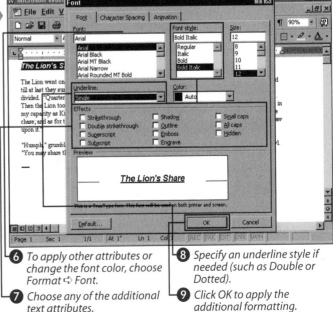

6 To apply other attributes or change the font color, choose Format ⇨ Font.

7 Choose any of the additional text attributes.

8 Specify an underline style if needed (such as Double or Dotted).

9 Click OK to apply the additional formatting.

115

Setting Paragraph Alignment and Spacing

Text alignment refers to the starting position of each line of text in a paragraph. Another term for text alignment is *justification*. The default alignment is Left, which means that each line begins at the same horizontal position. This results in a smooth left edge, and a ragged right edge (because each line has a different number of letters and spaces).

In Word, you can choose from three other alignments as alternatives: Align Right, Center, or Justify. Align Right makes the right text edge smooth and the left edge ragged. Center centers each line of the paragraph between the margins so that each line starts and ends in a different spot. Justify inserts small spaces between words and letters as needed so that both the right and left text edges are smooth and even. You can choose a paragraph's alignment by selecting it and clicking the appropriate toolbar button.

Line spacing refers to the amount of space between the lines in a paragraph and before and after the paragraph. For example, in a letter you might have single-spaced paragraphs with one blank line after each paragraph. In a manuscript, you might have double-spaced paragraphs and one-and-a-half blank lines after each one. Word lets you set any measurement for inter- and intra-paragraph spacing, using measurements as small as one point ($\frac{1}{72}$ of an inch). These measurements are set in the Paragraph dialog box, shown on the last two figures on the opposite page.

Indentation is the amount that a paragraph is moved in from the normal document margin. You might indent a paragraph to set it apart from the rest of the document — for example, a quotation. You can also set first-line indents for paragraphs, so that each paragraph's first line is automatically indented 0.5" (which is about five spaces, the amount you were probably taught to indent a paragraph in your high school typing class!) or some other measurement. That way, you don't have to press Tab at the beginning of every paragraph.

TAKE NOTE

INDENTATION SHORTCUT

You can find Increase Indent and Decrease Indent buttons on the toolbar, which indent and outdent based on the tab stops. For example, clicking the Increase Indent button indents the current paragraph to the first default tab stop (0.5" from the left margin).

WIDOW/ORPHAN CONTROL

It is considered bad desktop publishing to leave a single line of a paragraph hanging at the bottom (widow) or top (orphan) of a page. Word can watch for these and move a line or two to the next page to fix it. In the Paragraph dialog box, (Format ➪ Paragraph) click the Line and Page Breaks tab and ensure that the Widow/Orphan Control checkbox is selected.

CROSS-REFERENCE
See the next section "Setting Tabs," to learn about tab stops.

FIND IT ONLINE
Converting a document to HTML can mess up the alignment, see **http://support.microsoft.com/support/kb/articles/q162/9/22.asp** for a workaround.

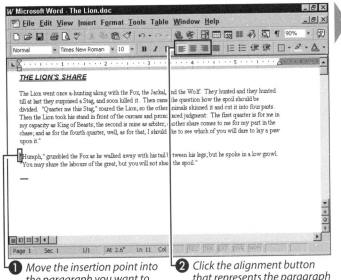

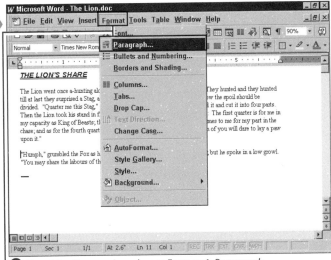

1 Move the insertion point into the paragraph you want to format. Or, if you want to format multiple paragraphs at once, select them.

2 Click the alignment button that represents the paragraph alignment you want.

3 To set the line spacing, choose Format ⇨ Paragraph. The Paragraph dialog box opens.

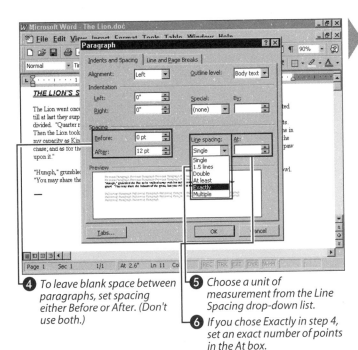

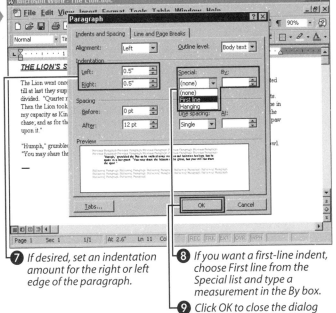

4 To leave blank space between paragraphs, set spacing either Before or After. (Don't use both.)

5 Choose a unit of measurement from the Line Spacing drop-down list.

6 If you chose Exactly in step 4, set an exact number of points in the At box.

7 If desired, set an indentation amount for the right or left edge of the paragraph.

8 If you want a first-line indent, choose First line from the Special list and type a measurement in the By box.

9 Click OK to close the dialog box.

117

Setting Tabs

Tab stops help you align your typing at the same horizontal point on multiple lines, to create multicolumn lists and tables. In Word, default tab stops occur every 0.5" starting at the left margin. Each time you press Tab, the insertion point moves to the next stop: 0.5", 1", 1.5", and so on. You can also place custom tab stops in a document, overriding these defaults, by clicking Word's ruler. If the ruler does not appear, choose View ⇨ Ruler.

The most common tab stop is Left. When you press Tab to move to its position, the insertion point jumps there and the text you type starts running to the right from that point on.

With a Right tab stop, the insertion point moves to the stop, but the text you type runs back toward the left, so that the last letter of your typed text aligns with the stop rather than the first letter.

With a Center tab stop, the typed text centers itself under the stop.

A Decimal tab stop acts just like a Right tab stop until you type a period (decimal point); then it aligns everything after that period to the left. The following table shows the symbols Word uses for each tab stop.

Tab Stop Symbols

⌐	Left
⌐	Right
⊥	Center
⊥	Decimal

You can also set up leaders for your tab stops. *Leaders* are repeated characters, such as periods or dashes, that stretch from the last bit of text before the tab stop to the first bit of text at the tab stop. Leaders help your eye follow a line across an open space.

TAKE NOTE

▶ CUSTOM TABS OVERRIDE DEFAULT TABS

When you place a custom stop, Word ignores the default stops to the left of the custom one, but all the default ones to the right of it remain in place. So, for example, if you placed a custom tab stop at the 2" mark on the ruler, your tab stops for the paragraph would be at 2", 2.5", 3", and so on. But if you placed another custom tab stop at the 5" mark, your tab stops would be at 2", 5", and 5.5".

▶ REMOVING OR MOVING TAB STOPS

To move a tab stop, drag its marker on the ruler to a different spot. To delete a tab stop, drag it below the ruler and drop it.

▶ BAR TABS

Available in the Tabs dialog box, the Bar tab stop creates a vertical bar on the page at the tab stop.

▶ FIND AND REPLACE TABS

Find and replace tabs using Word's Find and Replace feature. To specify the tab character use ^t.

CROSS-REFERENCE
See "Using Drag and Drop" in Chapter 5 for information on dragging things with the mouse.

FIND IT ONLINE
If tab stops are deleted during a spell check, see http://support.microsoft.com/support/kb/articles/ q183/6/23.asp for a workaround.

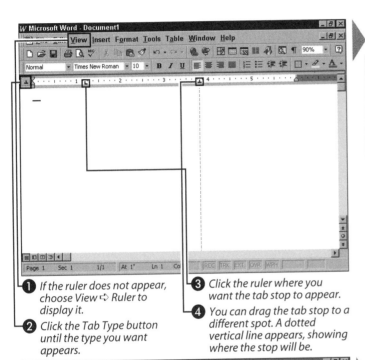

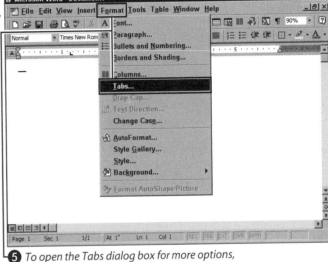

1 If the ruler does not appear, choose View ➪ Ruler to display it.

2 Click the Tab Type button until the type you want appears.

3 Click the ruler where you want the tab stop to appear.

4 You can drag the tab stop to a different spot. A dotted vertical line appears, showing where the stop will be.

5 To open the Tabs dialog box for more options, choose Format ➪ Tabs.

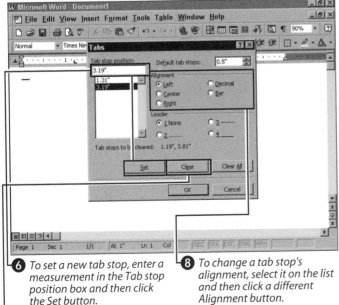

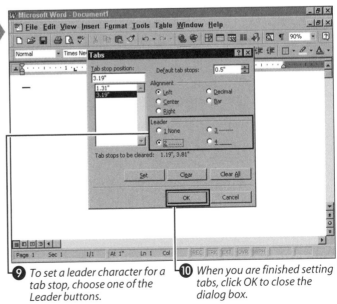

6 To set a new tab stop, enter a measurement in the Tab stop position box and then click the Set button.

7 To clear a tab stop, select it on the list and then click Clear.

8 To change a tab stop's alignment, select it on the list and then click a different Alignment button.

9 To set a leader character for a tab stop, choose one of the Leader buttons.

10 When you are finished setting tabs, click OK to close the dialog box.

119

Setting Margins and Paper Size

Margins are the blank spaces between the edges of the paper and the beginning of the printed text. The default margins for a Word document are 1" at the top and bottom and 1.25" at the left and right. These settings work well for business letters and most reports, but sometimes you may want to change them. For example, if you have a report that almost fits on a single page, you might slightly decrease the right and left margins (say, to 1" apiece, or even 0.9") to make it fit. Or perhaps you are writing a resume that looks a little bit short — you could increase the top margin to 1.25" to make it start just a bit further down on the page.

Paper size and orientation can also be adjusted for a document. The default paper size is 8.5" x 11", which is the size of a standard sheet of typing paper, but you can create a Word document to be printed on any size.

Paper source is an issue only if you have a multi-tray printer. For example, some business printers have two trays, and keep letterhead in one tray and plain paper in another, or second-page letter stationery.

The default page orientation is portrait, which means the page is taller than it is wide. The alternative is landscape, wherein the page is wider than it is tall. An easy way to remember which is which is to think about paintings and photographs. A portrait of a person is tall and thin because a person is taller than they are wide. A picture of a landscape is wide and short because there is more to see from side to side.

TAKE NOTE

SECTION BREAKS ENABLE DIFFERENT SETTINGS

The paper size, margins, and orientation settings in Word apply to the entire document, not to individual paragraphs. If you want a different margin setting for certain pages of the document, you must create a section break (choose Insert ➪ Break and then choose one of the options in the Section Break part of the dialog box). Section breaks enable each section to have its own document-wide settings, such as margins, number of columns, and so on.

OTHER DOCUMENT-WIDE SETTINGS

Some other formatting options that apply to the entire document (or the entire section, if you have created section breaks) include headers and footers, paper source, and vertical alignment. You can set all of these in the Page Layout dialog box (File ➪ Page Layout).

MARGINS V. INDENTS

It's important to understand the difference between margins and indents. Margins apply to the entire document (or section). Indents operate on individual paragraphs in relation to the margins.

CROSS-REFERENCE

See "Creating Headers and Footers" in Chapter 7 to learn more about headers and footers.

FIND IT ONLINE

See **http://support.microsoft.com/support/kb/articles/q108/4/56** for information on changing a table's width.

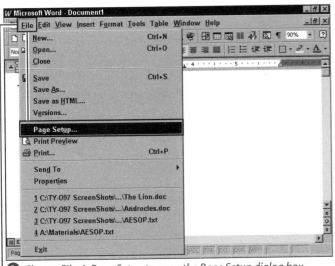

❶ Choose File ⇨ Page Setup to open the Page Setup dialog box.

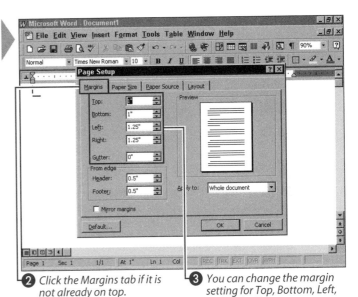

❷ Click the Margins tab if it is not already on top.

❸ You can change the margin setting for Top, Bottom, Left, and Right. Type a new number or use the up and down arrows.

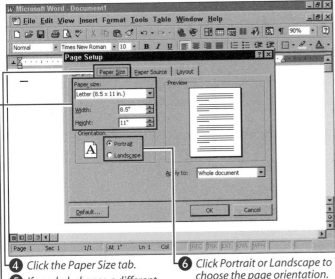

❹ Click the Paper Size tab.

❺ If needed, choose a different paper size from the drop-down list, or manually enter paper dimensions in the Width and Height boxes.

❻ Click Portrait or Landscape to choose the page orientation.

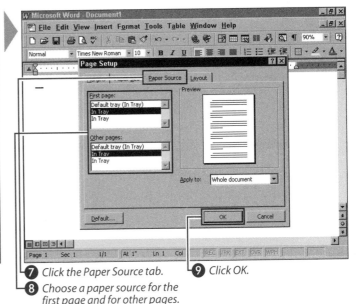

❼ Click the Paper Source tab.

❽ Choose a paper source for the first page and for other pages. If your printer has only one tray, skip to step 9.

❾ Click OK.

Using AutoFormat

utoFormat helps you create attractive, consistently-formatted documents. AutoFormat has two components: AutoFormat As You Type and AutoFormat. AutoFormat As You Type fixes minor formatting mistakes automatically, without issuing any special commands. AutoFormat is a command you issue. It goes through your document and finds/fixes formatting problems and inconsistencies. You can either accept the changes as a whole or review each one.

Using AutoFormat As You Type is completely effortless — the changes just happen. For example, after the first couple of paragraphs of a bulleted list, Word catches on and formats the next paragraph (the next time you press Enter) as a bulleted list item.

Some people find AutoFormat As You Type more of a hindrance than a help, because it makes changes that you don't necessarily want. To review the AutoFormat As You Type options and set it to use only the rules you want, choose Tools ⇨ AutoCorrect and then click the AutoFormat As You Type tab. In the dialog box that appears, you can turn on/off the following options:

▶ **Apply As You Type:** Choose whether or not you want automatic bulleted and numbered lists, and automatic borders, headings, and tables.

▶ **Replace As You Type:** Choose whether you want your regular typed characters replaced by special typesetting symbols, for example, two short dashes (−−) replaced by a long dash (—).

▶ **Automatically As You Type:** Choose from the miscellaneous formatting helpers here, such as whether to define styles based on your formatting.

The AutoFormat command, explained on the facing page, is totally separate from these AutoFormat As You Type options.

TAKE NOTE

AUTOFORMAT OPTIONS

AutoFormat has its own options you can set. Choose Tools ⇨ AutoCorrect and click the AutoFormat tab, or choose Format ⇨ AutoFormat and click the Options button.

AUTOFORMATTING AND STYLES

AutoFormatting works especially well when you have applied styles to your document headings, because it can then readily identify which text blocks are headings and which are regular paragraphs. If you have used styles (covered later in this chapter), try clicking the Style Gallery button in the AutoFormat dialog box (shown on the next page) and exploring how the formatting changes if you apply various templates.

CROSS-REFERENCE

AutoCorrect is another feature that replaces some of your typing with special symbols. See "Using AutoCorrect" in Chapter 7 for details.

FIND IT ONLINE

If an error message appears when formatting a table, see http://support.microsoft.com/support/kb/articles/ q108/4/56.asp for a workaround.

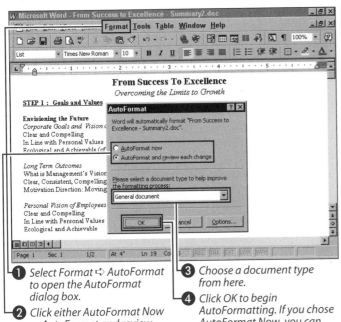

1 Select Format ⇨ AutoFormat to open the AutoFormat dialog box.

2 Click either AutoFormat Now or AutoFormat and review each change.

3 Choose a document type from here.

4 Click OK to begin AutoFormatting. If you chose AutoFormat Now, you can skip the rest of these steps.

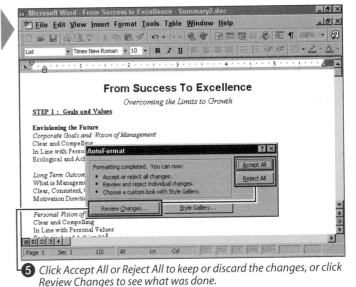

5 Click Accept All or Reject All to keep or discard the changes, or click Review Changes to see what was done.

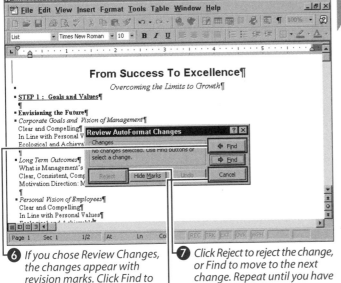

6 If you chose Review Changes, the changes appear with revision marks. Click Find to move to the first change.

7 Click Reject to reject the change, or Find to move to the next change. Repeat until you have examined all changes.

8 Click Cancel to return to the AutoFormat box.

9 Click Accept All to accept all remaining changes, or click Reject All if you decide not to keep any of them.

Using Styles

Styles are named sets of formatting that you can apply to individual paragraphs (or depending on the style type, to individual characters). For example, you might create a style called Chapter Title that contained the following specifications: Times New Roman font, 18-point size, Bold, Italic, and Centered. Then every time you assigned that style to a paragraph, it would immediately become formatted in the specified way.

As you can imagine, styles are extremely useful in longer documents, such as reports, for maintaining consistency. You don't have to remember whether you chose 14- or 16-point type for the headings on earlier pages; the style remembers that for you. All you need to do is apply the style to the headings. Additionally, when you decide to change a style, the changes apply automatically to all the text to which it has been applied. If you later decide that all headings should be 18-point, you merely change the style, and all the headings change.

A set of predefined styles comes with each template, including the one for a blank document (Normal). To see the list of available styles, open the Style drop-down list on the Formatting toolbar.

You can apply a style as-is, or you can modify the style's definitions or even create your own styles. The easiest way to modify a style is by example, as shown on the facing page. The procedure for creating a brand-new style is much the same.

TAKE NOTE

PARAGRAPH V. CHARACTER STYLES

You can create either paragraph or character styles. Paragraph styles contain both paragraph and text formatting (for example, center alignment and bold type); character styles contain only text formatting. Most of the predefined styles are paragraph formats, and the default type you create when defining styles by example is Paragraph.

CHANGING THE STYLES STORED IN A TEMPLATE

When you modify a style in a document, the change applies only to that document, not to the template on which the document was based. To make changes to a template, open the template (File ⇨ Open) and modify the template itself.

ANOTHER WAY TO DEFINE/MODIFY STYLES

You can also modify and create styles from a dialog box. Choose Format ⇨ Style and then click the style you want to redefine and click Modify, or click the New button to create a new style. Then click the Format button and choose a formatting aspect (Font, Paragraph, etc.). Specify your formatting changes and then click OK until all dialog boxes are closed. This more complicated than the "by example" method, but it is very powerful, providing access to all styles and all formatting options at once.

CROSS-REFERENCE
See "Using Templates" in Chapter 10 for more details on modifying templates.

FIND IT ONLINE
For information on the Style Gallery, see
http://support.microsoft.com/support/kb/articles/q142/7/50.asp.

FORMATTING DOCUMENTS

Using Styles

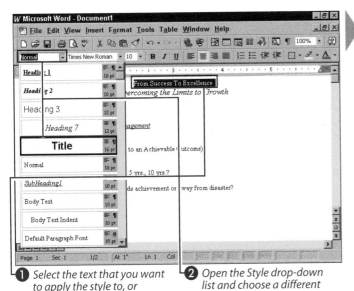

1 Select the text that you want to apply the style to, or position the insertion point in the paragraph.

2 Open the Style drop-down list and choose a different style to use.

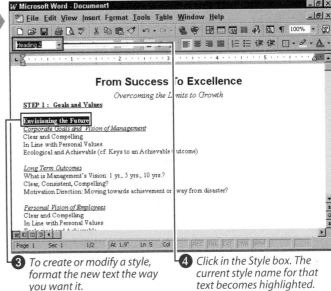

3 To create or modify a style, format the new text the way you want it.

4 Click in the Style box. The current style name for that text becomes highlighted.

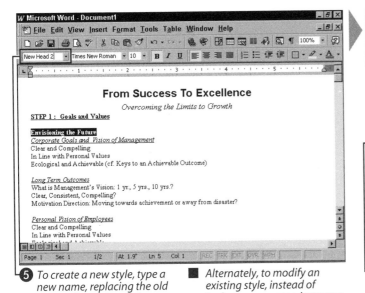

5 To create a new style, type a new name, replacing the old one, and press Enter. You can skip the rest of these steps.

■ Alternately, to modify an existing style, instead of typing a new name, just press Enter. A dialog box appears.

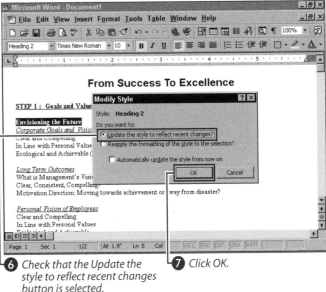

6 Check that the Update the style to reflect recent changes button is selected.

7 Click OK.

Personal Workbook

Q&A

1 What is the difference between character and paragraph formatting?

_____

_____

_____

2 What is the unit of measurement used to measure font size?

_____

_____

3 What are the four kinds of paragraph alignment that Word supports?

_____

_____

_____

4 At what interval are the default tab stops spaced?

_____

_____

_____

5 What are the four kinds of tab stops you can set on the ruler? (Bonus: What is the fifth kind of tab stop, available only from the Tabs dialog box?)

_____

_____

6 What are the default margins on a new, blank document in Word?

_____

_____

7 How can you have more than one set of margin settings in a single document?

_____

_____

8 What's the difference between a margin and an indent?

_____

_____

9 What's the easiest way to create a new style?

_____

_____

ANSWERS: PAGE 407

EXTRA PRACTICE

1 Type some text and format it in Arial font, 16-point, bold.

2 Use the Font dialog box to make the text double-underlined.

3 Create a paragraph and set it at 1.5 line spacing between lines, with 12 points of space after it.

4 Set tab stops for that paragraph at 1" and 3" on the ruler.

5 Set your document margins to 1" on all sides.

6 Create a style called New Heading that formats text as Times New Roman, 16-point bold, and italic.

REAL-WORLD APPLICATIONS

✔ A document you add to each week is formatted so that you need to press Enter twice after every paragraph. You can break that habit by formatting each paragraph to have one line of space after it. Depending on the font size you are using, one line is probably either 10 or 12 points.

✔ If you create the same type of documents on a regular basis, you can save time. Create styles that correspond to the formatting you use most often in those documents and create templates that contain them. (See Chapter 10.)

✔ If you use letterhead stationery for your business letters, measure the stationery with a ruler to see how many inches you need to leave at the top. Set your top margin in Word to that amount plus 0.5".

Visual Quiz

How do you display the dialog box shown here? Which controls in it are also available from the toolbar?

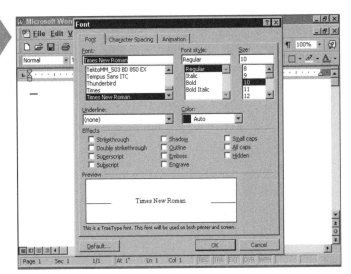

CHAPTER **9**

MASTER
THESE
SKILLS

▶ Using WordArt

▶ Using Clip Art

▶ Inserting a Picture

▶ Editing a Picture

Adding Graphics to Word Documents

Graphics can really enliven a dull document. Whether you want to publish a whole catalog full of graphics or you just want a simple clip art logo at the top, this chapter can help.

You can include many kinds of graphics in a document. Probably the most common kind is clip art — predrawn "generic" artwork that comes with Word. It got its name in the olden days (ten years or so ago) when graphic artists bought huge books of generic artwork with dozens of images crammed on each page. They would clip out the image they wanted with scissors and paste it into their layout. Word provides a Clip Gallery, a special program that organizes and helps you insert clip art. You can also use the Clip Gallery to connect to the Internet and download additional clip art free from Microsoft.

WordArt is a text manipulation program that enables you to stretch, bend, twist, squeeze, and color a word or phrase until it takes on an "artsy" quality. You can use WordArt to create logos, posters, advertisements — anything that needs to be flashy and memorable. *Warning*: Once you start playing with WordArt, you may not get anything else done for the rest of the day!

You can also insert your own scanned or purchased images, including photographs. Say your CEO wants his photo in the annual report? Or your staff artist works only on paper, not on a computer? No problem. Just use a scanner or digital camera to put the image into your computer and then place the image into your Word document with the Insert ⇨ Picture ⇨ From File command. This is also how you use clip art that you buy separately from Word, on one of those "10,000 Great Images" disks that always seem to be on sale at the local computer store. Word can accept graphics in a wide variety of formats, including JPG, TIF, PCX, BMP, and GIF.

Once the image has been placed in Word, you can move, resize, crop, and otherwise manipulate it to fine-tune the presentation to perfection. With some images, you can even change the colors from within Word, without opening a separate graphic-editing program. We spend some time at the end of this chapter looking at the many image editing controls in Word.

Using WordArt

WordArt is what's known as an applet — a separate little program that runs only from within Word (or one of the other Microsoft Office programs that supports it). You can use WordArt to create some stunning special effects for your text.

Back in Chapter 8, you learned the basics of text formatting — how to change the font, the size, the color, and so on. WordArt takes this formatting to a new level. Not only can you change the text color, you can add shading, patterns, and textures to it. You can resize letters, and bend and squeeze them into a swoosh, a triangle, or any of dozens of other shapes.

The WordArt Gallery provides 30 predesigned WordArt layouts; combinations of font and size choices, color choices, and shape choices. When you create a new piece of WordArt, you choose one of these. You are not tied to it, however; at any point you can choose a different layout for your text from among these 30, or you can change any attribute of your WordArt to fine-tune it for your own use (size, shape, color, font, and so on).

When you work with WordArt, a WordArt toolbar appears containing the buttons and controls you need for editing. Some of the most commonly used

WordArt buttons are:

Edit Text: Opens a dialog box so you can edit text.

Gallery: Enables you to choose a different layout.

Format: Enables you to change the color, size, position, and word wrapping.

Shape: Opens a palette of shapes to mold words into.

Free Rotate: Rotates or tilts words at any angle.

Same Letter Heights: Toggle between normal letter heights and uniform heights.

Vertical Text: Toggle the letters running vertically versus horizontally.

Alignment: Align words to the Center, Left, or Right, or choose one of the special effects such as Stretch.

Character Spacing: Select a spacing tightness, such as Tight, Normal, or Loose.

TAKE NOTE

FAST IDENTIFICATION OF WORDART TOOLBAR BUTTONS

As with other toolbars, you can find out what each WordArt button does by hovering the mouse pointer over it until a ScreenTip pops up with an explanation.

CROSS-REFERENCE
See "Formatting Text" in Chapter 8 for information about changing the font, size, and color of Word text.

FIND IT ONLINE
Earlier versions of Word don't support the same WordArt format, see **http://support.microsoft.com/support/kb/articles/q157/4/66.asp**.

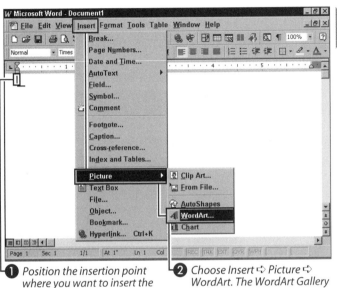

1 Position the insertion point where you want to insert the WordArt.

2 Choose Insert ⇨ Picture ⇨ WordArt. The WordArt Gallery dialog box appears.

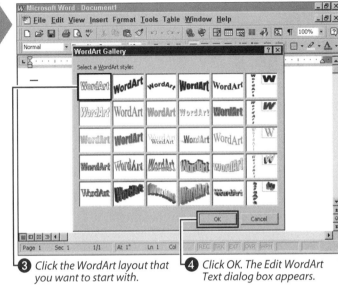

3 Click the WordArt layout that you want to start with.

4 Click OK. The Edit WordArt Text dialog box appears.

5 Replace the "Your Text Here" sample text with your own text.

6 If desired, change the font, font size, and attributes.

7 Click OK. The WordArt appears in your document.

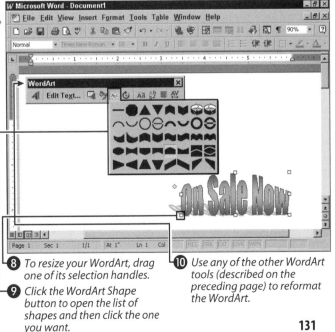

8 To resize your WordArt, drag one of its selection handles.

9 Click the WordArt Shape button to open the list of shapes and then click the one you want.

10 Use any of the other WordArt tools (described on the preceding page) to reformat the WordArt.

131

Using Clip Art

Many users don't realize it, but Word (and Office 97 as a whole) comes with thousands of beautifully drawn clip art images. These images are royalty-free, which means you can use them in any of your business or personal documents without paying any fees. You can also download hundreds more images free from the Microsoft Web site.

Clip art is organized in Word through an applet called the Clip Gallery. This program lists clip art by category, so when you are looking for a specific kind of image (such as pictures of computers or animals) you can find it quickly. Actually, clip art from Microsoft takes up only one of the four tabs in the dialog box; the other three tabs help you organize other graphic images, sounds, and videos. We don't cover these tabs explicitly in this chapter, but they work the same way as the Clip Art tab.

Once you have placed your clip art piece, you can move it by dragging it around onscreen. Just point to the art and drag. To resize the art, drag one of the selection handles (the little boxes) around the edges.

You can edit clip art by right-clicking it and choosing Format Picture. This opens a Format Picture dialog box, chock-full of controls that help you change the image's attributes, size, and positioning in the document. You can also use the buttons on the Picture toolbar, which appears whenever a picture (clip art or other) is selected. This works for all pictures, not just clip art. We look at the procedures later in this chapter.

TAKE NOTE

NO CLIP ART COMMAND?

If there is no Clip Art command on the Insert ⇨ Picture menu, clip art has not been installed. Rerun the Office 97 setup program and choose to install clip art.

MORE CLIP ART AVAILABLE

If the Office 97 CD is in your CD-ROM drive when you open the Clip Gallery, it automatically includes all the extra clips from the CD in the Clip Gallery window. For the best selection, try to remember to put this disk in every time you browse for clip art. Better yet, leave the disk in your drive whenever it is otherwise idle.

ASPECT RATIO

When you resize a picture, if you drag it by a corner, it maintains its aspect ratio, which is the ratio of width to height. This ensures that the picture does not become distorted. If you drag a side handle, rather than a corner, the aspect ratio is *not* maintained. Drag a side handle only if you really want to change the aspect ratio.

CROSS-REFERENCE

Learn about the controls for modifying a picture in "Editing a Picture" later in this chapter.

FIND IT ONLINE

To find more clip art on the Internet, click the Web button in the Clip Gallery window.

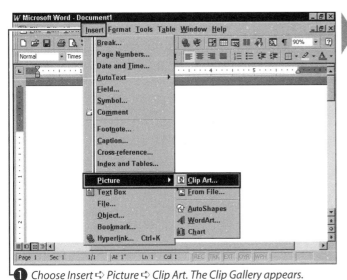

① Choose Insert ⇨ Picture ⇨ Clip Art. The Clip Gallery appears.

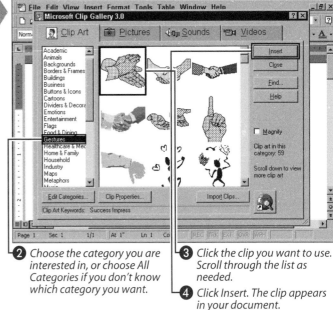

② Choose the category you are interested in, or choose All Categories if you don't know which category you want.

③ Click the clip you want to use. Scroll through the list as needed.

④ Click Insert. The clip appears in your document.

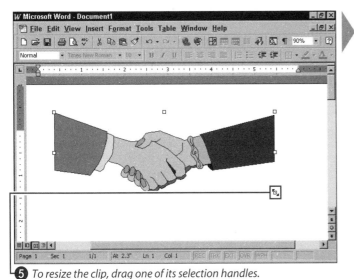

⑤ To resize the clip, drag one of its selection handles.

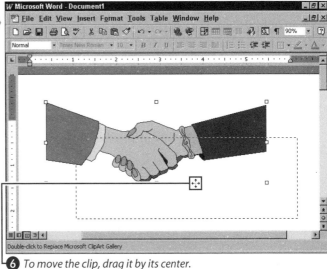

⑥ To move the clip, drag it by its center.

133

Inserting a Picture

You aren't limited to the clip art that the Clip Gallery provides; you can use almost any picture in Word. All you need to know is the file's name and where it is stored.

Getting the picture into your computer can be a bigger challenge than placing it in your document. If you have a hard copy of the picture (such as a printout of a logo or a photo), you can scan it in, if you have access to a scanner. A scanner is like a fax machine, except instead of sending the image over the phone lines, it saves it in a computer file.

If you need to scan an image, you can use the program that came with the scanner, or, if the scanner conforms to the TWAIN standard (and almost all do these days), you can scan directly from within Word. Use the Insert ⇨ Picture ⇨ From Scanner command. If you don't have that command on your menu, you don't have a compatible scanner installed.

If you don't have a picture to scan, consider using a regular camera to take a picture, or use a digital camera to take an electronic picture. Digital cameras are like regular cameras except they store the pictures on computer disks rather than film, eliminating the need to deal with a photo lab for processing. These digital cameras are still rather pricey ($200 and up), but if you take a lot of pictures for use in your Word documents and other Office programs, it may be worth it to you in terms of film and processing savings.

TAKE NOTE

▶ COLOR OR GRAYSCALE?

Don't worry if the picture you have is in color but you need it to be grayscale (that is, black and white with shades of gray). You can either scan it in grayscale mode or use Word to convert color to either grayscale or true black-and-white (no grays), as you learn to do in the following task.

▶ FILE FORMATS SUPPORTED

Word supports pictures in the following file formats: EMF, WMF, JPG, PNG, BMP, PCX, DIB, RLE, EPS, DXF, PCT, CGM, CDR, DRW, TIF, TGA, PCD, GIF, WPG, FPX, and MIX. If your Insert Picture dialog box does not list all these formats, you may not have all the filters installed. (They are not all installed with a default installation of Office 97.) Rerun the Office 97 setup program and choose to install all the text and graphics filters and you will never have to worry about it again.

▶ PICTURE SAMPLES

You can find many photo samples in the subfolders in the Clipart\Photos folder on the Office 97 CD.

CROSS-REFERENCE

Learn about the controls for modifying a picture in "Editing a Picture" later in this chapter.

FIND IT ONLINE

Print a graphic on your labels, see
http://support.microsoft.com/support/kb/articles/q123/3/12.asp.

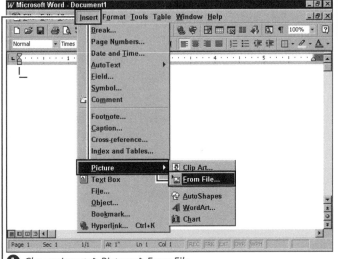

❶ Choose Insert ➪ Picture ➪ From File.

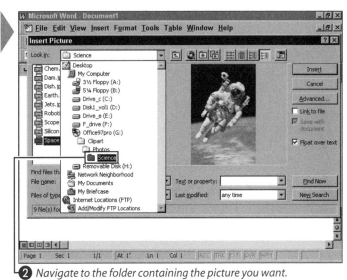

❷ Navigate to the folder containing the picture you want.

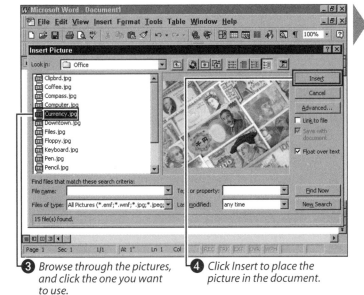

❸ Browse through the pictures, and click the one you want to use.

❹ Click Insert to place the picture in the document.

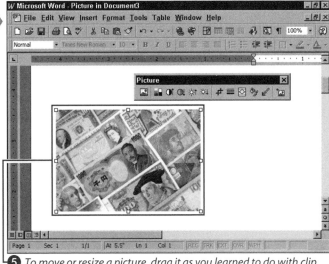

❺ To move or resize a picture, drag it as you learned to do with clip art in the preceding task.

Editing a Picture

After placing a picture (clip art or other) in a document, you have a wealth of controls at your disposal. You can make the image behave exactly the way you want it to.

You saw in the preceding sections how to move and resize graphics. Here's a quick review: To move, drag the image by its center when your mouse pointer looks like a four-headed arrow; to resize, drag one of the selection handles (the little boxes at the edges).

Most of the image editing commands are available in two ways: from the Format Picture dialog box, or from the Picture toolbar. The Format Picture dialog box offers all the controls in one convenient stop and includes some advanced options not available anywhere else. The Picture toolbar, in contrast, is easier and quicker to use, but not as powerful. In the steps on the following pages, we show you how to use the toolbar method whenever possible, jumping to the Format Picture dialog box only when needed.

Word controls enable you to actually change the picture's appearance. You can adjust the brightness and contrast, and you can switch among the following image types: *automatic* (color, if the image is color), *grayscale* (black, white, and shades of gray), *black-and-white* (no grays), and *watermark* (a semi-transparent color image that you can use as a backdrop for text). Depending on the image type, you may also be able to set one of the image's colors as transparent, so that the background color shows through.

You can crop the picture to remove extraneous parts of the image. This is useful when you have a snapshot that has an important detail that you want to spotlight but the detail is small and hard to see. By cropping out the unwanted parts, and then enlarging the remaining image, you can zoom in on the relevant part.

Continued

TAKE NOTE

▶ MULTISIDE CROPPING

Cropping works best when you crop from a side handle rather than a corner handle, but that means that you can do only one side at a time. Fortunately, when you click the Crop tool to turn it on, it remains on until you click it again to turn it off. That means you can crop each side of the image, one after the other, without having to turn on the Crop tool each time.

▶ PLACING TEXT OVER A WATERMARK

If you set an image's type to Watermark, you can place a text box over the image (Insert ➪ Text Box). This can look really cool! Try placing your company's slogan on top of a watermark-formatted logo, for example.

CROSS-REFERENCE

For more information about toolbars, see "Using the Toolbars" in Chapter 1.

FIND IT ONLINE

See **http://officeupdate.microsoft.com/ downloadDetails/sr1off97detail.htm** if an error message appears when editing pictures.

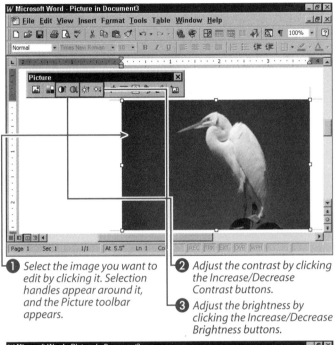

① Select the image you want to edit by clicking it. Selection handles appear around it, and the Picture toolbar appears.

② Adjust the contrast by clicking the Increase/Decrease Contrast buttons.

③ Adjust the brightness by clicking the Increase/Decrease Brightness buttons.

④ To change the image type, click the Image Control button and choose a different image type.

⑤ To crop the picture, click the Crop button.

⑥ Position the mouse pointer over the selection handle on the side you want to crop.

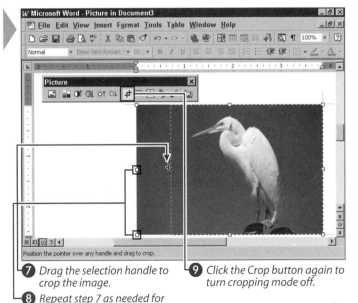

⑦ Drag the selection handle to crop the image.

⑧ Repeat step 7 as needed for other handles.

⑨ Click the Crop button again to turn cropping mode off.

Editing a Picture
Continued

Another feature you can apply to an image is a border. You can place a border (single, double, triple, or any of a variety of special designs) around the graphic frame to help it set off from the text a bit more.

Speaking of setting things off from the text, Word includes very good controls for controlling text wrapping — that is, the way that the surrounding text interacts with the graphic. The text wrapping types include: Square, which maintains a square block around the image; Tight, which wraps the text around the image itself (including any ragged edges); Through, which runs the text through any transparent parts of the image; and None, which runs the text behind the image. Additional wrapping settings, available on the Wrapping tab of the Format Picture dialog box, enable you to control wrapping on individual sides of the image.

A very handy command for wrapping text around an irregular-shaped graphic is Edit Wrap Points, the bottommost command on the Wrap drop-down list, shown on the opposite page. With this feature, you can mark off specific areas that the text should run into or stay away from. For example, suppose you have a picture of a triangle on a white background. You place that image in your document but the graphic box in which it sits is rectangular, so the text isn't able to wrap around it. If you edit the wrap points, showing the tool where the image is (and isn't), it can wrap closely around the shape.

The Format Picture dialog box does everything that the Picture toolbar does, and more. The last step on the next page begins to explore it by pointing out a couple of useful commands that are found exclusively there, but you will probably want to spend more time with this powerful dialog box on your own. In it, you can specify precise measurements for cropping, sizing, and positioning. Things that you can only "eyeball" with the mouse and the Picture toolbar's controls. This can be very useful for professional desktop publishers who may need to make their settings exactly match those of another person working on laying out other parts of the same document.

TAKE NOTE

▶ TRANSPARENT COLOR LIMITATION

The Transparent Color option is not available for most Word-supplied clip art. Only images of certain types can handle this special formatting. If you want to play with this feature, try using one of the photos in the Office 97 CD's Clipart\Photos folder.

▶ RESETTING THE PICTURE

It is easy to get carried away editing an image. If you want to go back to the original image, click the Reset Picture button, on the far right of the Picture toolbar.

CROSS-REFERENCE

Learn how to create documents with both text and graphics for the Web in Chapter 6.

FIND IT ONLINE

Check out **http://desktoppublishing.com/** for a giant list of clip art and image sites.

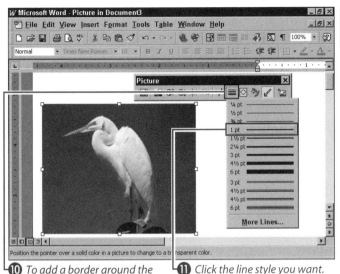

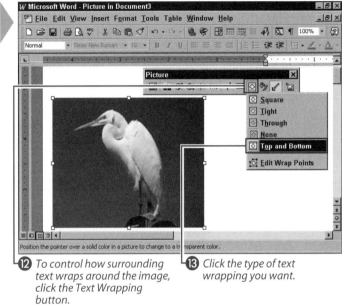

⑩ To add a border around the image, click the Line Style button to open a list of line styles.

⑪ Click the line style you want.

⑫ To control how surrounding text wraps around the image, click the Text Wrapping button.

⑬ Click the type of text wrapping you want.

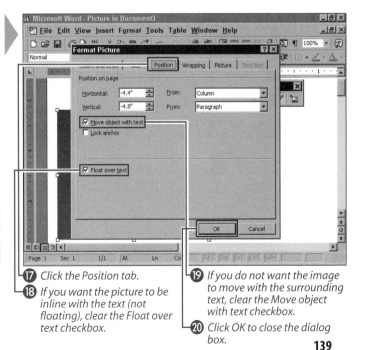

⑭ Click the Set Transparent Color button.

⑮ Click the color that you want to disappear. The color behind the picture shows through.

⑯ To change how the picture is anchored, click the Format Picture button to open the Format Picture dialog box.

⑰ Click the Position tab.

⑱ If you want the picture to be inline with the text (not floating), clear the Float over text checkbox.

⑲ If you do not want the image to move with the surrounding text, clear the Move object with text checkbox.

⑳ Click OK to close the dialog box.

139

Personal Workbook

Q&A

1 How would you change the wording of your WordArt?

_____

_____

_____

2 Besides clip art, what three types of files does the Clip Gallery allow you to manage?

_____

_____

_____

3 Name two sources of additional clip art besides the clip art that is installed on your hard drive in Office 97.

_____

_____

_____

4 What does it mean if your Insert ➪ Picture menu doesn't have the From Scanner command on it?

_____

_____

_____

5 Which of the following is not a valid image type that Word accepts: BMP, QIR, or JPG?

_____

_____

_____

_____

6 How would you reset a picture that you had tried to edit but made mistakes with?

_____

_____

_____

_____

7 What would be the advantage of editing a picture through the Format Picture dialog box rather than from the Picture toolbar?

_____

_____

_____

_____

ANSWERS: PAGE 407

EXTRA PRACTICE

1 Create some WordArt with your first name as the text. Try several different colors and shapes with it.

2 Locate some clip art of your favorite animal on the Office 97 CD and import it into a document.

3 Resize the clip art and move it around on the page.

4 If you have access to a scanner, scan in a picture of yourself and import it into a document. (If you can't do that, select a photo from the Office 97 Clipart\Photos folder.)

5 Crop the picture so you can see only the eyes.

6 Type some text around your picture. Move the picture around and see how the text reacts. Experiment with the Text Wrapping settings to see how it changes.

REAL-WORLD APPLICATIONS

✔ Create an advertisement for an upcoming event and use a big piece of WordArt at the top of it as an attention-getter. For example: "Important!" "Sale!" "Today!"

✔ Choose some clip art that expresses a feeling you want to convey and place it at the top or bottom of a memo or letter you are writing, to add personality to it. For example, for a fun letter to a friend, choose a cartoon character. To motivate a business team, choose a blue ribbon or a "thumbs up."

✔ Write a letter to potential clients selling your services, scan and include a photograph of yourself next to your name and address. People like to see who they are going to be doing business with. This works especially well in real estate and insurance sales.

Visual Quiz

What is wrong with this WordArt and how would you fix it?

_____

_____

_____

_____

_____

_____

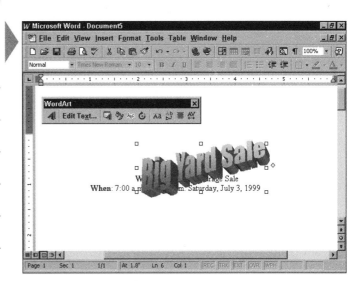

CHAPTER 10

MASTER THESE SKILLS

▶ Creating a Numbered or Bulleted List

▶ Controlling the Bullet or Number Format

▶ Creating Tables

▶ Formatting Tables

▶ Using Multiple Columns

▶ Using Templates

Learning Some Advanced Techniques

Are you ready for something a little more challenging? In this chapter, you learn how to take advantage of some of Word's greatest time-savers. These features aren't as obvious as, say, changing the font or setting a tab, but if you take the time to master them, you will be able to create superior documents with much less fuss.

We start out by looking at *lists*. How many times have you struggled on your typewriter or old word processor to get the numbers in a numbered list lined up just right? Or the indents in the lines following the first one? With Word 97, it's no longer a struggle. Not only does Word create perfect bulleted and numbered lists, complete with indents, but it even automatically numbers your list. You can also select from a variety of number formats and bullet characters, and control the spacing on both sides of the bullet or number.

Word 97 also excels (no pun intended!) at tables. A table is a grid of cells, sort of like a mini Excel spreadsheet. Tables can help you create parallel columns, and, in many situations, work much more neatly than simple tab stops.

You can format each row and column separately, changing its height, width, and other attributes, for great flexibility. Another neat thing about tables is that you can place borders around each individual table cell, creating a grid of boxes in which to type.

Typing text in multiple columns in a table is great, but what if you want the entire document to be in two or more columns? In that case, you would use the Columns feature to set up multiple columns. This takes your regular text and lays it out in columns, so you don't have to create a special table and move your text into it. There are some limitations to the Columns feature, and some caveats, discussed later on in the chapter.

We round out this chapter by revisiting templates. You can use other templates that come with Word, or you can create your own templates for documents that you create over and over, saving yourself quite a bit of prep time.

Creating a Numbered or Bulleted List

In Word, creating a numbered list is simple. When Word numbers a list for you, all the tab stops and indents are set perfectly, so that each line lines up correctly. The numbering is always correct; if you delete one of the numbered list items, all the other numbers shift to account for it.

Bulleted lists are pretty much the same as numbered lists except the numbers are replaced by bullets. A bulleted list is used when you want to display a list of items in which the order is not important. For example, you might use a bulleted list to show which departments are involved in the latest fund-raiser plans. In such a list, the order that you list them in is not significant. (In contrast, a numbered list is used when the order is important, such as the steps for baking a cake or performing a computer backup.)

You can create a numbered or bulleted list in any of these ways:

▶ Type the list and then select it and click the Numbering or Bullets button on the toolbar.
▶ Click the Numbering button on the toolbar to turn numbering or bullets on and then type the list. Every time you press Enter, Word starts the next number or bullet. Press Enter twice in a row to end the list, or click the Numbering or Bullets button again to turn numbering off.
▶ Type a 1 or an asterisk (*), press Tab and then type your first item. Press Enter and then type 2

or another asterisk (*) and a Tab. Word should recognize that you are creating a numbered or bulleted list and turn Numbering or Bullets on automatically. When you are finished, press Enter twice in a row to end the list or click the Numbering or Bullets button to turn numbering or bullets off.

The Numbering and Bullets buttons on the toolbar are on/off toggle switches, like a light switch. When you click one, if the selected paragraphs do not have numbers or bullets, it assigns them. If they already have numbers or bullets, it removes them. If you have selected a mixed group (some already numbered or bulleted, some not), it makes them all bulleted/numbered.

TAKE NOTE

TURN ON THE AUTOFORMATTING AS YOU TYPE

If Word doesn't work as described in the steps on the facing page, you need to make sure that Word knows you want automatic numbered and bulleted lists. Choose Tools ➪ AutoCorrect and click the AutoFormat As You Type tab and make sure that the Automatic numbered lists and Automatic bulleted lists checkboxes are marked.

CROSS-REFERENCE
Bulleted lists formatting is covered in "Controlling the Bullet Format" later in this chapter.

FIND IT ONLINE
Check out Alki Software's site dedicated to helping Word users at **http://www.wordinfo.com/**.

Starting and stopping

You can start a numbered list, stop it, and then start it a few paragraphs later, and Word remembers what number you left off with. To set this up, create the first part of the numbered list. Next, turn off numbering and type the regular paragraphs. Turn numbering back on and type the next numbered item. Word numbers it 1, thinking it is a new list, but don't fret. Right-click it and choose Bullets and Numbering. In the Bullets and Numbering box that appears, click the Continue previous list button and click OK.

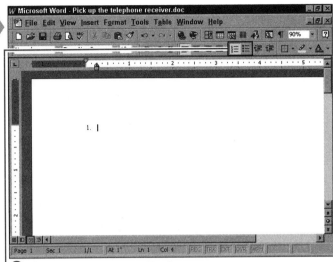

① *Click the Numbering or Bullets button to turn on numbering/bulleting. The first number or bullet appears.*

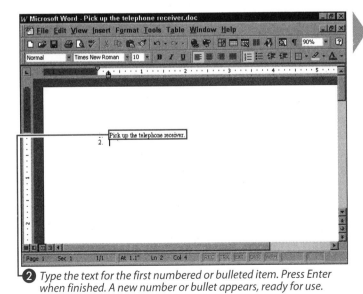

② *Type the text for the first numbered or bulleted item. Press Enter when finished. A new number or bullet appears, ready for use.*

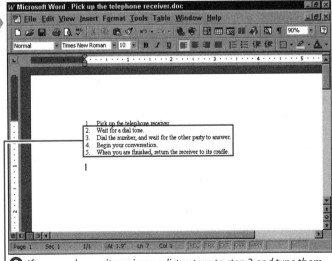

③ *If you need more items in your list, return to step 2 and type them. Otherwise, press Enter again to stop the numbering/bulleting.*

Controlling the Bullet Format

For everyday documents, the default bullet format may be all you need. But if you use Word for desktop publishing, where the look of the page is as important as the words, you will appreciate Word's ability to customize this look.

There are two levels of customization for bullets. At the basic level, you can choose from seven preset formats from the Bullets and Numbering dialog box (Format ➪ Bullets and Numbering). If all you want is a distinctive bullet character, this customization will meet your needs.

You are not limited to these presets, however. You can choose one of the seven presets and then click the Customize button to customize it. The Customize Bulleted List dialog box opens and you can redefine what that preset will look like from then on. (We usually try to redefine one of the presets that we don't think we will ever use, rather than messing up one that we might want later.)

In the Customize Bulleted List dialog box, you can set precise spacing between the left margin and the bullet, and between the bullet and the rest of the text. This is especially useful when you are using a non-standard size for your bullet and it throws off the first line of text when default settings are used. You can also choose any character (literally anything!) as your bullet, and change the font and size.

TAKE NOTE

▶ BULLET CHARACTER FONTS

If you have Windows 95 or 98 and Office 97, you already have several fonts from which to choose bullet characters. These fonts are specially designed to pull symbols from, rather than for regular typing: Marlett, Monotype Sorts, Symbol, Webdings, and Wingdings. You can find a mind-boggling number of bullet choices in these!

▶ USING A TEXT CHARACTER AS A BULLET

When you choose a bullet character from the Symbol dialog box (shown in the steps on the facing page), the Font drop-down list does not contain every single font on your system — only the ones that contain symbol characters commonly used for bullets. If you want to use a text character from a font not listed, click the Font button in the Customize Bulleted List dialog box, and select that font there. Then close that dialog box and click the Bullets button to reopen the Symbol dialog box. Now the font you want is there.

▶ EASY INDENTATION

If you want your bulleted list to be indented further than it currently is, you can highlight the entire list, right-click and then choose Increase Indent. Or, to indent one bulleted point at a time, position your insertion point at the beginning, between the bullet and the text, and press Tab. The entire bulleted paragraph, including the bullet, moves to the next Tab stop.

CROSS-REFERENCE

If you need to format a numbered list, see "Controlling the Number Format" later in this chapter.

FIND IT ONLINE

Join a newsgroup dedicated to Word users at news:bit.mailserv.word-pc.

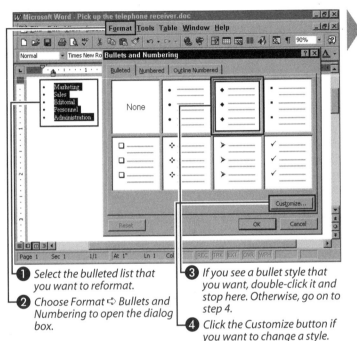

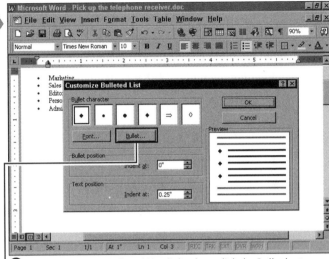

1 Select the bulleted list that you want to reformat.

2 Choose Format ➪ Bullets and Numbering to open the dialog box.

3 If you see a bullet style that you want, double-click it and stop here. Otherwise, go on to step 4.

4 Click the Customize button if you want to change a style.

5 In the Customize Bulleted List dialog box, click the Bullet button to open the Symbol dialog box.

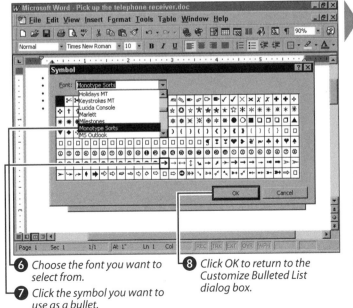

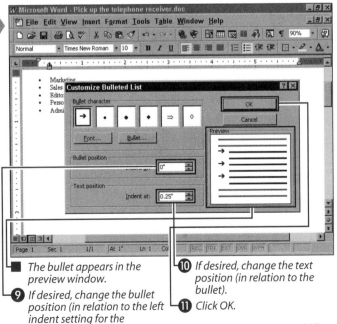

6 Choose the font you want to select from.

7 Click the symbol you want to use as a bullet.

8 Click OK to return to the Customize Bulleted List dialog box.

■ The bullet appears in the preview window.

9 If desired, change the bullet position (in relation to the left indent setting for the paragraph).

10 If desired, change the text position (in relation to the bullet).

11 Click OK.

Controlling the Number Format

The controls for the numbered list format are much the same as those for bullets. You can choose from one of seven preset formats, or set up your own.

The default number format is Arabic with a period (1. 2. 3.). You can choose a different number format, such as capital or lowercase roman numerals, alphabet letters (capital or lowercase), words (One, Two, Three), or places (1st, 2nd, 3rd). You can also choose what character follows each number — a period, a parenthesis, or any other character you choose (perhaps a dash or a colon?). You can also specify what number to start numbering at. (The default is 1.)

As with bullets, you can choose which font to use for the numbering, but most people leave this set to [Normal Text], which means that whatever font is chosen for the regular text in that paragraph will also be used for the number. This makes the numbering look more natural. However, sometimes you might want the numbering to stand out. If this is the case, you should change the font (perhaps to Arial Black, a very thick font, so the numbers get noticed).

You can choose a number position of Left (default), Centered, or Right. These settings are in relation to the Aligned At setting. For example, a setting of Left and 2" aligns the numbers to the left at a makeshift tab at the 2" mark on your ruler. Left-aligned numbers start at the same spot on the left; for example, 1 and 10 both start at the 2" mark. If you have a long numbered list that has more than 9 items, you must decide whether you want the first digit (left aligned) or the last digit (right aligned) of the numbers to align with one another.

TAKE NOTE

ANIMATED NUMBERS

If you are designing a document to be viewed onscreen (rather than printed), have some fun with animated numbers. In the Customize Numbered List dialog box, click the Font button and then the Animation tab. Choose one of the animations listed there (like Sparkle Text) and then finish selecting your number font normally. These special effects won't print, of course.

SAVING STYLES

If you create a rather complex format for your numbered lists, you might want to create a named style for that formatting. Your named style will include the formatting for the numbers along with any formatting for the text of the paragraph itself. Then you can apply that style from the Style drop-down list whenever you want to use it.

CROSS-REFERENCE

To learn about creating named styles, see "Using Styles" in Chapter 8.

FIND IT ONLINE

Join a newsgroup dedicated to word processing at news:comp.os.ms-windows.apps.word-proc.

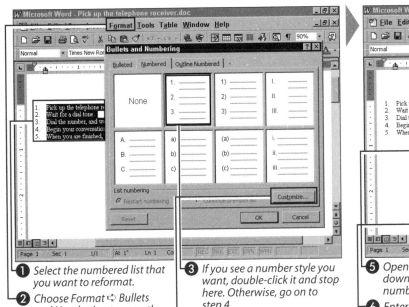

❶ *Select the numbered list that you want to reformat.*

❷ *Choose Format ➪ Bullets and Numbering to open the dialog box.*

❸ *If you see a number style you want, double-click it and stop here. Otherwise, go on to step 4.*

❹ *Click the Customize button to change a style.*

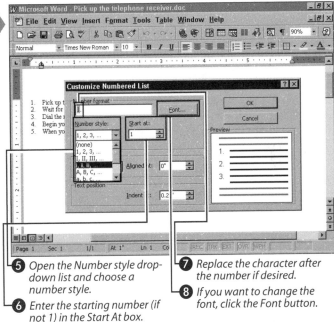

❺ *Open the Number style drop-down list and choose a number style.*

❻ *Enter the starting number (if not 1) in the Start At box.*

❼ *Replace the character after the number if desired.*

❽ *If you want to change the font, click the Font button.*

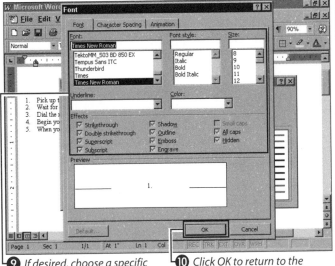

❾ *If desired, choose a specific font, size, and/or attributes that you want to use for the numbering.*

❿ *Click OK to return to the Customize Numbered List dialog box.*

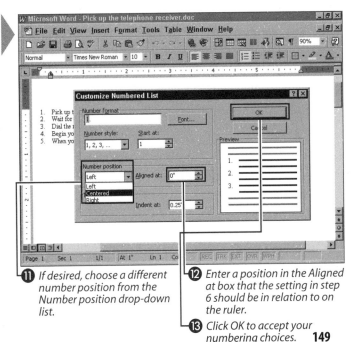

⓫ *If desired, choose a different number position from the Number position drop-down list.*

⓬ *Enter a position in the Aligned at box that the setting in step 6 should be in relation to on the ruler.*

⓭ *Click OK to accept your numbering choices.*

Creating Tables

The Tables feature is a powerful formatting tool that makes it easy to get professional-looking parallel column layouts.

There are two kinds of multicolumn layouts in desktop publishing: *parallel* and *newspaper*. Text in a newspaper-type column runs from top to bottom in one column, then fills the next column, and so on, until the article is finished. A parallel column layout, on the other hand, relies on text in one column aligning with text in the next column. For example, a list of names and addresses in multiple columns requires that the right name in Column A be next to the correct address in Column B. We're working with parallel columns when we work with tables in Word. (Newspaper columns are covered later in this chapter.)

A table in Word consists of a grid of boxes arranged in rows and columns, much like in a spreadsheet (as you learn in the next part of this book when you work with Excel). The following points show you how to move the insertion point from cell to cell in a table:

- ▶ Press Tab to move to the next cell (to the right, or to the beginning of the next row if in the rightmost cell).
- ▶ Press Shift+Tab to move to the previous cell.
- ▶ Use the arrow keys to move one cell in the arrow's direction.
- ▶ Click in the cell in which you want to type.

When you are working with a table, the commands on the Table menu become available. From this menu, you can add and remove rows and columns, and perform various formatting functions.

To insert a row or column, select the row or column that you want the new one to be above or to the left of. Then click the Insert Row or Insert Column toolbar button, or open the Table menu and choose Insert Rows or Insert Columns. Deleting a row or column is similar: Select the row or column to delete and click the Cut button on the toolbar, or choose Table ⇨ Delete Columns or Table ⇨ Delete Rows.

TAKE NOTE

▶ DRAWING A TABLE

Another way to make a table is with the Draw Table feature. Click the Draw Table toolbar button, or choose Table ⇨ Draw Table. Your mouse pointer becomes a pencil, and you can drag to draw the table gridlines exactly where you want them onscreen. This is a great way to create a table with columns of uneven widths; if you create the table with the Insert Table command, which you learn on the following page, all the columns are the same width, and you must change their widths manually.

▶ TABLE FROM TEXT

To create a table from existing text in your document, select the text and then choose Table ⇨ Convert Text to Table.

CROSS-REFERENCE

Moving around in a Word table is a lot like moving around in an Excel worksheet. See "Moving Around the Worksheet" in Chapter 14.

FIND IT ONLINE

To subscribe to receive daily tips on Word visit **http://www.dummiesdaily.com/**.

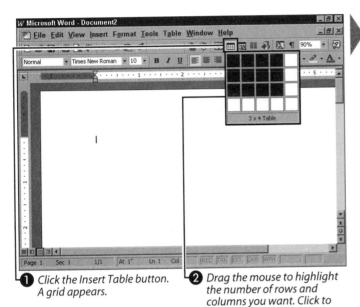

1 Click the Insert Table button. A grid appears.

2 Drag the mouse to highlight the number of rows and columns you want. Click to create the table.

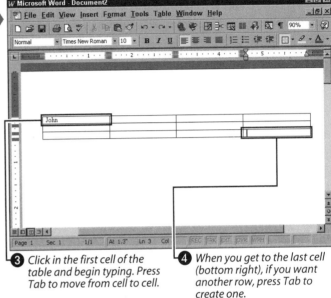

3 Click in the first cell of the table and begin typing. Press Tab to move from cell to cell.

4 When you get to the last cell (bottom right), if you want another row, press Tab to create one.

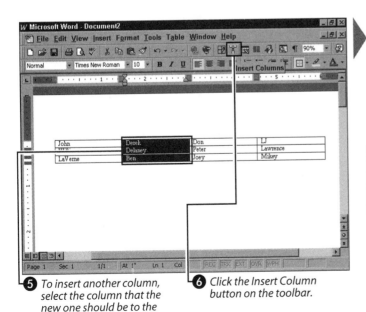

5 To insert another column, select the column that the new one should be to the left of.

6 Click the Insert Column button on the toolbar.

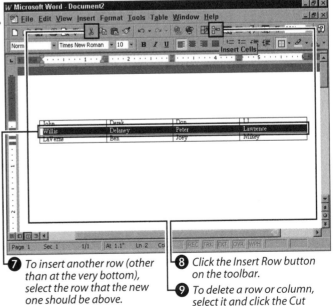

7 To insert another row (other than at the very bottom), select the row that the new one should be above.

8 Click the Insert Row button on the toolbar.

9 To delete a row or column, select it and click the Cut button.

Formatting Tables

In the preceding task, you learned how to add rows and columns; you can also resize these rows and columns. You can resize an entire row or column, or just one individual cell. (Beware, however, that resizing individual cells can result in a bizarre-looking table.) To affect only one cell, select it before you begin resizing.

The easiest way to resize cells is to drag the divider line between two cells. Position the mouse pointer between two cells; the mouse pointer turns into a vertical line with arrows on it. Drag the divider line to the right or left (holding down the left mouse button). If you drag this way, the overall width of the table remains the same; the dragging merely changes how the space between the two cells is divvied up. However, if you hold down the Shift key as you drag, it changes the size of the table, and all cells to the right of the line you are dragging maintain their current individual sizes.

You can also remove the gridlines from the table, so that the text in the cells looks like it is floating in multiple columns. Conversely, you can add gridlines to the table, so that certain lines are thicker or a different pattern for emphasis. (This works well, for instance, when the top row in your table contains column labels and you want to separate them from the others with a thick horizontal line.) You can control the gridline settings for each side of each cell individually, to create all sorts of interesting effects.

For example, you might remove the gridlines from all the cells except one, so that it looks like there is a box drawn around that cell's content.

TAKE NOTE

FORMATTING TEXT IN A TABLE

You can format the text in your table cells normally, as you do any other text. Simply select the text and then apply the formatting.

TABLE AUTOFORMAT

Word comes with several predesigned table formats that can help you make an attractive table. Try them out by choosing Table ⇨ AutoFormat.

EVEN DISTRIBUTION

If you get your rows and columns out of whack, you can bring them back into line by selecting the entire table and then choosing Table ⇨ Distribute Rows Evenly and/or Table ⇨ Distribute Columns Evenly.

BORDERS APPLY TO THE SELECTION

When you select cells before adding borders, the borders you choose will apply to that selected block as a block, not as individual cells. For example, if you select two rows and apply a bottom border, the border will be along the second row only. You can use the All or Grid buttons in the Borders and Shading dialog box (see the following page) to include the inside edges of cells in the range in your Border command.

CROSS-REFERENCE

To format text, see "Formatting Text" in Chapter 8.

FIND IT ONLINE

To find out more about Word macro viruses, visit http://www.look.com/vamacro.html.

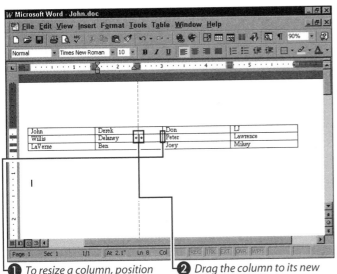

❶ To resize a column, position the mouse pointer to the left of that column.

■ If you want the column to the right to retain its size, hold down the Shift key.

❷ Drag the column to its new width. Repeat the steps for each column you want to resize.

❸ To change the gridlines for one or more cells, select them.

❹ Choose Format ➪ Borders and Shading.

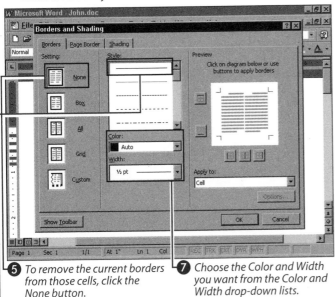

❺ To remove the current borders from those cells, click the None button.

❻ Click the border style you want.

❼ Choose the Color and Width you want from the Color and Width drop-down lists.

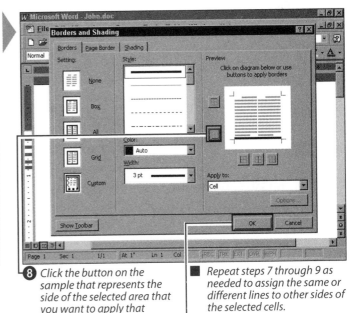

❽ Click the button on the sample that represents the side of the selected area that you want to apply that gridline to.

■ Repeat steps 7 through 9 as needed to assign the same or different lines to other sides of the selected cells.

❾ Click OK.

Using Multiple Columns

Have you ever wondered why newspapers print the news in multiple columns? It's because shorter lines are easier for the eye to follow. You can put multiple columns to work in your Word documents and help your own readers the same way.

As you learned back in Chapter 8, document-wide settings (like columns) affect the entire section, and by default, a document has only one section. That means the Columns setting affects the entire document. You can get around this by creating section breaks (use the Insert ➪ Break command) or by selecting text before you issue the Columns command.

What's the best way? It all depends on what you're doing. If you want the first half of your document to be in one column and the second half in two columns, it's fairly simple to just insert a section break where you want the number of columns to change. Position your insertion point in the second section before you issue the Columns command.

However, if you have a snippet of text in the middle of your document that should be multicolumn, with single-column text before and after, you must create two section breaks: one before that text and one after it. This time, position your insertion point in the middle section before changing the number of columns. In that case, it's much easier to select the snippet first and then issue the Columns command. Word assumes that the selected text should be in a section by itself and creates the required section breaks automatically.

You can create multiple columns with the Columns toolbar button; that's the easiest way. Just click the button to drop down a grid, like the one you saw in the "Creating a Table" section earlier in this chapter. Then drag across the number of columns you want. With that method, however, you don't get all the special controls, like specifying column width and gutter (the spacing between the columns). To set those controls, you must use the Format ➪ Columns command.

TAKE NOTE

▶ VERTICAL LINES BETWEEN COLUMNS

In a newspaper, vertical lines separate each column, making it easier to read. You can achieve this same effect by selecting the Line between checkbox in the Columns dialog box (seen on the facing page).

▶ UNEVEN COLUMNS

In professional desktop publishing, it is considered stylish to make one column larger than the other. For example, on the front page of a newsletter, you might have one column that takes up $2/3$ of the width and the other column that takes up the remaining $1/3$. You could put your lead story in the larger one and use the smaller one for little blurbs about the other stories on later pages.

CROSS-REFERENCE

To create parallel columns, use a table. See "Creating a Table" earlier in this chapter.

FIND IT ONLINE

Get tips on working with long documents in Word: http://www.wordinfo/how_to/nomaster.

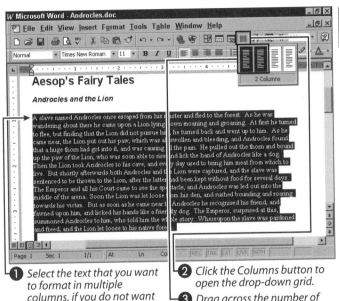

① Select the text that you want to format in multiple columns, if you do not want to do the entire document.

② Click the Columns button to open the drop-down grid.

③ Drag across the number of columns you want, and click to select them.

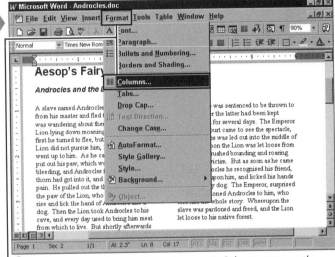

④ To format the columns, choose Format ➪ Columns to open the Columns dialog box.

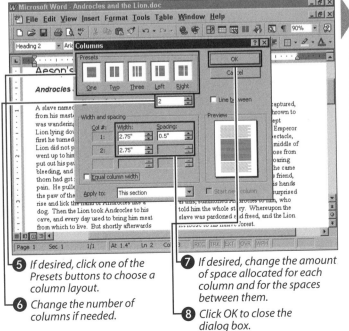

⑤ If desired, click one of the Presets buttons to choose a column layout.

⑥ Change the number of columns if needed.

⑦ If desired, change the amount of space allocated for each column and for the spaces between them.

⑧ Click OK to close the dialog box.

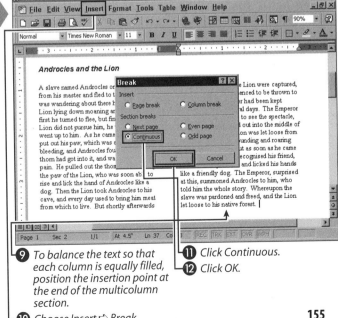

⑨ To balance the text so that each column is equally filled, position the insertion point at the end of the multicolumn section.

⑩ Choose Insert ➪ Break.

⑪ Click Continuous.

⑫ Click OK.

Using Templates

Every document is based on a template. The blank, default documents are based on a template called Normal.dot. Word comes with many special-purpose templates that you can use to save time in your document creation. Some of these include newsletters, fax cover pages, letters, memos, reports, and resumes.

To use a template, just choose File ➪ New and select the template you want from the New dialog box. The New dialog box has several tabs, each one for a different category of template. For example, there are tabs for Letters & Faxes, Memos, and Reports. Each of these tabs corresponds to a folder in the C:\Program Files\Microsoft Office\Templates folder.

Word also comes with several special templates called wizards. Wizards are Q&A sessions where Word asks you what you want and then creates it for you. For example, the Letter Wizard asks you about your preferences in formatting, layout, letterhead, and so on, and then creates a letter. All you do is fill in the body of it.

You can create your own template out of any document. Just create a document with any boilerplate text, styles, margins, and other settings you want, and then choose File ➪ Save As. Change the Save As Type to Document Template, give it a name, and click Save. You can use it, the same as the other templates, with File ➪ New. Another way to create a new template is to use File ➪ New and select a template that is close to the one you want. Then click the Template option button and click OK. A new template is created with the same settings as the one you chose; you can modify them and save it under a different name.

To modify an existing template, open it as you would a regular document file. Just use File ➪ Open and change the Files of Type setting to Document Templates. Navigate to the folder containing the template to open and double-click it to open it. Make any changes necessary and then save it.

TAKE NOTE

WHERE ARE TEMPLATES SAVED?

When you change the Save As Type to Document Template, the location changes to C:\Program Files\Microsoft Office\Templates, the default save location for templates. You can save any new templates you create in this folder or in any of its subfolders (Memos, Reports, and so on). You can save templates in other places too, but you won't be able to use them from the New dialog box if you do.

TEXT FIELDS

When you create a document with certain templates, gray shaded areas appear in the resulting document, with instructions in them. These are fill-in fields. Click one of them and type the text needed there. If you do not fill these in, nothing will print in those spots.

CROSS-REFERENCE

To recall how to change drives and folders in an Open or Save dialog box, see "Opening and Closing Office Files" and "Saving Office Files" in Chapter 3.

FIND IT ONLINE

Choose Help ➪ Microsoft on the Web ➪ Free Stuff and visit the Office Update page to learn how to get more templates.

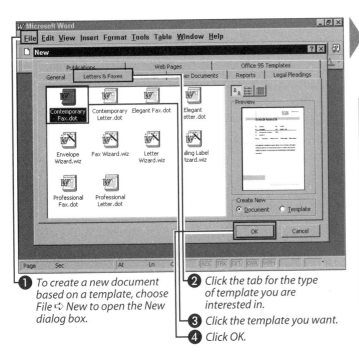

1 To create a new document based on a template, choose File ⇨ New to open the New dialog box.

2 Click the tab for the type of template you are interested in.

3 Click the template you want.

4 Click OK.

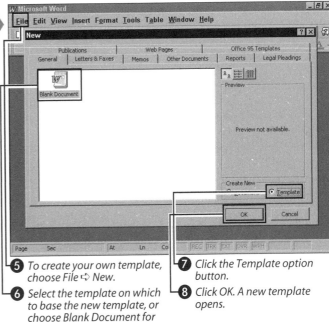

5 To create your own template, choose File ⇨ New.

6 Select the template on which to base the new template, or choose Blank Document for one based on Normal.dot.

7 Click the Template option button.

8 Click OK. A new template opens.

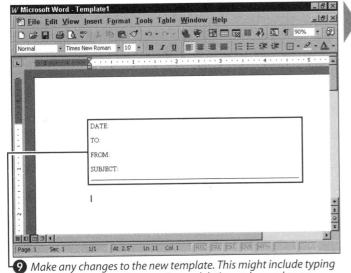

9 Make any changes to the new template. This might include typing text, changing margins, creating or deleting styles, and so on.

10 Choose File ⇨ Save. The Save As dialog box opens.

11 Type a name for the new template in the File name text box.

12 Click Save.

Personal Workbook

Q&A

1 If you want Word to create a bulleted list automatically, what symbol should you type in front of each paragraph?

_____

_____

_____

2 How would you turn off AutoFormatting, so Word did not create automatic bulleted and numbered lists?

_____

_____

_____

3 Name two fonts whose characters can be used for bullets.

_____

_____

_____

4 Name two ways to create a table in Word.

_____

_____

5 What effect does holding down the Shift key have when dragging a table column to resize it?

_____

_____

_____

6 How do you get a vertical line to appear between your columns when using multiple columns in a document?

_____

_____

_____

_____

7 What happens if you change the number of columns in a document and you don't select any text first? What happens if you do select text first?

_____

_____

_____

_____

ANSWERS: PAGE 408

EXTRA PRACTICE

1 Type several paragraphs and make them into a bulleted list with a bullet character chosen from the Wingdings font.

2 Reformat the list as a numbered list and change the number type to Roman numerals.

3 Create a table with two columns and four rows. In the first column, type the first names of four of your friends. In the second column, type their last names.

4 Add a row at the top of the table, and type column headings in it ("First Name" and "Last Name"). Add a thick bottom border on the first row, so a separator line appears between the column headings and the column content.

REAL-WORLD APPLICATIONS

✔ You could create a table with six columns that lists the names and addresses of a group of people that you mail things to frequently. Reserve the top row of the table for the field names: First, Last, Address, City, State, and ZIP.

✔ You could create and save (Letterhd.dot) a template that is just like Normal.dot except it has the extra amount of top margin that you need for your stationery.

✔ Create a professional newsletter with a section at the top formatted in one column. Insert a section break and format the following section in three columns, and type your articles there. Use Page layout view so you can see your work.

Visual Quiz

What is wrong with this numbered list? How would you fix it?

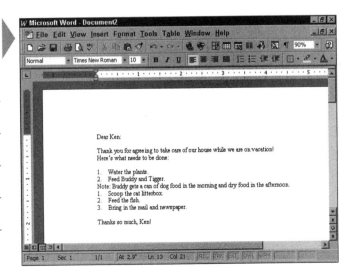

159

CHAPTER **11**

Creating Form Letters, Labels, and Envelopes

Mail merge is by no means a beginner's feature, but it's a very useful one. You can use it to create form letters, mailing labels, batches of preaddressed envelopes, and lots more.

During a mail merge, you combine a data file (usually containing a list of names and addresses, or similar data) with a form letter that contains markers to show where each bit of data should go. For example, you might have some text in your form letter like this:

Greetings, <<First Name>>! If the <<Last Name>> family has been contemplating a new air conditioning system, now is the time to take advantage of our Independence Day Weekend sale.

When you merged it with a data file containing first and last names, the result would be a series of personalized letters, one of which might look like this:

Greetings, Margaret! If the Colvin family has been contemplating a new air conditioning system, now is the time to take advantage of our Independence Day Weekend sale.

Mail merge takes some preparation. First, you need to create your data file. You can do this either by creating a table (see Chapter 10) and filling in your data, or using the Mail Merge Helper to create a new data source. In this chapter, you learn how to create the data source separately, but we point out where you could create a new data source instead.

After you prepare your data file, you start the merge itself. A merge has three main steps: creating the form document; selecting (or creating) the data file; and merging the two together. In this chapter, we work through each of these steps to create a finished merge.

At the end of this chapter, we take a break from merging and look at a quick way to print a single envelope for a letter you've written using Word's Envelopes command.

Selecting the Type of Merge

There are many variables in merging, such as what type of data file you are using, where the output should be directed, and so on, but the most important decision is what type of merge you want to perform. Word offers four types:

▶ **Form Letters** — This encompasses every kind of mass mailing document you might send, including sales flyers, personalized reports, letters, memos, and so on. If you want a document that includes paragraphs full of text, Form Letters is the way to go. This chapter focuses on form letters because they are the most common type of merge.

▶ **Mailing Labels** — This option creates sheets of names and addresses arranged to match up with the stickers on those blank mailing label sheets you can buy at an office supply store. You feed the sheets into your printer like regular paper, and Word prints on them. Then you can peel the labels off and stick them on boxes, envelopes, newsletters, or whatever. The labels don't necessarily have to be names and addresses for mailing; you could create price labels for products you sell, for example.

▶ **Envelopes** — This option also creates lists of names and addresses, but it prints them on envelopes rather than on sheets of labels. It's a very different thing, since only one envelope can pass through your printer at once. (In contrast, a single label sheet can hold 30 or more names and addresses.)

▶ **Catalog** — Most people don't use this option very often. You can use it to merge a list of products into a catalog-type listing. You might use it to print out a price list of the items you have in your inventory, for example.

Each of these merge types has its own quirks and special options. We focus on the most common type: Form Letters. Almost everyone in business has to print form letters at one time or another. Once you have learned how to create form letters, the other merge types should become very easy to figure out.

TAKE NOTE

MATCHING MAILERS

Have you given any thought to how you will distribute your form letters? After you have created them, and gained some experience with merging, you might want to try the Envelopes or Mailing Labels merge features on your own, to see if you can use that same data file to help you address your envelopes or packages.

LABEL TYPE

If you are buying labels to feed into your printer, make sure you get the right kind for your printer. The kind designed for ink-jet printers is not designed to stand up to the heat in a laser printer, and may melt inside your printer, causing great damage.

CROSS-REFERENCE
To enter names and addresses for your mail merge, create a table, see "Creating Tables" in Chapter 10.

FIND IT ONLINE
For an online tutorial of Merge Features, visit
http://www.ag.ndsu.nodak.edu/lessons/word.

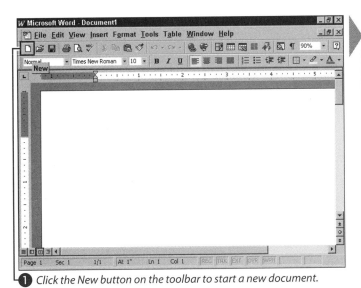

❶ Click the New button on the toolbar to start a new document.

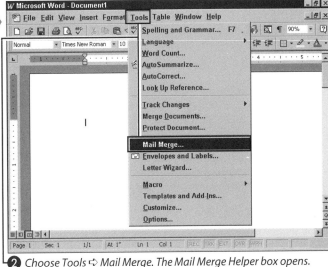

❷ Choose Tools ➪ Mail Merge. The Mail Merge Helper box opens.

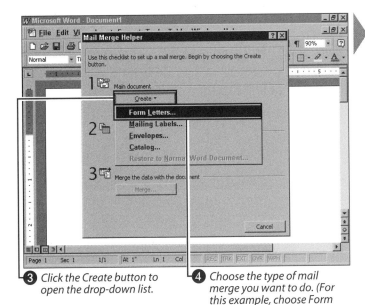

❸ Click the Create button to open the drop-down list.

❹ Choose the type of mail merge you want to do. (For this example, choose Form Letters.)

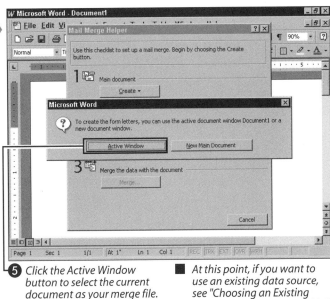

❺ Click the Active Window button to select the current document as your merge file.

■ At this point, if you want to use an existing data source, see "Choosing an Existing Data Source" (the next task). If not, see "Creating a New Data Source."

Choosing an Existing Data Source

The most time-consuming part of a mail merge is typing in the data, so you don't want to have to do it more than once. If you already have the data keyed in, you may be able to use it in its current format. If you created a table of names and addresses in the Extra Practice section at the end of Chapter 10, you can use it here. Word's Merge can pull from any of several sources, including the Address Book from Outlook, Schedule+, Outlook Express, or from an Excel worksheet or Word table. (A Word table is a good choice for data files.)

If the data is in a plain text file or a Word table, you need to make sure that the fields have names. The best way to accomplish this is to put the field names in the first row of the table or the first paragraph of the text file. Names such as First, Last, Address, and so on identify each column as a data field to be used in the merge. If the file is plain text, consider converting it to a Word table (Table ⇨ Convert Text to Table) to make it easier to examine to ensure that there aren't any errors in it (such as one or more lines missing data in some of the fields).

If you aren't sure whether your existing data will work, go ahead and try it; if it works, you have saved yourself quite a bit of data entry time. The worst that can happen is that Word won't be able to use it, and you will have to either import the data into a regular

Word document to clean it up or create a new data source as described in the next task.

The steps on the following page start in the Mail Merge Helper dialog box, and assume that you have just completed the task "Selecting the Type of Merge" earlier in this chapter.

TAKE NOTE

► IMPORTING DATA FROM A DIFFERENT FORMAT

If your data is in another format, you might be able to export it from whatever program it is in and then import it into a Word table. Try opening the file in Word and then selecting it and choosing Table ⇨ Convert Text to Table.

► USING A SPREADSHEET

If your data is in an Excel spreadsheet, open Excel and remove any titles or extra blank rows at the top; save your work and return to Word to continue the merge. This ensures that Word does not mistake a title for a column row.

► USING ACCESS DATA

Mail Merge doesn't directly support Access files, but you can easily copy an Access table (select it and choose Edit ⇨ Copy) and paste it into an Excel worksheet or a Word table.

CROSS-REFERENCE

To create a Word table, see "Creating a Table" in Chapter 10.

FIND IT ONLINE

To use an Outlook Express address book for a Word Mail Merge, see **http://support.microsoft.com/support/kb/articles/q191/2/64.asp**.

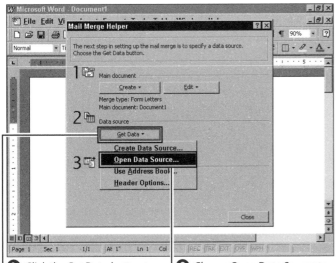

❶ *Click the Get Data button to open the drop-down list.*

❷ *Choose Open Data Source to open a Word or Excel document as the source (and skip to step 5) or choose Use Address Book to pull from an address book.*

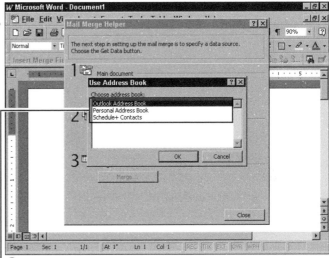

❸ *If you chose Use Address Book, double-click the type of address book it is.*

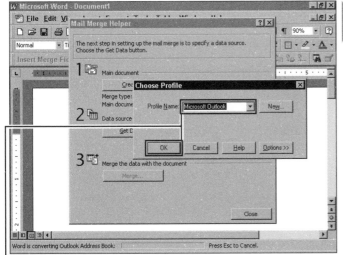

❹ *If prompted, choose the profile to pull the address book from, and click OK. (You may not see this, depending on your version of Windows and Outlook.) Skip to step 7.*

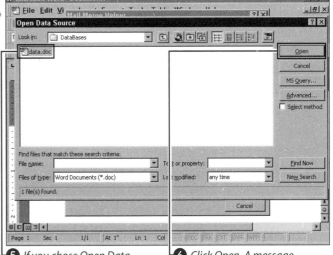

❺ *If you chose Open Data Source, select the data file to use.*

❻ *Click Open. A message appears saying that Word found no merge fields. Click Edit Main Document and then turn to "Creating the Main Document" later in this chapter.*

Creating a New Data Source

If you don't have any data in a usable format, you will have to create a new data source. Fortunately, Word's Mail Merge Helper makes it very easy by providing a data entry form. You select the fields you want to include and Word helps you fill in the information in each field for each person. Next, Word saves your work to a separate file, in a table. You can not only use this file for your data file in the current merge, but because it is saved separately, you can also use that same data in other merges you do in the future.

Word's Create Data Source dialog box, shown on the following page, helps you set up your field list. The field list will form the columns in the new table that Word creates for you. You need to make sure that all the fields you need for your merge appear on the list. Word provides a default list that includes Title, FirstName, LastName, JobTitle, Company, Address1, Address2, City, State, PostalCode, Country, HomePhone, and WorkPhone. Occasionally, you might create a merge where you need some other fields too. For example, if you are sending out expiration notices to insurance customers, you need to add a field that lists the date on which their policy expires.

The buttons at the bottom of the Data Form box (shown on the next page) move to the previous or next record (the plain arrows) or to the first or last record (the arrows with vertical lines). You should not have to use these unless you make a mistake and need to go back to a certain record or unless you want to browse back and check something in a record you entered.

The steps on the following page start in the Mail Merge Helper dialog box, and assume that you have just completed the task "Selecting the Type of Merge" earlier in this chapter.

TAKE NOTE

▶ CREATING A WORD TABLE MANUALLY

Instead of going through the procedure on the next page, you can create a new Word document containing a table and place your data to be merged in it. Make sure that the first row of the table contains the field names you want to use (FirstName, LastName, Address, and so on).

▶ EXTRA FIELDS

Word offers more fields than you will probably need for a simple mass mailing. For example, seldom would you include the recipients' home and work telephone numbers. If you don't think you need the information for a certain field, delete it when you set up the field list, or simply ignore it and don't fill it in or use it in your main document.

CROSS-REFERENCE

For more information about databases, see Chapter 23, "Creating a Simple Database."

SHORTCUT

If you have data in an Excel table, you can copy and paste it into Word, save it, and use that file as the data table.

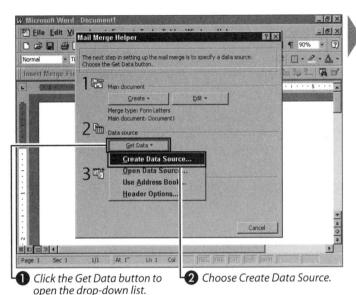

1 Click the Get Data button to open the drop-down list.

2 Choose Create Data Source.

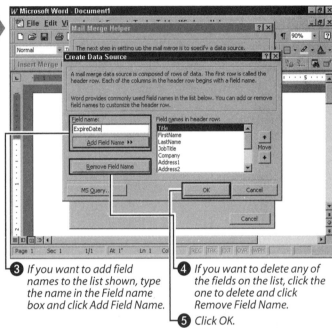

3 If you want to add field names to the list shown, type the name in the Field name box and click Add Field Name.

4 If you want to delete any of the fields on the list, click the one to delete and click Remove Field Name.

5 Click OK.

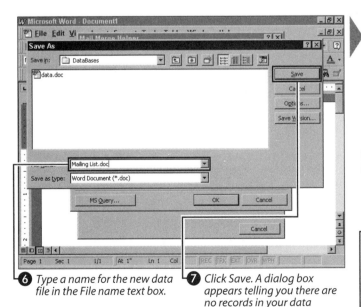

6 Type a name for the new data file in the File name text box.

7 Click Save. A dialog box appears telling you there are no records in your data source. Click Edit Data Source.

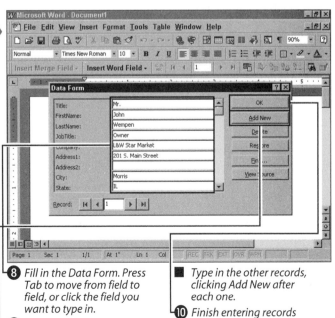

8 Fill in the Data Form. Press Tab to move from field to field, or click the field you want to type in.

9 Click Add New to start a new record.

■ Type in the other records, clicking Add New after each one.

10 Finish entering records and click OK. Move on to the next task.

Creating the Main Document

After you have told the Mail Merge Helper what data file you want to use, in either of the preceding two tasks, it tells you that "Word found no merge fields in your main document," as you can see in the first figure on the next page. This means that you have not yet created your form document. No problem; we create it in this task.

The main document is just a regular Word file with an additional toolbar at the top of the screen. The Mail Merge toolbar contains buttons for some of the most common mail merge commands, and it also has a drop-down list containing the names of the fields in your data file. You can select them from this list to drop them into your document in the right spots.

For example, suppose you are creating a letter. You'd type the date at the top, and perhaps your return address. In the spot where the recipient's name and address should go, you would insert the First Name field, type a space and then insert the Last Name field. Next, you'd press Enter to start a new line and insert the Address line. Keep building the address, inserting City, State, and ZIP.

The next part is easy — simply type the letter normally, including your closing and signature block. If you want to include merge fields in the body of the letter, do so. For example, you might want to say something like "Imagine how wonderful Christmas at the <<Last Name>> household will be this year with the Acme Christmas Tree Decorator Kit." By inserting the Last Name field strategically in the sentence, you can make each recipient's letter look personalized in content as well as in address and greeting.

Preview your letter (with File ➪ Print Preview) to make sure it looks good, and then you're ready to actually perform the merge, as explained in the next task.

TAKE NOTE

▶ SUBSEQUENT USES

The procedures outlined in this chapter for creating a data file and a main document are for a brand-new merge. You can save this merge file and reuse it, without having to set it up each time. In the future, just reopen the main document and perform the merge. Learn how to do this in the next task.

▶ DON'T TYPE THE FIELD NAMES

You can't just type the field names where you want them in the main document; you must select them from the drop-down list on the Mail Merge toolbar. That's because although those fields look like regular text when they're inserted, they are more than just text; hidden codes behind them perform the mail merge magic.

CROSS-REFERENCE

See "Starting a Merge with a New Data Source" and "Starting a Merge with an Existing Data Source," earlier in this chapter to learn how to manage both situations.

FIND IT ONLINE

For a lisitng of downloadable Word macros, check out: http://www.ikingston.demon.co.uk/ee/mac_01.

Don't Forget to Punctuate

As you insert your merge fields in your master document, remember to type spaces or punctuation between the fields. Many a beginner has despaired after printing a whole stack of letters addressed to JohnSmith and MaryJones. An especially tricky line is the City, State, ZIP line. Here's how to do it: Insert the City field, type a comma, type a space, insert the State field, type two spaces, and insert the ZIP field.

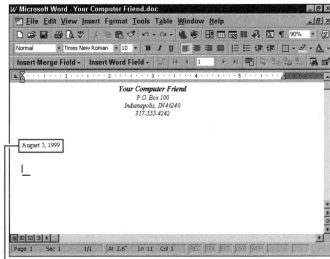

① *Type the date and any other opening text that should be the same on each letter (such as the return address, for example).*

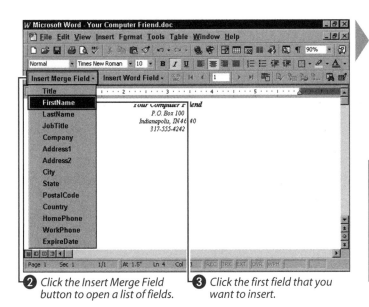

② *Click the Insert Merge Field button to open a list of fields.*

③ *Click the first field that you want to insert.*

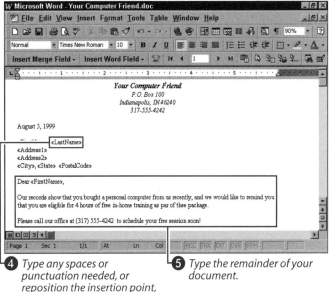

④ *Type any spaces or punctuation needed, or reposition the insertion point, and then insert other fields.*

⑤ *Type the remainder of your document.*

Checking and Printing Your Mail Merge

Now comes the big moment — doing the merge itself. You can do this in a couple of ways: you can merge to a new document onscreen, or you can merge directly to the printer. The latter is only for the very brave and confident, because if something goes wrong, there's no opportunity to catch it before you've wasted a lot of paper! In almost every circumstance, you should merge to a new document.

The toolbar buttons for these two actions are:

 Merge to New Document

 Merge to Printer

These options perform the merge immediately. If you want to exclude some of the records from the merge, or set any special options, you must use Mail Merge instead. This enables you to specify:

▶ Where to merge to (document, printer, or e-mail).

▶ Which records to merge (from 1 to 5, for example). You can also set Query Options that further delineate which records should be included.

▶ Whether or not to print blank lines when a certain record field is empty.

Since these special options are not very commonly used, we don't deal with them in the task on the next page, but you should be aware that they're available in case you need them.

CROSS-REFERENCE
For more information about printing, see Chapter 4, "Printing Documents."

FIND IT ONLINE
If you have trouble with phone numbers not printing in the correct format, see http://support.microsoft.com/support/kb/articles/q172/5/25.asp.

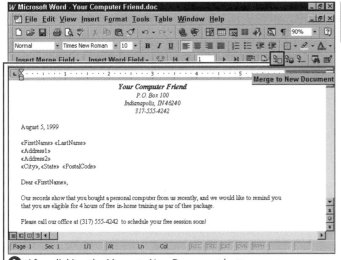

1 After clicking the Merge to New Document button, a new document appears with your letters in it, each letter on its own page.

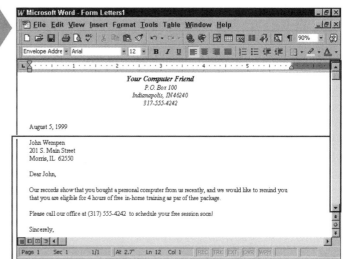

2 Scroll through the document, checking each letter to make sure it is addressed properly.

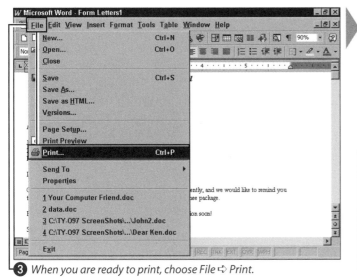

3 When you are ready to print, choose File ➪ Print.

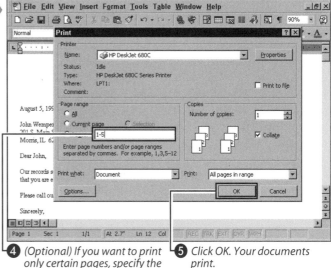

4 (Optional) If you want to print only certain pages, specify the page numbers.

5 Click OK. Your documents print.

Printing a Single Envelope

If you're just typing a single letter, you don't need to go through the rigmarole of a mail merge just to print an envelope for it. There's a much easier way: the Tools ⇨ Envelopes and Labels command. Using this command, you can create an envelope layout and attach it to your document, so it is always ready to print.

Word can even remember your return address for you and include it on every envelope you print. You can also store multiple return addresses and choose which one you want to use each time. Or, if you have a preprinted return address on your envelopes, you can omit the return address from the print job entirely.

Word can also print a bar code on each envelope, which the machines at the post office use to read the destination information. Using bar codes helps the post office deliver your letters more quickly.

Most business letters are sent in business-size envelopes, but you can print on any size envelope. Just let Word know what envelope size you want to use. To do so, click the Options button in the Envelopes and Labels dialog box, and choose the envelope size on the Envelope Options tab. You can enter custom envelope sizes to accommodate those that do not appear on Word's predefined list.

The trickiest part about printing an envelope in Word is figuring out which way to feed the envelope into your printer. Every printer is different! You might need to feed the envelope in sideways, upside-down, backwards, aligned with the right edge or left edge, or even centered. Your printer's manual may be able to tell you the proper method, or you may be able to test it, as explained in the note on this page.

TAKE NOTE

▶ TESTING YOUR PRINTER'S ENVELOPE FEED

If you can't find any information about envelope orientation in your printer's manual, the best way to check it is to feed in a single sheet of paper, and see where the address prints. Draw a little arrow on the paper first, and feed the paper in arrow-first and arrow-up. From looking at where the envelope address prints in relation to that arrow, you can deduce how to feed the envelope in.

▶ ADDRESS BOOK

You can pull addresses (either the recipient or the return address) from your Address Book in Outlook. Just click the Address Book icon in the Envelopes and Labels dialog box above either the Delivery Address or Return Address area.

CROSS-REFERENCE

To work with the address book in Outlook, see "Addressing E-mail and Faxes" in Chapter 20.

FIND IT ONLINE

To print multiple copies of an envelope, see http://support.microsoft.com/support/kb/articles/q155/1/98.asp.

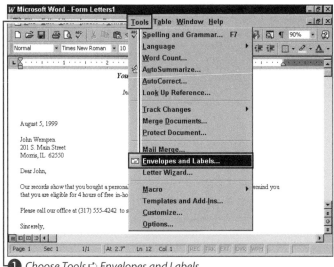

① Choose Tools ➪ Envelopes and Labels.

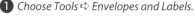

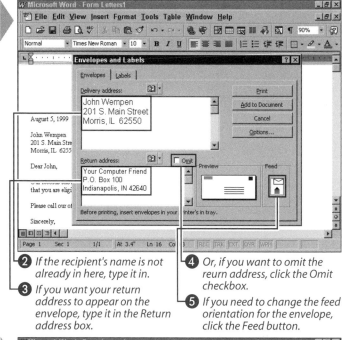

② If the recipient's name is not already in here, type it in.

③ If you want your return address to appear on the envelope, type it in the Return address box.

④ Or, if you want to omit the return address, click the Omit checkbox.

⑤ If you need to change the feed orientation for the envelope, click the Feed button.

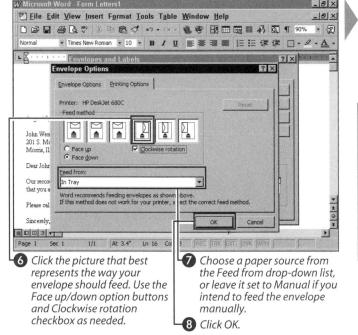

⑥ Click the picture that best represents the way your envelope should feed. Use the Face up/down option buttons and Clockwise rotation checkbox as needed.

⑦ Choose a paper source from the Feed from drop-down list, or leave it set to Manual if you intend to feed the envelope manually.

⑧ Click OK.

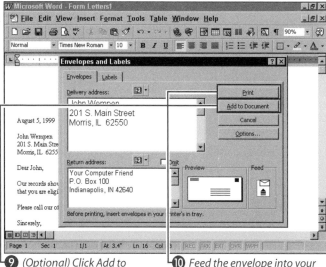

⑨ (Optional) Click Add to Document to store the envelope setup with the document. Then reopen the dialog box by reselecting Tools ➪ Envelopes and Labels.

⑩ Feed the envelope into your printer, and then click Print.

Personal Workbook

Q&A

1 Which of the following cannot be used directly for a merge data source: Word documents, Outlook address book, Excel worksheet, or Access database?

_____

_____

2 True or false: When you create a new data source with the Mail Merge Helper, the data becomes a saved part of the mail merge file, rather than being saved in a separate document.

_____

_____

3 What is the difference between a Mail Merge main document and a normal Word document?

_____

_____

_____

4 True or false: It is okay to type the field names into the main document, instead of selecting them from the drop-down list on the Mail Merge toolbar.

_____

_____

_____

5 True or false: If you click the Merge to Printer button, Word prints all the merged letters immediately, without creating a new Word file containing them.

_____

_____

_____

6 True or false: You should place your envelope in the printer in whatever way is shown on the Feed button in the Envelopes and Labels dialog box.

_____

_____

_____

7 Where do the addresses that appear when you click the Address Book button in the Envelopes and Labels dialog box come from?

_____

_____

_____

8 What must you do to save the envelope's information with the letter?

_____

_____

ANSWERS: PAGE 409

EXTRA PRACTICE

1. Try creating a mail merge that prints mailing labels using the table that you created in the Real-World Applications section of Chapter 10 as the data file.

2. Perform the same mail merge again, but this time use Envelopes as the merge type.

3. Try using the Catalog merge type on the same data and see what results you get. Think about how this feature might be useful for your home or business.

4. Start a new mail merge for a form letter and create your own data file using the Data Form dialog box. Enter the names of your family, friends, or pets as the recipients. (It's just for practice!)

5. Experiment with the envelope size settings. Try printing on nonstandard envelopes by setting the envelope size manually.

REAL-WORLD APPLICATIONS

✔ Make mail-merged labels for your holiday cards this year. Use a fancy script font and buy peel-off labels that are clear, or that match your card envelopes (red or green, perhaps?).

✔ Print some envelopes with just your return address on them — no recipient. Keep them on hand to mail your bills, or anything else that you hand-write the recipient address on.

✔ Print some envelopes with both your return address and the address where you send your monthly mortgage or rent. Keep these envelopes handy for bill-paying each month, so you don't have to address an envelope.

Visual Quiz

What is wrong with the merge fields in this letter and how would you fix them?

_____

_____

_____

_____

_____

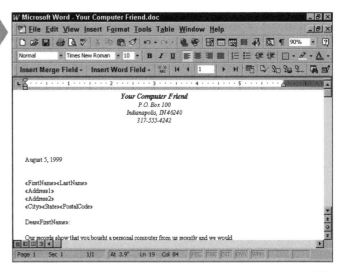

CHAPTER 12

MASTER THESE SKILLS

▶ Creating an Outline

▶ Editing an Outline

▶ Expanding and Collapsing Heading Levels

▶ Typing Text under Outline Headings

Creating an Outline in Word

Some authors never use an outline to plan their books. They simply sit down at the keyboard and start typing, and out come these wonderful stories! Others (most of us!) have to start with an outline to help remember what they want to say and in what order they want to say it. You should have seen the detailed outline that we came up with before we wrote this book!

When faced with the task of writing a lengthy project, rarely do you sit at the keyboard and have the text flow naturally in a logical order off the top of your head. This method also makes it more likely that your presentation of the material will not be balanced — you could, for example, spend a long time on one topic and not enough time on a related topic. It's also easy to leave out information that you would probably see the need for if you create an outline before beginning the writing. Creating an outline also helps you pinpoint topics that may not be substantial enough to stand on their own. You may instead decide to make such a topic a subtopic under a larger topic.

If you are planning a big writing project, more than a few simple pages, the Outline feature in Word can help. In Outline view, you can create a multilevel outline, and reorganize/replan to your heart's content. Word lets you collapse and expand the outline as needed, helping to focus either on the big picture or tiny details. When you're ready to write, you simply switch to Normal or Page Layout view and start typing your text. If you later need to rearrange sections in your document, you can easily jump back to Outline view and do the rearranging. When you return to Normal view, you'll find that Word has not only moved the headings, but any text that you had typed beneath them too.

In this chapter, you learn how to create and edit an outline, and how to view the outline exactly the way you want it onscreen. You can even print your outline for easier reference as you work. Then, when you're ready to write the document itself, we show you how to work with an outline in Normal or Page Layout view. We teach you how to customize the way Outline view works and make the most of Word's automatic numbering feature (from Chapter 10) on an outline.

Creating an Outline

Outline creation in Word is best accomplished in Outline view. (You can type a list of topics in any view you like, but you won't have the outlining tools available in any view except Outline.) You can switch to outline view from the View menu, or click the Outline View button on the toolbar located at the left end of the horizontal scroll bar (it's the fourth button from the left).

In Outline view, the Outlining toolbar appears. It includes buttons for promoting and demoting a line's outline level, moving a line up or down in the outline, and displaying/hiding various levels of headings.

Typing an outline in Word's Outline view is simple — just type. To start a new line, press Enter, as usual. When you press Enter, the new line has the same outline level as the one above it.

You can change a line's level by pressing Tab to indent (demote) it, or Shift+Tab to outdent (promote) it. You can have up to nine outline levels. You can also use the Promote and Demote buttons on the Outlining toolbar to change a line's outline level, but most people find the Tab and Shift+Tab more convenient because they don't have to take their hands off the keyboard. To change the level of a paragraph that you already typed, place the cursor anywhere inside it and then press Tab or Shift+Tab.

It is best not to try to number items on your outline manually because as you work, your numbering is likely to change, making your outline inaccurate. Instead, you should use Word's Automatic Numbering feature (discussed in Chapter 10) to number the items on your outline. That way, as you move and add/delete items, everything stays numbered correctly. To use it, just click the Numbering button on the toolbar, or choose Format ➪ Bullets and Numbering.

TAKE NOTE

▶ TAB STOPS

You can't use tab stops in Outline view because the Tab key does not function as it usually does; it changes the outline level. To use tabs, switch back to Normal or Page Layout view temporarily.

▶ NUMBERING FORMAT

To choose which numbering format you want to use in Outline view, choose Format ➪ Bullets and Numbering and click the Outline Numbered tab. Next, choose a numbering format and click OK. You can choose different numbering formats for different levels; select a heading of the level you want to format first.

▶ FORMATTING OUTLINE LEVELS

Each outline level takes its formatting from a style. For example, first-level headings use the style Heading 1, second-level headings use style Heading 2, and so on. To change how headings appear in Outline view, redefine the heading style, as you learn to do in Chapter 8.

CROSS-REFERENCE
See "Controlling the Numbering Format" in Chapter 10 to learn more about numbered list formatting.

FIND IT ONLINE
If you get an Invalid Page Fault error message when promoting or demoting outline items, you should install the Office 97 Service Release 1 patch. Find it at **http://officeupdate. microsoft.com/downloadDetails/sr1off97detail.htm**.

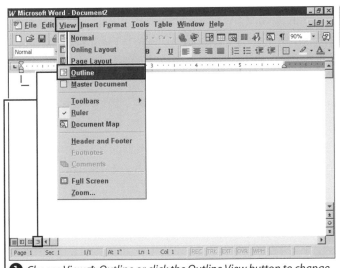

1 Choose View ➪ Outline or click the Outline View button to change to Outline view.

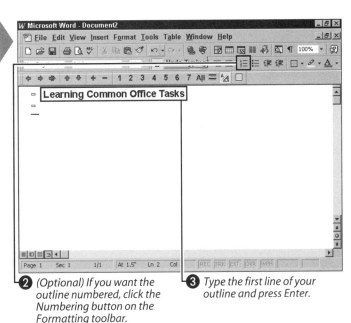

2 (Optional) If you want the outline numbered, click the Numbering button on the Formatting toolbar.

3 Type the first line of your outline and press Enter.

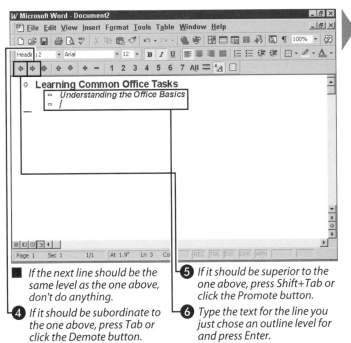

■ If the next line should be the same level as the one above, don't do anything.

4 If it should be subordinate to the one above, press Tab or click the Demote button.

5 If it should be superior to the one above, press Shift+Tab or click the Promote button.

6 Type the text for the line you just chose an outline level for and press Enter.

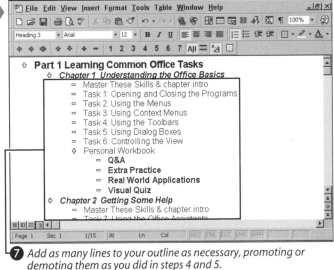

7 Add as many lines to your outline as necessary, promoting or demoting them as you did in steps 4 and 5.

Editing an Outline

An outline helps you organize your thoughts before you start writing the body of your text. Rearranging the outline headings after initially jotting them down is a natural part of the process. Almost nobody produces a perfect outline right off the bat.

When working in Outline view, you can select a line by clicking the minus sign next to it. Some lines have plus signs next to them, indicating that there are subordinate lines beneath them. When you click a plus sign, the entire block becomes selected: the heading and all its subordinates. You can use this feature to move, copy, or delete them as a group. You can rearrange your outline headings in several ways:

▶ Use Drag and drop to move entire sections. Drag a heading by the plus or minus sign to its left; the pointer changes to a four-headed arrow, indicating that you can move what's beneath it.

▶ Use Cut and Paste to move sections from one spot to another. (This works well if the destination is several pages away, making drag-and-drop impractical.) Simply select what you want to move and click Cut; then reposition the insertion point and click Paste.

▶ Use the Move Up and Move Down buttons on the Outlining toolbar to move one line at a time. Select the line(s) you want to move and then click the applicable button to go up or down one line (or one block, if the line directly above or below has subordinate lines that must stay together).

▶ Press Alt+Shift+Up Arrow to move a selection up, or Alt+Shift+Down Arrow to move it down.

Of course, all the normal editing tools are at your disposal too, such as text editing, text formatting (including text color changes and highlighting), the Find and Replace features (Edit ⇨ Find and Edit ⇨ Replace), and Undo.

TAKE NOTE

HIGHLIGHT FOR EMPHASIS

When writing a long document based on an outline, you might like to highlight (with the Highlight tool on the Formatting toolbar) the parts that you have finished writing. It can also be useful to highlight (in another color) parts that need special attention, enabling you to find them quickly on the outline.

INDENT BUTTONS ON THE FORMATTING TOOLBAR

In Outline View, the Increase Indent and Decrease Indent buttons do not work as they do in other views.

CROSS-REFERENCE

See "Using Drag and Drop" in Chapter 5 for more information about moving text in that way.

SHORTCUT

If you have trouble selecting with drag and drop, use the keyboard. Click where you want to begin, and then hold down Shift while pressing the arrow keys.

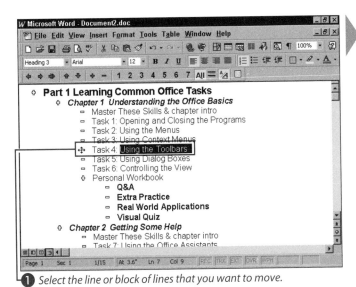

① Select the line or block of lines that you want to move.

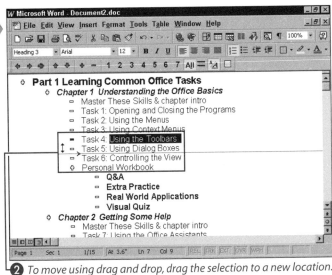

② To move using drag and drop, drag the selection to a new location. A line shows where it will go.

③ Release the mouse button. The selection is relocated.

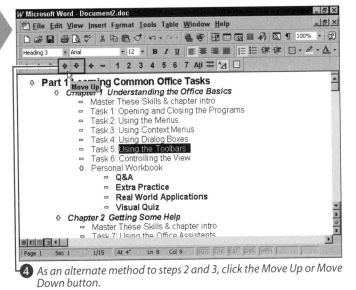

④ As an alternate method to steps 2 and 3, click the Move Up or Move Down button.

Expanding and Collapsing Heading Levels

Typically, you want to see everything that is in your outline. However, you can collapse certain levels of your outline, temporarily hiding them so that the big picture becomes clearer. There are two kinds of collapsing:

▶ You can collapse the outline globally at a certain level; for example, collapse all headings that are lower than level two.

▶ You can collapse the levels underneath a single heading.

Expanding is the same: you can expand the entire outline to show any number of heading levels again, or you can expand individual headings. To expand or collapse the outline levels, you can use the buttons on the Outlining toolbar. Each button, or set of buttons, is geared toward a different expanding/collapsing scheme:

Outlining Buttons

➕ ➖	Expand and Collapse
1 2 3	Numbered buttons (seven in all)
All	All
≡	Show First Line Only

The Expand and Collapse buttons expand or collapse all subordinate headings under the currently selected line, by one level each time you click them. The shortcut keys for these buttons are: Alt+Shift+plus sign for Expand, and Alt+Shift+minus sign for Collapse.

Clicking the numbered buttons (seven in all) changes the number of outline levels that you see. The shortcut keys for these buttons are Alt+Shift+the number. Use the numbers above the letter keys, not the numeric keypad keys.

The All button immediately displays all outline levels, fully expanding it. The shortcut key for this is Alt+Shift+A.

The Show First Line Only button collapses multi-line paragraphs (for example, if a heading is so long that it wraps to the next line) to take up only one line of space on the outline. The shortcut key for this is Alt+Shift+L.

TAKE NOTE

OUTLINE PRINTING

You can print the displayed outline levels using File ➪ Print. The hidden outline levels do not print.

DOUBLE-CLICK SHORTCUT

You can double-click a plus sign to quickly expand or collapse the subordinate items beneath it.

CROSS-REFERENCE

To use your outline to start typing your body text, see "Typing Text under Outline Headings" later in this chapter.

FIND IT ONLINE

To prevent collapsed outlines appearing distorted in Print Preview, see **http://support.microsoft.com/support/kb/articles/q160/8/42.asp.**

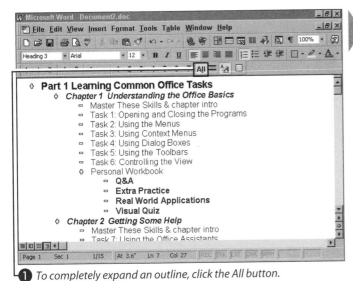

1 To completely expand an outline, click the All button.

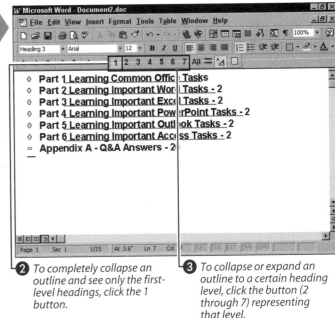

2 To completely collapse an outline and see only the first-level headings, click the 1 button.

3 To collapse or expand an outline to a certain heading level, click the button (2 through 7) representing that level.

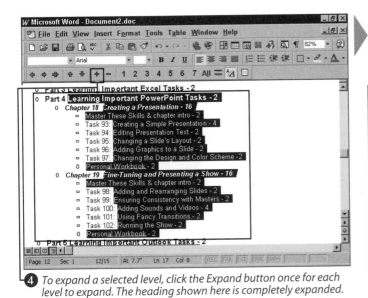

4 To expand a selected level, click the Expand button once for each level to expand. The heading shown here is completely expanded.

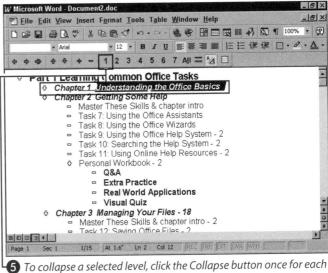

5 To collapse a selected level, click the Collapse button once for each level to collapse.

Typing Text under Outline Headings

When you are finished with your outline, you're ready to start typing your text. You can do this in a couple of ways:

▶ If your outline represents multiple chapters, you may want to break up each chapter into separate Word files. You can copy the portion of the outline that refers to each chapter using Edit ⇨ Copy.

▶ If your document will be short enough to manage in a single Word file, you can leave it all as it is. Many PCs start to perform sluggishly in Word when a document exceeds 50 pages or so.

In this task, we assume that your document is short enough to keep in a single Word file.

To type text, switch to Normal or Page Layout view. Your headings from the outline become regular text, formatted with one of the heading styles in your style list. You can type text beneath each heading and format it with a nonheading style (such as Normal).

If you decide later that you need to rearrange some topics in your document, you can jump back into Outline view and move them as demonstrated in the preceding task. The body text you typed beneath them moves with them. You can move body text separately from a heading in Normal or Page Layout view, using drag and drop or cut and paste.

TAKE NOTE

▶ REMOVE THE NUMBERING

You may have numbered items on your outline for reference, but once you start typing the actual body text in Normal or Page Layout view, the numbers (and the indentation that goes with them) may not be appropriate anymore. To get rid of the number on a line, select it and deselect the Numbering button on the toolbar to turn numbering off.

▶ NO STYLE CHANGE NEEDED

To type text under a heading, position the insertion point at the end of the heading line and press Enter to start a new paragraph. The new paragraph is automatically formatted with the Normal style; all of Word's default heading styles are set up with Style for Following Paragraph set to Normal. See Chapter 8 for more information about styles.

▶ GENERATING AN OUTLINE FROM TEXT

If you already have text but need to create an outline from the headings, use the Insert ⇨ Index and Tables feature to generate a Table of Contents. See Word's online help for details about this feature.

▶ OUTLINE LEVEL V. HEADING STYLES

If you don't want specific formatting applied to an outline entry, use the styles Level 1 through Level 9.

CROSS-REFERENCE

"Controlling the View" in Chapter 1 explains Normal, Page Layout, and other views.

FIND IT ONLINE

Outline view has limited support for formatting commands. See http://support.microsoft.com/support/kb/articles/q111/0/72.asp for more information.

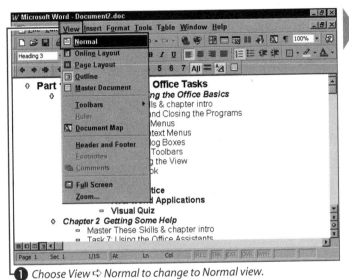

1 *Choose View ⇨ Normal to change to Normal view.*

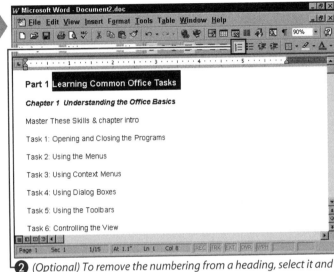

2 *(Optional) To remove the numbering from a heading, select it and click the Numbering button.*

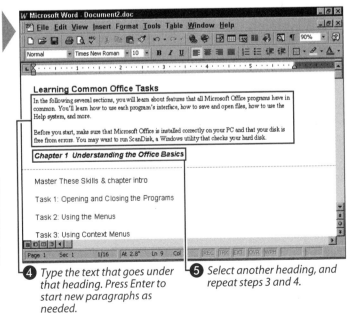

3 *Position the insertion point at the end of the line and press Enter, creating a new paragraph formatted as Normal style.*

4 *Type the text that goes under that heading. Press Enter to start new paragraphs as needed.*

5 *Select another heading, and repeat steps 3 and 4.*

Personal Workbook

Q&A

1 Which Word views can you use to create outlines in?

_____

_____

_____

2 Which key(s) do you press to demote an outline item?

_____

_____

_____

3 Which keys(s) do you press to promote an item?

_____

_____

_____

4 How would you change the numbering format used on your outline, if you did not like the default?

_____

_____

_____

5 The Heading 3 style on the Styles drop-down list corresponds to which outline level?

_____

_____

_____

6 How would you change the formatting of all first-level outline lines?

_____

_____

_____

7 True or false: A plus sign next to an outline item means that there are subordinate headings beneath it that you cannot see right now because they are collapsed.

_____

_____

_____

8 True or false: When you're ready to type the body text under your headings, you should change to Normal or Page Layout view.

_____

_____

_____

ANSWERS: PAGE

EXTRA PRACTICE

1 Create your own multilevel outline listing all the rooms in your house as first-level headings and the furniture in them as second-level headings.

2 Assign numbering to the first-level headings. Move the bottom heading to the top of the list.

3 Add third-level headings under any furniture items that contain other items (such as magazines in a magazine rack or knick-knacks on a coffee table).

4 Switch to Normal view and type a sentence of normal text under each first-level heading that provides some information about each room.

5 Change to Page Layout view and see how your work changes.

REAL-WORLD APPLICATIONS

✓ The next time you plan a party, make a "to do" outline in Word. Your first-level headings might be Food & Beverages, Decorations, Entertainment, and Invitations. You could make a second-level list of the things you need to do in each category.

✓ Help your child create an outline of the next school report he or she has to write, and show him or her how to change to Normal view and type his or her text afterwards.

✓ Use an outline to organize various Web addresses that you have collected. Make each address a third-level heading and use heading levels 1 and 2 to create an organizational structure for them. Word automatically formats Web addresses as hyperlinks, so you can click them in the document to jump immediately to the page on the Internet.

Visual Quiz

Based on what you can see in this figure, at least how many levels does this outline have?

_____

_____

_____

_____

_____

CHAPTER **13**

MASTER
THESE
SKILLS

▶ **Correcting Spelling and Grammar As You Type**

▶ **Checking Your Spelling**

▶ **Checking Your Grammar**

▶ **Customizing Spelling and Grammar Options**

▶ **Tracking Changes**

Checking Your Work

Like it or not, we are all judged by our spelling and grammar in everything we write. Some personnel managers throw out any resume or cover letter that has a typo. They rationalize that such a person would not be a careful, conscientious worker.

Word provides a number of tools for improving the quality of your writing. Chapter 7 demonstrated how Word uses AutoCorrect to correct common typing errors, such as automatically changing "teh" to "the." In this chapter, you learn about Word's spelling and grammar checking tools, further defenders of your professional image.

The spelling and grammar checkers operate in two ways: as you type (automatically) and whenever you issue the Tools ➪ Spelling and Grammar command (interactively with you). Both have their uses. You may want to use the automatic checking to identify obvious typos as you go along and then run a complete spelling and grammar check when you finish a document, before sending it anywhere.

In the spelling checker, you can create your own custom dictionary that contains all the words that you use frequently that aren't in Word's standard dictionary. The names of clients might be included there, as well as street and town names, product names, technical jargon, and other words unique to your profession.

With the grammar checker, you can decide which grammar rules to apply, from passive voice to verb tense. If you're not up on all those rules (and not many people are, save English professors and editors!), you can simply choose one of Word's Writing Styles (Standard, Casual, Formal, and so on) and let a predefined set of rules be your guide.

At the end of the chapter, you learn about a revision feature that helps you track changes and corrections that multiple people make to a document. Businesses find dozens of uses for this feature, from contract negotiation changes to report reviews. This feature was used extensively, for example, when this book was being prepared for publication! Each editor entered his or her changes with revision marks turned on, so everyone on the project could see who had changed what. Next, the final decision-maker on the project accepted or rejected each revision using the same tool.

Correcting Spelling and Grammar As You Type

As you have been typing in the preceding chapters, you may have noticed the wavy red and green underlines under some words and phrases. They are Word's way of letting you know that it thinks something is not quite right with them. The red ones are possible spelling errors and the green ones are possible grammatical errors.

The easiest way to ask Word "what do you mean?" is to right-click the underlined word or phrase. A pop-up menu appears, telling you what is wrong and in some cases suggesting a revision.

The menu that appears presents you with the following spell-check options:

▶ Select a revision (if one is presented).
▶ Choose Ignore All to ignore this and all other instances of the error (in this document only).
▶ Click Add to add the word to your custom dictionary, so it will no longer be considered misspelled in any documents.
▶ Choose AutoCorrect and then the correction to add this misspelling/correction pair to the list of AutoCorrect As You Type words.
▶ Choose Spelling to open the full-blown spelling checker, described in the task that follows this one.

For a grammar check, you can:

▶ Select a revision (if one is presented).

▶ Choose Ignore Sentence to skip this sentence when grammar checking (in this document only).
▶ Choose Grammar to open the full-blown grammar checker, described in "Checking Your Grammar" later in this chapter.

If the wavy underlines bother you, you can turn them off. Choose Tools ⇨ Options and click the Spelling & Grammar tab. On this tab, you can turn off as-you-type spelling and grammar checking altogether (by deselecting the Check spelling as you type and Check grammar as you type checkboxes). Or you can turn off the display of wavy lines for this document only by selecting the Hide spelling errors in this document and Hide grammatical errors in this document checkboxes.

TAKE NOTE

CHOOSING WHICH GRAMMATICAL ERRORS ARE MARKED

The grammar checker operates according to the rules chosen in the Grammar Options. To get there, choose Tools ⇨ Options and click the Spelling & Grammar tab. Next, click the Settings button in the Grammar section of the dialog box to open a dialog box where you can select the rules that you want to be applied.

CROSS-REFERENCE
To perform a full spelling or grammar check, see "Checking Your Spelling" or "Checking Your Grammar" later in this chapter.

FIND IT ONLINE
The spell checker does not flag single letters as misspelled. See http://support.microsoft.com/support/kb/articles/q87/8/57.asp.

Not Up on Grammar?

To get a hint as to why the grammar checker may have marked a particular phrase, right-click it and choose Grammar to open the full grammar checker. In the dialog box that appears, the error appears in a text box, and above that text box is a grammar category that can give you an idea of what Word thinks is wrong.

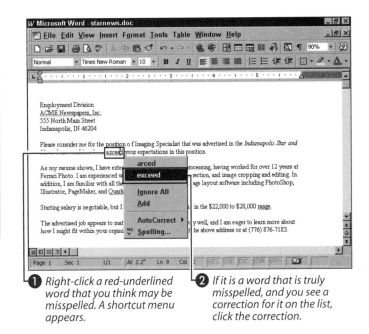

1 Right-click a red-underlined word that you think may be misspelled. A shortcut menu appears.

2 If it is a word that is truly misspelled, and you see a correction for it on the list, click the correction.

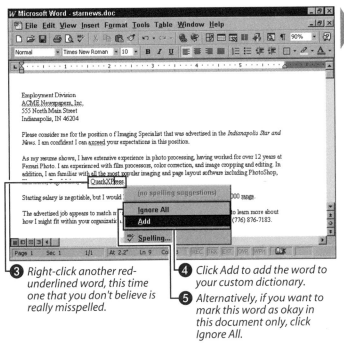

3 Right-click another red-underlined word, this time one that you don't believe is really misspelled.

4 Click Add to add the word to your custom dictionary.

5 Alternatively, if you want to mark this word as okay in this document only, click Ignore All.

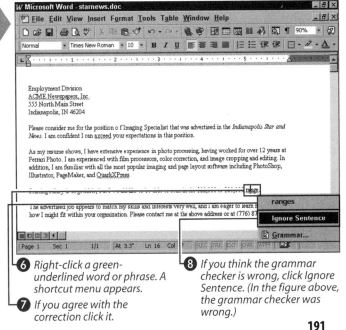

6 Right-click a green-underlined word or phrase. A shortcut menu appears.

7 If you agree with the correction click it.

8 If you think the grammar checker is wrong, click Ignore Sentence. (In the figure above, the grammar checker was wrong.)

Checking Your Spelling

I f your document is long, it can get tiresome to right-click each wavy-underlined word or phrase. In such cases, it's easiest to use the full-blown spell-check feature in Word. It checks all the words and sentences for both spelling and grammar. (You can perform both types of checks at once.)

To begin the spelling check, click the Spelling toolbar button, or choose Tools ⇨ Spelling and Grammar, or press F7. If you have no misspelled words or grammatical errors, Word presents a dialog box telling you that your spell check is complete. Click OK to close that dialog box.

If, on the other hand, Word finds a misspelled word, as it did on the following page, you can choose from the following options:

▶ Ignore: Skips over this occurrence of the word.
▶ Ignore All: Skips over all occurrences of the word in this Word session only.
▶ Suggestions: Lists words close to the spelling of the word you actually typed. Choose the correct one by clicking it.
▶ Not in Dictionary: This box shows the word in its context. You can double-click the misspelled word in this box and type a correction if none of the words in the Suggestions box is correct.
▶ Change: Changes the word in the document to the word highlighted in the Suggestions box. (Don't click this button until you choose the

correct word in the Suggestions box or type a correction in the Not in Dictionary box.)
▶ Change All: Changes all occurrences of the word in the entire document to the word highlighted in the Suggestions text box.
▶ Add: Adds the word to Word's custom dictionary so that it will recognize it in the future.
▶ AutoCorrect: Adds the word to the AutoCorrect list so that if you misspell it the same way in the future, Word automatically corrects it as you type.
▶ Undo: Reverses the last correction made (very handy if you are clicking through so fast that you make a mistake).

TAKE NOTE

USE AUTOCORRECT CAUTIOUSLY

Don't click the AutoCorrect button for misspellings that you may sometimes want to change to some other word, or you may introduce embarrassing mistakes into your document. For example, if you often type "pian" instead of "pain," but sometimes accidentally type "pian" instead of "piano," don't tell Word to always AutoCorrect to "pain," or you may find that Word has corrected your attempt at typing piano and made it a pain!

CROSS-REFERENCE
See "Checking Your Grammar" later in this chapter.

FIND IT ONLINE
Some fonts interfere with the spelling check. Check out http://support.microsoft.com/support/kb/articles/ q164/3/32.asp.

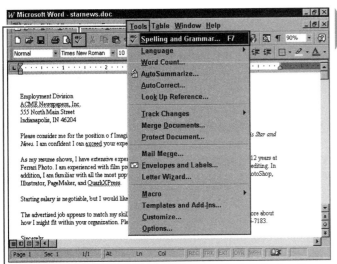

① Click the Spelling and Grammar button on the Standard toolbar, or choose Tools ▷ Spelling and Grammar.

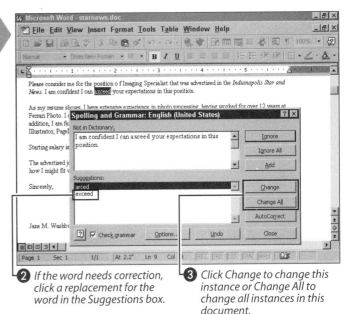

② If the word needs correction, click a replacement for the word in the Suggestions box.

③ Click Change to change this instance or Change All to change all instances in this document.

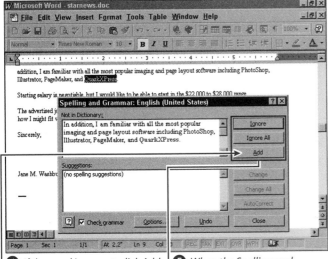

④ If the word is correct, click Add to add it to the dictionary, or Ignore or Ignore All to ignore one or all instances in this Word session.

⑤ When the Spelling and Grammar checker moves on to the next mistake, Correct, Add, or Ignore it as necessary.

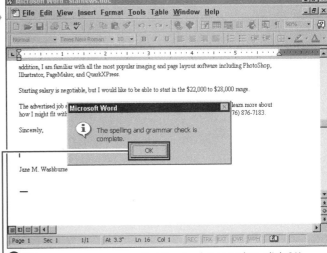

⑥ When you see a message that the check is complete, click OK.

Checking Your Grammar

As mentioned earlier, grammar checking takes place at the same time as spell checking, so you may see its dialog box interspersed with the spell-check dialog box as you go. You can tell the difference between the spelling controls and the grammar controls because there are fewer (and some different) grammar controls, as shown on the facing page.

The following are the controls you find when Word discovers a grammatical error:

▶ Ignore: Skips over this occurrence of the grammatical error (if indeed it is an error).

▶ Ignore All: Skips over all occurrences of the grammatical error in this Word session.

▶ Suggestions: Lists alternate wordings or punctuation corrections that might fix the problem. (*Warning*: using these blindly can introduce errors where there weren't any before.)

▶ Next Sentence: Skips the sentence currently identified as problematic, ignoring all additional grammatical errors that might be in that sentence. (Use this instead of Ignore if you know the sentence is right.)

▶ Change: If available, changes the text to read as the selection in the Suggestions box recommends.

▶ Undo: Reverses the last correction made and returns to that sentence so you can reevaluate it.

Notice that there is no Add, Change All, or AutoCorrect button. You cannot add a grammar construct to the dictionary, nor can you AutoCorrect one. And Change All wouldn't make sense because every sentence is different and needs to be evaluated separately.

TAKE NOTE

▶ DON'T COUNT ON THE GRAMMAR CHECKER

Grammar is much less precise than spelling and you will find that Word's grammar check is far from perfect. More than 50 percent of the time, the sentence identified as wrong is actually okay, and applying one of Word's suggested corrections will introduce an error. Use the grammar check only to make you think about whether something is right or wrong, not as a final arbiter of good grammar.

▶ GRAMMAR OPTIONS ABOUND

As you learn in the next task, you can set all kinds of parameters for the grammar check, so if Word applies a particular grammar rule that you don't want to check for, you can turn it off.

▶ WORD COUNT

To count the number of words in your document (or in a selection), choose Tools ⇨ Word Count.

CROSS-REFERENCE
If Word displays a spelling error as you are checking, refer to "Checking Your Spelling" earlier in this chapter.

FIND IT ONLINE
For more information about the grammar checker, see "http://support.microsoft.com/support/kb/articles/Q167/6/55.asp."

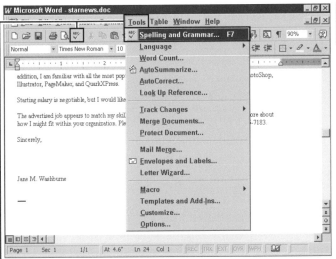

❶ *Click the Spelling and Grammar button on the Standard toolbar, or choose Tools ➪ Spelling and Grammar.*

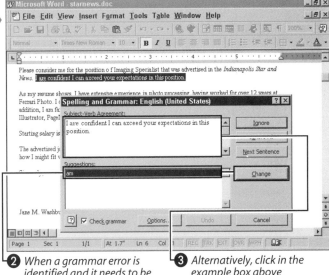

❷ *When a grammar error is identified and it needs to be changed, click the correct change in the Suggestions box and click Change.*

❸ *Alternatively, click in the example box above Suggestions (its name varies depending on the error found), type a correction and then click Change.*

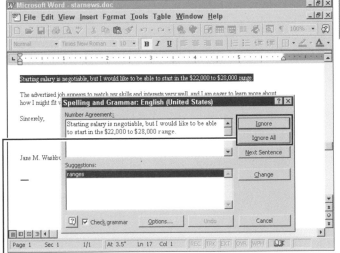

❹ *If an error is found that does not need to be changed, click Ignore to ignore it and move on, or Ignore All to stop applying that grammar rule in this document.*

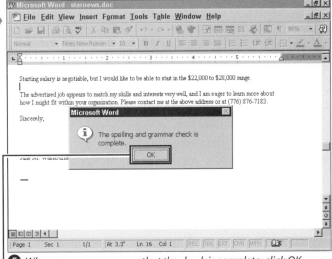

❺ *When you see a message that the check is complete, click OK.*

Customizing Spelling and Grammar Options

Word's spelling and grammar checkers are very customizable. For instance, you don't have to put up with Word continually asking you to correct sentences based on a grammar rule that you don't care about. And you have already seen how you can add words to the dictionary, so they are no longer marked as misspelled.

The spelling options and the grammar options are separate, but they are both set in the same dialog box, so we look at them together here.

The spelling options include:

▶ Checking spelling as you type: We looked at this earlier in the chapter; it turns on/off the automatic spell check.

▶ Hide spelling errors in this document: As you may remember from the first task in this chapter, this turns off the wavy underlines in the document that indicate errors.

▶ Always suggest corrections: If you turn this off, nothing will appear in the Suggestions area. This might help the spell-check speed on an extremely old and slow computer.

▶ Suggest from main dictionary only: The custom dictionaries, as you will shortly see, contain the words you've added. The Main dictionary is the one that comes with Word. By default, Word checks and suggests from both. Select this option to have it suggest only from the main dictionary.

▶ Ignore words in Uppercase: With this selected, Word does not check words that have the first letter capitalized, such as proper names.

▶ Ignore words with numbers: With this selected, Word ignores letters that are grouped together with numbers, such as license plate numbers (BRQR123).

▶ Ignore Internet and file addresses: With this selected, word doesn't check hyperlinks or strings of text that appear to be Web addresses (http://www.mysite.org).

Continued

Continued

TAKE NOTE

CREATING MULTIPLE CUSTOM DICTIONARIES

Click the Dictionaries button to open the Custom Dictionaries dialog box. To add a word to a dictionary, choose which custom dictionary you want to use (from the Custom Dictionary drop-down list), and then click OK to go back to the document. Type the word you want to add to the dictionary, right-click it and choose Add.

CROSS-REFERENCE

For information about automatically correcting spelling errors, see "Using AutoCorrect" in Chapter 7.

FIND IT ONLINE

To delete words from custom dictionaries, see the instructions at **http://support.microsoft.com/support/kb/articles/q86/5/57.asp**.

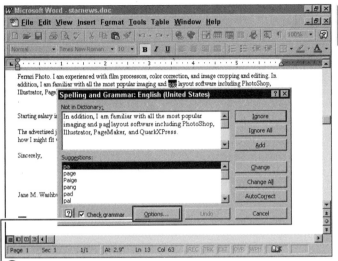

❶ Click the Options button in the Spelling and Grammar dialog box, or choose Tools ➪ Options and click the Spelling & Grammar tab.

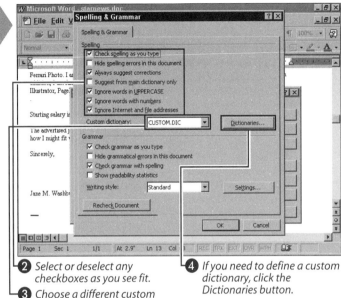

❷ Select or deselect any checkboxes as you see fit.

❸ Choose a different custom dictionary from the Custom Dictionary drop-down list.

❹ If you need to define a custom dictionary, click the Dictionaries button.

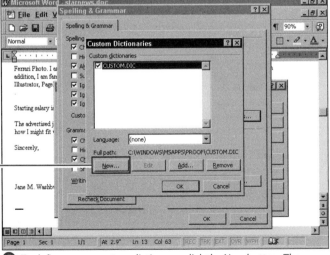

❺ To define a new custom dictionary, click the New button. The Create Custom Dictionary dialog box opens.

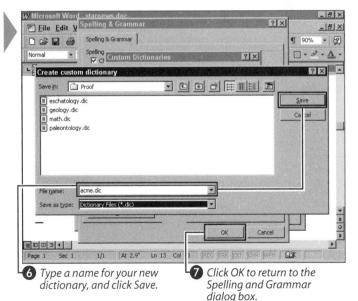

❻ Type a name for your new dictionary, and click Save.

❼ Click OK to return to the Spelling and Grammar dialog box.

Customizing Spelling and Grammar Options *Continued*

Setting Grammar Options

Now let's look at the grammar options. The settings for grammar include:

- ▶ Checking grammar as you type: This turns on/off the automatic grammar check.
- ▶ Hide grammatical errors in this document: This turns off the wavy underlines in the document that indicate errors.
- ▶ Check grammar with spelling: If you deselect this, your spelling checks will not include grammar checking.
- ▶ Show readability statistics: Turn this on to see a readability formula at the end of your check to tell you how understandable your writing will be to your reader.

Word's grammar options let you choose a formality level, which activates a certain set of grammar rules. Word offers the following Writing style choices: Casual, Standard, Formal, Technical, and Custom. Casual is most appropriate for friendly, conversational letters. Standard works well in most general business situations. Formal is great for important reports and legal documents. Technical works well when explaining math, engineering, or scientific concepts. And Custom lets you define your own specific set of grammar rules.

How do you set customized rules? Well, you click the Settings button to open a Grammar Settings dialog box. From there, you can pick the formality level you want to customize, and then choose the individual grammar rules you want to apply or ignore. We recommend that you customize only the Custom style and leave the others set at their default settings. That way, you can revert back to one of the preset levels at any time.

Also in the Grammar Settings box, you can find three Require settings. The first one, Comma before last list item, specifies whether you want to use what's called a serial comma. Punctuation with quotes enables you to specify where the punctuation mark goes when it is next to a quotation mark: inside or outside. According to most grammar sources, inside is the generally accepted placement. Finally, Spaces between sentences enables you to specify either one or two spaces after a sentence.

TAKE NOTE

▶ GRAMMAR V. STYLE

The grammar checker can not only check for real grammatical errors, but also stylistic issues, such as the overuse of cliches. When you customize the grammar rules, these stylistic rules are identified on the list as "Style — {rule}." If you don't want Word dictating good writing style to you, turn these checkboxes off, or use the Casual or Standard level, neither of which include these rules.

CROSS-REFERENCE

Learn how to best use Word's Help features in Chapter 2.

FIND IT ONLINE

For information on Grammar Slammer, an alternative grammar checker, visit **http://members.aol.com/ langvanq/gramdemo.htm**.

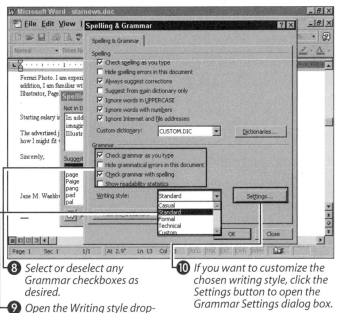

8 Select or deselect any Grammar checkboxes as desired.

9 Open the Writing style drop-down list and choose a writing style level.

10 If you want to customize the chosen writing style, click the Settings button to open the Grammar Settings dialog box.

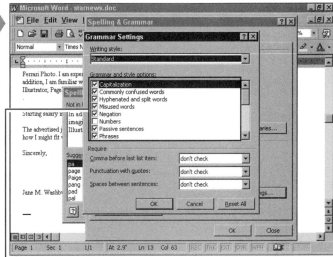

11 Select or deselect individual grammar rules as required.

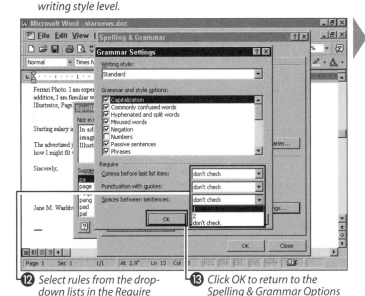

12 Select rules from the drop-down lists in the Require section.

13 Click OK to return to the Spelling & Grammar Options dialog box.

14 Click OK to close the dialog box and apply your settings.

Tracking Changes

Whenever more than one person makes edits to a document, the inevitable questions arise: Who changed what? And why? Was it the CEO who reworded that sentence, or the lowly intern? And whose head will roll if it's wrong?

To help with such situations, Word offers the Track Changes feature. When you turn on Track Changes, Word places revision marks in the document to show exactly what's been added, deleted, and changed. If more than one person edits the document, each person's revisions are shown in a different color. Then, when you are ready to consolidate all edits and publish your document, you can use the Accept or Reject Changes feature to whiz through them.

The revision marks that Word uses by default are strikethrough for deleted text (~~like this~~) and underline for added text (<u>like this</u>). As mentioned above, revisions appear in color, a different one for each editor. The color makes it very easy to skim through a multipage document onscreen to see what has changed. Revisions can get somewhat messy to interpret, so you must read them closely. Here's an example of a paragraph with revision marks:

The great ~~big~~ shaggy dog ~~lifted up~~ <u>raised</u> his head and sniffed toward the <u>w</u>~~W~~est. Barbe~~q~~cue…someone was cooking barbe~~q~~cue. Spare-ribs, from the smell of it. Then<u>,</u> sighing<u>,</u> he laid his head <u>back</u> down on the ~~patio~~ floor and ~~closed his eyes~~<u>slept</u>.

The Accept or Reject Changes feature moves through each change individually and you can accept or reject each one. For example, in the paragraph above, you would first choose whether to accept the deletion of "big," and then choose whether or not to replace "lifted up" with "raised," and so on. Or, you can accept all the changes in one swoop, without reviewing them individually.

TAKE NOTE

COMPARING DOCUMENTS

If you have two versions of a document and you want to see how they differ, use the Tools ➪ Track Changes ➪ Compare Documents command. Word generates a markup with revision marks that shows exactly what the differences are.

CHANGING THE REVISION MARK COLOR

If you don't want the revision marks to be different colors for each editor, you can choose a color to use for all marks. Choose Tools ➪ Options and click the Track Changes tab, and then choose a color from the Color drop-down lists. From here, you can also choose different colors for deleted versus inserted text and choose to apply a different color to reformatted text.

ADDING COMMENTS

People editing a document can also add comments to their edits that explain their rationale for the change. To add a comment, select the text to attach the comment to and choose Insert ➪ Comment.

CROSS-REFERENCE

For more information on changing the color of text, see "Formatting Text" in Chapter 8.

FIND IT ONLINE

To find out why Word may be marking separate revisions as single instances, see **http://support.microsoft.com/support/kb/articles/q112/1/65.asp**.

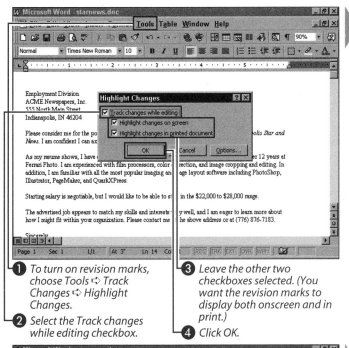

1 To turn on revision marks, choose Tools ➪ Track Changes ➪ Highlight Changes.

2 Select the Track changes while editing checkbox.

3 Leave the other two checkboxes selected. (You want the revision marks to display both onscreen and in print.)

4 Click OK.

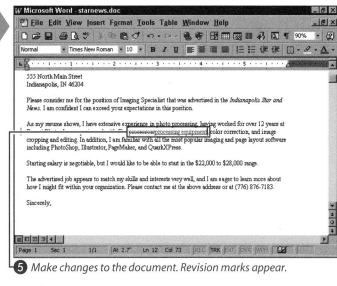

5 Make changes to the document. Revision marks appear.

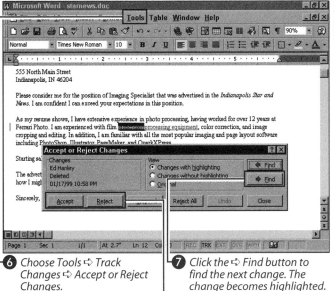

6 Choose Tools ➪ Track Changes ➪ Accept or Reject Changes.

7 Click the ➪ Find button to find the next change. The change becomes highlighted.

8 Click Accept or Reject.

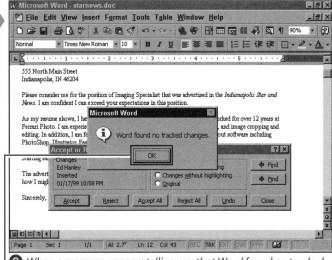

9 When a message appears telling you that Word found no tracked changes, you have seen them all. Click OK.

Personal Workbook

Q&A

1 What does it mean when a word has a green wavy underline?

_____

_____

_____

_____

2 What's the easiest way to look up the correct spelling for a single word that has a red underline?

_____

_____

_____

_____

3 What is a custom dictionary and how is it different from Word's main dictionary?

_____

_____

_____

_____

4 What is the difference between Ignore and Ignore All when checking spelling and grammar?

_____

_____

_____

5 True or false: Word's grammar suggestions are almost always worth taking.

_____

_____

_____

_____

6 How do you prevent Word from showing red wavy underlines as you type?

_____

_____

_____

7 True or false: When using revision marks, added text appears in bold.

_____

ANSWERS: PAGE 410

EXTRA PRACTICE

1 Open all the documents you have created and saved so far in Word, and perform a spelling and grammar check on them.

2 Create a new document and fill it with nongrammatical sentences. (Get creative!) See how many of them Word correctly identifies as wrong and how it suggests that you change them.

3 Review the explanations of the grammar rules in the Word Help file to make sure you understand them.

4 Count the number of words in a document you have typed.

5 Review the AutoCorrect list to make sure that you have not accidentally added any AutoCorrections that you should not have.

REAL-WORLD APPLICATIONS

✔ Add your clients' names to a custom dictionary all at once by opening a file containing their names (such as a Word table or Excel spreadsheet) and running a spell check, adding each misspelled word to the dictionary. In the future, when you type those names in documents, they will not be marked misspelled.

✔ Set up a Custom writing level in the grammar checker that uses only the grammar rules you are most interested in checking for.

✔ Add a button to your Formatting toolbar that toggles on/off the checkbox for Track Changes While Editing. To do so, right-click any toolbar and choose Customize. Click the Commands tab. Choose Tools from the Categories list, and drag the words "Track Changes" from the Commands list to your Formatting toolbar. Click Close to close the dialog box.

Visual Quiz

What command would you use to display this dialog box?

_____

_____

_____

_____

_____

_____

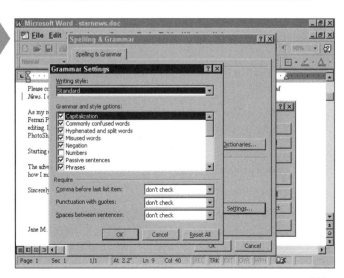

PART

III

Learning Important Excel Tasks

Many people use their computers to handle and manipulate data. Office 97 provides a program to help you perform this called Excel. Excel is a spreadsheet program, similar to programs such as Lotus 1-2-3 and Quattro Pro. A spreadsheet works much like an accountant's ledger book, in that it contains a grid where you can enter numbers and make calculations.

Of course, using a tool like this on a computer means that Excel goes far beyond the old "graph paper and slide rule" concept. The actual spreadsheet in Excel is called a *worksheet*, and you can manipulate the look and feel of worksheets to meet your specific needs. A single Excel document can contain many separate worksheets, creating what is called a *workbook*.

Excel worksheets and workbooks offer you many powerful tools. You can perform advanced calculations with your data and those calculations will be automatically updated whenever you edit data. You can also create graphs — called *charts* by Excel — out of your data to make it more presentable to other people. The chapters in Part III show you how to perform these seemingly complicated operations in just a few easy steps.

CHAPTER **14**

MASTER THESE SKILLS

▶ **Entering Numbers and Text**

▶ **Entering Dates**

▶ **Using Data Fill**

▶ **Moving Around the Worksheet**

▶ **Selecting a Range**

▶ **Creating References**

▶ **Inserting and Deleting**

Creating a Worksheet

Perhaps the greatest use for a computer is to track data and make calculations. Excel is a powerful tool for doing these kinds of operations. Excel is a spreadsheet program, similar to other programs such as Quattro Pro and Lotus 1-2-3. A spreadsheet works somewhat like the classic ledger that accountants and factors used to use.

But to say that Excel is similar to a ledger is like comparing Outlook (the Office 97 e-mail program covered later) to the old tin can and string you used to use to communicate with your neighbor's treehouse. It goes far beyond simply being a graph where you write down numbers for posterity. Excel can make both simple and complex calculations, predict trends, graph statistics, and much more.

Before you can accomplish any of the amazing tasks, you have to enter some data and understand a few basic concepts about *worksheets*. A worksheet is basically one page of data in Excel. Entering data is relatively straightforward and Excel offers some useful tools to help you format that data so that it displays the way you want it to. Excel also offers a feature called

Data Fill that automates many of your data entry tasks.

Besides entering data, you also need to know how to move around the worksheet, and the *workbook* in general. Excel allows you to have many different worksheets in a single file, and a multisheet file is called a workbook. If your worksheets get very large, you will have to learn some new techniques for moving around the worksheets beyond simply moving the cursor up and down with the arrow keys. You should also understand how to insert or delete cells, rows, and columns, so that you can modify your worksheets again later.

Another key skill is knowing how to work with a range of cells. A range consists of two or more cells, and although cells in a range are usually adjacent, they do not have to be. To work effectively in Excel, you must learn how to select ranges, and how to identify them properly in formulas and other Excel functions.

These skills and more are described in this chapter. The skills you learn here will provide the foundation for virtually every other task you perform in Excel, so mastering them now is critical.

Entering Numbers and Text

Excel is a spreadsheet program, and as such, it works kind of like an electronic ledger book. And like a ledger, you need to enter data for it to be of any use. So, one of your first steps in creating a worksheet is to enter some data. This data can be in the form of numbers, text, or something else, depending on your needs.

Entering text and numbers is relatively simple, and there are a couple of ways to do it. The simplest method is to click a cell and begin typing. Once you press Enter or click in a different cell, the data is actually entered into the cell.

Another way to enter data in a cell is to select it and type your data in the text box on the Formula bar, just above the document window. This is the better method, especially if you need to edit data that was previously entered. Otherwise, if you click a cell with data already in it and start typing, whatever was in there before will be replaced.

One thing that may surprise you as you enter data into the cells is that not all of the data you enter is actually displayed on the worksheet. The default size of the cells on your worksheet is fairly small, so you may need to resize them to view more of the data. At any rate, even if you can't *see* all of the data, as long as you typed it in, it's there. Just to be sure, click one of the "full" cells and check that all of your data is shown in the Formula bar.

The first two figures on the facing page show you how to enter data into cells. The third figure shows you how to edit existing data using the Formula bar, and the last figure shows you how to adjust the size of a cell to view more of the data.

TAKE NOTE

CELLS, COLUMNS, AND ROWS

If you're a little confused by the terminology here, fear not. As you look at an Excel worksheet, you can see that the document window is divided into a grid. A single box in this grid is called a cell, which is where your data actually resides. You should also know that the term *column* refers to a vertical (top to bottom) line of cells, and *rows* run across the screen from left to right.

ENTERING OTHER KINDS OF DATA

You can enter almost any kind of data into a cell, including pictures and other graphics. You do this using virtually the same methods you would in other Office 97 programs. Use options in the Insert menu of the Excel menu bar to insert other data types.

CROSS-REFERENCE

Learn how to automate much of the data entry process in "Using Data Fill" later in this chapter.

FIND IT ONLINE

Visit the main excel page at **http://www.microsoft.com/ excel/default.htm**.

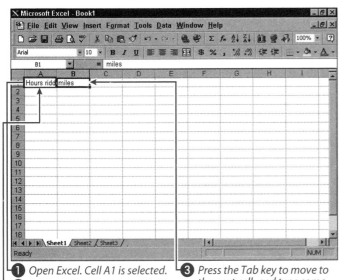

① Open Excel. Cell A1 is selected.

② Type some text to enter it in the cell. Type several words or a sentence.

③ Press the Tab key to move to the next cell, and type some more text in cell B1.

■ Notice that only the first part of the text you type is shown on the worksheet.

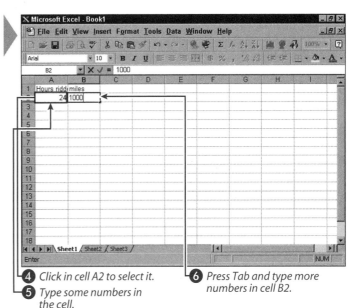

④ Click in cell A2 to select it.

⑤ Type some numbers in the cell.

⑥ Press Tab and type more numbers in cell B2.

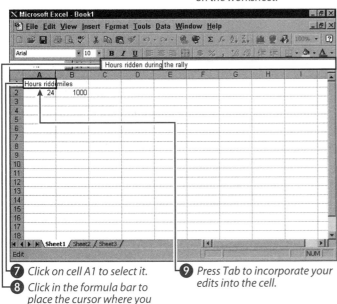

⑦ Click on cell A1 to select it.

⑧ Click in the formula bar to place the cursor where you want it. Edit the text you typed in earlier.

⑨ Press Tab to incorporate your edits into the cell.

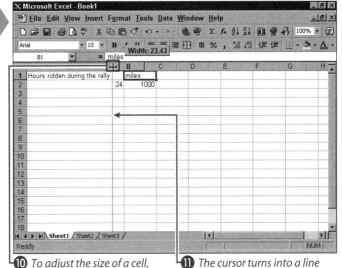

⑩ To adjust the size of a cell, move the cursor over the column border at the top of the worksheet window.

⑪ The cursor turns into a line with two arrows. Click and hold the left mouse button and drag the column border left or right.

209

Entering Dates

In the previous task, you learned how to manually enter numbers and text. This is the most basic method for entering data on a worksheet, and is probably the method you will use the most. There is nothing particularly challenging about it; simply click a cell and start typing.

Excel recognizes various types of data that are commonly entered into cells. One of the most common data types is a date. Dates can tell you when a payment was made, when an assignment is due, when an item was received, and much more. It is an important kind of data in most—if not all—of your Excel worksheets.

When you enter a date on your worksheet, it is much more than just a number to Excel. Excel recognizes the date format and can use it in a variety of applications. For example, Excel can calculate a length of time between two entered dates. It can also use dates in formulas when calculating maturity or compound interest.

You can enter dates in several different ways. The most basic method is to enter the date in a cell manually, using a technique similar to that described in the previous task. You can also have Excel enter dates automatically, and there is even a shortcut to allow you to quickly enter the current date. Once the dates are entered, Excel also enables you to format the cells so that the date is displayed the way you want it. For instance, if you only need the month and year displayed, you can format cells in a column to display only those parts of the date.

The figures on the following page show you several ways to enter dates into an Excel worksheet. The first two figures show you how to enter a date manually. The last two demonstrate how to format a cell so that the date is displayed a certain way.

TAKE NOTE

IS THE YEAR 2000 IN YOUR FUTURE?

You may have heard a lot about the "Year 2000 Problem" lately, but Excel (and all other Office 97 programs) is "Year 2000 Ready." Excel recognizes any date between January 1, 1900 and December 31, 9999. This does nothing to solve the "Year 10,000 Problem," but Microsoft figures you have plenty of time to figure that one out for yourself.

PROPER DATE FORMATS

To make sure that Excel recognizes dates you enter, make sure you stick to a proper format. In the United States, for example, you type the month, day, and year separated by a slash or hyphen. It should look something like this: 07/21/98. The format you use will depend on your country. You may use four digits for the year. If you use two digits, Excel assumes that all two-digit years between 00 and 29 refer to years in the twenty-first century.

QUICK DATE ENTRY

Press Ctrl+; to quickly enter the current date in a cell.

CROSS-REFERENCE

If you want to format more than one cell at a time, see "Selecting a Range" later in this chapter.

FIND IT ONLINE

Subscribe to receive Excel tips at **http://www.tipworld.com/**.

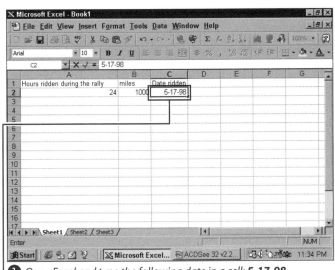

1 Open Excel and type the following date in a cell: **5-17-98**. Press Enter when done.

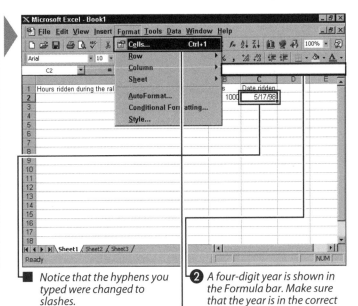

■ Notice that the hyphens you typed were changed to slashes.

2 A four-digit year is shown in the Formula bar. Make sure that the year is in the correct century.

3 Select the cell and click Format ⇨ Cells.

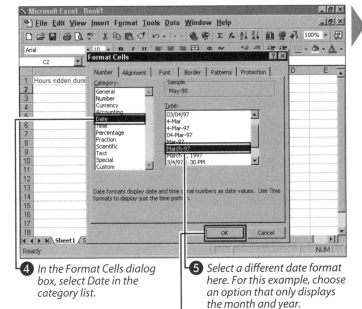

4 In the Format Cells dialog box, select Date in the category list.

5 Select a different date format here. For this example, choose an option that only displays the month and year.

6 Click OK.

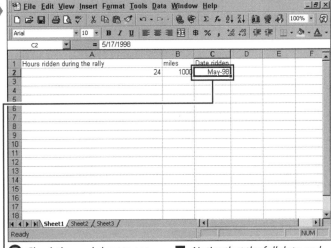

7 Check the worksheet to see that the date is now shown in the desired format.

■ Notice that the full date and four digit year is still shown in the formula bar.

211

Using Data Fill

Entering data manually—as shown in the first task in this chapter—is the most basic method for adding data to a worksheet. You can manually enter virtually any kind of data you want, mainly because it is so simple and versatile. This is fine for many circumstances, but it can also be time-consuming. Whereas manually entering a piece of data in a cell takes only a few seconds, adding that same data to dozens or even hundreds of cells can consume a significant period of time. Before you know it, you've spent an entire day performing one simple, repetitive task.

As you can see, manually entering all of your data is often not the most efficient way to go about your work. A more effective way is to use the tools that Excel provides which automate the data entry process. One of the most useful features is Data Fill, which lets you quickly fill in a range of cells based on something already entered in an adjacent cell. For example, suppose entries in a worksheet are based on daily inputs. Rather than manually typing the date on every single row, you can use Data Fill to automate the process.

Data Fill can work in a couple of different ways. The two most basic uses involve either copying a cell or creating a series based on a cell. If you use Data Fill to copy a cell that has the date 5/17/98, all of the cells you choose to fill will have the same date entered in them. On the other hand, if you use Data Fill to create a series, the next cell will have 5/18/98, the one after that will be 5/19/98, and so on.

The figures on the facing page show Data Fill in action. The first two figures show you how to use Data Fill to copy a cell. The last two figures demonstrate how to use Data Fill to create a series, first with just one cell, and then with a series of cells.

Continued

TAKE NOTE

USING THE FILL HANDLE

When you want to use Data Fill, you need to use the Fill Handle for the sample cell or range. The Fill Handle is a little square on the lower right-hand corner of the selection, and when you move the mouse pointer over the handle it changes to a skinny plus sign.

USING THE DATA FILL CONTEXT MENU

If you drag the Fill Handle while holding the left mouse button, Excel makes some assumptions about what kind of fill you want. Usually this is just a copy. If you want more options, hold the right mouse button when you drag the fill handle to bring up the Data Fill context menu.

CROSS-REFERENCE
You will probably use the Data Fill context menu a lot. Learn more about this in "Using Context Menus" in Chapter 1.

FIND IT ONLINE
Click Help ⇨ Microsoft on the Web ⇨ Free Stuff and find the Power Utility Pak to upgrade Excel.

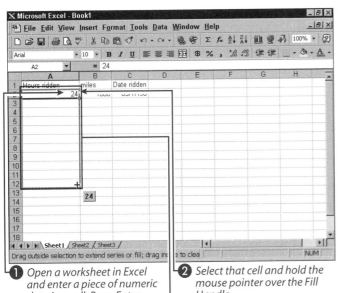

1 Open a worksheet in Excel and enter a piece of numeric data in a cell. Press Enter when done.

2 Select that cell and hold the mouse pointer over the Fill Handle.

3 Click and hold the left mouse button and drag it down several rows.

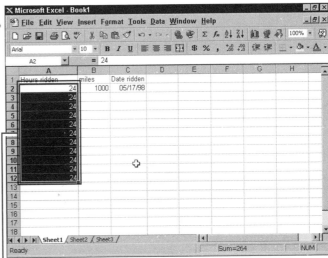

4 Release the mouse button to fill in the data.

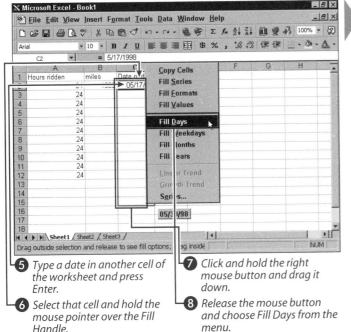

5 Type a date in another cell of the worksheet and press Enter.

6 Select that cell and hold the mouse pointer over the Fill Handle.

7 Click and hold the right mouse button and drag it down.

8 Release the mouse button and choose Fill Days from the menu.

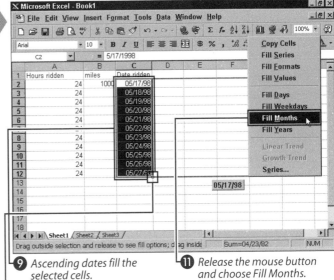

9 Ascending dates fill the selected cells.

10 Hold the mouse pointer over the Fill Handle of the range you just created, click and drag it to the right.

11 Release the mouse button and choose Fill Months.

■ Notice that the columns you just created show ascending months as you move to the right.

213

Using Data Fill
Continued

So far in this task, you have learned the basics of using Data Fill. First you learned how to use Data Fill to copy the contents of a cell, the most basic method of using this feature. Copying cells in this manner can save a great deal of time, and ultimately will be more effective than simply using Copy and Paste commands like you might have in other Office 97 programs.

After you used Data Fill to copy a cell, you moved on to learn about creating a series with Data Fill. This is a little more advanced and perhaps represents the true beauty of this feature. A series goes far beyond simple copying; it acts in an intuitive manner to help you accomplish in seconds what might otherwise take hours.

In the example given on the previous page, you created a series using a date. From a software developer's point of view, this is an easy kind of series to create because just about everyone on the planet uses the same clock and calendar. Everyone knows what day comes after August 1, and deciding which year follows 1999 is equally simple.

But the real challenge in creating a series comes when you use other kinds of data that are not so standardized. Whether you are entering the cost of an expense, a length of time spent in training, a measure of pounds gained or lost, a quantity of inventory, an annual percentage rate, or whatever, the data you enter into a cell will be a number. How does Excel know what this number actually represents? How can it tell how to increment the series? Should it be incremented at all?

The key is that you must tell Excel what kind of number it is and how to increment it. You can increment in a linear or nonlinear manner, and you can adjust the interval of the increment. You can even increment items that are not purely numbers.

The figures on the following page show you how to use Data Fill to create several different kinds of series. The first two figures show how to create an ascending series using data that is not purely numeric. The remaining figures demonstrate how to create a series based on your own criteria.

TAKE NOTE

▶ LINEAR V. GROWTH TRENDS

Excel can predict trends for you with Data Fill in either a linear or growth format. Linear growth means that the number increases by a fixed amount. For example, a linear growth trend extrapolated from the numbers 1 and 2 would produce 3, 4, 5, and so on. But a growth trend multiplies by a constant factor, so the results from 1 and 2 would be 4, 8, 16, and so on.

▶ QUICK FILLS

Press Ctrl+D to quickly fill one cell down, or Ctrl+R to fill one cell to the right.

CROSS-REFERENCE
If you have created a range with Data Fill, learn how to use it in a formula in Chapter 15.

FIND IT ONLINE
Search **http://www.pcworld.com/** for articles, software libaries, and more.

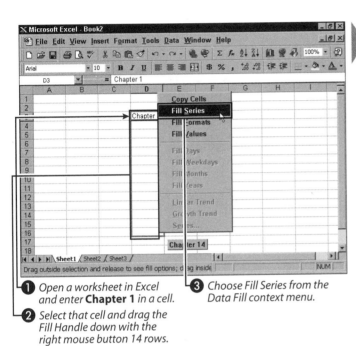

① Open a worksheet in Excel and enter **Chapter 1** in a cell.

② Select that cell and drag the Fill Handle down with the right mouse button 14 rows.

③ Choose Fill Series from the Data Fill context menu.

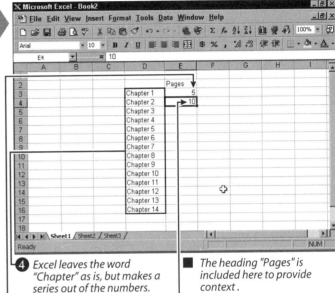

④ Excel leaves the word "Chapter" as is, but makes a series out of the numbers.

⑤ In the next column enter the number **5** in the same row as Chapter 1.

■ The heading "Pages" is included here to provide context.

⑥ Enter the number **10** in the next row.

① Select the cells that you just entered the numbers in.

⑦ Click the right mouse button and drag the Fill Handle down to the cell next to Chapter 14.

⑧ Choose Series from the context menu that appears. In the Series dialog box, click the Trend checkbox to select it.

⑨ Click OK.

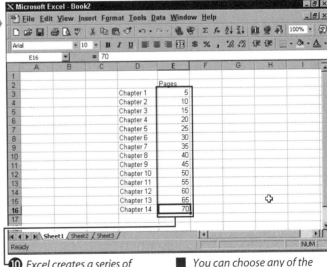

⑩ Excel creates a series of numbers based on the trend set by the first two cells.

■ You can choose any of the other options in the Series dialog box to customize your series.

215

Moving Around the Worksheet

Depending on what you will be using Excel worksheets for, some of those sheets can become quite large. On a single worksheet you can have as many as 256 columns and — are you sitting down? — 65,536 rows. As you might guess, scrolling to the end of a large worksheet using only the Tab and arrow keys can become quite time-consuming.

Fortunately, Excel offers you many convenient ways to move around your worksheets. But before you can start scrolling around aimlessly in Worksheet Land, you must understand a few basic concepts about how the worksheet is laid out. First of all, understand that an Excel file is not necessarily a single worksheet. One file can, and often does, contain multiple worksheets; each containing different kinds of data and formulas that all rely on each other to function properly. Such a file is called a *workbook*. You can switch to another worksheet in a workbook by clicking the tabs along the bottom of the document window. The sample workbook shown on the facing page actually has three available worksheets, as will any new Excel file you create. You can create additional worksheets by choosing Insert ⇨ Worksheet from the menu bar.

Like all other Office 97 programs, the Excel document window has scroll bars to help you move around in the window. You can click on either side of the scroll bar to move one whole screen up, down, left, or right. You can also move to the very last available row or column by holding the Ctrl key while you press the left or down arrow keys. Press Ctrl+right arrow or Ctrl+left arrow to return to the top.

The figures on the facing page demonstrate several ways to move around within your worksheets. The first figure shows you how to switch to another worksheet within the same workbook. The second and third figures demonstrate how to move around using just the keyboard, and the final figure illustrates the use of the scroll bars.

TAKE NOTE

WHY IS THE SCROLL BAR SO SMALL?

One thing to note about the scroll bars is that they will only be scaled to your existing document. If you don't have any data way out in cell IV65536, then the scroll bars won't let you scroll all the way there. Use Ctrl+an arrow key if you're just dying to see what's out there.

REMEMBER TO PLACE THE CURSOR

If you have moved a significant distance in a large worksheet, make sure you click a cell in your current view to place the cursor nearby. Otherwise, even though you are looking at rows 230–260, if the cursor is all the way back up in row 5 the view will jump back up there as soon as you press a key on the keyboard.

QUICK RETURN TO THE TOP

From anywhere in a worksheet you can quickly return to the top (cell A1) by pressing Ctrl+Home.

CROSS-REFERENCE
See Chapter 16 to learn how to improve your view as you move around the worksheet.

FIND IT ONLINE
Search **www.idgbooks.com** for more IDG books on Excel.

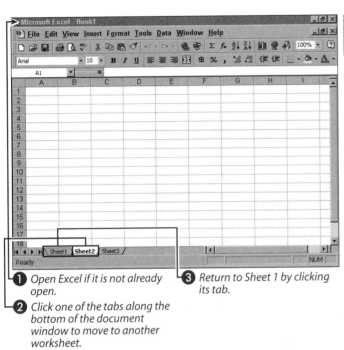

① *Open Excel if it is not already open.*

② *Click one of the tabs along the bottom of the document window to move to another worksheet.*

③ *Return to Sheet 1 by clicking its tab.*

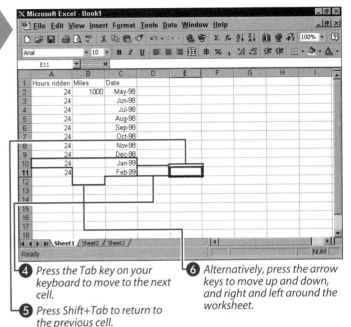

④ *Press the Tab key on your keyboard to move to the next cell.*

⑤ *Press Shift+Tab to return to the previous cell.*

⑥ *Alternatively, press the arrow keys to move up and down, and right and left around the worksheet.*

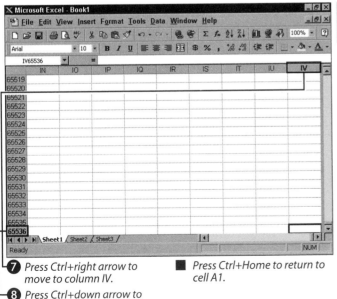

⑦ *Press Ctrl+right arrow to move to column IV.*

⑧ *Press Ctrl+down arrow to move to row 65536.*

■ *Press Ctrl+Home to return to cell A1.*

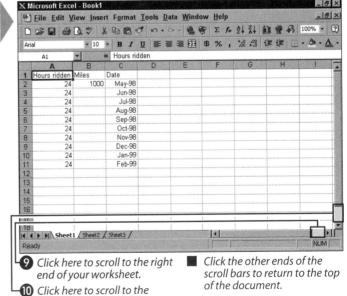

⑨ *Click here to scroll to the right end of your worksheet.*

⑩ *Click here to scroll to the bottom of your worksheet.*

■ *Click the other ends of the scroll bars to return to the top of the document.*

Selecting a Range

Usually, when you enter data into an Excel worksheet, each piece of data goes in its own cell. If you are making a list of expenses, for example, each individual expense needs to go in its own cell. This way, it will be easier to use and work with later on.

When you *do* enter related pieces of information into cells — such as in the expenses example previously mentioned — it's usually best to enter them into adjacent cells. This means that you should list all expenses in the same column or row of the worksheet. If you prefer to read the numbers up and down, place all expense numbers in a single column. Likewise, if you prefer to read these numbers left to right you can use a single row instead.

Lining up related pieces of data in an adjacent manner has many advantages. It stands to reason that since these pieces of data are related to each other, you will probably use them together later on. If you have a list of many different expenses, you may want to add them all up to see what your total expenses are. To do this, you will probably end up selecting this range of cells at some point. Selecting a range of cells instead of just one is easy. It usually involves just a few easy mouse clicks or keystrokes to make it happen.

Of course, cells don't have to be adjacent for you to select them in a range. You can select cells all over a worksheet whether they are connected or not. This may be desirable if you need to add up numbers from a variety of sources spread out across the worksheet. You can do this by holding the Ctrl key down as you click each desired cell.

The figures on the facing page show several techniques for selecting a range of cells. The first three figures demonstrate how to select adjacent cells using first the mouse and then just the keyboard. The last figure shows you how to select a range of nonadjacent cells.

TAKE NOTE

▶ WATCH OUT FOR THE FILL HANDLE

When you are using the mouse to select a range, watch out for the Fill Handle. It is the little square at the bottom-right corner of every Excel selection. If you click-and-drag the fill handle, much more than a simple range selection will take place.

▶ SELECTING ROWS AND COLUMNS

You can select an entire row or column by clicking its heading at the top or side of the document window. If one cell in the selection is different — such as a label — Excel ignores that cell in its calculations.

CROSS-REFERENCE

Learn about selecting other kinds of objects in "Selecting Objects and Graphics" in Chapter 5.

FIND IT ONLINE

Join the spreadsheet news group at **news:comp.apps. spreadsheets.**

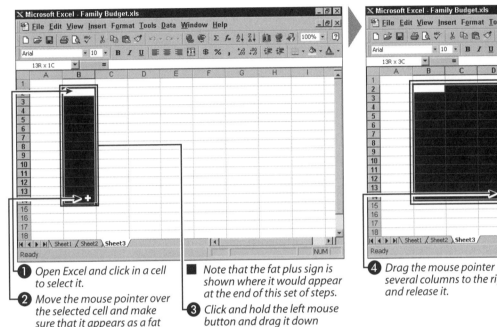

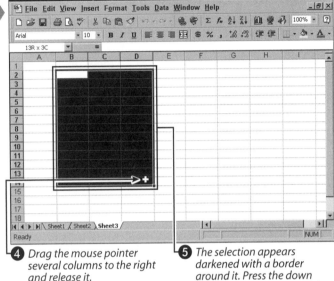

① Open Excel and click in a cell to select it.

② Move the mouse pointer over the selected cell and make sure that it appears as a fat plus sign.

■ Note that the fat plus sign is shown where it would appear at the end of this set of steps.

③ Click and hold the left mouse button and drag it down several rows.

④ Drag the mouse pointer several columns to the right and release it.

⑤ The selection appears darkened with a border around it. Press the down arrow key to move out of the currently selected range.

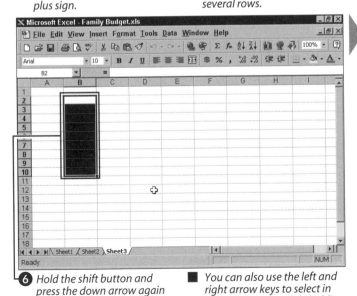

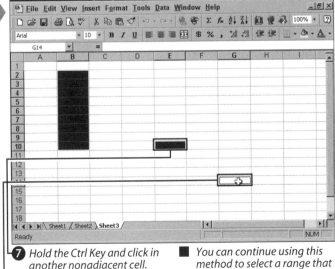

⑥ Hold the shift button and press the down arrow again to add cells to the new range.

■ You can also use the left and right arrow keys to select in those directions while holding down the Shift key.

⑦ Hold the Ctrl Key and click in another nonadjacent cell.

⑧ Continue holding Ctrl and click another cell.

■ You can continue using this method to select a range that includes as many cells as you want.

Creating References

Excel is a truly versatile program because it can perform a huge variety of operations and calculations with your data. If you want to perform any of these operations, you are going to have to provide Excel with instructions and formulas to help it do the work. When you do this, you need to tell Excel where to get data from. If you are using Excel to track your family's budget, for instance, you need to tell it which cells represent income and which ones represent expenses.

You do this by creating *references* to data. A reference may only apply to a single cell, or it may apply to a range of cells. It can also refer to cells on other worksheets within the workbook, or even to data from other programs. You can use one worksheet to store data, and use another worksheet within the workbook to actually perform calculations. You may even set up a third worksheet to provide a neatly formatted report of your calculations in the other worksheets. Whatever the case, you need to create references to cells and ranges before you can make all of this happen.

Cells in an Excel worksheet are named based on their location in the grid of columns and rows. The first cell in any worksheet is called *A1*, because it is in column A, row 1. A range of cells is named by using the first and last cells in the range, separated by a colon. So a range of cells from A1 down to A7 would be called A1:A7. If the range covers a block of several rows *and* columns, it might be referred to as A1:C7. You can also refer to all of the cells in a given column or row. For instance, to refer to all of the cells in column A, you would enter **A:A**. Or, if you want to refer to all cells in rows 2 and 3, you would enter **2:3**.

The figures on the following page show you how to create references. The first two figures show how to refer to another cell within the same worksheet. The last two figures show how to create a reference to a cell on another worksheet within the same workbook. Both examples assume you are using the reference in a formula, but these techniques are used in many other functions as well.

TAKE NOTE

OTHER SHEETS IN THE WORKBOOK

To refer to a cell on another worksheet within the same workbook, you start the reference by using the worksheet's name. This is separated from the cell reference with an exclamation mark (!). A reference to a range of cells on another worksheet would look something like this: Sheet2!B2:B7.

SIMPLER REFERENCE CREATION

To simplify creating a reference, select a range before you create a formula.

CROSS-REFERENCE

Learn more about formulas in "Creating Basic Formulas" in Chapter 15.

FIND IT ONLINE

Read PC World's spreadsheet column at: **http://www.j-walk.com/ss/pcworld/index.htm**.

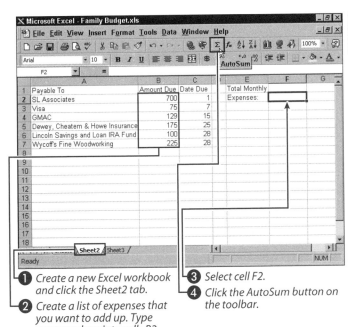

① Create a new Excel workbook and click the Sheet2 tab.

② Create a list of expenses that you want to add up. Type your numbers into cells B2 through B7.

③ Select cell F2.

④ Click the AutoSum button on the toolbar.

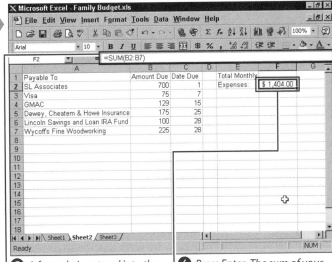

⑤ A formula is entered into the cell, but the reference isn't correct. Change the reference in the Formula bar so that it reads **=SUM(B2:B7)**.

⑥ Press Enter. The sum of your expenses should now appear in cell F2.

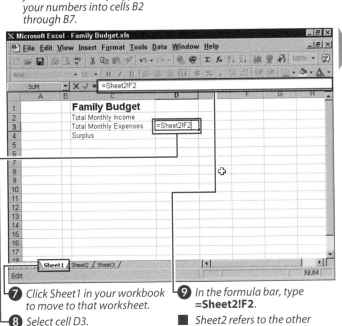

⑦ Click Sheet1 in your workbook to move to that worksheet.

⑧ Select cell D3.

⑨ In the formula bar, type **=Sheet2!F2**.

■ Sheet2 refers to the other worksheet and F2 refers to the actual cell.

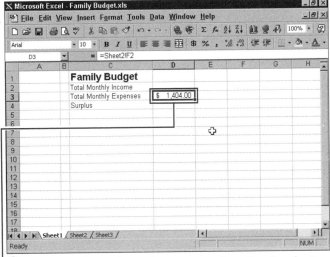

⑩ Press Enter. The total sum of your expenses from the other sheet is displayed in cell D3.

Inserting and Deleting

As you work more with Excel and enter data, you will get familiar with the column and row formats used in the worksheets. These provide a useful grid to help you keep your information organized and in order. It also helps you keep related data together in a way that will be easy to make use of later.

Inevitably, you will find the need to change how your worksheets are laid out. For instance, suppose you are tracking training accomplishments for workers in your office. You might list the names of each person in rows along the left side of the window, and the training topics in the columns along the top. What if you need to add a new employee to the list, or remove someone who has left? What if you no longer need to train on a certain topic and need to remove it from the list?

Making changes like this isn't nearly as complicated as you might think. Excel gives you the ability to insert or delete as many rows and columns as you want in a worksheet, without negatively impacting the rest of the workbook. No matter how many changes you might make, the worksheet will maintain the same continuity that it had before.

The figures on the facing page show you how to insert or delete rows or columns. The first two figures demonstrate how to insert an entire column into a worksheet, and the last two figures demonstrate the procedure for deleting a row. You can also insert or delete one cell at a time if you wish.

TAKE NOTE

▶ INSERTING A SINGLE CELL

If you do not want to insert a row or column across the entire worksheet, right click a cell in the worksheet and choose Insert from the context menu. In the Insert dialog box choose Shift cells right or Shift cells down to insert a cell just in that row or column.

▶ DELETING CELLS

Just as you can insert a single cell into a column or row, you can delete a single cell from a column or row without affecting the rest of the worksheet. Simply right-click the cell you want to get rid of and select Delete from the context menu. Make a selection from the Delete dialog box just as you would to insert a cell.

▶ USING CUT AND PASTE

Besides inserting and deleting, you can also move cells, columns, and rows by using selection methods and context menus. Right-click the column, row, or cell selection you want to move and choose Cut from the context menu. The selection remains in place, but with a flashing border around it, until you paste it to a new location.

CROSS-REFERENCE
Learn more about using Copy-and-Paste and Cut-and-Paste in "Copying and Moving Objects" in Chapter 5.

FIND IT ONLINE
Visit the spreadsheet page at **http://www.j-walk.com/ss/index.html**.

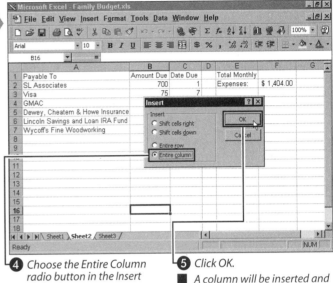

❶ Open an Excel worksheet with data in several rows and columns.

❷ Select any cell in the column that is just to the right of where you want to insert another column.

❸ Right-click the cell and choose Insert from the context menu.

❹ Choose the Entire Column radio button in the Insert dialog box.

❺ Click OK.

■ A column will be inserted and all the existing columns will shift to the right.

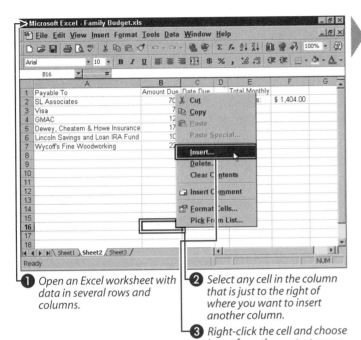

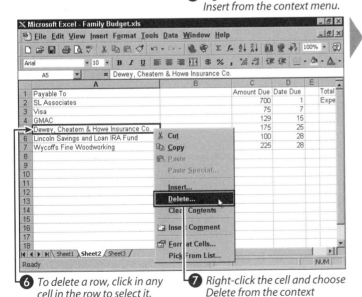

❻ To delete a row, click in any cell in the row to select it.

❼ Right-click the cell and choose Delete from the context menu.

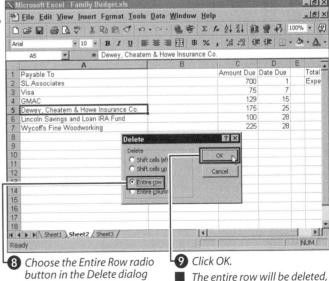

❽ Choose the Entire Row radio button in the Delete dialog box.

❾ Click OK.

■ The entire row will be deleted, and rows under it will be shifted up.

Personal Workbook

Q&A

1 What kind of data can you enter in a cell?

_____

_____

2 Should you use a specific format when you enter a date into a cell?

_____

_____

3 How can you quickly enter the current date in a cell?

_____

4 Where is the Fill Handle located?

_____

5 What happens if you select a cell with a date in it and then drag the Fill Handle down several rows?

_____

_____

6 How do you specify a series to increase by an increment of five?

_____

7 What is the quickest way to move back to the top of a worksheet?

_____

_____

8 How do you move to another worksheet within a workbook?

_____

_____

9 Can you select nonadjacent cells in a range? How?

_____

_____

10 If you want to refer to cells A1 through B7 in Sheet3, how should the reference look?

_____

_____

11 How do you delete an entire row in a worksheet?

_____

_____

ANSWERS: PAGE 411

EXTRA PRACTICE

1 Create a workbook with at least two different worksheets.

2 On the first worksheet, enter the current date in cell A1.

3 Use Data Fill to make a list of ascending dates down to cell A10.

4 Switch to the second worksheet and create a list of numbers.

5 In the first worksheet, make the total of the numbers you entered in the second sheet appear in cell B1.

6 Delete row 7 from the first worksheet.

REAL-WORLD APPLICATIONS

✔ You might create multisheet workbooks in Excel for many important tasks. If you are tracking your company's inventory, you might want to create a separate sheet for each warehouse. You can then use references to report total inventory figures on the front sheet.

✔ If you need to create a worksheet that tracks daily numbers for an entire year, you can use Data Fill to fill in many of the cells. This will save you from having to manually type a lot of repetitive information 365 times.

✔ If you have created a worksheet with daily entries for an entire year, it will be quite large. You can use some of the techniques you learned here to move about the worksheet more efficiently.

Visual Quiz

Cell C2 displays only a month and year, but in the formula bar a day is also given. Why is the day not displayed on the actual worksheet? How can this be changed? How was the series of dates created? What is the easiest way to create the series of numbers in column A?

_____

_____

_____

_____

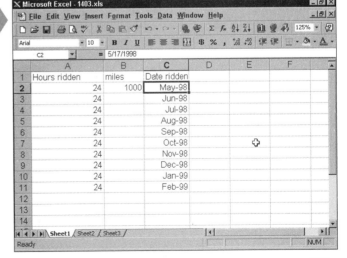

CHAPTER 15

MASTER
THESE
SKILLS

▶ **Creating Basic Formulas**

▶ **Using Ranges in Formulas**

▶ **Using Absolute, Relative, and Mixed References**

▶ **Using Formula Wizards**

▶ **Using Functions**

Creating Formulas

If all you ever did with Excel was type numbers and text into cells, it would be nothing more than a glorified piece of graph paper, a veritable waste of electrons and cathode rays. But storing information in this manner is not what Excel, excuse the pun, excels at. Excel is a spreadsheet program, which means it is capable of performing advanced calculations using your data, producing some truly amazing results.

Excel performs these tasks through the use of formulas. A formula is a set of instructions that tells Excel what to do, and in what order to do them. In this respect, it is like a mathematic equation. An equation can be as simple as 1+1=2, but is often far more complex. A formula in Excel might find the total of hundreds of cells and then multiply that figure by a percentage and filter it based on logical criteria.

Understanding how to create formulas is critical to accomplishing anything in Excel. Fortunately, Excel provides a number of tools to make that process easier. Wizards guide you through some of the most complex calculations, and features like AutoSum automate the most mundane and repetitive ones. Functions are another interesting feature, and offer a sort of "prepackaged" way to create formulas. Further combating the mundane, Excel can act intuitively when you copy formulas to simplify what could otherwise be very time-consuming.

Before you can create formulas, you need to have a solid grasp on the basics of creating an Excel worksheet. Of particular importance are cell and range references, and data entry techniques. If you haven't yet mastered these skills, check out Chapter 14 first. Once you've done this, you're ready to begin creating formulas.

This chapter guides you through the creation of a wide variety of formulas. A single worksheet is used and developed throughout the chapter, so for best results you should begin with the first task and follow along, in order, with the rest of the chapter. After completing all the tasks, you will have a worksheet that you can use to track your own expenses and income, if you so desire.

Creating Basic Formulas

As a spreadsheet, Excel is expected to perform a wide variety of calculation and number crunching tasks. Once you have created a worksheet in Excel, the real work happens in the background; all you should have to do is type in the numbers and watch the magic occur. Entering one single number might change totals, update graphs, and may even affect other programs.

How does Excel do all of this? It does its job through the use of formulas. If numbers and data are the life blood of Excel, then a formula is the heart that pumps those numbers and keeps the worksheet alive. A formula can be either simple or complex, depending on our needs. If all you need to do is add up a list of expenses, the formula to perform that task will simply find a sum. If, on the other hand, you need those numbers to predict a trend of expenses over a period of time, the formula will get much more complex.

You have many options for entering formulas into a worksheet. Generally speaking, you enter a formula into a cell just like you would a piece of data. The result of the formula is displayed in whichever cell you placed the formula in. So, if you entered a formula to find the sum of one plus one into cell A1, the cell would only display the number "2." However, in the formula bar just above the worksheet window the actual formula would be displayed, which would look something like this:

=1+1

If you were to change the formula in the formula bar by adding another "+1" to it, cell A1 would then display the number "3." Also, notice the equal (=) sign. This must precede the formula so that Excel knows you want the formula's result displayed.

The figures on the following page show how to perform a basic calculation on a worksheet using a formula. Once you have mastered this basic single operation formula, you can move on to more complicated formulas on the following pages.

Continued

TAKE NOTE

▶ ARITHMETIC OPERATORS

To perform certain calculations, Excel must be given a correct arithmetic operator. This is the symbol that tells Excel what kind of calculation to make, such as subtracting or multiplying. Valid operators in Excel are addition (+), subtraction (-), multiplication (*), division (/), percentage (%), and exponentiation (^).

▶ ORDER OF CALCULATION

Calculations in Excel generally conform to the rules of arithmetic. Calculations are read from left to right, with multiplication and division operations performed before addition or subtraction. Also, calculations inside parentheses will be done first. For example, (2+2)*3 would equal 12 because the operation in parentheses is done first. But in the case of 2+2*3, the result is 8 because the multiplication happened first.

CROSS-REFERENCE

Learn more about cell references in "Creating References" in Chapter 14.

FIND IT ONLINE

http://www.tucows.com/ has a number of HTML tools for publishing online Excel spreadsheets.

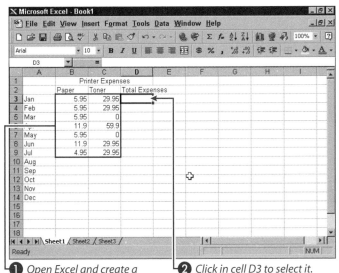

① Open Excel and create a worksheet with numeric data in several rows of columns B and C.

② Click in cell D3 to select it.

③ Type the following in cell D3: =B3+C3.

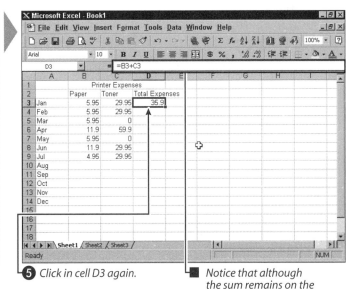

④ Press Enter. Notice that the sum of cells B3 and C3 is now displayed in cell D3, rather than the formula you typed.

⑤ Click in cell D3 again.

■ Notice that although the sum remains on the worksheet, you can see the actual formula in the Formula bar.

Creating Basic Formulas
Continued

As you have learned so far, formulas have the power to bring your Excel worksheets alive. On the previous two pages, you learned how to create a basic formula involving a single calculation. You added together numbers from two specific cells on the worksheet.

One of the most important things to understand about formulas is the proper syntax. As in the previous example, your formulas should begin with an equal (=) sign. This is followed by a simple arithmetic formula using cell references as variables. The wonderful thing about using references in your formulas is that if any of the data in those cells changes — say, you found another receipt that needs to be added to your expenses — the formula's result is automatically updated.

Besides the equal sign and arithmetic operators you have already learned about, you will probably make use of parentheses on a regular basis. Think back for a moment to that algebra class you had in school. You probably learned to calculate from left to right, and to perform multiplication and division before you did addition and subtraction.

Furthermore, you also learned that calculations inside parentheses should be done first. Well, Excel formulas work exactly the same way. You can use parentheses to control how the calculations are performed.

The figures on the following page show you how to create a more complex formula. Notice that a formula is being created on a different worksheet of the same workbook that was used before. A cell reference is used to get information from a cell on another worksheet within the workbook.

TAKE NOTE

▶ USE AUTOSUM

Adding numbers together is one of the most common tasks in Excel. Because of this, the program offers a feature called *AutoSum* that automates much of the process. Select the cells you want to add up (they must be adjacent) and click the AutoSum button on the Excel toolbar. The total of the selected cells appears in the cell that immediately follows the range. For example, a formula will look something like this: =SUM(B3:C3), and the actual sum (and hence the formula) will appear in cell D3. This formula does the same thing as the formula you created on the previous page, but it uses the SUM function instead of the plus sign operator.

▶ WORDS IN CELLS

Some of the cells you select may have a word in them instead of numbers. This is common when you write a formula that tells Excel to add up the numbers in all of the cells in a single column or row. If that column or row has a text label in one of the cells, Excel automatically ignores that cell during calculation.

CROSS-REFERENCE
Learn a quick way to copy formulas in "Using Absolute, Relative, and Mixed References" later in this chapter.

FIND IT ONLINE
Click Help ⇨ Microsoft on the Web ⇨ Free Stuff to download templates that make many calculations easier.

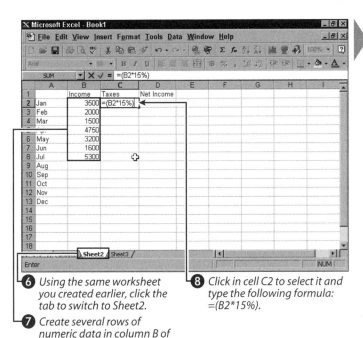

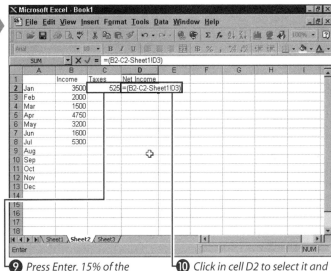

6 Using the same worksheet you created earlier, click the tab to switch to Sheet2.

7 Create several rows of numeric data in column B of Sheet2, beginning with cell B2.

8 Click in cell C2 to select it and type the following formula: =(B2*15%).

9 Press Enter. 15% of the amount shown in cell B2 is now displayed in C2.

10 Click in cell D2 to select it and type the following formula: =(B2-C2-Sheet1!D3).

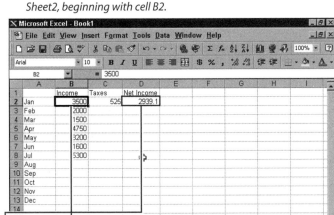

11 Press Enter. Notice that the result shown in cell D2 is equal to B2 minus the numbers referred to in the formula.

12 Click in cell B2 again.

13 Increase the number shown in cell B2 by 500 and press Enter.

■ Notice that the cells that use the data in B2 have been automatically updated to reflect your change.

Using Ranges in Formulas

At this point, you have learned how to make simple and more complex formulas in Excel. So far, those formulas have referred specifically to each cell used. That is, if you created a formula that used cell B2, it only read cell B2. For many simple operations this is effective, but more often than not, you need to perform calculations using information from multiple cells.

You can assign multiple cells in a formula by creating a reference to a range. As you learned in Chapter 14, a range encompasses multiple cells, whether it be 2 cells or 200,000. This is another commonly used technique because it can be used for a variety of purposes. You can use a large group of cells together in the formula, as if they were one cell. For instance, if we need to determine total monthly income for the year, we could just create a range that refers to all of the monthly figures.

Using ranges saves a lot of time and productivity. If you needed to add up a column of 42 pieces of data, for example, it would take a long time indeed to type each and every cell reference. With a range reference, you only need to type the first and last cell references in the range.

Range references are usually separated by a colon, as in B2:B13. This means that the range reference uses the information in every cell from B2 to B13.

You can also use a range in a formula that encompasses an entire column or row. If you wanted to display the total of all cells in column B, you would use the reference B:B in your formula. Just be careful, you should only use this if the cell displaying the actual total is not in that same column. This would create what is called a *circular reference*.

The figures on the following page demonstrate how to use ranges within formulas. You will use the worksheets that you created in previous tasks in this chapter, so if you haven't been following along, you might want to go back and create those worksheets now. The first two figures show how to use a specific range of cells in a formula. The last two figures create a formula using all of the cells in a column.

TAKE NOTE

CREATING FORMULAS FOR NONADJACENT CELLS

You can create a formula for nonadjacent cells in a range by simply separating them with a comma instead of a colon. So the formula =SUM(B2, C3) would add only cells B2 and C3. You can combine both kinds of ranges in a formula. The formula =SUM(B2:B13, C3) adds cells B2 through B13 and cell C3 together into a single total.

CROSS-REFERENCE

Learn how to select a range in "Selecting a Range" in Chapter 14.

FIND IT ONLINE

K2 Enterprises offers courses geared for CPAs. Visit http://www.k2e.com/.

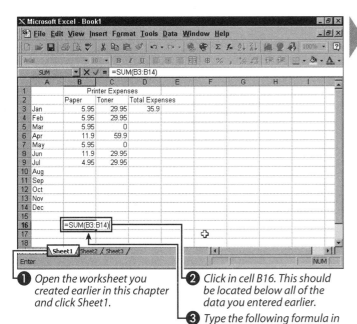

1 Open the worksheet you created earlier in this chapter and click Sheet1.

2 Click in cell B16. This should be located below all of the data you entered earlier.

3 Type the following formula in cell B16: =SUM(B3:B14).

4 Press Enter. The total of all of the cells in the range B3:B14 is displayed in the cell.

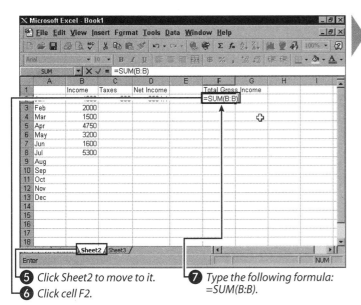

5 Click Sheet2 to move to it.

6 Click cell F2.

7 Type the following formula: =SUM(B:B).

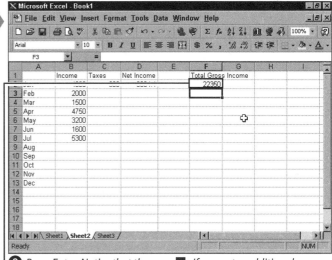

8 Press Enter. Notice that the total of all the cells in column B is now displayed in cell F2.

■ If you enter additional numbers in the blank cells of column B later on, the sum in cell F2 will reflect those changes.

Using Absolute, Relative, and Mixed References

If you have been following along with the examples given earlier, you might have noticed that there are many more formulas left to add to the spreadsheets you have created. Manually entering all those repetitive formulas is not the most efficient way to work. You would be better off to copy those formulas into the other cells that need them. But here you may notice a problem: On Sheet1 you created a formula in cell D3 that adds cells B3 and C3. It stands to reason that you will want a similar formula in the cells below D3 to perform a similar calculation. But if you simply copy the formula from cell D3 into the cells below, it will contain references to the cells up in row 3, right?

Wrong. Excel anticipates the need to copy formulas in this manner and makes use of *absolute*, *relative*, and *mixed* references. So far, the references you have created are all relative references because they can change relative to where they are copied. If you copy the formula from D3 into the cell in row 4, the references in the formula will automatically change to 4 as well. This greatly speeds up the formula creation process because it enables you to create formulas in a more intelligent way.

Of course, you may not always want Excel to automatically change your formulas like this when you copy them. If you anticipate copying a formula that you do not want to change relative to its position in the worksheet, you should use an absolute reference. This is done by placing a dollar sign ($) in front of the portion of the reference that should not change. So, if you want to copy the formula =B3+C3 to another cell without changing the references, it should look like this: =$B$3+$C$3. Both the column and row references here are absolute, meaning they will not change no matter where you copy them.

You can mix absolute and relative references to create mixed references. If you want the row reference to change, but not the column, you would write the formula thus: =$B3+$C3. Now the columns are fixed, but the row numbers can change.

The figures on the facing page show you how to copy formulas. The first two figures demonstrate how to copy using mixed references, and the last two figures make use of relative references.

CROSS-REFERENCE

See "Creating References" in Chapter 14 to learn more about working with references.

FIND IT ONLINE

http://www.computerimages.com/sup_xl.html provides technical support for Excel.

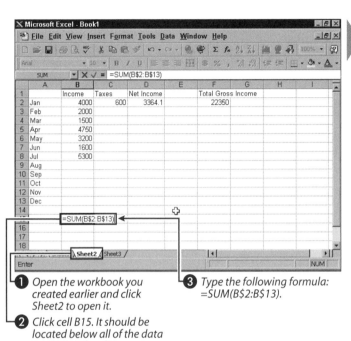

① Open the workbook you
created earlier and click
Sheet2 to open it.

② Click cell B15. It should be
located below all of the data
you entered earlier.

③ Type the following formula:
=SUM(B$2:B$13).

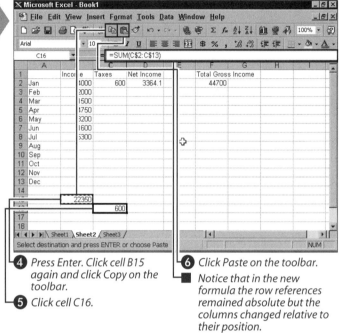

④ Press Enter. Click cell B15
again and click Copy on the
toolbar.

⑤ Click cell C16.

⑥ Click Paste on the toolbar.

■ Notice that in the new
formula the row references
remained absolute but the
columns changed relative to
their position.

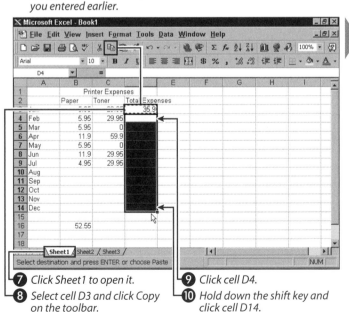

⑦ Click Sheet1 to open it.

⑧ Select cell D3 and click Copy
on the toolbar.

⑨ Click cell D4.

⑩ Hold down the shift key and
click cell D14.

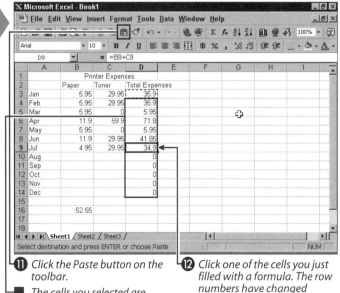

⑪ Click the Paste button on the
toolbar.

■ The cells you selected are
filled with a formula similar to
what was copied from cell D3.

⑫ Click one of the cells you just
filled with a formula. The row
numbers have changed
relative to their position on
the worksheet.

235

Using Formula Wizards

By now you have performed calculations that are on the most basic level. Excel is capable of creating much more complicated formulas, and to describe them all would be beyond the scope of this book. Check out IDG Book's *Excel 97 Bible* by John Walkenbach for exhaustive coverage of Excel formulas.

Nevertheless, Excel provides some wizards to simplify some of the more complicated calculations you might have to make. One of those wizards is the Conditional Sum Wizard, which you practice using here. A conditional sum calculation only adds up numbers from a range of cells based on conditions that you specify. A condition lets you specify what kind of data is displayed or used, ensuring that erroneous data does not occur.

A conditional sum calculation might be used in the workbook that has been created throughout the course of this chapter. Recall that in column C of Sheet2 you calculated a percentage of income to be used for taxes. But what if you had negative income one month? This could easily happen if you had greater expenses than income, but you wouldn't want Excel to calculate a negative tax amount. You could apply a condition to the formulas in that column that only calculates taxes when positive income is earned.

The Conditional Sum Wizard uses conditions in making calculations. Looking back at Sheet1 of the workbook you have created, suppose that you have a total supply budget of $40. In some months you went over budget, and you need to calculate how much was spent in the over-budget months. You can do this using the Conditional Sum Wizard.

The figures on the facing page show you how to use the Conditional Sum Wizard to perform the calculation described here. As you can see, the wizard takes you through the process of creating the formula step by step, asking you some relatively simple questions about what you want the result to be. It then uses this information to create what would otherwise be a complicated formula.

Continued

TAKE NOTE

▶ USING COMPARISON OPERATORS

The example shown here makes use of a comparison operator, namely the greater than (>) sign. This means that it only looks for values that are greater than the amount you specify. Other comparison operators are less than (<), greater than or equal to (>=), less than or equal to (<=), not equal to (<>), and of course equal (=).

▶ OTHER USES FOR CONDITIONAL SUM

Conditional Sum is quite versatile. You can use it to determine totals that only meet certain values. For instance, suppose you have a worksheet that lists all kinds of office expenses, but you only want to find out what you spent on pens. The Conditional Sum Wizard helps you cull this information from an otherwise large worksheet.

CROSS-REFERENCE
Learn more about wizards in "Using the Office Wizards" in Chapter 2.

FIND IT ONLINE
Get some online tips from the Excel help page at **http://www.lacher.com/**.

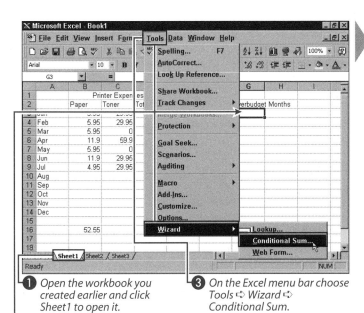

① Open the workbook you created earlier and click Sheet1 to open it.

② Click cell G3.

③ On the Excel menu bar choose Tools ⇨ Wizard ⇨ Conditional Sum.

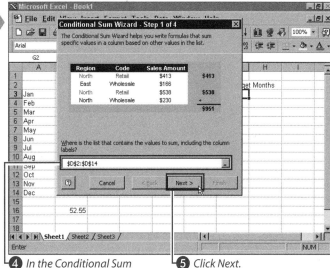

④ In the Conditional Sum Wizard dialog box, specify a range to look in. In this case, use $D$2:$D$14.

⑤ Click Next.

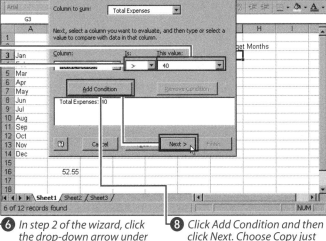

⑥ In step 2 of the wizard, click the drop-down arrow under "Is:" and choose greater than (>).

⑦ Under "This value:" type 40.

⑧ Click Add Condition and then click Next. Choose Copy just the formula to a single cell, in the third dialog box, and click Next.

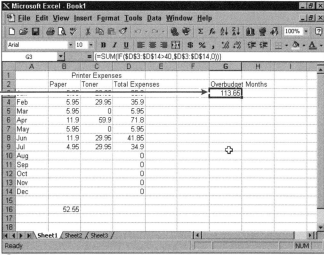

⑨ In the final dialog box, type G3 in the text box and click Finish. (Note that the figure shows the results of this step.)

■ Cell G3 will show the total of only those cells in column D that are greater than $40.

Using Formula Wizards

Continued

The Conditional Sum Wizard is but one of several wizards available to you in Excel. Wizards are actually little add-in programs for Excel, much like Web browser plug-ins, such as RealAudio Player or NetMagnet. Excel comes with several of these add-ins as standard, but you can add in other wizards and plug-ins as you see fit.

Add-ins aside, a lesson in Excel formula wizards just wouldn't be complete without looking at the AutoSum feature. There are no big surprises here; in fact, you've already used AutoSum several times. As you saw, AutoSum makes short work of what is, without doubt, the most common type of calculation you are likely to make in Excel: adding numbers.

AutoSum is a very powerful tool, yet it is quite simple to use. Still, you should know a few special things to make AutoSum work better for you. You need to understand that AutoSum only creates one basic kind of formula. If you want it to automatically create a formula that does anything other than find the sum of adjacent cells, you're out of luck. Your best bet may be to use AutoSum as a starting point to create your basic formula. You can always edit it manually by typing in new instructions and references in the formula bar.

The figures on the following page show you how to create a formula with AutoSum, and then how to manipulate that formula to better suit your specific needs. You begin by using AutoSum to find the total of a column of data you created earlier in this chapter.

In the last two figures, you perform some manual edits to the basic AutoSum formula.

TAKE NOTE

▶ AUTOSUM AND RELATIVE REFERENCES

As you create formulas with AutoSum, notice that references in these formulas are all relative. This means that if you copy the formula to another cell, the references change relative to the new position.

▶ RANGES IN AUTOSUM

When you create a formula using AutoSum, you can only use a range of adjacent cells. If you try to select nonadjacent cells using the Ctrl key and then click AutoSum, the formula will not be correct. For better results, create the basic formula using AutoSum, and then add in any nonadjacent cells manually.

▶ UNDERSTANDING FUNCTIONS

You might notice that whenever you create a new formula with AutoSum, the formula always begins with SUM, followed by a range reference in parentheses. The word SUM is actually a *function*. An Excel function contains a predetermined set of instructions to perform calculations associated with the function in question. In the case of SUM, the instructions add up all of the cells in the range reference.

▶ INSERT AUTOSUM FORMULAS IN A FLASH

Press Alt+equal sign (=) to quickly insert an AutoSum formula.

CROSS-REFERENCE

AutoSum formulas use relative references. See "Using Absolute, Relative, and Mixed References" earlier in this chapter.

FIND IT ONLINE

Get more Excel tips at: **http://spreadsheets. home.mindspring.com/exceltips.htm.**

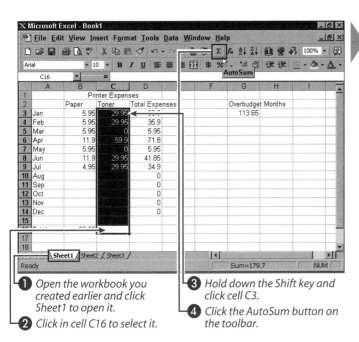

① Open the workbook you created earlier and click Sheet1 to open it.

② Click in cell C16 to select it.

③ Hold down the Shift key and click cell C3.

④ Click the AutoSum button on the toolbar.

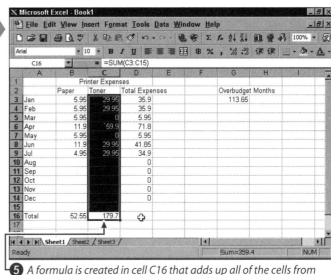

⑤ A formula is created in cell C16 that adds up all of the cells from C3 to C15.

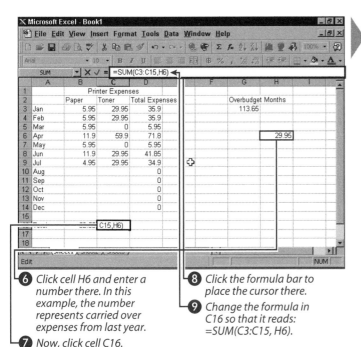

⑥ Click cell H6 and enter a number there. In this example, the number represents carried over expenses from last year.

⑦ Now, click cell C16.

⑧ Click the formula bar to place the cursor there.

⑨ Change the formula in C16 so that it reads: =SUM(C3:C15, H6).

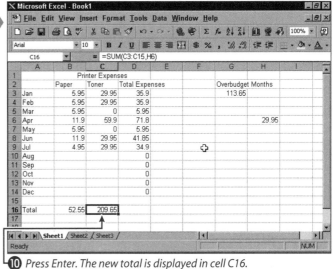

⑩ Press Enter. The new total is displayed in cell C16.

Using Functions

During the formative years of your education you probably learned how to make calculations using only constants. That is, you were given arithmetic problems such as "1+1=?" and you had to figure out the answer. Eventually you learned algebra and with it a whole new way of making calculations. With algebra, you no longer had a neat set of numbers to add, subtract, multiply, or divide. Instead, you were presented with variables, and you were forced to make decisions about how those variables fit into the equations. You have probably noticed that cell references work a lot like variables in algebraic equations. True to form, the value of a cell reference varies every time you change the data in that cell.

Now with Excel, you get to learn yet another way of looking at calculations. Excel makes use of tools called *functions* in many — if not most — of the formulas on every worksheet. A function is a short keyword that tells Excel to perform a predetermined set of calculations. For instance, suppose you want to find the average of a range of cells. You probably know that finding an average involves adding together a group of numbers and then dividing by the quantity of the group, and so does Excel. You can use the AVERAGE function to find the average of a range of cells without having to manually enter a lot of complicated operators and instructions.

To use a function in a cell, all you have to do is press the equal sign key (=), choose a function name,

and place your cell references within parentheses right after the function. Excel does the rest. The figures on the facing page show you how to use a function in a formula. Using the workbook you have been working on throughout this chapter you can determine average monthly expenses for certain items.

Continued

TAKE NOTE

MAKING CALCULATIONS ON FUNCTIONS

Sometimes, you may need to make other calculations in a formula in addition to the function. You can do this by enclosing the entire function formula (including the function name) inside parentheses and making it part of a bigger formula. The result would look something like this:
=(AVERAGE(B3:B14))+(AVERAGE(C3:C14))

THE DIFFERENCE BETWEEN AVERAGES AND TRENDS

The example shown here finds the average monthly cost of some supplies using the AVERAGE function. An average in this case simply tells you what your monthly cost for that item has been, spread evenly over a number of months. The somewhat more advanced TREND function, on the other hand, gives you a better indication about whether prices seem to be going up, down, or nowhere, based on what has been happening recently. Try them both to see which one works best in a variety of situations.

CROSS-REFERENCE

Get the full scoop on cell references in "Creating References" in Chapter 14.

FIND IT ONLINE

Check out Unistat, a statistical package you can add to Excel, at **http://www.unistat.com/**.

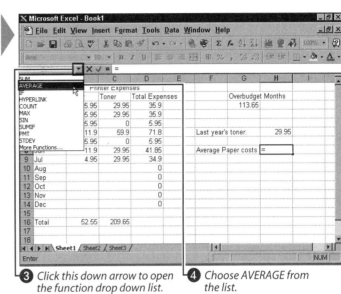

① Open the workbook you
created earlier and click
Sheet1.

② Click cell H8 and type an
equal sign (=).

③ Click this down arrow to open
the function drop down list.

④ Choose AVERAGE from
the list.

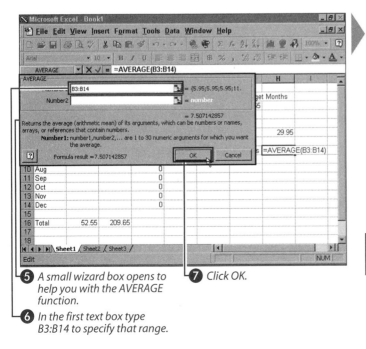

⑤ A small wizard box opens to
help you with the AVERAGE
function.

⑥ In the first text box type
B3:B14 to specify that range.

⑦ Click OK.

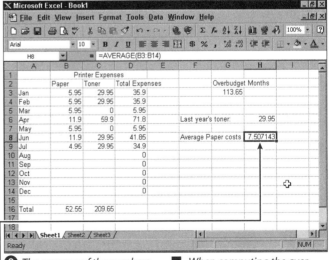

⑧ The average of the numbers
in cells B3 through B14 is
displayed in cell H8.

■ When computing the average, Excel ignores empty cells.
If those cells contained the
number 0, they would have
been included and would
bring the average down.

Using Functions
Continued

Excel offers many other functions that you can use. So far you've learned about the AVERAGE — and SUM functions. Another very useful function that you should learn about is IF. Simply stated, the IF function helps you make more logical decisions about what kind of data is, and is not, displayed on your worksheets.

To illustrate, consider the workbook you have been working on throughout this chapter. In that book you calculated monthly expenses on Sheet1, and subtracted that amount from gross income on Sheet2. Sheet2 also calculates the amount of tax to be paid each month, based on the gross income for that month. However, a problem occurs when you have negative income. What if a major expense occurs during the year that results in negative income? Obviously, tax will not be paid if there is a loss, but since the current tax calculation is based solely on gross income, tax could end up getting paid anyway.

The simple solution is to calculate tax-to-pay based on net income. This gives a more realistic number, but again you have a problem. If net income during a given month is negative, the formula will calculate negative tax. To avoid this, you can use the IF function to provide an exception. IF performs a *logical test* on you data, based on criteria you set. In the case of the tax calculation discussed above, you want to test net income to make sure it is greater than 0. The formula must contain this logical test, and then it must tell Excel what to display in the cell if the value is *true* (in this case, greater than 0) or *false* (not greater than 0). Results of a logical test are always expressed as either true or false because the result must be one or the other.

The figures on the following page demonstrate how to use the IF function in this situation. Obviously, you can use IF in many other situations as well. It can be used whenever you need to test data for a specific condition.

TAKE NOTE

▶ IF FUNCTION SYNTAX

Proper syntax with the IF function is important. You begin the formula like any other, with an equal sign and the function name. Within the parentheses, you must place the logical test, value if true, and value if false, in that order. It should look something like this: =IF(D2>0, D2*15%, 0).

▶ COMPARISON OPERATORS

Excel provides several comparison operators that you can use in the logical test portion of IF formulas. They are equal to (=); greater than (>); less than (<); greater than or equal to (>=); less than or equal to (<=); or not equal to (<>).

CROSS-REFERENCE

If the cells on your worksheets aren't big enough, see "Controlling Column Widths" in Chapter 16.

FIND IT ONLINE

Visit **http://www.add-ins.com/** to find some excellent Excel add-in tools and programs.

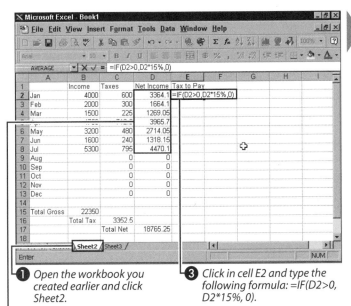

① Open the workbook you created earlier and click Sheet2.

② If you haven't already done so, fill in column D by copying the formula from cell D2.

③ Click in cell E2 and type the following formula: =IF(D2>0, D2*15%, 0).

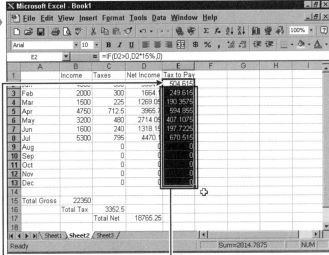

④ Press Enter. Notice that 15% of the net income for January is now displayed in cell E2.

⑤ Copy the formula from cell E2 into the remaining cells in column E, down to row 13.

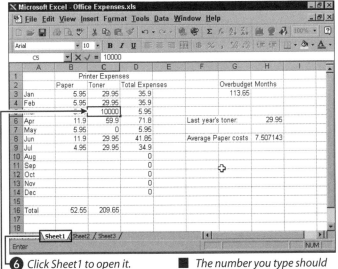

⑥ Click Sheet1 to open it.

⑦ In cell C5, change the existing expense number to an exorbitant amount.

■ The number you type should be larger than the income for that month, as reported back on Sheet2.

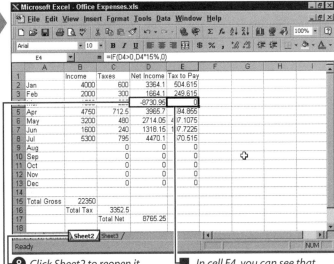

⑧ Click Sheet2 to reopen it.

⑨ Notice that the Net Income shown in cell D4 is now a negative number.

■ In cell E4, you can see that the Tax-to-pay amount is 0, because you used the IF function to avoid a negative value.

243

Personal Workbook

Q&A

1 Which character must precede any formula?

_____

_____

2 In a formula, what is the order of arithmetic calculations?

_____

_____

_____

3 Do ranges used in formulas have to contain adjacent cells?

_____

_____

_____

4 What is the quickest way to find the total of a column of numbers?

_____

_____

_____

5 What does a dollar sign ($) in front of a column reference mean?

_____

_____

_____

6 Do formulas change if you copy them to different cells?

_____

_____

_____

7 What is a function?

_____

_____

_____

8 What function lets you perform a logical test on a piece of data?

_____

_____

_____

ANSWERS: PAGE 412

EXTRA PRACTICE

1 Create a worksheet with 3 columns and 10 rows of numeric data.

2 Make the totals of each column appear underneath the data.

3 Make the totals of each row appear along the right side of the data.

4 Use the Conditional Sum Wizard to find the total of all cells with a value less than 5.

5 Find the average of all the cells in the middle column.

REAL-WORLD APPLICATIONS

✔ You can use an Excel worksheet to score a competition where contestants earn points. Using formulas you can determine each contestant's total score, average score, and even the average score of all contestants in the competition.

✔ Use the TREND function to analyze monthly sales over a period of several years and determine if sales appear to be increasing or decreasing. This information can then be translated into a graph that is presented at a shareholders' meeting.

✔ Simple SUM formulas can be used to track income and expenses, and you can even calculate the interest you are paying on various loans. See how many months or even years could be cut off your mortgage loan by paying $25 extra each month? Plug it into the formula!

Visual Quiz

What is the quickest way to display the column totals shown near the bottom? In the formula shown in the formula bar, what does the asterisk (*) mean? What does IF mean in that formula? Based on the information displayed in cell E4, is the result true or false?

_____

_____

_____

_____

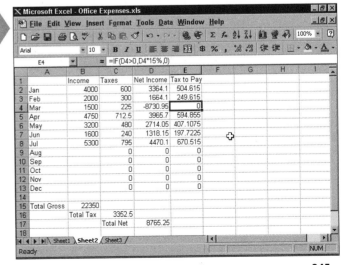

CHAPTER 16

MASTER THESE SKILLS

▶ **Formatting Text and Numbers**

▶ **Aligning Text and Numbers**

▶ **Controlling Column Widths**

▶ **Changing Row Heights**

▶ **Keeping the Titles in View**

▶ **Using AutoFormat**

Changing Appearances

As computer programs go, Excel is not what most people think of as terribly fun. It is a program of pure function, performing calculations and logical operations without drama or excitement. Indeed, most of the worksheets you create in Excel will probably end up with an aggressively bland appearance.

But it does not always need to be this way. You can do many things to spice up the look and feel of your Excel worksheets to give them a more custom — and attractive — appearance. You can change the way that titles are displayed so that they look more appealing and are easier to read on the page. You can make those titles remain visible even as you scroll around the document, making the whole sheet easier to understand. Finally, you have complete control over the size of columns and rows within your worksheets, an important skill in improving how your data is displayed.

Performing these tasks to improve the look of your worksheets does more than make your worksheets more appealing to the eye. If your data should conform to a specific format — say, your numeric data needs to be displayed as dollar values — it is important that it is displayed as such on the worksheet. Excel lets you control formatting so that data is always displayed the way you need it.

This chapter shows you how to control and improve the look of your Excel documents. You start by learning about text and number formatting. Text formatting in Excel is similar to text formatting in Word, and helps you make your worksheets easier to read and even eye-catching. Number formatting is important to ensure that your data displays properly. You learn about aligning numbers and text within the cells, techniques that often preclude the need to resize columns and rows. Nevertheless, you learn how to change the width of worksheet columns and the height of worksheet rows. You also learn how they are measured so that you can control them more easily later on.

Another very useful skill you are introduced to here is a method for keeping your column and row titles in view, even as you scroll far down in the worksheet. Finally, we show you how a feature called AutoFormat can help you automate much of the formatting process.

Formatting Text and Numbers

If you have spent any amount of time using a word processor like Word, you've probably already learned about formatting text. In Word, you can dramatically change the appearance of your document by changing the formatting of your text. These changes may come in the form of a different font set, a larger print size, bold or italic characters, and a myriad of other options.

Just as formatting in Word documents is important, you should learn how to format numbers and text in Excel as well. Formatting in Excel often goes beyond simply changing the appearance of the worksheet; it can have functional repercussions as well. Having data appear in a way that is easy to absorb and understand makes your work more efficient and appear more professional to others.

One example of formatting used within a worksheet that you have probably already worked with is date formatting. When you enter a date into a cell, Excel automatically recognizes that and formats the date accordingly. In Chapter 14 you even learned how to change the formatting for dates so that they are displayed the way you want them.

Excel doesn't always recognize other types of data that warrant special formatting. Monetary units are a good example. Suppose you need to enter the dollar amount $11.90 into a cell. If you type 11.90, Excel assumes it is a regular number and displays it as 11.9. While this may not seem like a big deal, it does make it harder to recognize this number as a dollar amount at first glance. You can make Excel keep that extra zero — and maybe even display a dollar sign — by applying formatting to the number.

While you're at it, you can also apply formatting, such as bold, italics, and different typefaces, to text in a worksheet. This helps improve the asthetics of the worksheet, which become especially important if others need to read it. The figures on the facing page demonstrate how to apply formatting to several different kinds of data. If you followed along through Chapter 15 you may notice that this is the same workbook that was created there. You can use that same workbook, or create a similar one from scratch.

TAKE NOTE

FORMATTING ENTIRE ROWS AND COLUMNS

It makes sense to save a bit of time and effort to format an entire column or row at once, rather than format one cell at a time. To do this, click the column or row heading to select the whole thing, right-click it, and choose Format Cells from the context menu.

AUTOMATIC FORMATTING

Excel automatically formats some things for you. For instance, if you type a dollar sign with a number, that cell is automatically formatted as currency. You can also apply some of the most common formatting, such as currency, using buttons on the Formatting toolbar.

CROSS-REFERENCE

Learn more about text formatting in "Formatting Text" in Chapter 8.

FIND IT ONLINE

Contact **news:comp.apps.spreadsheets**, a news group dedicated to spreadsheets.

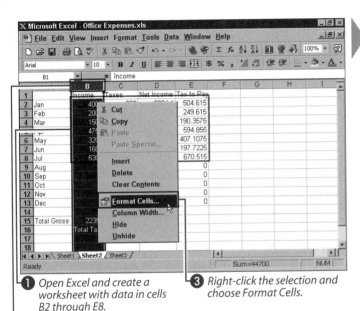

① Open Excel and create a worksheet with data in cells B2 through E8.

② Click the heading for column B to select the entire column.

③ Right-click the selection and choose Format Cells.

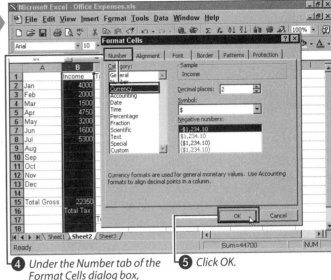

④ Under the Number tab of the Format Cells dialog box, choose Currency.

⑤ Click OK.

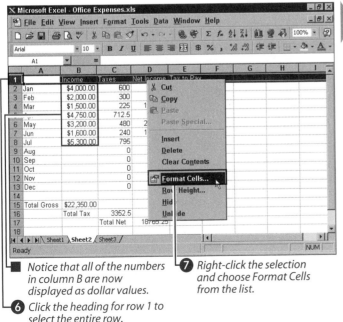

■ Notice that all of the numbers in column B are now displayed as dollar values.

⑥ Click the heading for row 1 to select the entire row.

⑦ Right-click the selection and choose Format Cells from the list.

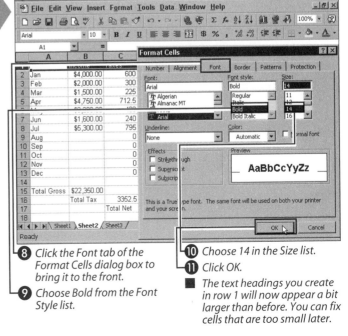

⑧ Click the Font tab of the Format Cells dialog box to bring it to the front.

⑨ Choose Bold from the Font Style list.

⑩ Choose 14 in the Size list.

⑪ Click OK.

■ The text headings you create in row 1 will now appear a bit larger than before. You can fix cells that are too small later.

Aligning Text and Numbers

Formatting text and numbers is the first step towards making your worksheets a bit more presentable and easy to read. Having data appear in the correct format is vital to effective worksheet creation, as is the ability to make your headings and labels stand out.

Another thing you can do to make your worksheets look their best is to adjust the alignment of text and numbers. Alignment is the positioning of the data within a cell. Data — whether text, numbers, or some other kind of data — can be aligned left, right, or centered. It can also be oriented near the top or bottom of a cell if you wish.

This can be useful in more cases than you might think. Recall the exercise you performed in the last task, where you increased the font size of column labels in your worksheet. Depending on how long those labels were, some of them are probably overlapping or hidden now because they are too big for the cell. This detracts from the overall appearance of your worksheet, and viewers may not be able to read all of the labels.

One common solution to this problem is to make the columns physically wider, a procedure described later in this chapter. But in the case of columnar labels, that's not always the best answer. Stretching a column out to fit a long label may result in a rediculously wide column with lots of white space down the page. A better solution might be to change the orientation of the labels so they fit better in a narrow column.

You can also change the alignment of numbers if you wish. More often than not, you will want most numbers to line up along the right side of their respective cells, but if you want to change that you certainly can. The figures on the facing page show you how to change the alignment of text within a worksheet. The text labels that were modified in the last lesson are reoriented for more efficient use of space. Although aligning numbers is not demonstrated, it uses the same techniques shown here.

TAKE NOTE

CONSIDER NUMBER FORMATS

If you want to change the alignment of some numbers, consider what kind of format the numbers are supposed to be in. If the numbers denote currency, they will probably be easier to read if aligned along the right side of the cell. On the other hand, binary numbers can be read more easily from the left, so you might want to realign those accordingly.

MERGE AND CENTER

If you have a long heading that overlaps several cells, you can select it and choose Merge and Center from the Formatting toolbar. This centers the text, and merges any overlapped cells with the original one.

CROSS-REFERENCE

See "Justifying and Aligning Text" in Chapter 8 to learn more about text alignment.

FIND IT ONLINE

Visit **http://planmagic.com/thebest/excel.html** to download, or find out more about, Excel add-ins.

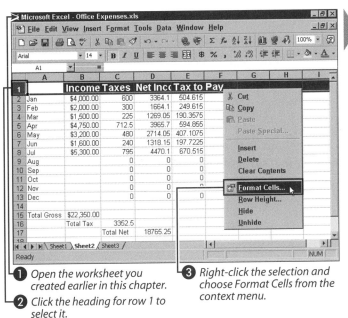

❶ Open the worksheet you created earlier in this chapter.

❷ Click the heading for row 1 to select it.

❸ Right-click the selection and choose Format Cells from the context menu.

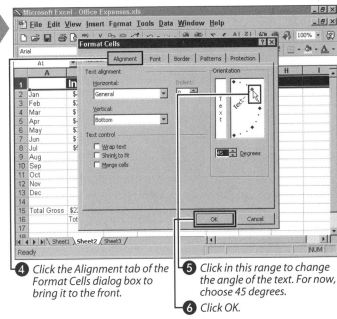

❹ Click the Alignment tab of the Format Cells dialog box to bring it to the front.

❺ Click in this range to change the angle of the text. For now, choose 45 degrees.

❻ Click OK.

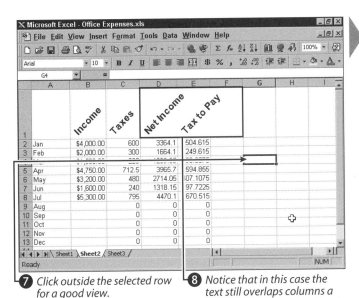

❼ Click outside the selected row for a good view.

❽ Notice that in this case the text still overlaps columns a bit. This is evidenced by the missing column borders.

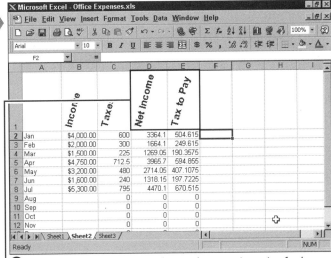

❾ Follow the previous steps to change the text orientation further and eliminate overlapping.

Controlling Column Widths

In the previous task, you learned how to adjust the contents of cells so that they fit better into the columns. This is an effective way of making your worksheets look better because it allows the labels to be read completely without impacting the rest of the worksheet.

But there will be times when you want to adjust the width of columns on a worksheet. This is especially true if the data displayed in the cells is too wide to be completely viewed within the standard column width. You may also decide that a wider column is preferable to changing the alignment of text as shown in the previous task.

Sometimes, you might want to make a column narrower instead of wider. You might do this if all the data in the cells of a column consists of only one or two digits. A narrower column will clean up the appearance of your worksheet by getting rid of unnecessary white space and moving related pieces of data closer together.

You can adjust column width using a couple of different techniques. The simplest way is to simply click and drag the borders on the column headings. When you hold the mouse pointer over a border in the headings, it changes to a line with two arrows. All you have to do is click and hold the left mouse button, and drag the border to a new width. Another

way to adjust column width involves the Column Width dialog box. This dialog box measures width in terms of how many characters of the standard font fit in the normal view of a cell. The standard font in Excel is Arial, so if you choose a different font then a different number of characters might be displayed.

The figures on the facing page show you how to adjust the width of columns in Excel. The first two demonstrate how to use click and drag to adjust columns one at a time, and the last two figures show you how to change the default width for all columns in the worksheet.

TAKE NOTE

▶ COLUMN WIDTHS REMAIN CONSTANT

When you do adjust the width of a column, you need to keep in mind that all of the cells in a column must have the same width. Changing the width of one cell in a column changes the width of all other cells in that column.

▶ DEFINING THE DEFAULT WIDTH

The default width of columns in Excel is such that 8.43 characters of the Arial font can fit in each cell. You can change the default width by choosing Format ⇨ Column ⇨ Width from the Excel menu bar and typing in a new number.

CROSS-REFERENCE
You can change the size of rows as well as columns. See the next task, "Changing Row Heights" to learn more.

FIND IT ONLINE
Kona Systems at **http://www.konasys.com/** offers Hula, a Web database that integrates with Excel.

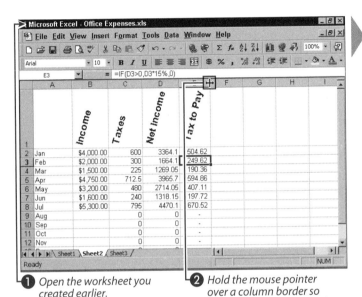

① Open the worksheet you created earlier.

② Hold the mouse pointer over a column border so that it becomes a line with two arrows.

③ Click and hold the left mouse button, and drag the pointer to increase or decrease the column width.

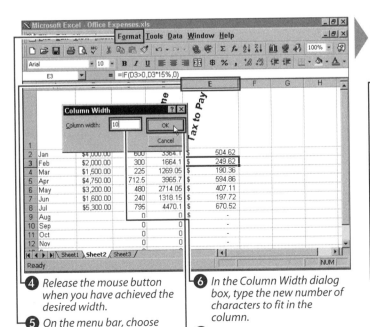

④ Release the mouse button when you have achieved the desired width.

⑤ On the menu bar, choose Format ➪ Column ➪ Width.

⑥ In the Column Width dialog box, type the new number of characters to fit in the column.

⑦ Click OK.

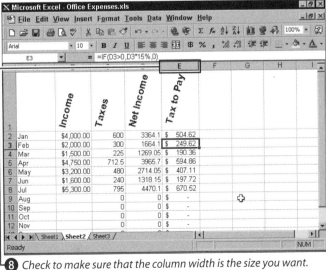

⑧ Check to make sure that the column width is the size you want.

Changing Row Heights

Columns aren't the only worksheet element that can be resized. Besides adjusting the width of columns, you can also change the height of rows in your worksheet. This has many uses and can do just as much to enhance the look of your worksheets as column width adjustments.

By default, rows in Excel are set at 12.75 points high. A point is a standard unit of measure used by typesetters for many years. The most common point sizes used in Office 97 programs are 10 and 12. The default font size used in Excel worksheets is 10 points, so you can see that each row normally has 2.75 points of free space to provide a margin at the top and bottom of text and numbers. As a point of reference, six 12-point cells would fit in one inch if printed out on paper.

If you apply a different font size to characters in a row, that row is automatically resized to fit the characters. You can also manually adjust the size of rows, using techniques similar to those used to resize columns. You might want to do this if you don't like the default size that Excel has assigned to a row. A taller row can also be used to provide a visual cushion between elements on your worksheet.

Just as you did when you adjusted the width of columns, you can click and drag row borders to resize them. There is also a Row Height dialog box where you can adjust the height by typing a new number. And just as with columns, you cannot adjust the height of cells independently. When you adjust the height of one cell, you adjust the height of all the other cells in that row at the same time.

The figures on the facing page show you how to adjust row heights. The first two figures show you how to click and drag a row border, and the last two figures demonstrate how to adjust height using the Row Height dialog box. You can access this dialog box via the Excel menu bar, or using a context menu as shown here.

TAKE NOTE

MEASURING ROW HEIGHT V. COLUMN WIDTH

As mentioned, row height is expressed in terms of point size rather than the number of characters that are displayed, as in column widths. Because a standard character in Excel is 10 points tall, the numbers shown in the Row Height dialog box tend to be much larger than those in the Column Width box.

ADJUSTING MULTIPLE ROWS

To adjust the height of several rows at once, simply select all of the rows you want to change. Remember to hold the Shift or Ctrl key as you select each row.

QUICK ROW RESIZING

Double-click the lower border of a row to quickly resize it to fit the contents of the cells.

CROSS-REFERENCE

See "Formatting Text and Numbers" earlier in this chapter to learn more about changing the look and size of cell data.

FIND IT ONLINE

News:microsoft.public.excel.misc is a news group that covers miscellaneous Excel topics.

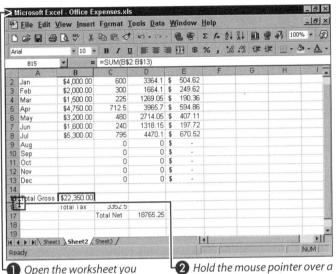

❶ Open the worksheet you created earlier.

❷ Hold the mouse pointer over a row border until it becomes a horizontal line with two arrows.

❸ Click and hold the left mouse button and drag the row border to a new height.

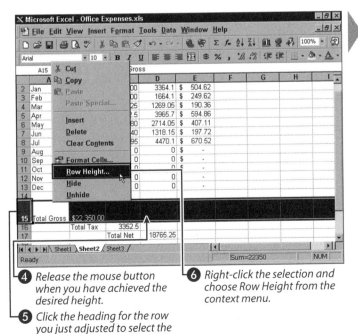

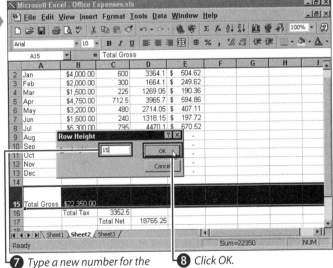

❹ Release the mouse button when you have achieved the desired height.

❺ Click the heading for the row you just adjusted to select the entire row.

❻ Right-click the selection and choose Row Height from the context menu.

❼ Type a new number for the row height.

❽ Click OK.

■ Make sure that the row is now the desired height.

255

Keeping the Titles in View

As you create larger and more complex worksheets, you may have to spend a lot of time scrolling around to see all of the data you need. This is usually not a problem because Excel gives you such a wide range of columns (256) and rows (65,536) to utilize. Unfortunately, scrolling down or across a worksheet can cause some view problems, primarily as they relate to how your column and row labels are displayed. You can rely on Excel's zoom feature to get a bird's eye view of a spreadsheet, but this feature isn't too helpful if you need to read what is in each cell.

You have probably noticed that no matter how far down or across you scroll on the worksheet, the column and cell labels — that is, the letters across the top and numbers across the left side of the screen — are always visible. This way, you always know which cell you are in. But you probably don't think of your data in terms of these labels. If you list monthly gross income in the cells of column B, you probably think of that data as your income figures, not as the contents of the B column. That's why you probably assigned your own column titles at the top of the worksheet, so you can determine at a glance what the numbers in that column represent.

As you scroll farther and farther down the worksheet, the column titles you created in row 1 disappear. When you're working way down in row 142, how do you know what belongs in column C?

Scrolling all the way back to the top just to see the title wastes a lot of time, so Excel lets you freeze portions of your worksheet so that they stay in view.

The figures on the facing page show you how to set your titles so that they remain in view even as you scroll away from the rows where they were originally input. The example used here assumes that you have created a worksheet similar to that used in the figures. In other words, it assumes that you have arranged data in a grid, with titles along the tops of the columns as well as down the side.

TAKE NOTE

▶ DECIDING WHAT TO FREEZE

To freeze your titles so they stay in view, you must use the *freeze panes* feature of Excel. To freeze the top row of your worksheet, click in a cell in row 2 to freeze everything above it. If you have titles along row 1 and in column A, select cell B2 before you freeze the panes.

▶ SPLITTING V. FREEZING PANES

Instead of freezing panes, you can also split them using the Split option in Excel's Window menu. This splits the worksheet so that an entire copy of the sheet exists on either side of the split. You can scroll through each copy of the worksheet individually, but if you edit one they are all updated.

CROSS-REFERENCE
See "Moving Around the Worksheet" in Chapter 14 for more on viewing different parts of the worksheet.

FIND IT ONLINE
Visit The Excel Sheet Magazine at **http://www.sheet.com/** for articles and tips on maximizing Excel.

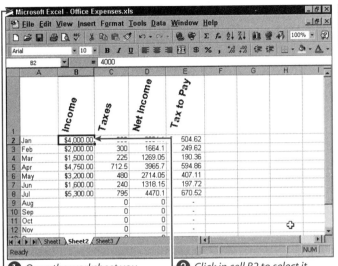

1 Open the worksheet you created earlier.

2 Click in cell B2 to select it.

3 On the Excel menu bar choose Window ➪ Freeze Panes.

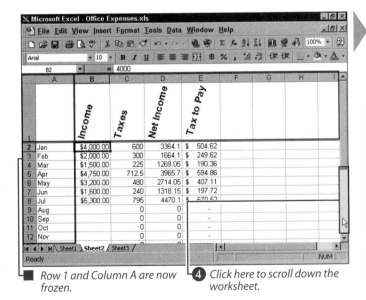

■ Row 1 and Column A are now frozen.

4 Click here to scroll down the worksheet.

■ Notice that row 1 remains in view even though you have scrolled down the worksheet.

5 To unfreeze the panes, choose Window ➪ Unfreeze Panes on the Excel menu bar.

257

Using AutoFormat

S o far in this chapter, you have learned how to manipulate the appearance of your Excel worksheets so that they look just the way you want them to. You have learned how to format text and numbers, align data within the cells, and adjust the size of columns and rows. You can use any of these techniques to give your worksheets a custom yet professional appearance.

Now that you've learned how to change appearances manually, it's time to learn how to perform much of this formatting automatically. Excel offers a feature called AutoFormat that automates much of the formatting process so you can spend more time actually working with your data and less time trying to make it look good.

Like the AutoFormat feature offered in other Office 97 programs such as Word, AutoFormat functions through a simple dialog box that presents a number of predetermined formats for your worksheet. As you scroll through the various preformatted tables available to you, you may recognize them from the table AutoFormat feature in Word. The table formats available in AutoFormat are designed and named to suit a variety of purposes, but just because you are formatting a worksheet that contains information about expenses and income doesn't mean you have to use one of the formats called "Accounting."

Once you have applied AutoFormat to a range on your worksheet, you may notice that the worksheet in the normal document window does not look exactly the way it did in the AutoFormat dialog box. Don't worry; your formatting went fine. Excel continues to show you where the cell borders are for ease of editing. But if you print the worksheet out, or embed it into a Word or PowerPoint document, it will look as it did in AutoFormat. If you're not sure, click the Print Preview button on the toolbar to preview it.

The figures on the facing page show you how to change the appearance of a worksheet using AutoFormat. The example uses the worksheet developed earlier.

TAKE NOTE

REPLACING MANUAL FORMATTING

If you apply AutoFormatting to a worksheet it will replace any prior formatting that was manually applied to it. Of course, after you have applied AutoFormatting you can go back and make any formatting changes you want.

FORMATTING "IMPERFECT" WORKSHEETS

Often when you apply AutoFormatting to a worksheet, the data in the sheet does not conform exactly to the sample you choose. This is not a problem; Excel is pretty intuitive and will guess as best it can, how to apply the formatting. For this reason, make sure you review the worksheet to make sure that formatting was applied the way you want it.

CROSS-REFERENCE

Before you can apply AutoFormatting, you must select a range. Learn how in "Selecting a Range" in Chapter 14.

FIND IT ONLINE

Check out Quixl by Legend Software, an Excel plug-in that lets you download stock quotes and other financial data.

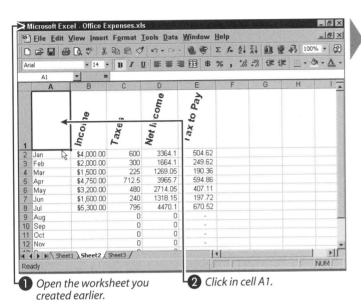

1 Open the worksheet you created earlier.

2 Click in cell A1.

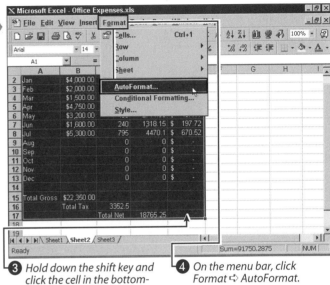

3 Hold down the shift key and click the cell in the bottom-right corner of your worksheet. You may need to scroll down a bit.

4 On the menu bar, click Format ➪ AutoFormat.

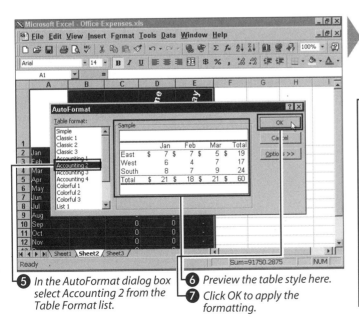

5 In the AutoFormat dialog box select Accounting 2 from the Table Format list.

6 Preview the table style here.

7 Click OK to apply the formatting.

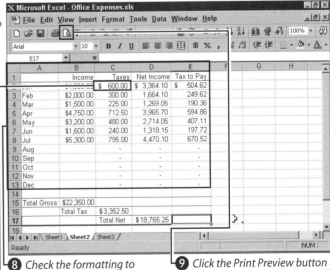

8 Check the formatting to ensure it suits your needs.

▪ Notice that because this was meant to be an accounting table, the number values are displayed as currency.

9 Click the Print Preview button to see what the worksheet will look like on paper.

Personal Workbook

Q&A

1 How do you format a number so that it displays as currency?

_____

_____

2 Can you apply special formatting to text in worksheet cells?

_____

_____

3 How do you align text so that it reads vertically in a cell rather than horizontally?

_____

_____

_____

4 What is the quickest way to change the width of a column?

_____

_____

_____

5 Can you change the width of only one cell in a column?

_____

_____

_____

6 How is row height measured?

_____

_____

_____

7 What is a frozen pane?

_____

_____

_____

8 How do you automatically apply formatting to a range of cells in a worksheet?

_____

_____

_____

ANSWERS: PAGE 413

EXTRA PRACTICE

1 Create a worksheet with 4 columns and 12 rows of numeric data.

2 Create titles for the columns in row 1 and titles for the rows in column A.

3 Make the Titles stay visible even when you scroll down the worksheet.

4 Apply the Colorful 2 format to the worksheet.

5 Make the numbers in your worksheet display as dollar values.

6 Use Print Preview to check the spreadsheet's format.

REAL-WORLD APPLICATIONS

✔ If you are preparing a worksheet to be used in your company's quarterly report, you can use formatting to make the worksheet look more professional. You can even apply the company colors to that worksheet, providing a more custom appearance.

✔ Suppose you are using a worksheet to track information about clients. Make the titles for each column and row stay in view as you scroll around the worksheet so that it is easier to use on a daily basis.

✔ You might sometimes use blank columns or rows as visual separators in an Excel worksheet. If you do this, try changing the size of the row or column so that it is much smaller. This way it won't take up as much space on the screen, yet the two closely spaced lines still provide a good visual break.

Visual Quiz

How do you make the text in the heading appear as it does here? How do you make the numbers appear as dollar values? Why are rows 2 through 6 not shown? How was row 1 kept in view? Some AutoFormatting was applied to this worksheet; was the special formatting of the labels created before or after the AutoFormat feature was used?

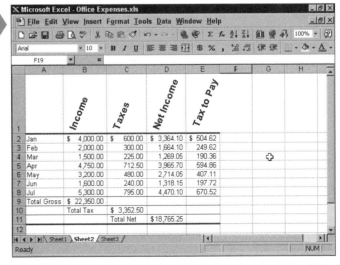

CHAPTER **17**

MASTER
THESE
SKILLS

▶ **Graphing Your Data**

▶ **Modifying Your Charts**

▶ **Using a Chart in Other Programs**

▶ **Changing the Size of Charts**

Creating Graphs

By now you might have figured out that Excel is an extremely verstile and capable program. You have learned how to create formulas, enter text, manipulate the way your data is displayed, and more. But perhaps the greatest feature of Excel hasn't even been tapped yet: the ability to graph data.

Graphs exist virtually everywhere you look. A graph is nothing more than a visual representation of data, a representation that is imprecise yet highly effective at getting a point across. Graphs are used for everything from describing how your tax dollars are spent to how the nutritional value of your cereal stacks up. Looking at numbers and data on the actual worksheet is often not very interesting and to get any real information out if it you have to stare at it for a while. But with a graph, you can represent that data in a way that is instantly recognizable and appealing to the eye. Graphs can be used in reports, on Web pages, or anywhere else where you need to present your data to others.

Using Office 97 you can even share your Excel graph with other programs to produce more advanced documents. You can link your graph to the original data source, such as an Excel database, so that as the information in the database is updated, the graph will be updated automatically.

Before you move on and learn how to create graphs, you should understand a bit about the terminology used here. You will seldom, if ever, see the term "graph" in Excel. Microsoft has chosen instead to call them *charts*. So when you want to create a graph in Excel, you will actually be creating a chart. You say potato, Microsoft says potaahhhto.

In this chapter you start by learning the basics of creating a chart. You learn to create two of the most basic forms of charts, and then move on to learn how to manipulate those charts so they conform to your specific needs. Next, you learn how to use Excel charts in other programs, a process that is easy to do thanks to the linking technology that is available in Office 97 programs. Finally, you learn how to further change the appearance of charts by changing their size and position.

Graphing Your Data

The ability to create graphs or charts has been a mainstay of spreadsheet software technology virtually from the very beginning. Even early versions of programs such as Lotus 1-2-3, Symphony, and Enable offered the ability to create simple graphs of data in the worksheet. Of course, these early graphs were not terribly fancy. Often you were stuck with using simple line charts that did little more than connect dots on a two-axis grid.

The graphing features of Excel go far beyond those humble beginnings. Sure, you can still create a simple line chart if you wish, but Excel offers many other styles to choose from as well. You can create pie charts, columnar charts, area charts, bar charts, and more. Your charts can be two-dimensional, or you can create a three-dimensional chart for a different visual effect. The style you choose will depend on your needs and tastes, so experiment a little before you make any final decisions.

When you begin to create a chart, there are several key things to consider. Perhaps the most important thing to consider is the type of data you are graphing. For instance, suppose you want to create a graph that illustrates stock prices for your company during the course of a year. In this case, you probably want to be able to see all of the ups and downs in stock prices, so a line chart or area chart would probably be best. Or, suppose you need to graph how your income is spent. In this case, you probably want to see what percentage of your income is spent on groceries, car insurance, utilities, tennis lessons, and so on. For this application, a pie chart or stacked column would work best.

The figures on the facing page show you how to create a simple chart using the Chart Wizard. The example utilizes data from a worksheet created in Chapters 15 and 16, but you can follow along using any worksheet that has data in it.

Continued

TAKE NOTE

USING GRIDLINES

Generally speaking, if you can live without gridlines, leave them out. Too many lines clutter your charts and make them difficult to read. Use the Gridlines tab on the Chart Wizard dialog box (Step 3) to change which lines are displayed.

UNDERSTANDING THE AXES

Most chart styles use two axes to orient data. The horizontal axis along the bottom of your charts is refered to as the X axis and the vertical one on the side is the Y axis. Three-dimensional charts also have a Z axis to express 3-D data.

CROSS-REFERENCE

See "Selecting a Range" in Chapter 14 to learn more about selecting a range of data to graph.

FIND IT ONLINE

Give and receive charting advice at
www.news:microsoft.public.excel.charting.

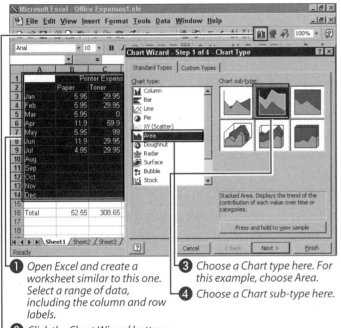

① Open Excel and create a worksheet similar to this one. Select a range of data, including the column and row labels.

② Click the Chart Wizard button.

③ Choose a Chart type here. For this example, choose Area.

④ Choose a Chart sub-type here.

⑤ Click Next. For now, leave the options on Step 2 alone and click Next again.

⑥ On Step 3, click the Titles tab to bring it to the front.

⑦ Type a Chart title here.

⑧ Type a label for the Y axis here.

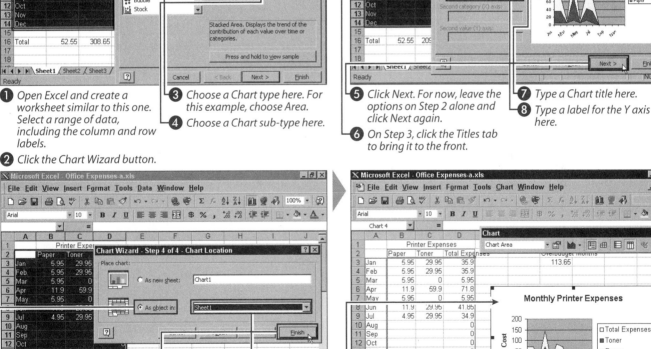

⑨ Click Next again to move to Step 4. Choose As object in: to create this chart on the same worksheet as the data.

⑩ Make sure the correct sheet is listed here.

⑪ Click Finish.

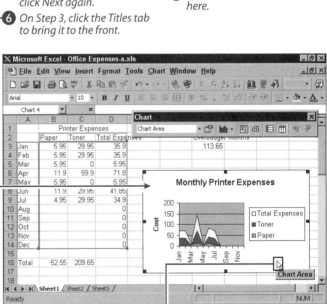

⑫ The chart appears, floating over your data. Click the chart to select it.

⑬ Hold the mouse pointer over the chart and click and hold the left mouse button. Drag the chart to a new location.

Graphing Your Data
Continued

As you saw in the previous example, creating a chart is quite simple. Credit this to the Chart Wizard, which makes the whole process a matter of answering a few questions and clicking an option or two. With relatively little effort, you have already created a professional-looking chart that greatly enhances the appeal of your worksheet.

Take a look at the chart you just created. Notice that the data ranges on the X and Y axes are labeled appropriately. The Chart Wizard picks up these labels directly from the worksheet, as long as you select them along with your data. Sometimes, you won't want or need those labels to be displayed. You can change this during Step 3 of the Chart Wizard by clicking on the Axes tab and changing the settings you find there.

Of course, some chart styles don't even have axes, per se. One example of this is the pie chart. A pie chart is usually round, and data is divided up into wedges. This kind of chart is popular for illustrating percentages and how a fixed quantity of something is distributed.

One way in which a pie chart differs from the area chart you created on the previous page is in labeling. On the area chart, range labels are perhaps the most important. In the previous example, the range labels made it possible to see the monthly breakdown of expenditures for printer supplies. In a pie chart, range labels are less important, but the data labels are critical. Each slice of a pie chart has its own label, providing a visual answer to questions such as "How much?" For example, the pie chart that comes with your government tax forms every year, illustrates how your tax money is being spent, so it is important to have a label on each pie slice. It would be difficult to illustrate this kind of information on something like an area chart.

The figures on the facing page show how to create a pie chart. Although the Chart Wizard is shown, notice that different options are available because you are working with a different style of chart. Most notable is the fact that Step 3 has fewer tabs to choose from.

TAKE NOTE

▶ USING COLORED CHARTS

Many Excel charts rely on colors to differentiate between different types of data. This usually makes sense, but may cause problems if you need to print it out and you only have a black-ink printer. If you need to make a black and white printout of a chart, choose one of the chart styles that is designed to be black-and-white in the first place.

CROSS-REFERENCE
See "Selecting Objects and Graphics" in Chapter 5 to learn more about working with charts.

FIND IT ONLINE
Download a "Bill Gates Pie Chart" wallpaper for your Windows desktop at **http://www.jokewallpaper.com/**.

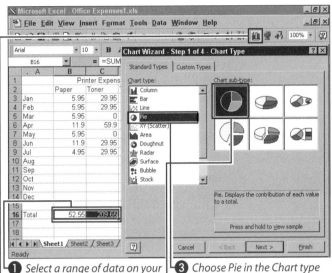

① Select a range of data on your worksheet. To keep things simple for now, just select two cells.

② Click the Chart Wizard button on the toolbar.

③ Choose Pie in the Chart type list.

④ Choose a Chart sub-type here and then click Next.

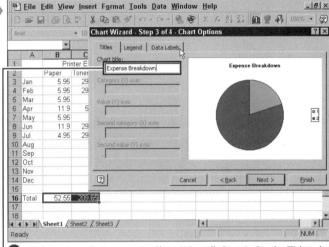

⑤ Click Next again to move to Chart Wizard's Step 3. On the Title tab, type a chart title here.

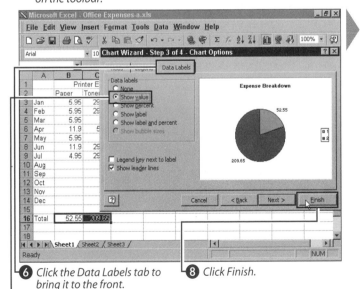

⑥ Click the Data Labels tab to bring it to the front.

⑦ Choose the Show value radio button.

⑧ Click Finish.

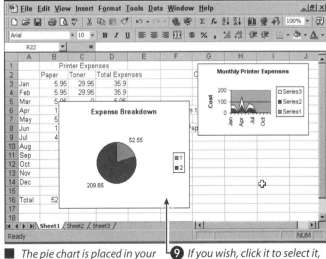

■ The pie chart is placed in your worksheet.

⑨ If you wish, click it to select it, and drag it to a new location.

267

Modifying Your Charts

Wonderful though the Chart Wizard may be, there is a good chance that you eventually become a little dissatisfied with your charts. This is not necessarily because the charts are bad or don't serve their intended purpose, but the simple fact is that things change.

Perhaps the most likely time for you to make changes is immediately after you create a chart. This is the time to review the chart, judge its overall appearance and make those minor tweaks and modifications to make it look just right. Also, some chart elements are actually intended for modification *after* the Chart Wizard has done its job.

You will want to modify the chart window itself. If you chose to have the chart inserted into an existing worksheet, it will appear as a white or clear window that floats over the sheet. You may need to move the chart around so that it does not block your data. On the other hand, you may actually prefer that it does block your data. That's not a problem; you can always move the chart out of the way if you need to edit.

Within the chart window are a number of elements that you can modify. The actual chart is but one element in the window, but you can still move and resize it as you see fit. You can also modify the chart legend by moving it, resizing it, or getting rid of it altogether. The chart title is fair game, because you

can move it, resize it, or edit the text. This goes for virtually any text in the chart window.

Finally, you can modify the appearance of the chart itself, even so far as choosing a different chart style. The figures on the facing page show you how to modify the basic appearance of your charts. Once you have performed some basic modifications, you can move on to learn about the more advanced modifications you can make.

Continued

TAKE NOTE

▶ USING THE CHART TOOLBAR

The Chart toolbar should automatically appear whenever you click in the chart window (if not, right-click the Chart Wizard icon and select Chart). It contains many of the options you need to modify your chart, including a drop-down list to select different chart areas to modify, and another drop-down list that enables you to quickly choose a different chart style.

▶ CHANGING THE PLOT AREA

Most worksheet styles have a background area, often containing a grid. This is also refered to as the *plot area*, and you can dramatically change the look of your worksheet just by changing the plot area color. Select the chart plot area, right-click the selection and choose Format Plot Area from the context menu.

CROSS-REFERENCE
You usually have to select chart elements to modify them. See "Selecting Objects and Graphics" in Chapter 5 to learn how.

FIND IT ONLINE
Check out the fascinating Experimental Analysis at **http://www.uni-sb.de/philfak/MZ/graph/titel.html**.

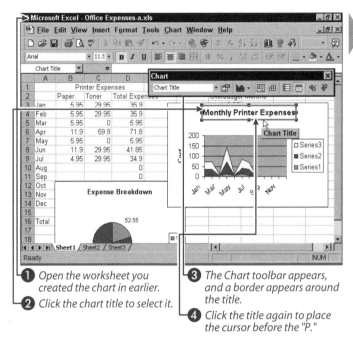

① Open the worksheet you created the chart in earlier.

② Click the chart title to select it.

③ The Chart toolbar appears, and a border appears around the title.

④ Click the title again to place the cursor before the "P."

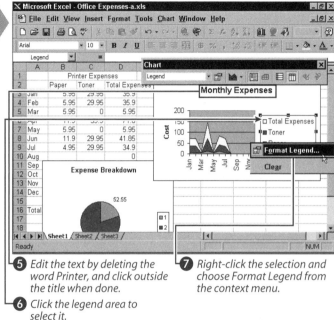

⑤ Edit the text by deleting the word Printer, and click outside the title when done.

⑥ Click the legend area to select it.

⑦ Right-click the selection and choose Format Legend from the context menu.

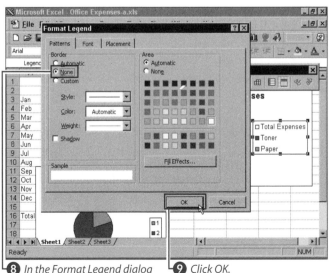

⑧ In the Format Legend dialog box, click the None radio button under Border to remove the border from the legend.

⑨ Click OK.

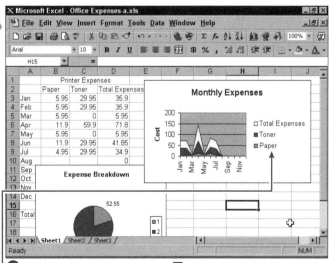

⑩ The legend border has gone. Hold the mouse pointer over the chart and click-and-drag it to a new location.

■ Click outside the chart window to hide the Chart toolbar and check the view.

Modifying Your Charts
Continued

In the previous example, you learned how to make some basic modifications to a chart. Those modifications were cosmetic and had little or nothing to do with how the chart actually works.

However, aesthetics aren't the only things you can change in your charts. One of the most important aspects of graphing data with a spreadsheet program like Excel, is that it does not remain a fixed object once you've created it. What if your data changes? In the days before computerized spreadsheets, such a change meant hiring artists to redraw the graph. But now, Excel automatically updates your graphs for you every time you change any of the data used by the chart.

Changes to your data may necessitate other changes as well. For instance, changes to the values of your data may impact the scales that are assigned to chart axes, but Excel automatically updates those when you modify data. The data on the chart itself is also updated whenever the data on the actual worksheet changes. And therein lies the real beauty of graphing with Excel.

You must also consider that, when you change data, you may decide that the actual chart style just doesn't suit your needs any more. Changing the chart style is an easy thing to do, but keep in mind that you are probably not the only person who will read this. Make sure you keep the new chart style simple and

easy to read. Use the same considerations you used when you first created the chart.

The first two figures on the facing page show you how to modify data in a chart. The last two figures show you how to change the style of the chart.

TAKE NOTE

▶ WHAT IF YOUR DATA MOVES?

Sometimes, you may need to move the data that is being used in a cell. This often happens when you need to insert a new row or column into a worksheet. When you move data, Excel automatically corrects the chart range references so that the correct data is still used.

▶ FORMATTING AXES

It is highly probable that the axes of your chart don't look exactly the way you would like them to. Perhaps they need new labels, or you don't want the numbers/units displayed. You can change these things and more in the Format Axis dialog box. Click the chart axis to select it, right-click the axis and choose Format Axis from the context menu.

▶ FLIP YOUR CHARTS

If the chart looks good but the data isn't displaying correctly, try clicking By row or By column on the Chart toolbar. This changes the overall orientation of the chart, kind of like choosing Portrait or Landscape orientation in a Word document.

CROSS-REFERENCE
Modifying data is simple. See "Entering Numbers and Text" in Chapter 14.

FIND IT ONLINE
Legend Software offers Excel charting software for financial analysis at **http://cgibin1.erols.com/ aadegan/**.

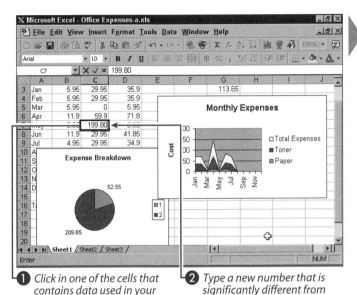

1 Click in one of the cells that contains data used in your charts.

2 Type a new number that is significantly different from the old one and press Enter.

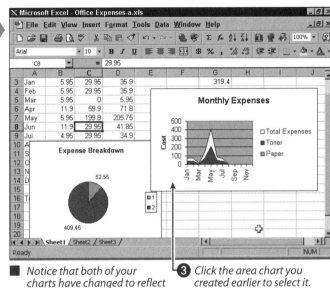

■ Notice that both of your charts have changed to reflect the new data.

3 Click the area chart you created earlier to select it.

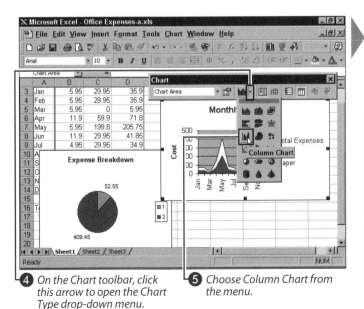

4 On the Chart toolbar, click this arrow to open the Chart Type drop-down menu.

5 Choose Column Chart from the menu.

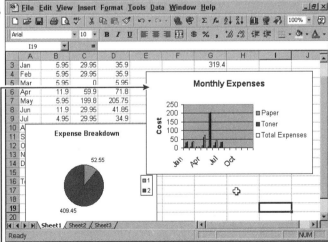

6 The chart now appears in the new style. Click outside the chart window to get a better view.

Using a Chart in Other Programs

Throughout this book, you have heard a lot about how versatile Office 97 programs are and how the suite programs can work together. This ability to share resources is one of the key strengths of modern programs such as those that come with Office 97. The programs use a concept called Object Linking and Embedding (OLE) to make office integration a true reality.

A chart is often the last step in your handling of important data. A chart keeps all your data in a neat, presentable package ready for show and tell. You can share an Excel chart with other programs to produce more advanced documents. For instance, if you were writing an article in Word about the North American Buffalo population, you could include an Excel line chart that illustrated the many ups and downs of these animals. Or you could include fiscal data charts in a PowerPoint presentation for your company's board of directors.

Basically, you can place an Excel chart into another document in two ways. The simplest is to copy the chart and then paste it into a Word document. If you want to edit a chart you've pasted into a document of another application, simply double-click it. A new Excel document window opens and allows you to edit the chart. However, you should note that if using the copy and paste method, you're editing only a *copy* of the original chart.

The other method involves *linking* the chart. When you link a chart, it retains a link to the original source of the data. If you update data in the original source document, the chart you copied will be automatically updated as well. With this method, when you double-click the chart to edit it, the chart's original source document opens.

The figures on the following page show you how to link a chart from your Excel document into a Word document. (Although not specifically demonstrated, the technique for simply pasting a chart into a document is quite similar.)

TAKE NOTE

▶ THE OLE CONCEPT

With OLE, elements of every program you use in Windows become known as objects. These objects are interchangable between programs, so that a program becomes little more than a toolbox, and the objects are the tools. In practical terms, it means that you can use an Excel worksheet in virtually any other Office program you wish, and vice versa.

▶ UPDATING LINKED FILES

Linked files should update every time you open the document where the linked object was pasted. If you believe that linked items have not been updated, click Edit ⇨ Links on the menu bar. Click Update Now in the dialog box that appears, and then click OK.

CROSS-REFERENCE

See "Copying and Moving Objects" in Chapter 5 to learn more about copying-and-pasting.

FIND IT ONLINE

Accounting Advisors offer Excel tips at
http://www.accountingadvisors.com/exceltip.html.

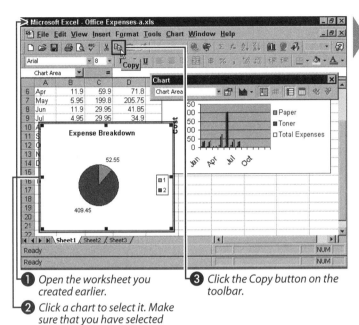

1 Open the worksheet you created earlier.

2 Click a chart to select it. Make sure that you have selected the whole chart, rather than just an element within it.

3 Click the Copy button on the toolbar.

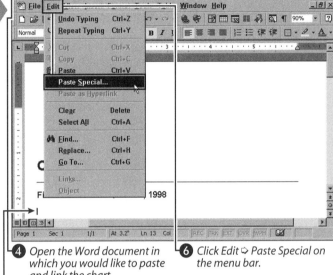

4 Open the Word document in which you would like to paste and link the chart.

5 Place the cursor where you want the chart to appear.

6 Click Edit ➪ Paste Special on the menu bar.

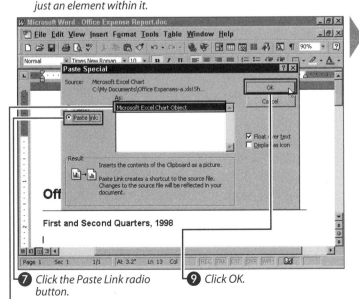

7 Click the Paste Link radio button.

8 Select Microsoft Excel Chart Object here.

9 Click OK.

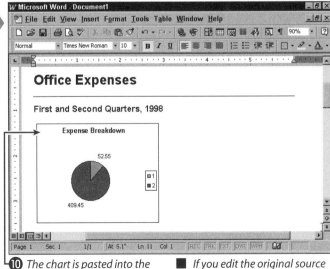

10 The chart is pasted into the document. Click outside the object to deselect it.

■ If you edit the original source document, or open the chart from within Word and edit it, both original and linked charts are updated.

Changing the Size of Charts

So far in this chapter, you have learned how to graph data in Excel by creating charts and how to change the appearance of those charts so that they better conform to your specific needs. You have even learned how to use Excel charts in other programs, an important skill if you want to take advantage of the powerful application sharing technology available to you with Office 97.

However, before your Excel documents are complete, you should check one more thing. Are all of the beautiful charts you've worked so hard to create the right size for you? Are they in the best position within the document? Chances are, most of the charts you have created still need a little tweaking in this area.

When you change the size of a chart, you have many things to consider. For example, when you resize a chart window, keep in mind that you are really only resizing the white space that the chart lives in. All of the elements within the chart — the legend, title, axis labels, and the chart itself — can be individually sized. Although at first this may seem like a pain, it can actually be a good thing. This way you can choose the size of the chart elements, shrinking things you think are less critical, and making the most important elements more prominent.

Generally speaking, most of the moving and resizing you will do with Excel charts is done in the same way as objects such as pictures and graphics. When you select the chart, it gains a border and handles on the sides and corners. These handles are used to change the size and shape of the chart window and elements. The corner handles change the size of two sides at once.

The first two figures on the facing page show you how to change the size of your Excel charts and chart elements. The last two figures demonstrate a method for moving items around inside a chart to change its appearance.

TAKE NOTE

▶ MOVING CHART ELEMENTS AROUND

When you select a chart element to move it, notice that a flashing border also appears around the chart window. Excel will not let you move elements, such as the title and legend, outside of the chart window.

▶ CONTROLLING THE HORIZONTAL AND THE VERTICAL

If you hold down the shift key as you move the chart window around your worksheet, it only moves directly on a horizontal or vertical plane, depending upon which direction you're moving your mouse.

CROSS-REFERENCE
See "Using Drag and Drop" in Chapter 5 to learn more about dragging items with the mouse pointer.

FIND IT ONLINE
Virtual Data at **http://www.virtualdata.com/** offers a VRML (Virtual Reality Modeling Language) charting plug-in for Excel.

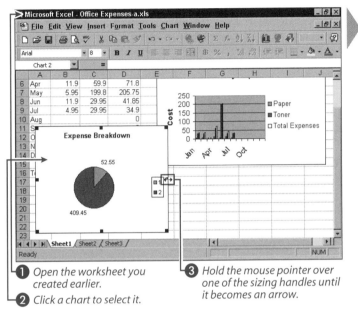

① Open the worksheet you created earlier.

② Click a chart to select it.

③ Hold the mouse pointer over one of the sizing handles until it becomes an arrow.

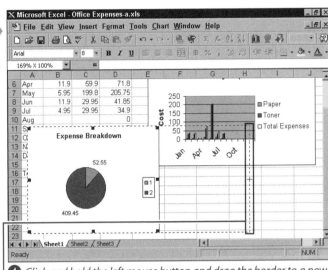

④ Click and hold the left mouse button and drag the border to a new size. Release the mouse button when you have achieved the desired size.

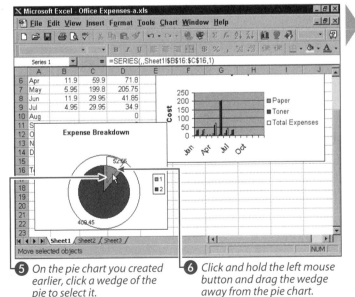

⑤ On the pie chart you created earlier, click a wedge of the pie to select it.

⑥ Click and hold the left mouse button and drag the wedge away from the pie chart.

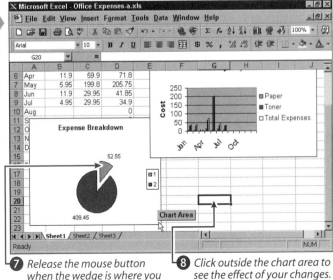

⑦ Release the mouse button when the wedge is where you want it.

⑧ Click outside the chart area to see the effect of your changes.

275

Personal Workbook

Q&A

1 What must you do before starting the Chart Wizard?

_____

_____

2 What kind of data works best with a pie chart?

_____

_____

_____

3 Why would a month-by-month record of expenses not work very well with a pie chart?

_____

_____

_____

4 What will happen to your chart if you update the data on the worksheet?

_____

_____

_____

5 How do you change the text of a chart title?

_____

_____

_____

6 Can you use an Excel chart in a Word document? How?

_____

_____

_____

7 How do you move chart objects around on your worksheet?

_____

_____

_____

8 Can the size of a chart be modified?

_____

_____

_____

ANSWERS: PAGE 414

EXTRA PRACTICE

① Create a worksheet that lists the number of hours you spent sleeping each day for the past week.

② Graph that data so that it shows a day-by-day trend.

③ Insert a copy of your graph into a Word document.

④ Change the size of the graph so that it is bigger.

⑤ Change the data on your worksheet and confirm that the charts were updated as well.

⑥ Change the position of your graph.

REAL-WORLD APPLICATIONS

✔ Charts and graphs are an important part of your professional life, especially if you have to present information to large groups of people. If you need to convince a room full of prospective customers, bring along some charts that illustrate the benefits of your product or service.

✔ If you need to produce a productivity report for your office, use a chart to graph how much work was done when. You may even be able to use that chart to analyze and identify slow trends in production that need to be improved.

✔ Managing your personal budget is an important task, but challenging to do well. Try making a pie chart that represents your monthly income and how it is spent to better see where all your hard-earned cash is going!

Visual Quiz

What kind of chart is the round one? What do the different colored areas represent? How do you move a chart like this so that it's not in the way? How do you change the style of chart being used? Can you change the data labels on the round chart? How?

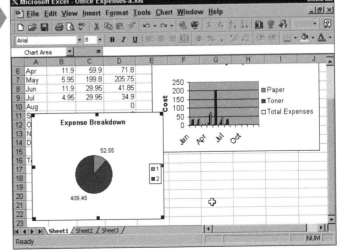

PART

IV

Learning Important PowerPoint Tasks

PowerPoint is a business tool for creating visual aids for presentations. You can either print the information on transparencies, create 35mm slides, or show the presentation on a computer screen. The latter provides the most punch because with an onscreen computerized show, you can include sounds, video clips, and animations that make your audience sit up and take notice.

In this part of the book, you learn how to create a basic presentation on any subject and dress it up with the perfect color scheme and formatting choices. PowerPoint comes with many design templates containing formatting and coloring schemes, and you can apply them to your presentation with a few simple mouse clicks. You also learn about adding sounds and videos to spice up a presentation, transitioning between slides, and rearranging the order of your slides.

Lastly, you learn how to work the controls to show your presentation on a computer screen. You can do much more than just shuffle forward and backward! You can jump to a particular slide quickly, blank out the screen temporarily during a discussion, and even draw on the screen with the mouse pointer to emphasize important points.

CHAPTER **18**

MASTER THESE SKILLS

▶ **Creating a Simple Presentation**

▶ **Editing Presentation Text**

▶ **Adding Graphics to a Slide**

▶ **Changing a Slide's Layout**

▶ **Changing the Design and Color Scheme**

Creating a Presentation

PowerPoint is a presentation creation program; it creates good-looking slides, overhead transparencies, or computer-screen shows that can help you sell your product, inform people about organizational changes, motivate workers, or just about any other business communication task.

This chapter and the next one are closely related. In this chapter, you start a new presentation, and start building your content. In the following chapter, you learn how to add special effects to your show and how to present it to your audience using PowerPoint.

Die-hard do-it-yourselfers can start out with a blank PowerPoint presentation and build just what they want from scratch, but the majority of us don't have that kind of time. So this chapter will focus on using one of PowerPoint's pre-designed templates to start a new show. These templates include background designs and fonts chosen to work well together, and in some cases they include sample text, also, to help folks who aren't sure what information needs to be included.

After you've chosen your template, the next task is to enter your text. Text, usually in the format of bulleted lists, forms the bulk of most presentations. A typical slide might contain a heading and several bullet points, which would be discussed and expanded upon in the lecture given by a live speaker. If you are designing a presentation for distribution on the Internet or in some other non-live way, you will need to put more information on each slide.

After you enter your text, you will want to take a look at each slide's layout. Does it adequately present the message? If not, you'll want to change its layout, perhaps to include a graphic, chart, or other object, or to lay out its bulleted list in two columns. Many layout options are available, and you can also create your own layout by starting with a blank layout and manually adding items to it.

Sometimes text is not enough; you may need graphics to drive home your message. This chapter will show you how to place a graphic on your slide, which can include clip art, a graphic image from a file, a graph, or an organizational chart.

Creating a Simple Presentation

You can start a presentation in one of three ways: by using the AutoContent Wizard, by using a template, or by starting from scratch. Hardly anybody ever starts from scratch because it's a lot of work; most people start from a template.

The AutoContent Wizard is the most foolproof, full-service method, and it's great for beginners! It takes a bit more time than the other methods, and you don't get to choose the formatting you want, but it is a good idea for first-time users who don't have a clue about how PowerPoint works. The first time you use PowerPoint, you should create a dummy presentation using the AutoContent Wizard, just to see what it's like. (We won't cover this step-by-step in this book, because it really is foolproof.)

The next-easiest method is using a Presentation template. These templates contain both formatting and sample text, so when you start a presentation based on one of them, you already have over a dozen slides in place, with text suggestions on each one. All you have to do is edit the sample text. This is the method demonstrated in this chapter.

Most Presentation templates have two versions: Standard and Online. Unless you are designing a presentation for Internet use, stick with the Standard ones.

More complicated than the Presentation template method is the use of Presentation Design templates. These templates contain formatting only, no sample slides, so you have to add your own slides, but you can add exactly the slides you want. When you first create such a presentation, the New Slide dialog box pops up right away, so you can choose the first slide layout. After that, you can add new slides by clicking the New Slide button, or typing text in Outline view (as explained in the next task, "Editing Presentation Text").

TAKE NOTE

▶ NEW BUTTON ON TOOLBAR

The New button on the toolbar starts a new, blank presentation. Don't use it unless you want a presentation that doesn't use a template.

▶ STEALING FORMATTING FROM ANOTHER TEMPLATE

If you need sample text, choose a Presentation template that has the appropriate text. Don't worry about its formatting. Then, after creating the new presentation, steal the formatting from a different template with the Format ⇨ Apply Design command.

▶ POWERPOINT DIALOG BOX AT STARTUP

When you start PowerPoint, a PowerPoint dialog box appears, in which you can choose to create a blank presentation, use a template, or use the AutoContent Wizard. This dialog box opens only when you start the program. If you close it, you will not see it again until next time you start PowerPoint. If you see it onscreen, click Template and start at Step 2 on the facing page.

CROSS-REFERENCE

To learn how to start PowerPoint, see "Opening and Closing the Programs" in Chapter 1.

FIND IT ONLINE

Download additional Presentation templates from the Microsoft Web site. Choose Help ⇨ Microsoft on the Web ⇨ Free Stuff.

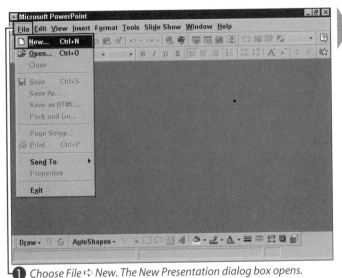

❶ *Choose File ⇨ New. The New Presentation dialog box opens.*

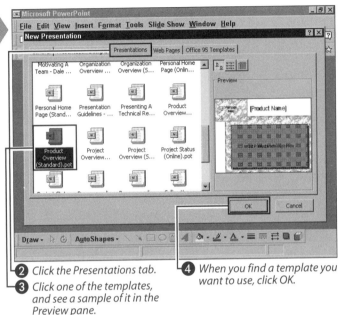

❷ *Click the Presentations tab.*

❸ *Click one of the templates, and see a sample of it in the Preview pane.*

❹ *When you find a template you want to use, click OK.*

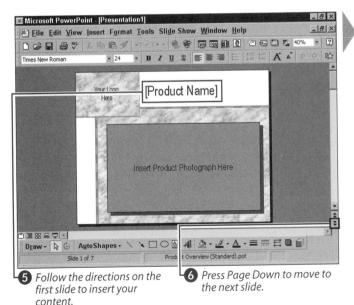

❺ *Follow the directions on the first slide to insert your content.*

❻ *Press Page Down to move to the next slide.*

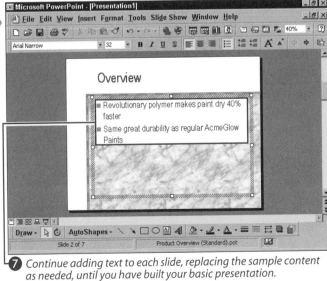

❼ *Continue adding text to each slide, replacing the sample content as needed, until you have built your basic presentation.*

Editing Presentation Text

Text editing is best done in Outline view, where you can see all the text from all the slides in a single outline. If you are creating a presentation from scratch, or using a Presentation Design template, you may want to type your text first in Outline view, and then switch to Slide view to check it out. To change to Outline view, choose View ➪ Outline or click the Outline View button in the bottom-left corner of the PowerPoint window, and then edit your text. Here's where the outlining skills discussed in Chapter 12 of this book will come in handy; a PowerPoint outline works a lot like a Word one. You can see in a Slide Miniature window how the slide will look in Slide view.

From within Outline view, you can also rearrange and delete text (and even entire slides). Just drag content up or down, as demonstrated with Word outlines in Chapter 12. If you promote a line of text to a first-level heading in the outline, it becomes its own slide. If you delete all the lines of text for a slide, the slide is removed from the presentation (unless the slide has some other content, such as a graphic, that you have added).

You can also edit text in Slide view, as you saw in the preceding task. Just select the existing text and type over it. (The other two views, Slide Sorter and Slide Show, do not allow text editing. You get a chance to look at those views in Chapter 19.) To add a new block of text to a slide in Slide view, click the Text Box button on the Drawing toolbar (the toolbar at the bottom of the screen) and drag your mouse pointer on the slide to show where you want the text box to go. You can then click inside it and type text.

TAKE NOTE

▶ FORMATTING TEXT

You can use all the usual toolbar tools for formatting text: the Font and Font Size drop-down lists and the Bold, Italic, and Underline buttons. The Formatting toolbar also includes Increase Font Size and Decrease Font Size buttons, as well as a Shadow button that adds a shadow effect to text. However, try not to make formatting inconsistent from slide to slide.

▶ TEXT BOX PLACEHOLDERS

On a simple Bullet list slide, there is one placeholder box for body text. If you want two bulleted lists side-by-side, change the slide's layout (Format ➪ Slide Layout) to a two-list layout.

▶ THE MIRACLE OF UNDO

Don't forget to take advantage of the Undo and Redo buttons (located on the Outline view toolbar) as you edit your presentation text.

CROSS-REFERENCE
To learn more about working with outlines, see "Editing an Outline" in Chapter 12.

FIND IT ONLINE
For information on text and outline view, see http://support.microsoft.com/support/kb/articles/q186/7/28.asp

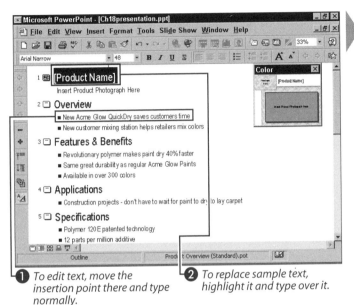

① To edit text, move the insertion point there and type normally.

② To replace sample text, highlight it and type over it.

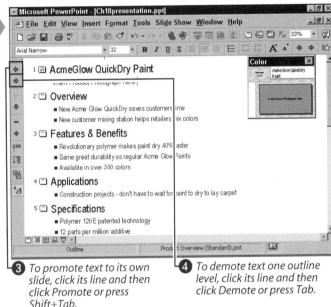

③ To promote text to its own slide, click its line and then click Promote or press Shift+Tab.

④ To demote text one outline level, click its line and then click Demote or press Tab.

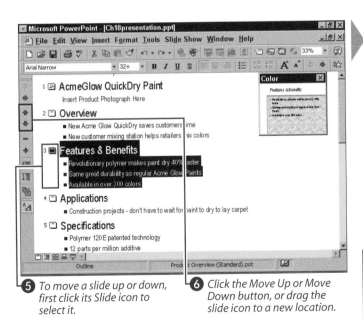

⑤ To move a slide up or down, first click its Slide icon to select it.

⑥ Click the Move Up or Move Down button, or drag the slide icon to a new location.

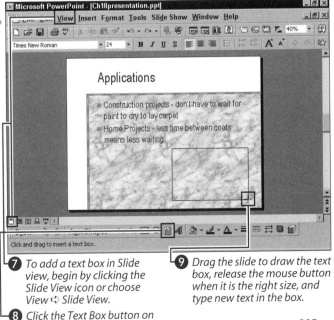

⑦ To add a text box in Slide view, begin by clicking the Slide View icon or choose View ➪ Slide View.

⑧ Click the Text Box button on the Drawing toolbar.

⑨ Drag the slide to draw the text box, release the mouse button when it is the right size, and type new text in the box.

Adding Graphics to a Slide

Graphics can be important components of a presentation. Clip art and other graphics files, as mentioned in Chapter 9, can add interest to an otherwise dull page. Charts can illustrate numerical data graphically, and organizational charts can help people understand a structure or a flowchart.

When you add new slides to a presentation using the New Slide button (or the Insert ⇨ New Slide command), you can choose a layout that contains clip art, a chart, or an organization chart placeholder. You can just click that placeholder to open a dialog box that enables you to choose the graphic. There are different layouts for bullets plus graphics, bullets plus charts, charts alone, and organizational charts alone.

You can also manually place any kind of graphic object on a slide, without a specific placeholder area to put it in. The way you do this depends on the type of object you want to place; the Insert ⇨ Picture submenu has separate commands that enable you to insert clip art, graphics from a file, an organization chart, an AutoShape, an image from a scanner, WordArt, and a Microsoft Word table. Many of these object types have already been dealt with earlier in this book. (Chapter 9 is especially rich in information about graphics.) You can insert a chart with the Insert ⇨ Chart command.

When you place a graphics image, a text box, a chart, or another item on a slide, it becomes an object. *Object* is PowerPoint's generic term for something that sits on a slide in its own box. As discussed in Chapter 9, you can resize an object by dragging the selection handles on its box. And you can move an object around by clicking within the object box and dragging. You can also change the properties of an object by right-clicking it and choosing Properties or one of the other editing commands on its shortcut menu.

TAKE NOTE

▶ PLACING AUTOSHAPES

The Insert ⇨ Picture ⇨ AutoShapes command opens an AutoShapes toolbar, from which you can select from dozens of predrawn shapes on your slide, such as caption bubbles, starbursts, arrows, and flowchart symbols.

▶ ORGANIZATION CHARTS

Placing an organization chart opens a separate program called Microsoft Organization Chart. You can use it to create great-looking organization charts. You can fudge a simple flowchart with it, too, but if you make lots of flowcharts, consider using a separate program to create them and then pasting them into PowerPoint.

▶ CHARTS AND GRAPHS

When you add a chart, Microsoft Graph, a separate program that helps you create charts and graphs, opens. If you already have a chart that you have created in another program (Excel, for example), you may prefer to insert it instead; just use the Clipboard to copy it over to PowerPoint.

CROSS-REFERENCE

For information about WordArt, clip art, and image files, see Chapter 9.

FIND IT ONLINE

An excellent flowchart program called RFFlow can be found at **http://www.rff.com**.

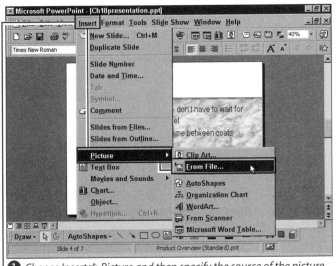

1 Choose Insert ➪ Picture and then specify the source of the picture you want to insert. For this example, choose From File.

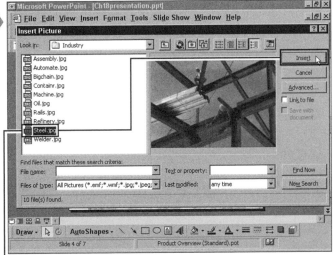

2 Using the dialog box that appears, choose a picture and place it on your slide. (The exact procedure varies depending on the graphic type.)

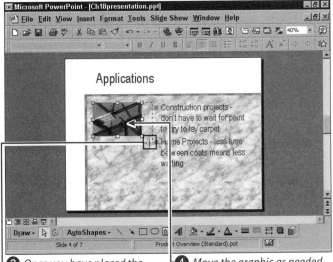

3 Once you have placed the graphic on the slide, resize it as needed by dragging its corner selection handles.

4 Move the graphic as needed by dragging it by any part except a selection handle.

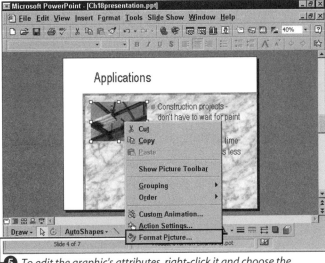

5 To edit the graphic's attributes, right-click it and choose the Format command from the shortcut menu. (The commands vary for different graphic types.)

Changing a Slide's Layout

A slide's layout refers to the size and position of the default text and graphic object boxes that appear on it. You choose a slide's layout each time you create a new slide with the Insert ⇨ New Slide command. If you create new slides from Outline view, they are assigned a default layout, which is a simple heading plus a single-column bulleted list. If you created your presentation based on a Presentation template, the slides may have all been created for you, so you may not have had the opportunity to create new slides yet.

You can change a slide's layout at any time. For example, suppose you have several slides that use the heading-plus-bullets default layout. This layout can get pretty boring if your whole presentation consists of nothing but that! You can add interest to your presentation by making some slides with a different layout. It can be as simple as taking a plain bulleted list slide, converting it to a bullets-plus-clip art layout. Then choose a relevant piece of clip art to be placed beside the bullets, and violà! Instant interest. The figures on the facing page show how to change a slide's layout.

You can also make changes to a slide layout manually, without selecting a different layout. Just move or resize the frames on the slide, the same way you do

any other objects. (Drag the selection handles to resize; drag any other part to move.) The only thing you cannot do on a layout is delete a frame completely; for example, if you have selected a layout that consists of a placeholder for text and a placeholder for a piece of clip art, and you decide you don't want the clip art after all, you can't delete the clip art placeholder box. You must instead change the layout to one that doesn't employ clip art.

TAKE NOTE

▶ MORE LAYOUTS

Many more layouts are available than those you see at first glance in the Slide Layout dialog box. A scroll bar appears to the right of the layouts; scroll down for several additional choices. Some of the placeholders on the layouts you see when you scroll down are designated for Objects, which can be anything, as you learned in the preceding task. When you double-click on one of these placeholders, the Insert Object dialog box appears, and you can choose any object type for any program installed on your PC.

▶ TOOLBAR BUTTON ALTERNATIVE

Instead of choosing Format ⇨ Slide Layout, you can click the Slide Layout button on the toolbar.

CROSS-REFERENCE

To change the placement of the placeholders on each slide, see "Ensuring Consistency with Masters" in Chapter 19.

SHORTCUT

Use the scroll bar to see more AutoLayout choices.

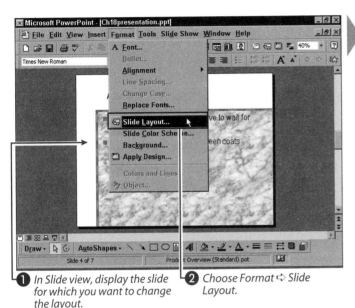

1 In Slide view, display the slide for which you want to change the layout.

2 Choose Format ⇨ Slide Layout.

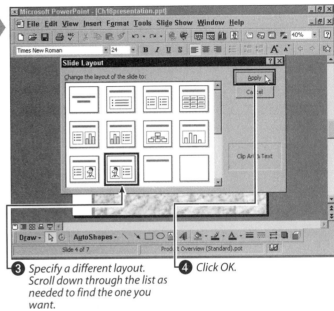

3 Specify a different layout. Scroll down through the list as needed to find the one you want.

4 Click OK.

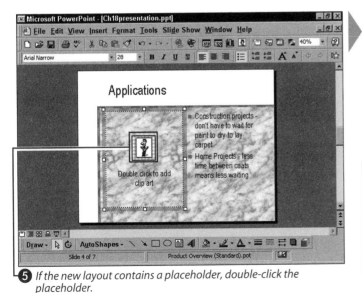

5 If the new layout contains a placeholder, double-click the placeholder.

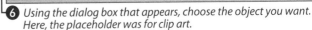

6 Using the dialog box that appears, choose the object you want. Here, the placeholder was for clip art.

Changing the Design and Color Scheme

The design of the presentation consists of the collection of formatting it inherited from the template you started with. The design includes the background colors and images, the positioning of the text and graphics placeholder boxes on the various layouts, and the fonts and font sizes/colors used. You can change any of these features manually for any and all slides, but it is faster and ensures more consistency to simply borrow the design from a different template.

Use the Apply Design dialog box to change to a different template's design (as shown on the facing page). The first time you use this dialog box, the contents of the Presentation Designs folder will probably appear. You aren't limited to these designs; you can switch to the Presentations folder and choose from among the designs that come with those templates, too. (To quickly switch to the Presentations folder, click the Up One Level button and then double-click on the Presentations folder.) Borrowing the design from a Presentation template will not impose the sample text from that template on your presentation; it merely copies the formatting from it.

You can also change the color scheme for your slides, without changing the whole design template. Each design comes with at least three color scheme choices: dark background, light background, and black-and-white. Dark background is best for slides shown on a slide projector or computer screen; light background is best for overhead transparencies and handouts. Black-and-white may be your only recourse if you are going to print the slides on a black-and-white printer. The bottom figures on the facing page demonstrate how to change color schemes.

TAKE NOTE

UNDO IS AVAILABLE

If you decide you don't like a design or color scheme, press Ctrl+Z after selecting it to undo it.

MULTIPLE LEVEL UNDO

Ctrl+Z undoes the most recent action. To undo multiple previous actions, such as the last four actions you've performed, open the Undo toolbar button's drop-down list and select the actions you want to undo.

CUSTOM COLOR SCHEMES

The Custom tab in the Slide Color Scheme dialog box enables you to specify exact colors to be used for various elements on your slides. This is an awful lot of work, however, unless you need to be picky about individual colors for some reason (such as to match your company's official colors).

CROSS-REFERENCE

See "Using Fancy Transitions" in Chapter 19 for information on all kinds of fun ways to get from slide A to slide B.

FIND IT ONLINE

Check out **http://www.dccc.edu/frr/HTML/PwrPoint** for a tutorial on changing slides.

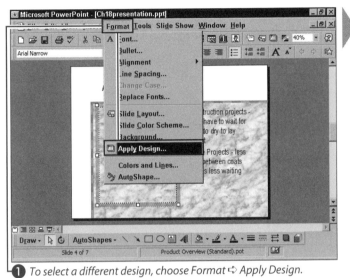

1 To select a different design, choose Format ➪ Apply Design.

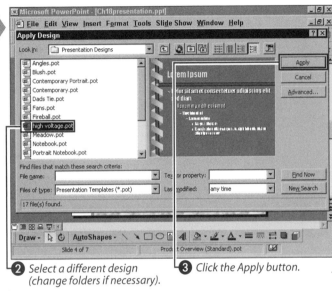

2 Select a different design (change folders if necessary). **3** Click the Apply button.

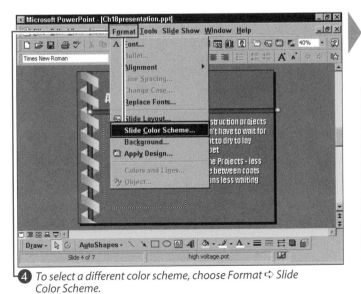

4 To select a different color scheme, choose Format ➪ Slide Color Scheme.

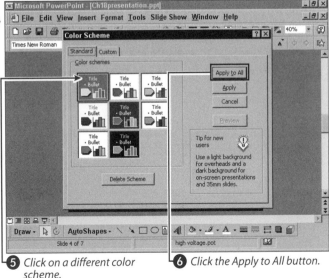

5 Click on a different color scheme. **6** Click the Apply to All button.

Personal Workbook

Q&A

1 What are the two kinds of templates you can use to create a presentation and how are they different?

_____

_____

_____

2 Once you've started a presentation in a particular template, how do you pick up a design (colors, background, and so on) from a different template?

_____

_____

_____

3 After you close the PowerPoint dialog box that appears when you start the program, how do you open it again?

_____

_____

4 Which view is best for editing slide text?

_____

_____

_____

5 There are three ways to place a graph on a slide. Name two of them.

_____

_____

_____

6 True or false: To move a picture, drag one of its selection handles.

_____

_____

7 True or false: The New button on the toolbar inserts a new slide in your presentation.

_____

_____

8 What is the difference between a layout and a design?

_____

_____

_____

ANSWERS: PAGE 414

EXTRA PRACTICE

1. Create a presentation with the AutoContent Wizard. Try to create the same presentation using a Presentation template.

2. Change the design of your presentation to one from a different template.

3. Insert a text box manually on a slide. Type some text in it. Change the layout of the slide and notice what happens to your text box.

4. Insert a graphic manually on a slide that uses a heading-and-bullets layout. Resize the text box to make room for the graphic.

5. Take the slide you created in Step 4 and apply a layout to it that includes a placeholder for a graphic. Notice what happens to your manually placed one.

REAL-WORLD APPLICATIONS

✔ Because you're the most computer-savvy employee in the sales department of XYZ company, it is your responsibility to use PowerPoint to create sales presentations. To streamline the process, you create a basic presentation containing slides that are always used, such as a title slide with the company's name and logo. You or others can customize the basic presentation by inserting new slides in the appropriate places. In addition, you create a new folder for presentations that are used frequently in the C:\Program Files\Microsoft Office\Templates folder.

✔ A coworker who was responsible for creating the presentation for an important potential client is out sick, and the boss has drafted you to do the work. Fortunately, you're familiar with the various Presentation Design templates, so you are able to finish the presentation in a snap.

Visual Quiz

This slide uses a very dark color scheme. What kinds of presentations would it be good for? What would it not be appropriate for?

_____

_____

_____

_____

_____

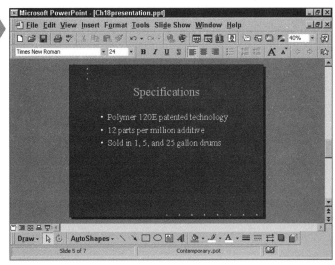

CHAPTER **19**

Fine-Tuning and Presenting a Show

Now that you have a basic PowerPoint presentation, you're ready to polish it up and present it to your audience. And what, exactly, does that entail? For one, you will want to check for consistency in all of your slides, for example, you'll want to see that all your backgrounds and fonts are the same so the audience is not distracted by the differences. You'll also want to run through your presentation to make sure you are happy with the arrangement of slides, to ensure the order is logical. You can also use advanced techniques to add sound and animations to your presentation, to make things more lively. That's what you learn in this chapter.

If you need to make a global change to the layout of all the slides in your presentation, such as adding page numbers or the company name, the best approach is to make the change on the Slide Master. Besides the Slide Master, there are also masters for handouts, speaker notes, and title slides.

You can enhance an onscreen presentation by adding transitions and animations to your show. Transitions are animated movements between slides. For example, when you advance from slide 1 to slide 2, a transition can make slide 1 appear to be dropping down as slide 2 drops in from the top. Dozens of transition effects are available. Animations are similar to transitions, except they affect individual objects on a slide. For example, you can animate a bulleted list so that each bullet point flies in from the left one by one.

Sound and video clips can enhance your show, too. You might include a video clip you recorded with a video camera of your CEO giving a speech, for example. Also, you might use whimsical sounds to lighten the mood, or play an audio track from a CD as a soundtrack to your presentation. You can even create your own video clips (called movies in PowerPoint parlance) with a 3-D animation program.

When you're ready to go, start the presentation by entering Slide Show view. Various navigational techniques, presented in this chapter, enable you to move quickly to any slide in the presentation. After the last slide, Normal view automatically reappears, but you can end the slide show early if you want by pressing Esc.

Ensuring Consistency with Masters

When you're presenting a slide show, you want people to focus on the content of each slide. If you have different backgrounds, colors, and so forth on each slide, the first thing people may notice is the formatting, and your message will get lost. That's why it's important to make the formatting of each slide consistent, so the only thing the audience will notice is the message.

Applying the designs presented in the preceding chapter is one way to ensure consistency. Another way is to work with the Slide Master rather than individual slides whenever you make formatting changes.

The Slide Master is like the presentation-wide layout template; it specifies where text boxes, graphics, and so on will be placed. Every slide that has a single bulleted list, for example, starts that list in exactly the same position on each slide, because that's where the Slide Master indicates it should start.

The Slide Master stores whatever formatting your chosen template design specifies. If you want to modify something about the design template you are using, such as switching the font used for headings, make the change on the Slide Master to apply the change to every slide.

If you want to add something to every slide, such as your company logo, you could manually place a graphic on every slide. However, you would not be able to ensure the placement will be exactly the same on each page. If, on the other hand, you place that graphic on the Slide Master, every slide in your presentation will show that graphic in the same spot.

To make changes, open Slide Master, make any alterations to the sample text there, and add any graphics that you want to include on each slide. After making your changes, exit Slide Master and return to normal slide editing.

TAKE NOTE

NEW DESIGN OVERRIDES CUSTOM SLIDE MASTER SETTINGS

If you make changes to the Slide Master, and then choose a different design (Format ⇨ Apply Design), your changes will be overridden by the new design. Make sure you have chosen the correct design for your presentation before you edit the Slide Master.

TITLE MASTER

The Title Master enables you to edit slides based on the Title layout which is different from the others. If you do not edit the Title Master (View ⇨ Master ⇨ Title Master), the title slides will have the same formatting as the regular slides.

IMPORT CONSIDERATIONS

When you import an outline created in a word-processing program, the slide master in the current presentation determines the format for the title and text.

CROSS-REFERENCE

If you want to add a graphic to the Slide Master, see Chapter 9.

FIND IT ONLINE

More on Title Master: http://support.microsoft.com/support/kb/articles/q158/4/44.asp.

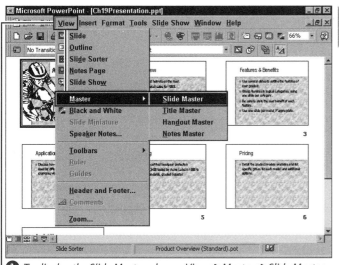

① To display the Slide Master, choose View ➪ Master ➪ Slide Master.

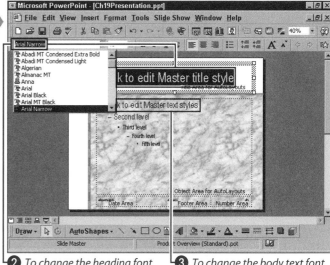

② To change the heading font or size, select the heading and use the controls on the Formatting toolbar to change its formatting.

③ To change the body text font or size, select the text and change its formatting the same way.

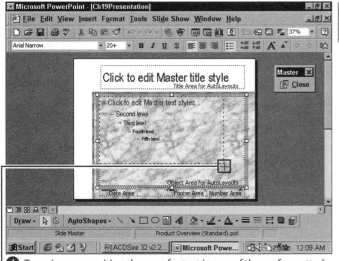

④ To resize or reposition the area for text in one of the preformatted slide layouts, move or resize the large text box in which the bulleted items appear.

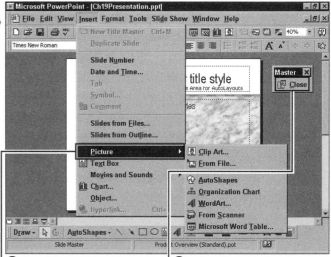

⑤ To add a graphic to the Slide Master, use the Insert ➪ Picture command and insert the graphic.

⑥ When finished editing the Slide Master, click the Close button.

Rearranging and Deleting Slides

If you created your presentation based on a design, you are already familiar with adding slides. You can add them either by typing new text in Outline view (and promoting the lines to the highest outline level to make them slides), or by using the New Slide toolbar button or menu command and choosing a new slide layout (as detailed in Chapter 18).

The best way to rearrange slides is to do so in Slide Sorter view. In this view, the slides in your presentation appear in thumbnail view. A thumbnail is a miniature version of your slide. So, the Sorter view displays as many slides in your presentation as it can. You can move the thumbnails around on the screen to different positions, just as you would rearrange pasted-up artwork by hand. Rearranging slides in Slide Sorter allows you to determine the best flow of your presentation. To move a slide in Slide Sorter view, just drag it and drop it where you want. PowerPoint automatically updates the order of your slides.

After you have created your slides, you may decide that you want to delete some of them. There are a number of ways to delete a slide. In addition to the methods on the facing page, you can display the slide in Slide Sorter or Outline view, select the slide's text, and use the Delete command.

CROSS-REFERENCE

Slide Sorter view is best for assigning transitions to slides, as discussed in the section, "Using Transitions."

FIND IT ONLINE

More hidden slides: **http://support.microsoft.com/ support/kb/articles/q119/5/77.asp.**

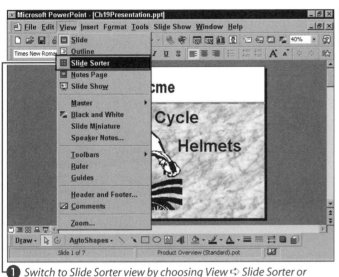

① *Switch to Slide Sorter view by choosing View ⇨ Slide Sorter or clicking the Slide Sorter View button.*

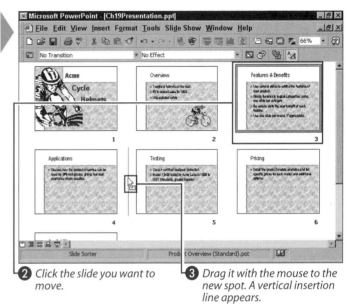

② *Click the slide you want to move.*

③ *Drag it with the mouse to the new spot. A vertical insertion line appears.*

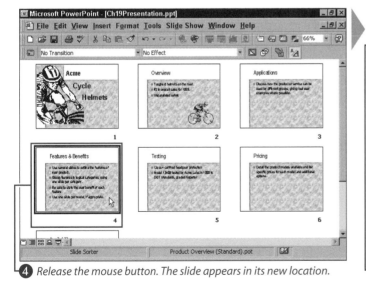

④ *Release the mouse button. The slide appears in its new location.*

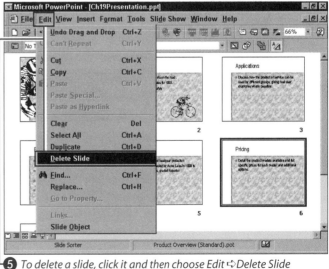

⑤ *To delete a slide, click it and then choose Edit ⇨ Delete Slide or press the Delete key.*

Using Fancy Transitions

Transitions are how you get from slide A to slide B. Back in the old slide projector days, there was only one transition: The old slide got pushed out and the new slide plunked into place. But with a computerized presentation, you can choose from all kinds of fun transitions, including wipes, blinds, dissolves, and much more.

Your best bet is to play with these transitions and see what each one does. The default transition is No Transition, which simply replaces one slide with another. To set up a transition, you use the Slide Transition dialog box.

In Slide Sorter view, you can open the Slide Transition dialog box as explained on the facing page. In the Slide Transition dialog box, a sample picture appears in the Effect area. Choose an effect from the drop-down list, and PowerPoint shows that effect in action on the sample. If you miss it, click the picture to see it again.

On the list of transitions that you work with, you'll notice that many of the transitions have multiple directions or orientations. For example, you might see Wipe Left, Wipe Right, Wipe Up, and Wipe Down. You can also choose the transition speed from the option buttons below the drop-down list of effects. That way you can specify exactly how you want the transition to work.

The Advance controls at the bottom of the Slide Transition dialog box influence when the move from one slide to the next will occur. The default is On mouse click, which means PowerPoint will wait for a mouse click before advancing the show. This is best for a speaker-led presentation. If you prefer, you can make the slide advance automatically by choosing Automatically, after ___ seconds and supplying a number. You can have both options selected to have the slide show advance either on your signal or after the specified time, whichever comes first.

TAKE NOTE

▶ TRANSITION SOUNDS

You can also associate a sound with the transition. Just choose a sound from the Sound drop-down list in the Slide Transition dialog box. When you assign a sound to the transition, the sound simply plays whenever the transition occurs. There is no special icon on the slide to click to play the sound. This is different from placing a sound or video clip on the slide itself, so that the sound is part of the slide content.

▶ TRANSITION SHORTCUT

You can open the Transition drop-down list on the Formatting toolbar in Slide Sorter view to choose a transition quickly. With this method, though, you don't get to set any of the other options shown in the steps on the following page.

CROSS-REFERENCE

To view the slide show as a whole, see "Running a Show" later in this chapter.

SHORTCUT

In Slide Sorter view, you can choose a transition from the Transitions drop-down list on the toolbar.

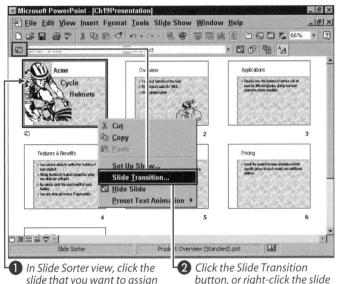

1 In Slide Sorter view, click the slide that you want to assign a transition to. The transition will be between this slide and the one that follows it.

2 Click the Slide Transition button, or right-click the slide and choose Slide Transition.

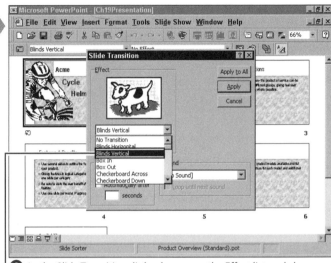

3 In the Slide Transition dialog box, open the Effect list and choose an effect.

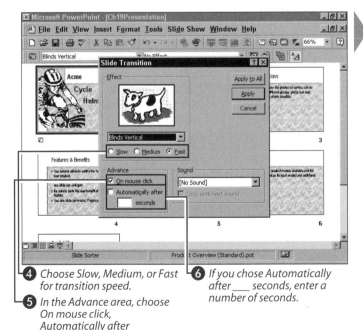

4 Choose Slow, Medium, or Fast for transition speed.

5 In the Advance area, choose On mouse click, Automatically after ___ seconds, or both.

6 If you chose Automatically after ___ seconds, enter a number of seconds.

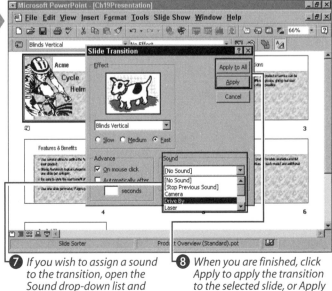

7 If you wish to assign a sound to the transition, open the Sound drop-down list and choose a sound.

8 When you are finished, click Apply to apply the transition to the selected slide, or Apply to All to use the same transition for all slides.

301

Using Animations

If transitions are the big picture, then animations are the close-up view. Transitions are actions that happen to move from one slide to another, and animations are actions that happen to move the focus from one object on a single slide to another object on that same slide.

For example, suppose you have a slide that contains a bullet list of three items. You could show all three bullets at once, but wouldn't it be more interesting to have each bullet fly in one at a time? That's easy to do with animation. You can also dim each bullet point when the next one comes into view, so you are, in effect, highlighting the current one. You can also animate parts of a Microsoft Graph chart, or make certain objects appear on the slide for a while and then disappear.

The easiest animation to assign is preset animation. This kind of animation is applied only to text, and it can be applied only in an all-or-nothing way to a slide. If you have more than one text box on the slide, you can pick any text box to apply animation to, and the rest of the text boxes will have that same animation.

You can assign preset animation from Slide Sorter view. A Text Preset Animation drop-down list appears on the Formatting toolbar in Slide Sorter view, and you can choose one of the dozens of preset text animations from it.

TAKE NOTE

CUSTOM ANIMATION

Custom animation is harder to set up, but much more powerful. With custom animation, you can animate each object on your slide separately, set animation timings, animate the elements on a chart, and more. You set custom animation from Slide view, not Slide Sorter. That's because custom animation must be set up separately for each slide. This book doesn't cover custom animation, but if you want to try it yourself, switch to Slide view and click the Animation Effects button on the toolbar or choose Slide Show ⇨ Custom Animation.

WHICH ITEMS ARE ANIMATED?

When you animate in Slide Sorter view, you don't get to choose which object on the slide is animated. If there is text on the slide, the text is animated. If there are two text boxes, one from a slide layout and one manually placed, the one from the layout is animated. For more control, set up the animation from Normal view with the Slide Show ⇨ Custom Animation command. This way you can choose exactly which elements are animated and which are not.

ANIMATING A CHART

To animate a chart you have created in Microsoft Graph, select it and then open the Custom Animation dialog box (Slide Show ⇨ Custom Animation). Use the Chart Effects tab's introduce Chart Elements drop-down list to specify how the elements of the chart should appear.

CROSS-REFERENCE

To control transitions between slides, see "Using Transitions" earlier in this chapter.

FIND IT ONLINE

See **http://support.microsoft.com/support/kb/articles/q171/6/82.asp** for help with Slide Sorter view.

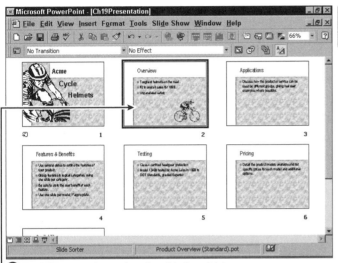

1 In Slide Sorter view, select the slide for which you want a preset animation. It must be a slide with a bulleted list on it.

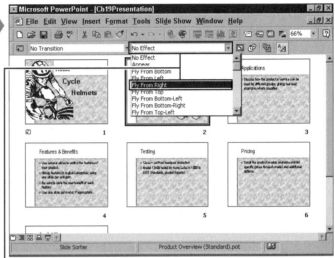

2 Open the Text Preset Animation drop-down list and choose an animation effect.

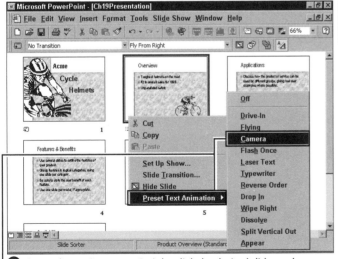

3 As an alternative to step 2, right-click the desired slide, and select Preset Animation. Click on the animation you want to use on the list.

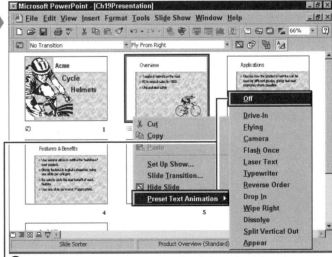

4 To remove a preset animation, right-click on the slide, select Preset Animation, and then select Off.

Adding Sounds and Videos

Sounds and videos can be added to a slide in much the same way that graphics are. And like graphics, sound and video clips sit on the slides in their own little resizable, movable frames.

When you place a sound clip on a slide, a little speaker icon appears on the slide to represent it. You can then click on that speaker during the presentation, or just point to it with the mouse, to hear the sound clip. When you place a video on a slide, the first frame of the video appears in a box. Then, during the presentation, you point to or click on that first frame to play the video. (You can specify which action — pointing or clicking — will activate the clip.)

You can insert sound or video clips either from the Clip Gallery or from your own files. The Office 97 CD comes with several video clips suitable for business presentations; if you place your Office 97 CD in your PC before opening the Clip Gallery, those extra clips will be available to you. (If you forget to put the CD in until after you have opened the Clip Gallery, you must close the Gallery and reopen it.) The facing page shows how to open the Clip Gallery to insert a sound or video. Next, use the Clip Gallery, as demonstated in Chapter 9, to select and insert a clip.

You can also insert sound or movie files of your own (ones you've created or recorded, or ones you've bought or downloaded from the Internet). To do this, use the Insert ⇨ Movies and Sounds ⇨ Movie from File or Sound from File command. Next, insert the clip the same way that you learned to insert a picture from a file in Chapter 9.

The steps on the following page show you how to insert a movie clip from the Clip Gallery. Insert your Office 97 CD in your computer before performing these steps.

TAKE NOTE

ASSOCIATING A SOUND WITH A GRAPHIC

Perhaps you would rather have your own picture than a speaker icon on the slide, on which you can click to play the slide. To do this, place the graphic where desired, right-click it and choose Action Settings. In the Action Settings dialog box, click the Play Sound checkbox on the Mouse Click tab, and choose a sound from the Play Sound drop-down list. If the sound you want doesn't appear on the list, click Other Sound and use the dialog box that appears in order to locate it.

CROSS-REFERENCE
To associate sounds with a transition, see "Using Transitions" earlier in this chapter.

FIND IT ONLINE
More on sounds: **http://support.microsoft.com/ support/kb/articles/q165/4/16.asp**.

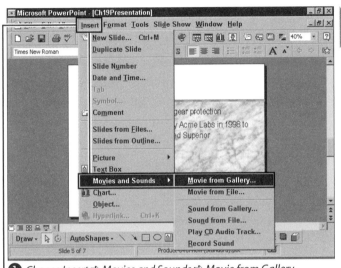

1 Choose Insert ➪ Movies and Sounds ➪ Movie from Gallery. The Clip Gallery opens.

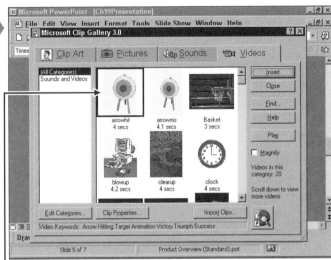

2 Click the movie you want and click Insert.

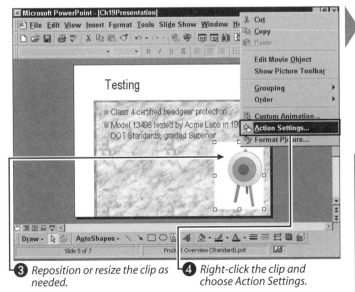

3 Reposition or resize the clip as needed.

4 Right-click the clip and choose Action Settings.

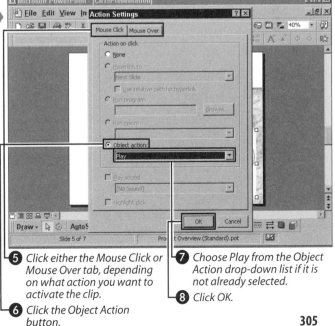

5 Click either the Mouse Click or Mouse Over tab, depending on what action you want to activate the clip.

6 Click the Object Action button.

7 Choose Play from the Object Action drop-down list if it is not already selected.

8 Click OK.

305

Running a Show

If you are going to show your presentation from printed transparencies or 35mm slides, you can skip this task. It pertains only to running a slide show using your computer. You can run a show on any computer monitor that you can hook your computer up to. If you are travelling, you can transfer your presentation file to a laptop computer to take with you.

To run a presentation, change to Slide Show view. The first slide in the show displays in full-screen view. You can move from slide to slide using the navigational techniques on the facing page. To exit from the show, press Esc or move forward past the last slide.

Many powerful controls are hidden behind that deceptively simple full-screen view. Right-click, or click on the embossed arrow in the bottom-left corner of the screen, to display a menu of choices designed to help you manage your presentation, some of which are listed here:

▶ Go — This submenu has commands that take you to: a Slide Navigator, a list of all the slides in the presentation from which you can choose; and By Title, a pop-up list of the slide titles from which you can choose.

▶ Meeting Minder — This command opens the Meeting Minder dialog box, from which you can take meeting notes and assign action items to people. It even has a link to Microsoft Outlook, so you can schedule activities.

▶ Speaker Notes — This command opens a window that displays any notes to yourself you have entered for that slide. You can enter more notes from here, or change them.

▶ Arrow and Pen — The default is Arrow, but you can change to Pen to use the mouse to draw on the slide. You can also select a pen color with the Pointer Options ⇨ Pen Color command.

▶ Black Screen — You can choose Screen ⇨ Black Screen to temporarily black out the display, so you can have a discussion in the middle of the presentation without leaving the current slide onscreen, for example.

TAKE NOTE

▶ POWERPOINT VIEWER

You do not have to have PowerPoint on the laptop that you travel with in order to show presentations. You can simply install the PowerPoint Viewer that comes free with Office 97. The PowerPoint Viewer is a much more compact program, and it runs presentations just as well as the full version of PowerPoint. It doesn't edit presentations, however, so make sure you finalize your presentation content before you hit the road. If you need to make changes to the presentation as you travel, load the full version of PowerPoint on your laptop.

CROSS-REFERENCE

See "Using Animations" earlier in this chapter to set up slide animation.

FIND IT ONLINE

To use the mouse as a pen, see http://support.microsoft.com/support/kb/articles/q190/3/44.asp.

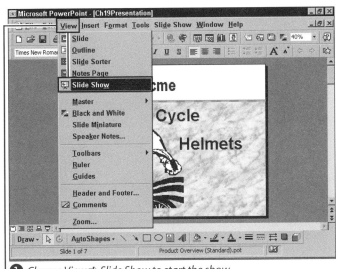

1 Choose View ➪ Slide Show to start the show.

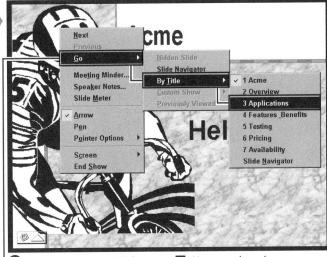

2 Jump to a certain slide by right-clicking and choosing Go ➪ By Title and then the slide name.

■ You can also advance through the slides by clicking the mouse or pressing Page Down or Page Up.

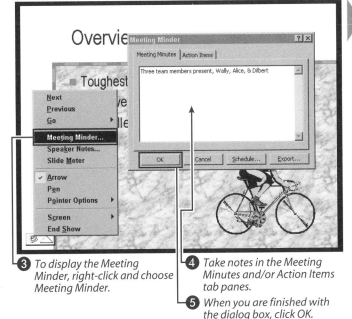

3 To display the Meeting Minder, right-click and choose Meeting Minder.

4 Take notes in the Meeting Minutes and/or Action Items tab panes.

5 When you are finished with the dialog box, click OK.

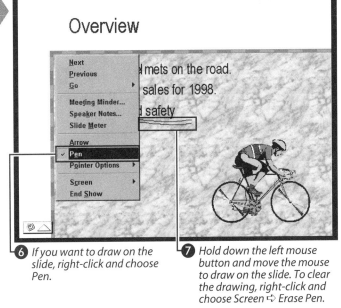

6 If you want to draw on the slide, right-click and choose Pen.

7 Hold down the left mouse button and move the mouse to draw on the slide. To clear the drawing, right-click and choose Screen ➪ Erase Pen.

■ To exit, press Esc.

Personal Workbook

Q&A

1 Why would you want to edit the Slide Master?

_____

_____

_____

2 How do you get out of the Slide Master and back to your regular presentation editing?

_____

_____

_____

3 Name two ways to delete a slide from a presentation.

_____

_____

_____

4 What is the difference between transitions and animations?

_____

_____

_____

5 True or false: You can animate only bulleted text with preset animations.

_____

_____

_____

_____

6 True or false: To associate a sound with a transition, use the Insert ➪ Movies and Sounds command.

_____

_____

_____

_____

7 How do you jump to a specific slide during a presentation?

_____

_____

_____

_____

_____

ANSWERS: PAGE 415

EXTRA PRACTICE

1 Add a piece of clip art to the Slide Master. View the presentation in Slide Show view and look at several slides to confirm that each contains that clip.

2 Apply a different design template. Note what happens to the clip art on the Slide Master.

3 Rearrange your presentation to put the slides in the opposite order.

4 Assign a different transition to each slide in the presentation. Run the show to see them.

5 Animate a slide that contains a bulleted list. Run the show to see the effect.

6 Associate a sound with a graphic so you can click on the graphic to play the sound. Run the show to see the effect.

REAL-WORLD APPLICATIONS

✔ You're the presentation whiz at your startup, so you know that consistency keeps audiences focused on the message rather than on special effects. When creating a presentation, you usually choose one transition effect and apply it to all the slides.

✔ You want to stop the presentation for a while and have a group discussion, so you use the Screen ⇨ Black Screen command to black out the screen. Then you use the Pen command to sketch a diagram that supports the discussion with white ink on the black screen.

✔ You are not sure what kind of questions your audience will be asking at your big sales pitch, and you are in a quandary over whether to delete some of the more technical slides. Rather than deleting them, hide them until you have further clarification.

Visual Quiz

What are two ways you could run your slide show from here?

_____

_____

_____

_____

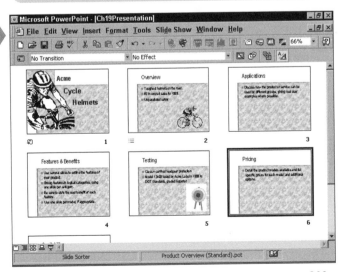

Contents of 'Desktop'

Name

My Computer

Network Neigh

Internet Explore

Microsoft Outloo

Recycle Bin

My Briefcase

3252-9

3259-6

3261-8

3262-6

3281-2

3286-3

DE Phone List

Device Manager

In

Iomega Tools

PART

V

Learning Important Outlook Tasks

Most people think of Outlook as just a communication tool. Outlook handles network and Internet mail services, serving as a communications center in your office. It even includes an address book called Contacts that stores e-mail addresses, phone numbers, mailing addresses, and other information about your friends and associates.

However, Outlook does much more than simply communicate. It also contains a calendar that enables you to plan your schedule for the day, week, month, and even the whole year! The calendar also integrates a task list that serves as a virtual "to do" list on your computer. Outlook keeps records of the work you have done in all Office 97 programs. All of these features are integrated in such a way that you may come to think of Outlook as a virtual secretary. Just don't ask it to get you a cup of coffee!

The chapters in Part V show you how to use the most important Outlook features. You start by learning Outlook's messaging capabilities, and then move on to learn about the Calendar and other features. Finally, you learn some basic housekeeping skills to help you keep Outlook working at its best.

CHAPTER **20**

MASTER
THESE
SKILLS

▶ **Creating Messages**

▶ **Addressing Messages Using the Address Book**

▶ **Sending and Receiving Attachments**

▶ **Sending, Receiving, and Replying to Messages**

Understanding E-Mail Basics

The last century has seen some truly profound advances in communication technology. Radios, televisions, and satellite communications were unfathomable 100 years ago. To those ancestors who saw the beginnings of the first telephone networks, the computers and the Internet we connect to using those networks would seem like something straight out of an H.G. Wells novel.

Communication has been significantly impacted by the proliferation of personal computers. For example, communication between colleagues, clients, friends, and family can all take place with much greater efficiency.

Outlook is an Office 97 program designed to help you communicate more effectively, and it serves this task in a number of ways. To help you organize your life a little better, it takes the place of many traditional office fixtures such as a calendar, appointment book, personal journal, phone dialer, and an address holder. In other words, it does almost everything a secretary might do, except make coffee.

Apart from all of the potential uses for Outlook, you will probably want to use it to send and receive electronic mail — e-mail — over the Internet or your company's Intranet. E-mail makes communicating with others much simpler and eliminates the need for many of the paper memos you might have used in the past. It also effectively shrinks the world down into a single office, because you can exchange and share virtually any kind of information using e-mail. Need to show a worksheet to your boss in Tahiti? No problem — just e-mail it to him using Outlook! Outlook makes an excellent e-mail program because it offers a number of useful enhancements over other more basic programs, and automates some of the most important features. This chapter discusses how to use Outlook's messaging features. Here you learn how to create and send e-mail messages to your associates, friends, family, or whomever you choose. You also learn how to attach files to your e-mails, enabling you to share your work with others more efficiently.

Creating Messages

First and foremost, Outlook is a program to help you communicate. If you plan to take advantage of those communication capabilities, you need to learn how to create a message. If you have a standard Internet e-mail account, you can generally send messages to anyone with an e-mail address. If you are on your company's network, you may be limited to exchanging mail only with others on the network. Either way, Outlook works the same.

E-mail is pretty basic in that you need two things: an address and the text of the message. Once you put those in, you send off your message. Other people can also send messages to you. These incoming messages are downloaded by Outlook whenever you open it, and they are sent to the Inbox area of the program. Your Inbox displays the name of the person who sent the message, along with the subject of the message and the time it was received. You can read these messages by double-clicking them in the Inbox.

If you want to reply to a message that someone sent you, you can simply click the Reply button on the toolbar. A new message window opens where you can compose your response. Although using the Reply button is simple, there will come a time when you need to compose a new message from scratch. Outlook makes this procedure relatively simple.

When you are actually composing your new message, you can type it much like you would any other text file. Outlook gives you some options for styling your text if you are using the HTML or RTF (rich-text format) format, or MS Word as your e-mail editor, including italics and special fonts. However, you should remember that unless the recipients are using e-mail clients that also support HTML or RTF, they will not be able to see the formatting.

The figures on the facing page show you how to create a basic message, and how to select Word as your editor. The last figure shows you some options you can select for sending the message. Once you have mastered the basics, we move on to more advanced techniques for creating and styling messages.

Continued

TAKE NOTE

GET AN E-MAIL ACCOUNT

Before you can receive e-mail, you need to have some kind of e-mail account. This may be provided over your company's network or intranet, or you may get e-mail along with an Internet account. Look in the yellow pages under *Internet Service Providers* for one in your area, or try one of the national companies such as Prodigy or Earthlink.

REPLY TO ONE OR ALL

When replying to a message sent to you, check if the message was also sent to other people. This is indicated by additional addresses in the To: and CC: fields of the message window. Decide if you want your reply to go to everyone or just the originator. Choose Reply or Reply to All on the toolbar.

CROSS-REFERENCE
Learn how to send the message in "Addressing Messages" later in this chapter.

FIND IT ONLINE
Get some great advice on writing e-mail messages at **http://www.webfoot.com/advice/email.top.html**.

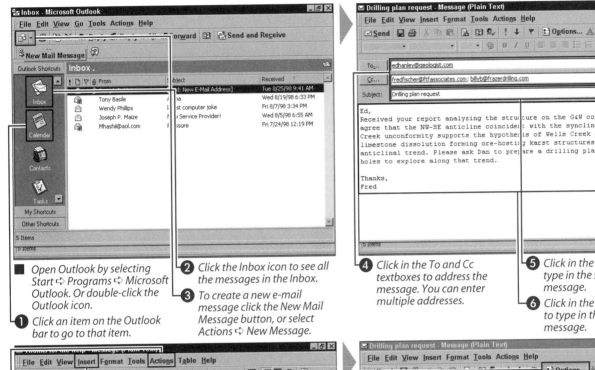

■ Open Outlook by selecting Start ➪ Programs ➪ Microsoft Outlook. Or double-click the Outlook icon.

❶ Click an item on the Outlook bar to go to that item.

❷ Click the Inbox icon to see all the messages in the Inbox.

❸ To create a new e-mail message click the New Mail Message button, or select Actions ➪ New Message.

❹ Click in the To and Cc textboxes to address the message. You can enter multiple addresses.

❺ Click in the Subject box to type in the subject of your message.

❻ Click in the message area to type in the text of your message.

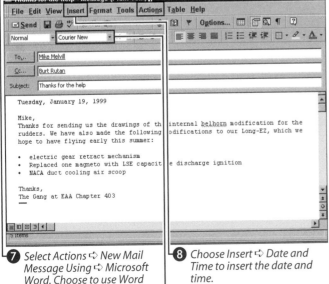

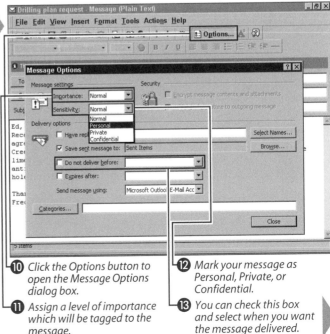

❼ Select Actions ➪ New Mail Message Using ➪ Microsoft Word. Choose to use Word just this once, or choose to make it your default e-mail editor.

❽ Choose Insert ➪ Date and Time to insert the date and time.

❾ Click the arrows to open drop-down menus to change the font and the font size.

❿ Click the Options button to open the Message Options dialog box.

⓫ Assign a level of importance which will be tagged to the message.

⓬ Mark your message as Personal, Private, or Confidential.

⓭ You can check this box and select when you want the message delivered.

315

Creating Messages

Continued

The steps given on the previous two pages show you the most basic techniques for creating a message. Modern e-mail programs such as Outlook make the message composition process simple, so that all you really need to do is type the words and click a toolbar button or two.

Credit much of this simplicity to the fact that e-mail messages have classically been, by nature, simple. From the beginning, an e-mail was nothing more than an ASCII text file, which means it uses an International character set that can be recognized and read by any computer. These text files contain no formatting to speak of, and some would say they are quite bland. On the other hand, text files are usually small, so they can be uploaded and downloaded quickly.

Some newer e-mail programs — including Outlook — enable you to do a lot more with your e-mail messages. The text is still there, but now, as long as you use HTML or RTF format, you can also choose different fonts, add boldface or italics, add colors, and even place a spiffy wallpaper behind your message. Outlook's message creation interface is similar to Word so if you are already familiar with Word you will already be a step ahead of the game. And, as we pointed out earlier, if you love Word, you can use Word as your e-mail editor in Outlook. Word takes a lot longer to load though, so some Outlook users shy away from using it.

Before you decide to go wild with formatting in your messages, you must first consider your audience. Many e-mail clients still cannot handle special character formatting or even graphics. At best, your recipient will just receive the text without any of the formatting you worked so hard to create. At worst, the message may be so full of tags, errors, and weird attachments that it can be difficult or impossible to read. Also, keep in mind that formatting and graphics take up greater bandwidth during download, and some recipients may not appreciate receiving messages from you that take too long to download.

The figures on the facing page show some of the options available to you for spicing up your messages. These techniques can be applied to any message, but remember to consider whether your recipient will be able to read it.

TAKE NOTE

BEWARE OF THE E-MAIL VIRUS

After getting an e-mail account, you may start to receive virus warnings in your inbox. These are, almost without exception, hoaxes, and often warn you not to open any message with a certain subject ("Good Times" is a popular one). You are also advised to forward these messages to as many people as possible to "spread the word." It's the oldest joke on the Net; don't do it!

CROSS-REFERENCE

Learn more about spicing up text in "Formatting Text" in Chapter 8.

FIND IT ONLINE

Join a mailing list to learn more about Outlook at the MS Exchange forum located at **http://www.msexchange.org/**.

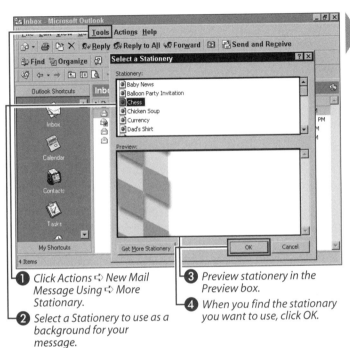

❶ Click Actions ➪ New Mail Message Using ➪ More Stationary.

❷ Select a Stationery to use as a background for your message.

❸ Preview stationery in the Preview box.

❹ When you find the stationary you want to use, click OK.

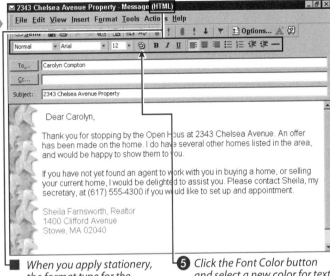

■ When you apply stationery, the format type for the message becomes HTML, and the formatting toolbar becomes available to allow you to format text.

❺ Click the Font Color button and select a new color for text you will add to the message.

■ To change the color of existing text, highlight the text first.

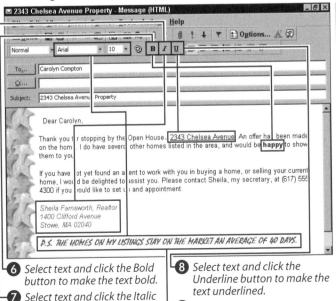

❻ Select text and click the Bold button to make the text bold.

❼ Select text and click the Italic button to italicize the text.

❽ Select text and click the Underline button to make the text underlined.

❾ Select text and choose a new font and font size from the Font drop-down menus.

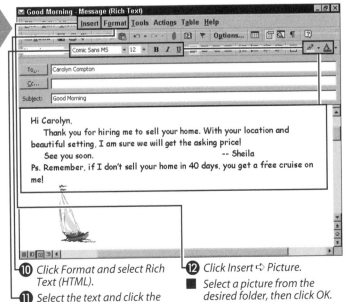

❿ Click Format and select Rich Text (HTML).

⓫ Select the text and click the Font, Font Size and Font Color buttons to format it.

⓬ Click Insert ➪ Picture.

■ Select a picture from the desired folder, then click OK. Move it by clicking and dragging, and resize it by dragging one of its handles.

Addressing Messages Using the Address Book

Think of the Internet as a giant postal service: Everything needs an address on it to ensure that it gets delivered to the right place. No address means no delivery.

E-mail addresses used on the Internet follow a fairly standard format. The address usually has two parts: The first part identifies the specific person or organization that the e-mail account is for, and the second part identifies the Internet Domain Name Server where that e-mail address is located. Using the analogy of the postal service, you can think of this second part of the e-mail address as being like a ZIP or Postal Code, which tells the postal service which post office to deliver the letter to. The two parts of the e-mail address are separated by an @ (pronounced "at") symbol. It looks something like this: kcunderdahl@idgbooks.com.

When you enter an e-mail address, you must be exact; if even one letter is wrong or missing, your message won't go to the right place. Entering addresses into the Address book and then using the Address book is much safer than typing them in each time.

Your default address book is actually your Contacts list (you learn more about entering contacts in the next chapter). When you enter someone into your address book, you are actually creating a contact for them in your contact list at the same time.

So, if you haven't entered any contacts into Outlook yet, you won't have anyone in your address book. However, if you are using Outlook in a company, you will almost certainly have at least company personnel in your address book.

Often, messages are sent to a group of people, such as everyone in the marketing department. Outlook Contacts enables you to create groups of addresses for just such a purpose. You give the group a name (Marketing), and then add the names to the group. When you send an e-mail to the group, every person in the group gets the e-mail. This is much easier than typing in 20 names or selecting 20 names from the address book.

TAKE NOTE

▶ ADDING A NEW ADDRESS FROM A RECEIVED MESSAGE

You can quickly add the address of a person who sent you e-mail to your address book by right clicking the address and selecting Add to Contacts. The New Contact dialog box opens with the name and e-mail address filled in. Type in the rest of the information, click OK, and the person is now in your Contacts Address book.

▶ IMPORTING AND EXPORTING ADDRESS FILES

Outlook also lets you import and export addresses from other files, such as Act and Goldmine. When you import these files, Outlook automatically enters the properties and addresses into Contacts, so you don't have to type anything.

CROSS-REFERENCE

Learn how to save addresses for future use in "Adding Contacts" in Chapter 21.

FIND IT ONLINE

Search for e-mail addresses of long lost friends by using Yahoo's People Search option at http://www.yahoo.com.

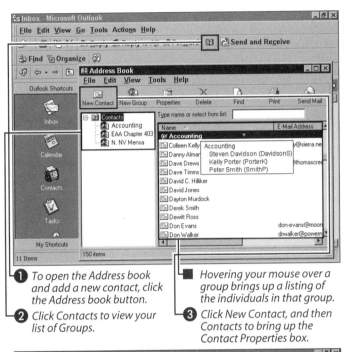

① To open the Address book and add a new contact, click the Address book button.

② Click Contacts to view your list of Groups.

■ Hovering your mouse over a group brings up a listing of the individuals in that group.

③ Click New Contact, and then Contacts to bring up the Contact Properties box.

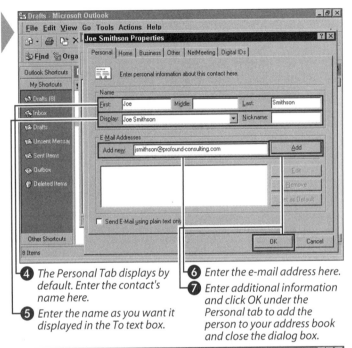

④ The Personal Tab displays by default. Enter the contact's name here.

⑤ Enter the name as you want it displayed in the To text box.

⑥ Enter the e-mail address here.

⑦ Enter additional information and click OK under the Personal tab to add the person to your address book and close the dialog box.

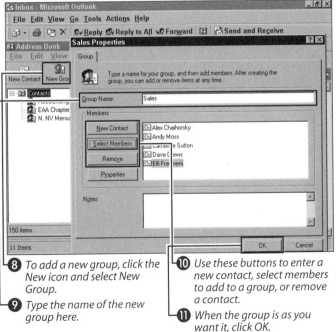

⑧ To add a new group, click the New icon and select New Group.

⑨ Type the name of the new group here.

⑩ Use these buttons to enter a new contact, select members to add to a group, or remove a contact.

⑪ When the group is as you want it, click OK.

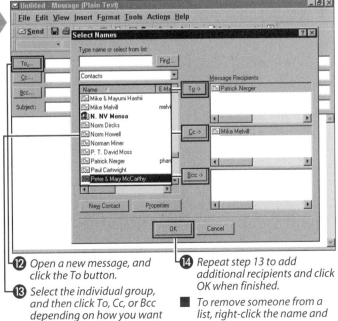

⑫ Open a new message, and click the To button.

⑬ Select the individual group, and then click To, Cc, or Bcc depending on how you want the message addressed.

⑭ Repeat step 13 to add additional recipients and click OK when finished.

■ To remove someone from a list, right-click the name and then select Remove.

319

Sending and Receiving Attachments

Computers and the Internet have greatly enhanced both personal and business communication. Many offices can no longer be defined by the strict geographical boundaries they once were, thanks primarily to this enhanced long distance communication.

But working with others involves more than simply communicating with them. Often you need to be able to work on the same items, and for this, simple e-mail messages will not suffice. Fortunately, Outlook makes it easy to exchange any computer file via a modem or Internet connection by attaching it to an e-mail message.

The applications of this technique are almost limitless. Do you need your company president to review an important document, but she's currently on an expedition to climb Mt. Everest? No problem — simply e-mail the document to her laptop. It doesn't matter if your coworker is across town, across the country, or flying in the space shuttle. If she is able to receive e-mail you can forward a file to her using Outlook.

One minor limitation is that you must remember that the recipient of your attached file has to have some way of opening it. If you e-mail someone an Excel spreadsheet, but that person does not have Excel on his computer, he will not be able to open the file. Just remember that when you send an attached file, you are only sending the file itself and not the whole program.

The first three figures on the following page show you how to attach a file or files to a message in Outlook. The last figure shows you how to save a file attachment that is sent to you.

TAKE NOTE

▶ COMPRESS YOUR FILES

Files and documents that seem relatively small on your computer may take a significant length of time to transfer via e-mail. Even with a relatively fast Internet connection, a 10MB file could take more than an hour to download. To conserve bandwidth, try compressing larger files with a program such as WinZip before you send them. Note that the person receiving your file must have WinZip in order to expand the compressed WinZip file.

▶ SENDING MULTIPLE ATTACHMENTS

Although not necessary, if you have more than one or two files to send, you may want to send them in separate messages. Doing this will simplify the download process if you or the recipients have problems with poor Internet connections and get disconnected frequently.

▶ OPENING ATTACHED FILES

Just as you can send out attachments, other people can send attachments to you. If you receive a message with an attachment, simply double-click the icon for the file to open it. Make sure you know who sent you the file; attachments from unknown parties might contain viruses!

CROSS-REFERENCE
To learn about saving attached files on your own hard drive see "Saving Office Files" in Chapter 3.

FIND IT ONLINE
You can download WinZip from the Internet from TUCOWS at **http://www.tucows.com/**.

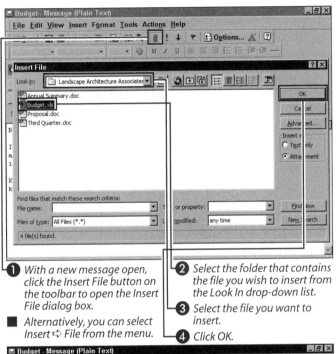

❶ With a new message open, click the Insert File button on the toolbar to open the Insert File dialog box.

■ Alternatively, you can select Insert ➪ File from the menu.

❷ Select the folder that contains the file you wish to insert from the Look In drop-down list.

❸ Select the file you want to insert.

❹ Click OK.

❺ The file appears as an icon. Double-check it to make sure it is the correct file. (If you did not insert the correct file, select the file and press the Delete key.)

■ Outlook creates a file area at the bottom of the message and inserts the file icons.

■ The icon of the attached file represents the type of file it is. This is an Excel file.

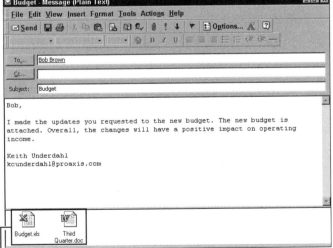

❻ You can attach multiple files to a message by repeating steps 1 through 4. This message has an Excel and a Word file.

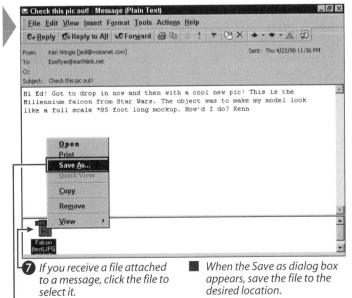

❼ If you receive a file attached to a message, click the file to select it.

❽ Right-click the file and choose Save As from the context menu.

■ When the Save as dialog box appears, save the file to the desired location.

Sending, Receiving, and Replying to Messages

Sending your messages in Outlook is almost as easy as sending a letter the traditional way, thanks to some user-friendly features. Generally speaking, all you have to do is perform a single click of the mouse to send your messages.

But watch out: Just like traditional mail, when you send it, it's *sent*. Drop something in the mailbox, and it's gone. You won't find an *Un*send button. Make sure the mail is addressed correctly *before* you click the button, and if the content of your message is controversial, make sure you really want to send it before it's too late. Any files you have attached to an e-mail are also sent when you click the Send button.

Receiving messages from others is also quite simple. Although Outlook automatically checks for new messages when you first start the program and periodically afterwards, you can also check for messages yourself using a simple menu command. Opening a message to read it and replying to that message are also easy tasks. Outlook also makes it easy to forward messages to other people and to reply to everyone who received a message.

If you are composing a message and find that you need to save it and come back later to edit it or add to it before you send it, Outlook offers a Drafts folder where you can store works in progress.

The first figure on the facing page demonstrates how to send a message when you are done composing it. The second figure shows you how to check the status of a message once you have clicked Send. The last two figures show how to receive and open messages that are sent to you.

TAKE NOTE

▶ OUTLOOK CHECKS YOUR MAIL FOR YOU

Outlook automatically checks for messages in your e-mail account every ten minutes. Some people love this feature because they don't have to remember to check on their own. Others are aggravated because it means that Outlook tries to tie up their phone line every ten minutes. If you want Outlook to wait longer than 10 minutes to check your e-mail, simply change the time in the Check for new mail messages every box.

▶ SENT MESSAGES ARE SAVED

Any messages you send will be saved in the Sent folder of Outlook. This way, if you need to refer back to a message you sent some time ago, you can find a record of that message in the Sent folder. Or, if you left someone off the address list, you can open the message from the Sent folder and simply forward it to that person. Sure beats typing the message again!

▶ SETTING OUTLOOK TO ALERT YOU OF NEW MESSAGES

You can tell Outlook to display a notification of a new message, or make a sound when you get new mail by going to Tools ➪ Options, Preferences Tab, E-mail Options, and Advanced E-mail options.

CROSS-REFERENCE

Once you have read a message, you can move it to another folder as described in "Moving Items" in Chapter 22.

SHORTCUT

You can quickly check for new messages by pressing F5.

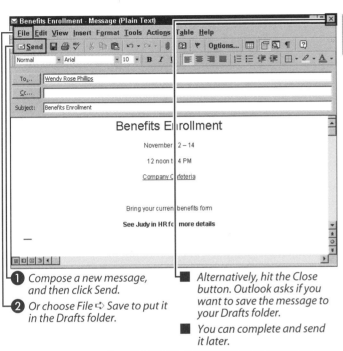

1 Compose a new message, and then click Send.

2 Or choose File ➪ Save to put it in the Drafts folder.

■ Alternatively, hit the Close button. Outlook asks if you want to save the message to your Drafts folder.

■ You can complete and send it later.

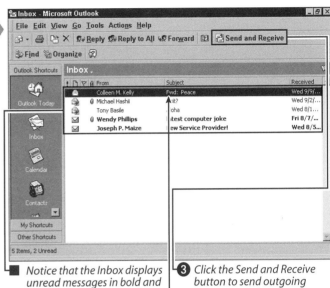

■ Notice that the Inbox displays unread messages in bold and messages you've opened already in normal text. Messages with attachments have a paper clip icon.

3 Click the Send and Receive button to send outgoing messages and receive incoming messages.

4 Double-click a message to open it.

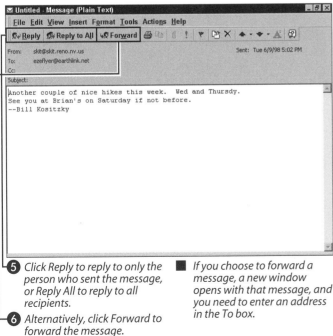

5 Click Reply to reply to only the person who sent the message, or Reply All to reply to all recipients.

6 Alternatively, click Forward to forward the message.

■ If you choose to forward a message, a new window opens with that message, and you need to enter an address in the To box.

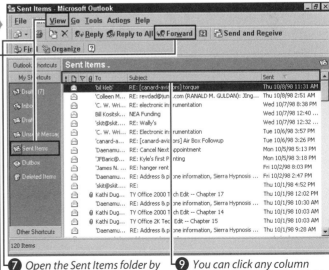

7 Open the Sent Items folder by selecting View ➪ Folders list and clicking Sent Items.

8 Click a message and then click the forward button to forward the message.

9 You can click any column heading to sort the Sent folder messages. This can help you find a message quickly.

323

Personal Workbook

Q&A

1 Describe two ways of opening a window and creating a new message.

_____

_____

_____

2 Can you apply special formatting to text in a message?

_____

_____

3 Will all message recipients be able to see that formatting?

_____

_____

4 Where does the address for the primary recipient go?

_____

_____

5 How do you send a copy of the message to additional recipients?

_____

_____

6 How do you send a "secret" copy to another recipient?

_____

_____

_____

7 What kind of files can be attached to an e-mail?

_____

_____

8 How do you unsend a message?

_____

_____

9 How do you check for new messages?

_____

_____

10 How do you know if a message in your Inbox is new?

_____

_____

ANSWERS: PAGE 416

EXTRA PRACTICE

① Create a new message in Outlook.

② Address the message to someone, and address a copy to someone else.

③ Address a copy of the message to someone in such a way that others will not know he or she is getting it.

④ Attach a small file to the message.

⑤ Send the message. When the recipients reply, open and then delete their responses.

⑥ Begin composing a message and then save it to your Drafts folder.

REAL-WORLD APPLICATIONS

✔ If your partner just traveled across the country and forgot to bring an important file, you can send the file directly to your partner by attaching it to an e-mail message.

✔ Create a group that includes all members of your weekly sports team so you can quickly send e-mails about games and weather reports.

✔ When you are sending out a message about an important deadline to your supervisor, add yourself to the Cc: list to give yourself an extra reminder about the project.

Visual Quiz

How do you open a window to create this message? How were the addresses entered in the To:, Cc:, and Bcc: fields? What does Bcc: mean? What does the icon at the bottom of the page called "SHistory.rtf" represent? How did it get there? How can you send this message?

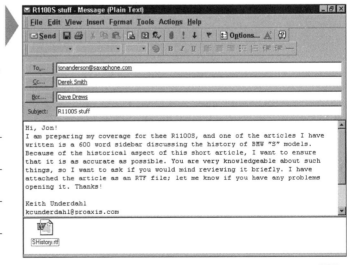

CHAPTER **21**

MASTER
THESE
SKILLS

▶ **Adding Contacts**

▶ **Sorting and Viewing Contact Lists**

▶ **Using the Calendar and Understanding Scheduling Basics**

▶ **Using Advanced Scheduling Features**

▶ **Using the Task List**

▶ **Using the Journal**

Managing Your Contacts and Appointments

In the previous chapter you learned how to use Outlook for sending and receiving messages. For many, that may be the only feature of Outlook they take advantage of, and that is a shame. One thing is for sure, there are plenty of other perfectly good e-mail clients out there, including Netscape Mail Eudora Pro, and Microsoft's own Outlook Express.

Outlook differs from those other clients in that it is much more than a simple e-mail client. Outlook contains a variety of features to help you increase your productivity and keep track of important events. It can serve as a virtual desktop in a way that the regular Windows Desktop never could.

One of the most important features of Outlook is the Contacts list. The Outlook Contacts list is similar in concept to the electronic address books used in other e-mail clients, but it can contain a lot more information about each person. The list can also be displayed in a more user-friendly interface, making it easier for you to read and use. You can also incorporate information from the Contacts list into most other Outlook functions.

Another very useful feature is the Calendar, which keeps track of important dates and events for you. The calendar can serve as an adequate replacement for the ubiquitous desk planner, a large calendar that many people use at their desks. The calendar works in conjunction with the Appointments feature, which helps you keep track of special engagements.

Two more useful tools are the Task List and Journal. The Task List can serve as an electronic "to do" list, but one that helps you meet your goals a little more effectively. And the Journal lets you record those important events that you just know will come back to haunt you again some day.

This chapter discusses how to use these various features and gives you some interesting ideas on how you can put Outlook to work for you. You don't have to use any of these features if you don't want to, but you might find that all of them are integrated so effectively that they can vastly improve your sense of organization, and restore sanity to the office.

Adding Contacts

Most people have a hard enough time just remembering names; trying to memorize addresses and phone numbers for everyone you might need to contact is virtually impossible.

Creating an electronic address book is a natural extension of computer technology. Computers store and process data, and what are addresses but data pertaining to all the people you know? Outlook provides you with just such an electronic address book called Contacts. It offers a number of advantages over an old-fashioned paper address book, not the least of which is that you will never have to worry about filling up all the blocks of the Contact list with scribbled out obsolete addresses.

The Outlook Contact list can do a lot of things that address books in other e-mail clients can't do. For example, suppose you are scheduling a meeting for next Thursday at 10:00 a.m. with six colleagues. You can use Outlook to schedule the meeting into your calendar and choose the six attendees from your Contact list. Outlook even goes so far as to automatically send reminders to those persons so they know about the meeting.

Besides the more advanced uses, your Contact list can still be used for the more mundane tasks, such as addressing messages, storing phone numbers, etc. Obviously, before you can actually use the Contact list for any of these things, you need to add some

people into the list. This can be done in several ways. One way is to add them in automatically when you reply to a message from them. You can also type the information in from scratch, which can be useful if you just got a business card from someone.

The figures on the opposite page show you how to add people to your Contact list. The first figure shows you how to add someone that has contacted you via e-mail, and the second figure demonstrates how to begin typing the information in manually. The last two figures point out some of the most important information you should enter about each contact.

TAKE NOTE

LOOKING UP CONTACTS

If you are not sure if a person who sent you an e-mail has already been added to your Contact list or not, you can look up the person. Right-click the person's name in the message window and choose Look up Contact from the context menu that appears.

ADDING A NEW CONTACT FROM THE SAME COMPANY

There might be times when you have several contacts at one company. Thankfully Outlook doesn't require you to type in the same information twice. Select Actions ⇨ New Contact from Same Company to have a new contact information sheet appear with Company, Address, Business Phone and Business Fax already filled in. You just add the unique information for that contact.

CROSS-REFERENCE

Learn how to enter your contacts into the Address Book in Chapter 20.

SHORTCUT

With the Contacts list displayed, double-click the text that says "Welcome to Contacts!" to quickly begin entering a new contact.

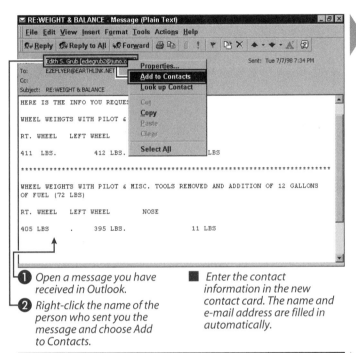

① Open a message you have received in Outlook.

② Right-click the name of the person who sent you the message and choose Add to Contacts.

■ Enter the contact information in the new contact card. The name and e-mail address are filled in automatically.

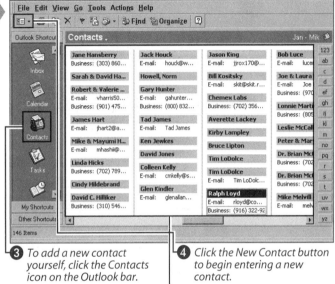

③ To add a new contact yourself, click the Contacts icon on the Outlook bar.

■ The Contact list appears. Notice that contacts are listed alphabetically.

④ Click the New Contact button to begin entering a new contact.

■ A new Contact card opens. Follow the steps listed below to enter information.

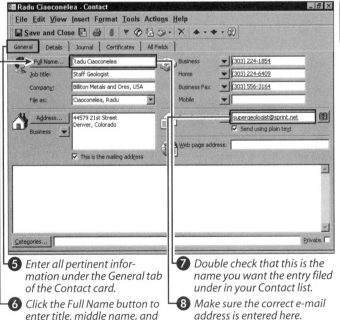

⑤ Enter all pertinent information under the General tab of the Contact card.

⑥ Click the Full Name button to enter title, middle name, and suffix.

⑦ Double check that this is the name you want the entry filed under in your Contact list.

⑧ Make sure the correct e-mail address is entered here.

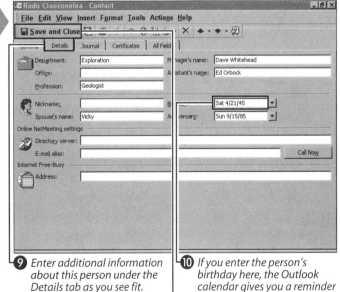

⑨ Enter additional information about this person under the Details tab as you see fit.

⑩ If you enter the person's birthday here, the Outlook calendar gives you a reminder when the big day gets close!

⑪ When you are done click Save and Close.

Sorting and Viewing Contact Lists

If you have only added a couple of people listed in your Contact list you may not be thinking to much about organizing them or rearranging the view. However, once your list has grown, there will come a point when you will want to have more control over the whole thing.

The Outlook Contact list gives you a number of useful options to help you better manage your addresses. One thing you can do is sort people by category. For example, suppose you want to be able to contact all of your family members in a hurry. Or, perhaps you might group together some business associates from a particular company. Outlook helps you sort contacts in this manner by letting you assign categories to each person. If you have a category called *Family*, you could add that category to the contact card for each of your family members. That way, you can tell Outlook to display only your family members, so you don't have to spend a lot of time weeding through the entire Contact list for them.

This is but one of several useful options. You can also change the way that Outlook displays your contacts. The format that Outlook uses by default may or may not appeal to you, and you can change the view as you see fit. You can choose from a couple of different views in a drop-down list on the toolbar, and by default it displays Address Cards. You can choose another view from this list, such as Detailed Address Cards or Phone List. You can also use this drop-down list to sort contacts by company, category, or location.

The figures on the following page introduce you to some of the view options available for the Contact list and demonstrate one way to organize the people in your list. Fortunately, customizing Outlook is pretty easy, and you should have no problem tailoring it to your own needs.

TAKE NOTE

▶ USING FILTERS

Another way to narrow the number of cards that are displayed is to filter them by clicking View ⇨ Filter. You can enter a name or word to search for on the Contacts tab, or even choose a category on the More Choices tab. When you click OK, Outlook filters through the address cards and displays only the ones you asked to look for.

▶ SPECIFY WHICH FIELDS ARE SHOWN

You can specify which fields to show by clicking View ⇨ Current View ⇨ Customize Current View and then clicking the Fields button. The list on the left side of the Show Fields dialog box shows all possible fields, and the list on the right shows which ones are selected for display now. Use the Add and Remove buttons to change which fields are displayed.

CROSS-REFERENCE

Learn how to add people to your list in the previous task, "Adding Contacts."

FIND IT ONLINE

Locate contact information for associates with Infoseek's People Find system at http://www.infoseek.com/.

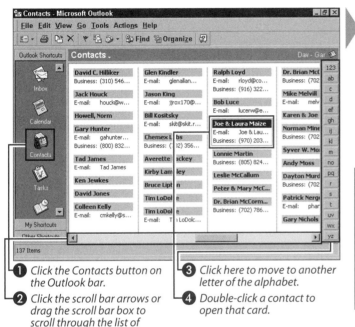

① Click the Contacts button on the Outlook bar.

② Click the scroll bar arrows or drag the scroll bar box to scroll through the list of contacts.

③ Click here to move to another letter of the alphabet.

④ Double-click a contact to open that card.

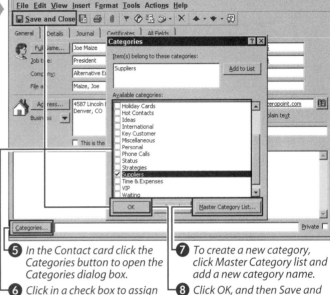

⑤ In the Contact card click the Categories button to open the Categories dialog box.

⑥ Click in a check box to assign a category to this person.

⑦ To create a new category, click Master Category list and add a new category name.

⑧ Click OK, and then Save and Close to close the Contact card for that person.

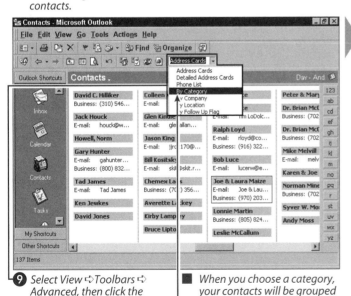

⑨ Select View ⇨ Toolbars ⇨ Advanced, then click the Current View drop-down list to see the various ways you can look at your contacts.

■ When you choose a category, your contacts will be grouped or sorted accordingly.

⑩ Click By Category to sort your contacts by categories.

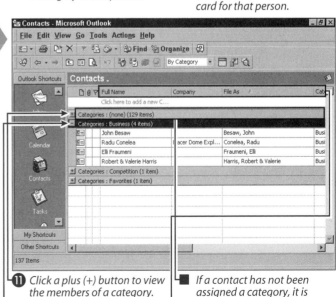

⑪ Click a plus (+) button to view the members of a category.

■ When a category is selected to display its members, a minus sign appears next to the category.

■ If a contact has not been assigned a category, it is placed in the None category.

⑫ Click one of these field headings to sort the people by that field.

Using the Calendar and Understanding Scheduling Basics

I f you have been working in an office setting for many years, you know that the ubiquitous desk calendar has been a trusted friend. Not only has it been a place for you to keep track of how long it is until Friday, but it is also the traditional place to make a note of meetings and appointments, jot phone numbers at a moment's notice, plan your next vacation, and any number of other important day-to-day items.

But, if the desk calendar has always been useful, it has also suffered from a few drawbacks. All those little notes and phone numbers you scribbled on it in a big hurry add up, and by October or November the corners are getting dog-eared or torn off completely. Pretty soon your most used tool becomes a source of desktop clutter.

Outlook provides a replacement for the good old desk calendar in the form of Calendar, an easy to use electronic planner. The Calendar is easy to read, and you can customize the view to suit your personal needs and tastes. You can display appointments only for the current day, or for the entire month. Outlook even improves on the desk calendar concept by providing you with a reminder in the form of a dialog box, 15 minutes before your scheduled event or meeting takes place. The figures on the following page show you how to view your Calendar and schedule a basic meeting. By default, Calendar opens showing a page for the current day, but you can change the view settings using the techniques shown in the last figure.

TAKE NOTE

▶ ADDING HOLIDAYS

Your Outlook Calendar does not mark any holidays. You can add holidays by selecting Tools ⇨ Options, clicking Calendar Options, clicking Add Holidays, selecting your country, and clicking OK. Outlook adds all the holidays that your country observes into your Calendar.

▶ REARRANGE YOUR WORKING WEEK

By default, Outlook assumes that you work from 8:00 a.m. to 5:00 p.m., Monday through Friday. You can change this setting to suit your actual work schedule by clicking Tools ⇨ Options. On the Calendar tab, place a check next to your workdays, and adjust your working hours as appropriate.

▶ SIMPLIFY CHOOSING THE DATE AND TIME

By default, Outlook assigns a date and time for your appointment based on which block the cursor was in when you opened the dialog box. Although the date and time are easy to change once the dialog box is open, you can still save yourself a step by clicking in the time block in which you want to schedule the appointment *before* you actually begin to schedule it.

CROSS-REFERENCE

Your tasks are an integral part of the calendar. See "Using the Task List" later in this chapter.

FIND IT ONLINE

Learn more about effective time management from the Daytimer Library at **http://www.daytimer.com/resource/library/**.

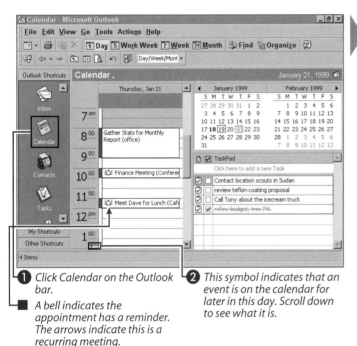

1 Click Calendar on the Outlook bar.

■ A bell indicates the appointment has a reminder. The arrows indicate this is a recurring meeting.

2 This symbol indicates that an event is on the calendar for later in this day. Scroll down to see what it is.

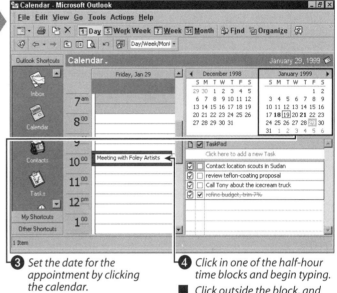

3 Set the date for the appointment by clicking the calendar.

■ Bold indicates appointment; a red rectangle highlights the current date.

4 Click in one of the half-hour time blocks and begin typing.

■ Click outside the block, and then double-click your new entry to open the Appointment window.

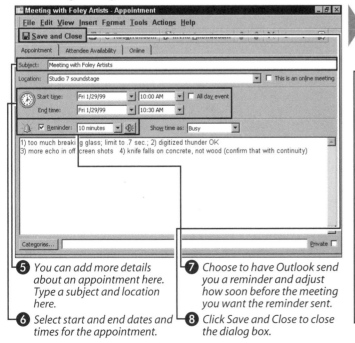

5 You can add more details about an appointment here. Type a subject and location here.

6 Select start and end dates and times for the appointment.

7 Choose to have Outlook send you a reminder and adjust how soon before the meeting you want the reminder sent.

8 Click Save and Close to close the dialog box.

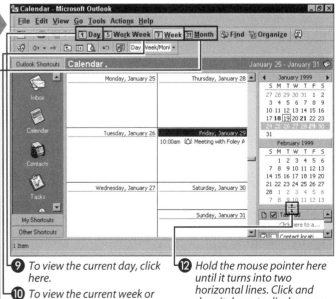

9 To view the current day, click here.

10 To view the current week or work week, click here.

11 To view the current month, click here.

12 Hold the mouse pointer here until it turns into two horizontal lines. Click and drag it down to display more months. (The TaskPad adjusts its size.)

333

Using Advanced Scheduling Features

Whether at work or at home, your life probably revolves around a seemingly endless series of meetings, appointments, and scheduled events. Because you have so many things to do at specific times, it can be all too easy to lose track of some important things.

Outlook's Calendar makes keeping one step ahead of important events easy. The meetings and appointments you schedule are automatically integrated into the rest of Outlook as needed.

Outlook enables you to enter recurring meetings all at one time. If you have a Marketing meeting every Monday at 10:00 a.m., you can tell Outlook that it's a recurring meeting and Outlook will fill in 10:00 a.m. for every Monday. This saves you an incredible amount of time and means you don't have to continually duplicate your efforts. Another neat feature of the Meeting dialog box is that it can help you plan your meetings as well. This feature goes far beyond simply choosing a time for the meeting and entering it in the calendar; you can also pick attendees for your meeting from your contact list. Outlook will automatically produce and send an e-mail message to each person you assign, reminding them of the meeting.

The figures on the following page show you how to schedule a recurring meeting and invite others to the meeting using Outlook's Calendar. The first figure shows you how to set up a recurring meeting dialog box, and the second one shows you how to edit a recurring meeting. The last two figures show you how to schedule a group meeting using the Meeting Planner tab of the same dialog box.

TAKE NOTE

▶ DRAGGING AND DROPPING A RECURRING MEETING

You cannot drag and drop a recurring meeting to a new day as you can a nonrecurring meeting. If you drag and drop a recurring meeting from Monday to Tuesday, Outlook tells you that you can only move this one occurrence of the meeting, and that you need to open the meeting series (explained below) and make the change in the dialog box.

▶ SCHEDULE AN ALL DAY EVENT

If you need to schedule an appointment or other event that will last all day, click the All Day Event check box in the Appointment dialog box. The Start Time and End Time options for the appointment will no longer be available.

▶ GROUP ATTENDANCE DESIGNATIONS

When scheduling a meeting for a group, you have three designations for attendees. Required, means the attendee must be at the meeting. Optional, means the attendee can attend the meeting but it's not mandatory. Resource, means that the attendee is designated as an information resource for anyone attending the meeting to call on if they need information about the meeting.

CROSS-REFERENCE

Before scheduling appointments you should understand the Calendar. See "Using the Calendar" earlier in this chapter.

SHORTCUT

You can find tips on conducting a good meeting at http://www.wordconnection.com/meeting.htm.

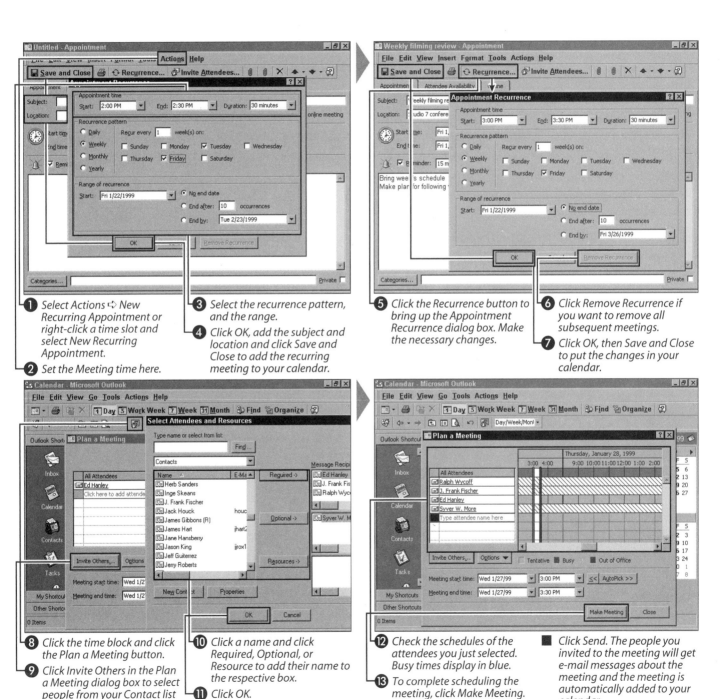

1 Select Actions ➡ New Recurring Appointment or right-click a time slot and select New Recurring Appointment.

2 Set the Meeting time here.

3 Select the recurrence pattern, and the range.

4 Click OK, add the subject and location and click Save and Close to add the recurring meeting to your calendar.

5 Click the Recurrence button to bring up the Appointment Recurrence dialog box. Make the necessary changes.

6 Click Remove Recurrence if you want to remove all subsequent meetings.

7 Click OK, then Save and Close to put the changes in your calendar.

8 Click the time block and click the Plan a Meeting button.

9 Click Invite Others in the Plan a Meeting dialog box to select people from your Contact list to attend the meeting.

10 Click a name and click Required, Optional, or Resource to add their name to the respective box.

11 Click OK.

12 Check the schedules of the attendees you just selected. Busy times display in blue.

13 To complete scheduling the meeting, click Make Meeting.

■ Click Send. The people you invited to the meeting will get e-mail messages about the meeting and the meeting is automatically added to your calendar.

Using the Task List

In the previous two tasks you learned about the Outlook Calendar and how to schedule appointments and meetings in the calendar. You saw how Outlook could improve organization within your office by replacing some of the traditional paper fixtures on your desk such as a calendar and appointment book.

Yet another traditional productivity item you probably use at home and at the office is a "to do" list. A "to do" list contains important things you need to get done, and as you complete items on the list you can scratch them off. Not surprisingly, Outlook provides you with a good replacement for these old-fashioned lists. Outlook has an area called *Tasks* that serves as a central location for you to record and monitor all of your goals and accomplishments. A task in Outlook can be anything from buying a new toothbrush to conquering the world. If you need to get it done, you can create a task for it in Outlook and just like the paper lists, place a check next to each item when you've completed it.

Besides being a place to record the things you need to get done, Outlook improves on the "to do" list concept in many ways. For one thing, you can assign a due date to tasks, and that due date will appear on your Outlook Calendar. You can also set periodic reminders for yourself to help you keep on schedule with a major task. Finally, Tasks serves as a place to keep permanent records of such things as the number of hours you dedicated to a given task, when you completed the task, how many miles you drove in connection with the task, who you sent your invoice to, and more. The Tasks feature is versatile enough to fit virtually any need.

The first figure on the following page shows you how to create a new task. The second and third figures show you how to record important information for a task, and the last figure demonstrates how to keep track of your tasks within Outlook.

TAKE NOTE

REPORT YOUR STATUS

You may often find that you need to report your status on a task to someone else, such as a supervisor or partner. You can do this quickly and efficiently by clicking the Send Status Report button on the task toolbar. An e-mail message is automatically generated, and includes the current status, hours worked, and any notes you have made. Just address it and send like any other e-mail message!

VIEW TASKS FROM THE CALENDAR

The Calendar contains an area called Taskpad that displays a brief list of all of your tasks. If you wish, you can actually perform most task management tasks from here.

CROSS-REFERENCE

If you plan to send a status report, see "Addressing Messages" in Chapter 20 to learn more.

SHORTCUT

Press Ctrl+Shift+K to quickly create a new task.

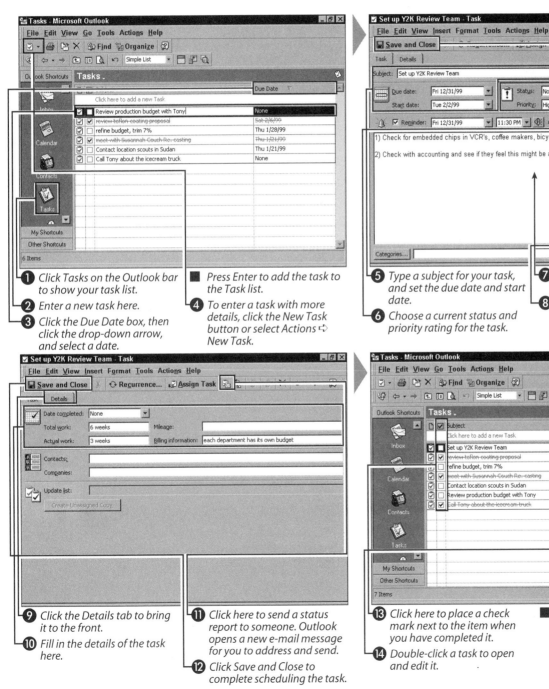

① Click Tasks on the Outlook bar to show your task list.

② Enter a new task here.

③ Click the Due Date box, then click the drop-down arrow, and select a date.

■ Press Enter to add the task to the Task list.

④ To enter a task with more details, click the New Task button or select Actions ➪ New Task.

⑤ Type a subject for your task, and set the due date and start date.

⑥ Choose a current status and priority rating for the task.

⑦ Set a reminder and enter notes about the task.

⑧ If you don't need to enter any more details, click Save and Close to enter the task into your task list.

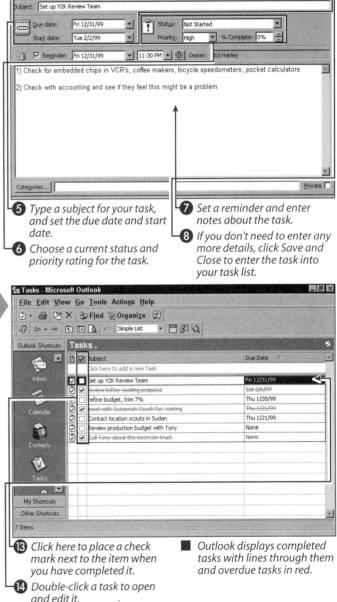

⑨ Click the Details tab to bring it to the front.

⑩ Fill in the details of the task here.

⑪ Click here to send a status report to someone. Outlook opens a new e-mail message for you to address and send.

⑫ Click Save and Close to complete scheduling the task.

⑬ Click here to place a check mark next to the item when you have completed it.

⑭ Double-click a task to open and edit it.

■ Outlook displays completed tasks with lines through them and overdue tasks in red.

337

Using the Journal

Most professionals understand the importance of organization within the office, so time is set aside for such things as keeping a list of contacts, monitoring a calendar, making appointments, and keeping track of important tasks. But there is one area in which many people fall behind: record keeping.

Ask yourself this question: What is and is not worth keeping a record of? Should you keep track of how many hours are spent working on an Excel worksheet? What about e-mail messages you get from prospective clients, or phone calls to the pizza delivery guy? Only you can decide for certain what is worth keeping on record and what isn't, but consider this: Even something that seems totally insignificant or easy to remember can come back to haunt you later on.

For example, suppose you keep a diligent record, including what time the call was made, who you called, and what was said, of every phone call you make. That is, every time you pick up the phone and get a busy signal, or leave a message on the answering machine, or even order a pizza pie. Now, suppose that a customer calls your supervisor and complains that you were rude and insensitive to them during a call made last Friday. Not only does your exhaustive phone call journal list no phone calls for that day, but

according to the Calendar you were on the other side of the country! Your career is saved by the diligent recording of everything that happens to you.

Outlook's Journal helps you keep a record of such things, in a format that is easy to use and maintain. Since it's part of Office 97 on your computer, you won't have to worry about storing bulky log books all over your workspace. Also, some things will be entered into your Journal automatically. When you work on a file in any Office 97 program, a record is kept in the Outlook Journal. This will help you keep track of what you did and when.

The first two figures on the following page show you how to review automatic entries in the Journal. The last two figures show you how to make your own entries manually, such as when you need to make a record of a phone call.

TAKE NOTE

▶ TRACK OTHERS' WORK WITH THE JOURNAL

All Journal entries are keyed to the person who made them, so if other people use your computer — and they log on as a different user with Windows — you can track their work in the Journal as well. You can prevent others from reviewing your Journal entries by choosing Private in the Journal Entry dialog box.

CROSS-REFERENCE

Learn how to open files that are attached to automatic Journal entries in "Opening and Closing Office Files" in Chapter 3.

SHORTCUT

Make a new Journal entry from anywhere in Outlook by pressing Ctrl+Shift+J.

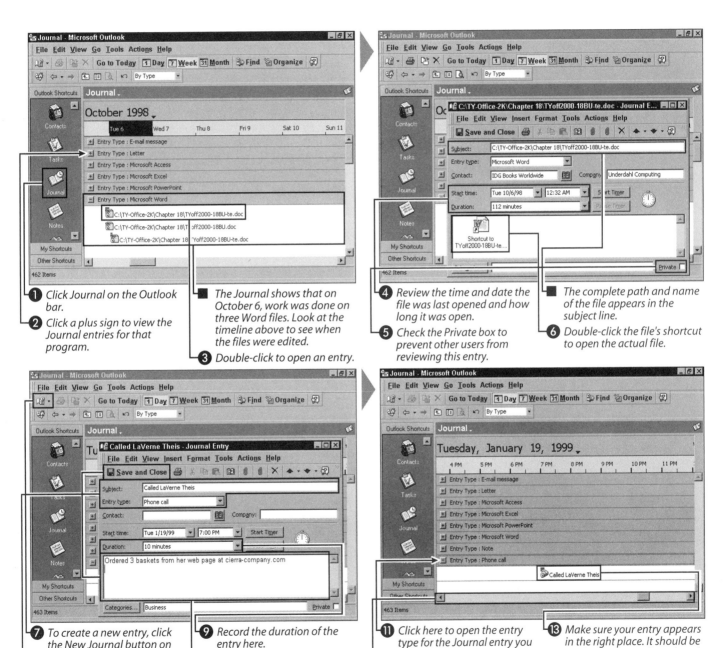

① Click Journal on the Outlook bar.

② Click a plus sign to view the Journal entries for that program.

■ The Journal shows that on October 6, work was done on three Word files. Look at the timeline above to see when the files were edited.

③ Double-click to open an entry.

④ Review the time and date the file was last opened and how long it was open.

⑤ Check the Private box to prevent other users from reviewing this entry.

■ The complete path and name of the file appears in the subject line.

⑥ Double-click the file's shortcut to open the actual file.

⑦ To create a new entry, click the New Journal button on the toolbar.

⑧ Type a subject for the entry here. Select a type of entry from this drop-down list.

⑨ Record the duration of the entry here.

⑩ Enter notes here. When you are done, click Save and Close to close the entry.

⑪ Click here to open the entry type for the Journal entry you just made.

⑫ Use the scroll bar to scroll back and forth through the current day.

⑬ Make sure your entry appears in the right place. It should be on the date you selected, and the entry should start at the approximate time of day that you made the call.

Personal Workbook

Q&A

1 What kind of information is stored in Contacts?

_____

_____

_____

2 How can categories help you better organize your contacts?

_____

_____

_____

3 What is one way to change the view of the Contact list?

_____

_____

_____

4 How do you add an event to your calendar?

_____

_____

_____

5 Other than placing a note in your calendar, what can the Meeting Planner do for you?

_____

_____

_____

6 How do you add something to your task list?

_____

_____

_____

7 What should you do when a task has been completed?

_____

_____

_____

8 What kind of things are recorded in the Outlook Journal automatically?

_____

_____

_____

ANSWERS: PAGE 417

EXTRA PRACTICE

1 Create a new contact card for William J. Clinton and add him to the VIP category. Type in your own e-mail address on his card for now.

2 Schedule a dental appointment for next Friday at 3:30 p.m. in the Outlook Calendar.

3 Schedule a meeting just after your dental appointment and notify Mr. Clinton that he needs to attend.

4 Add two items to your Task list. One of them should have a deadline and one should not.

5 Call your closest friend on the telephone and make a record of the call in the Outlook Journal.

REAL-WORLD APPLICATIONS

✔ Using a centralized contact list like the one in Outlook prevents you from having to rifle through a desk drawer full of business cards trying to find a phone number when you need it.

✔ You can use all of the features of Outlook to plan a meeting and then assign some of your coworkers to attend. Use the task list to make a note of things you need to get prepared before the meeting starts.

✔ If a coworker calls you to see if you're free for a round of golf this afternoon, check your Calendar to see if you have anything scheduled.

Visual Quiz

How do you open the section of Outlook shown here? Why are there seven days shown in the middle instead of just one? How do you get four months to display in the upper-right frame rather than just two? What do the bold numbers on the calendar indicate? What does the check mark next to the last task indicate? How do you schedule a meeting from this window?

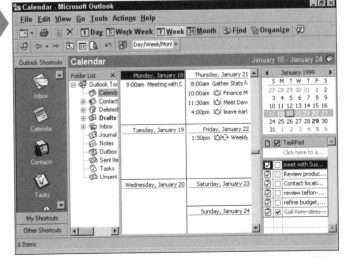

_____

_____

CHAPTER 22

MASTER
THESE
SKILLS

▶ Deleting Old Items

▶ Creating New Folders

▶ Moving Items

▶ Adding Outlook Services

Managing Your Outlook Folders

Throughout Part V of this book you have learned how Outlook can make your work easier and more organized. Outlook provides one central location on your computer from which to communicate, plan events, keep on schedule, record important information, and just generally make sense out of your day.

Outlook keeps you on top of things by eliminating much of the clutter and confusion that once plagued many office desks. That clutter diminished productivity because important figures were lost, reports misplaced, and meetings forgotten. Outlook solves many of these problems, but you should know that even Outlook can become cluttered and unwieldy if you don't perform some basic housekeeping chores from time to time.

A common mistake made by many users is to let messages pile up in the Outlook Inbox. Just like the classic mile high in-basket that haunts so many desks around the workplace, the Inbox on your computer can become disorganized and impossible to make any real sense out of. The key is to organize, and Outlook has some useful options to help you. You can create new folders within Outlook just like you create folders on your hard drive, and you can move items around to organize them into your new folders.

When you are done with something, you can delete it to get it out of the way. Deleting messages is easy; in fact, it may be too easy. Fortunately, Outlook provides a safe place to store recently deleted items, similar to the Windows Recycle Bin. If you decide that you deleted something you should have saved, you can easily restore it.

Besides offering ways to organize your messages, Outlook makes the process of adding services easy. Occasionally you may find the need to add a new mail account, or perhaps you may want to add fax capabilities.

This chapter shows you ways of organizing your messages within Outlook. You learn how to delete items, and then how to view the things you just deleted. You also learn how to create new folders within Outlook, and how to move messages into those new folders. Finally, you learn how to add more services to Outlook when you need them.

Deleting Old Items

When it comes to handling incoming messages, there seem to be two main schools of thought. One sends most messages straight to the garbage, often without even reading them. The other takes a "pack rat" approach and keeps a copy of every message ever sent, for any reason, from any one.

Neither of these approaches is terribly effective. As you begin receiving vast quantities of e-mail — it's only a matter of time — you will notice that some of them are obviously not relevant to you. Often you can tell just by looking at who the message is from, or what the subject is, that it is not worth your valuable time. In this case, you can delete the offending messages without ever even reading them.

Even if you *do* go to the trouble of opening a questionable message, deleting it from within the message window is still a matter of a single mouse click. If you delete a message from within the message window, Outlook saves you some time by automatically displaying the next unread message. This way, even if you download a large list of messages, you should only need to manually open the first one.

Besides getting rid of unwanted messages, you can delete items from other areas of Outlook as well. This includes Tasks, Contact cards, and Calendar appointments. Once you delete something, it is not completely deleted. Outlook moves these dregs to a folder called Deleted Items. You can restore messages from the Deleted Items folder almost as easily as you put them there in the first place.

The figures on the opposite page show you how to delete items in Outlook. The first figure demonstrates how to delete e-mail messages from the Inbox. The second figure shows how to delete a Contact card, and the third one shows you how to delete an appointment from your Calendar. The last figure shows you how to view items that have already been deleted.

TAKE NOTE

WHAT'S ALL THIS SPAM, THEN?

A term you may hear floating around the online community is *Spam*. According to 'net lore the term originated from a *Monty Python* skit, but whatever the etymology, it now applies to unsolicited advertisements sent to you via e-mail. If Spam messages irritate you, just delete them without ever opening them.

CLEAN OUT THOSE FOLDERS

It's a good idea to sort through all of your folders and delete irrelevant messages from time to time. Don't forget to look in Sent Items, and all of the other folders you might have created.

DELETING DELETED ITEMS

By default, items are cleared out of the Deleted Items folder after two months. You can also get rid of everything by right-clicking Deleted Items in the folder list and choosing Empty "Deleted Items" Folder.

CROSS-REFERENCE

See "Sending and Receiving Messages" in Chapter 20 to learn more about receiving things to delete.

FIND IT ONLINE

Find more useful Outlook add-ins at
http://nitty.rmit.usf.edu/usfit/exchange/addins.shtml.

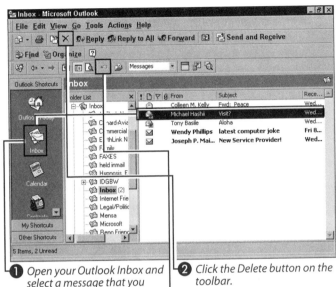

1. Open your Outlook Inbox and select a message that you wish to get rid of.

■ You can select multiple messages using Shift+click or Ctrl+click.

2. Click the Delete button on the toolbar.

3. Click the Undo button if you accidentally delete the wrong message.

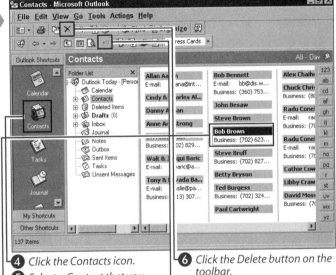

4. Click the Contacts icon.

5. Select a Contact that you want to get rid of.

■ You can select multiple contacts using Shift+click or Ctrl+click.

6. Click the Delete button on the toolbar.

7. Click the Undo button if you accidentally delete the wrong contact.

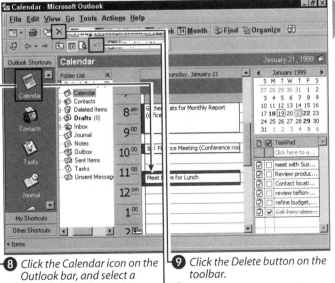

8. Click the Calendar icon on the Outlook bar, and select a canceled appointment.

■ You can select multiple appointments using Shift+click or Ctrl+click.

9. Click the Delete button on the toolbar.

10. Click the Undo button if you accidentally delete the wrong appointment.

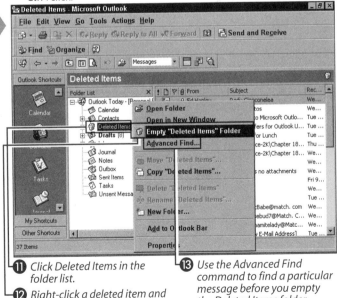

11. Click Deleted Items in the folder list.

12. Right-click a deleted item and choose Empty "Deleted Items" Folder from the context menu.

13. Use the Advanced Find command to find a particular message before you empty the Deleted Items folder.

■ Restore an item by dragging it to the correct folder.

345

Creating New Folders

I f you have spent any amount of time organizing things in an office, you know that proper categorization is the key to success. You file important records using a standard system that will be easy to interpret again some time in the future. For example, you would probably file employee personnel records in separate folders, organized in alphabetical order, in a drawer in a file cabinet. If you have a large company, you might even break these records down further and file them by department. On the other hand, suppose you work at home as a consultant for several different companies. It would make sense to use separate folders for each company's respective paperwork.

Files on your computer are organized in much the same way. Your hard drive has folders in it to help keep related files and documents together, and you learned how to create your own folders back in Chapter 3. This system makes perfect sense on your computer because it avoids a lot of potential organizational problems.

Outlook lets you create a similar system of folders within the program. You can create folders within folders, and even more subfolders within those folders. Messages can be filed wherever you want them; if you don't see a logical place for a certain item, simply create a new folder! When you are done with a folder, you can delete it just as easily as you created it, so go ahead and create folders even for temporary items.

When you create new folders, keep in mind how you would like things organized within Outlook. To keep things simple, it's usually best to create all of your folders as subfolders of the Inbox. Try to create just a few folders within the Inbox, and branch off from those with additional subfolders.

The figures on the facing page demonstrate how to create and delete new folders in Outlook. The first figure shows how to actually create a folder, and the second shows how to give that folder a name. The third figure demonstrates how to create a subfolder within a folder, and the last figure shows how to delete a folder that is no longer needed.

TAKE NOTE

▶ DELETING OLD FOLDERS

Folders help you stay organized, but a clutter of too many folders can defeat the purpose of trying to get organized in the first place. If you have folders that aren't being used anymore, select them and click the Delete button on the toolbar. Any files left in those folders will be deleted as well.

▶ RENAMING FOLDERS

Renaming folders is simple. Right-click the folder's name in the folder list and choose Rename from the context menu. Type a new name for the folder and press Enter when you are done.

CROSS-REFERENCE

Learn a similar procedure for creating new folders on your hard drive in "Creating New Folders" in Chapter 3.

FIND IT ONLINE

Get some great Outlook tips from smalloffice.com at **http://www.smalloffice.com/expert/archive/tesoft42.htm.**

■ If the folder list isn't displayed, select View ➪ Folders List.

1 Right-click the Inbox in the folder list.

2 Choose New Folder from the context menu.

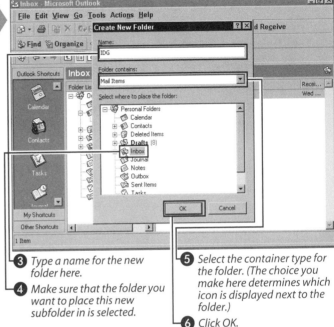

3 Type a name for the new folder here.

4 Make sure that the folder you want to place this new subfolder in is selected.

5 Select the container type for the folder. (The choice you make here determines which icon is displayed next to the folder.)

6 Click OK.

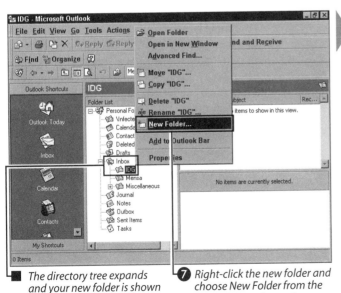

■ The directory tree expands and your new folder is shown as a subfolder of the Inbox.

7 Right-click the new folder and choose New Folder from the context menu to create a subfolder for it.

■ Repeat steps 3–5 to create as many folders as necessary.

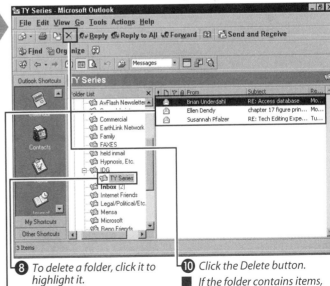

8 To delete a folder, click it to highlight it.

9 View the contents of the folder here to make sure it doesn't contain anything important.

10 Click the Delete button.

■ If the folder contains items, Outlook asks you if you want to delete the folder and move its contents into the Deleted Items folder.

347

Moving Items

In the previous task, you learned how to create new folders, a critical step toward getting organized in Outlook. Now that you have created some new folders for your messages and other items, it is time to actually put some items in those folders. You can do this by moving items from one folder to another. Moving items is very easy, but surprisingly it is something that many users never take the time to do. For the most part it is something you can do using context menus, from virtually anywhere in Outlook.

One thing you should know is that the techniques described here only apply to moving messages. Keep in mind that you can also select appointments in the Calendar, contact cards in Contacts, or even Tasks, and select Move to Folder from their context menus to move the item.

The figures on the facing page show you how to move a message to another folder. The first three figures show you how to move several items from the Deleted Items folder back to your Inbox. You'll find this to be an extremely important thing to know how to do. It can be all too easy to delete important e-mail messages. The last figure demonstrates how you can create a new folder during a move.

CROSS-REFERENCE

You will probably perform most moving tasks using context menus. Learn more about them in "Using Context Menus" in Chapter 1.

SHORTCUT

To quickly move an item, select it and press Ctrl+Shift+V to open the Move Items dialog box.

1 Click Deleted Items in the Folder List.

2 Select one or more messages to move out of this folder.

3 Right-click one of the messages and choose Move to Folder from the context menu.

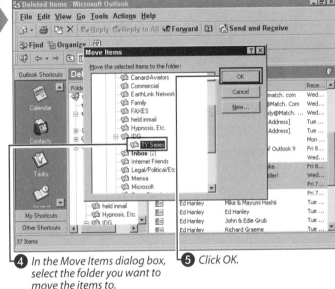

4 In the Move Items dialog box, select the folder you want to move the items to.

5 Click OK.

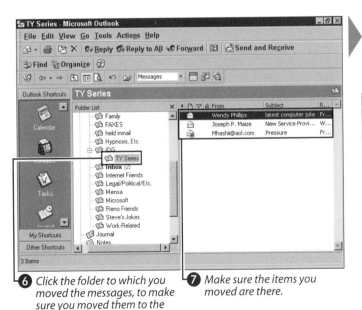

6 Click the folder to which you moved the messages, to make sure you moved them to the correct folder.

7 Make sure the items you moved are there.

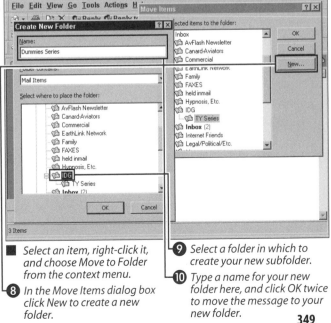

■ Select an item, right-click it, and choose Move to Folder from the context menu.

8 In the Move Items dialog box click New to create a new folder.

9 Select a folder in which to create your new subfolder.

10 Type a name for your new folder here, and click OK twice to move the message to your new folder.

Adding Outlook Services

When you think about it, Outlook is a pretty amazing tool for improving your efficiency around the office. It provides a calendar to help you plan your personal and professional schedule, keeps track of important tasks, reminds you when it's time for an appointment, maintains a record of the work you have done, and handles most of your messaging needs.

Believe it or not, Outlook is capable of even more. With only a few clicks of the mouse, you can upgrade Outlook to make it even more versatile than it already is. This process is called *adding services*. Services are things that Outlook can do; Internet Mail and your personal address book are services that are built-in to Outlook. You can add additional services, such as faxing capabilities, while installing Outlook, or, after you are up and running with Outlook. You can add services from an outside software vendor using menu commands.

Adding a service is relatively simple, but you have to know what you are doing. You can follow some simple menu commands as described here to add a service, be it from Microsoft or another vendor. If you are installing a service provided by another vendor, just click the Have Disk button in the Add Service dialog box. Locate the file that you have purchased or downloaded from the Internet, and install it. Generally speaking, you have to close and restart Outlook before any added services work.

You can look for Outlook 98 add-ins using the online Help system. There are many add-ins available at the Microsoft site, which can be accessed by clicking Help ⇨ Microsoft on the Web.

The faxing capability is very handy. You don't have to wait in line at the company fax, or even get up from your seat. Simply compose the fax and send it right from your computer. You can also receive faxes on your machine; no more lost faxes, or hunting for your fax through the company fax bin, or missed opportunities with clients due to fax problems.

TAKE NOTE

▶ SENDING FANCY FAXES

You can format your faxes by choosing Format ⇨ Rich Text (HTML) after the new fax message box appears. You can make text bold, underline, or italic, change the font or font size, or create bulleted lists. Remember that not many fax machines have color capabilities, so be careful about changing the color of the text.

▶ ADDING A FAX NUMBER TO A CONTACT

You can add a fax number to a contact's information without going to the contact manager. After bringing up the New Fax box, select To, click the contact's name, and select Properties. Click the Home tab and enter the fax number. Click OK.

CROSS-REFERENCE

Learn how to use the Online Help system in "Using Online Help Resources" in Chapter 2.

FIND IT ONLINE

You can find the WinFax Support Frequently Asked Questions at: **http://www.symantec.com/techsupp/ winfax/faq_winfax.html.**

1 Click Actions ⇨ New Fax Message. Alternatively, select File ⇨ New Fax message.

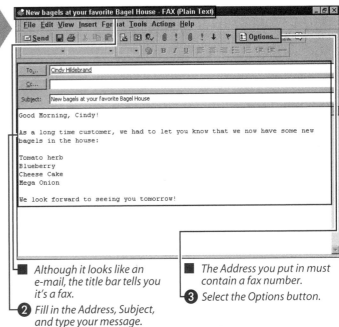

■ Although it looks like an e-mail, the title bar tells you it's a fax.

2 Fill in the Address, Subject, and type your message.

■ The Address you put in must contain a fax number.

3 Select the Options button.

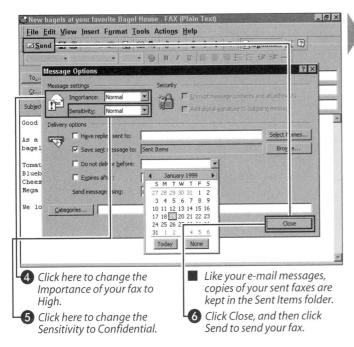

4 Click here to change the Importance of your fax to High.

5 Click here to change the Sensitivity to Confidential.

■ Like your e-mail messages, copies of your sent faxes are kept in the Sent Items folder.

6 Click Close, and then click Send to send your fax.

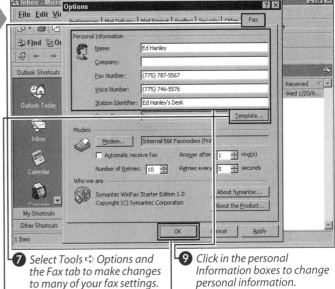

7 Select Tools ⇨ Options and the Fax tab to make changes to many of your fax settings.

8 Click Template to change your cover page.

9 Click in the personal Information boxes to change personal information.

10 Click Automatically receive fax, and then click OK.

351

Personal Workbook

Q&A

1 How do you delete a message in Outlook?

_____

_____

_____

2 How do you delete a Contact card?

_____

_____

_____

3 How do you create a new folder in Outlook?

_____

_____

_____

4 Where should you create new folders for your Outlook messages?

_____

_____

5 How do you move a message into another folder?

_____

_____

_____

6 When should you create a new folder?

_____

_____

_____

7 Can you move appointments from your Calendar into a different folder?

_____

_____

_____

8 How do you send a fax?

_____

_____

_____

ANSWERS: PAGE 417

EXTRA PRACTICE

1. Delete a message from your Inbox.

2. Restore that message back to the Inbox.

3. Move that same message into a folder called Sasquatch. If such a folder does not already exist, create one.

4. Create a subfolder in Sasquatch called Yeti.

5. Delete the folders called Sasquatch and Yeti.

6. Delete a Contact card.

7. Delete an appointment from your Calendar.

REAL-WORLD APPLICATIONS

✔ You will always be looking for new ways to organize your messages in Outlook. If you are currently corresponding with three or four different clients, create a separate folder for each one.

✔ Right now, you may only be connected to your company's network. But if you get Internet access in the future, you will probably want to add the Internet Mail service.

✔ If you receive a lot of e-mail messages with attachments, you might find that Outlook loads and shuts down a lot slower as time moves on. If this is the case, check to see if you have a lot of large messages with attachments in the Deleted Items folder. Getting rid of them should make Outlook run much more efficiently.

Visual Quiz

This message is currently stored in a folder called Office 97 stuff. How was this folder created? How did the message get here? How can the message be deleted? Can it be restored? How?

_____

_____

_____

_____

PART

VI

Learning Important Access Tasks

Access is a *database* — software that enables you to manage, access, and control information. When you use Access to create a database, you're organizing your information so that it will be both available and useful. You might want to think of an Access database as a highly structured storage system for your data. Because the database has a clearly defined structure, it's possible to find exactly the information you need without wading through all sorts of unrelated data.

Even if you've never worked with a database before, you probably have worked with data that was organized in spreadsheet fashion — in rows and columns. If so, you'll be pleased to learn that you can think of a database in much the same manner. In fact, database information is often displayed in a format that looks just like your old familiar spreadsheet.

In this part of the book, you learn some of the basics of using Access to manage information. You learn how to create a simple database, how to add information to the database, and how to get information from the database. None of these tasks is very difficult, and you'll soon be on your way to using Access for your information management needs.

CHAPTER 23

MASTER THESE SKILLS

▶ Creating a Database

▶ Modifying the Database Structure

▶ Adding Records to a Table

Creating a Simple Database

Think about the types of information you need to manage and it won't take long to realize that you could probably save yourself a lot of time and effort by using a database. A database is perfect for organizing related information and making it accessible. For example, suppose you purchase a list of several thousand potential customers for a new service business you are thinking of starting. You probably want to locate your new office so that it is convenient for the largest percentage of those potential customers. A database manager such as Access lets you examine the list in an organized fashion, enabling you to determine the best location for your new office.

Two primary types of databases exist. These are often referred to as *flat-file* and *relational* databases. Flat-file databases are the simplest type of database, and that's what you see in this chapter. Flat-file databases have one *table* that holds all of the information in the database.

Relational databases build on this by adding additional tables that contain information that is somehow related to the information in the first table. You might start out with a table containing information about your customers, and then later add a table containing information about customer orders. If you assign each customer a unique customer number, you can find every order a customer placed by looking in the orders table using the customer number as your search key. But why not simply expand the customer table to include customer order information? Because you'd have to enter all the information about a customer whenever you entered an order. In Access you can begin with a simple, single table flat-file database and later add additional related tables to enhance your database. You can find additional information about relational databases in other fine books from IDG Books Worldwide, such as *Access 97 Bible* by Cary N. Prague and Michael R. Irwin.

Creating a Database

Access provides two methods for creating a database. There's really no reason to begin the hard way — starting with a blank database and creating everything from scratch. Using the Database Wizard gives you a big head start on the process, and you can always modify the wizard-created database later, once you're more comfortable with Access.

The Database Wizard creates a complete database that includes at least one table and usually one or more data entry forms and reports. You may want to examine these components to learn more about how they are constructed; they make a very good learning tool.

When you use the Database Wizard, you'll discover that the process of creating a new database may vary somewhat, depending on the type of database you've chosen to create, and in some cases, the selections you made earlier. When in doubt, answer the Database Wizard's questions as well as possible, and then click the Next button to continue. Eventually the Database Wizard runs out of questions and the Next button is grayed out. When this happens, click the Finish button and wait while the Database Wizard creates the various database components.

Once the Database Wizard finishes creating a database, it displays a database form titled Main Switchboard. This form provides you with the means of entering and editing data, viewing and printing reports, and so on. Using your new database is as simple as just clicking the correct button and filling in a form.

TAKE NOTE

THE DATABASE WIZARD MAY NOT BE INSTALLED

If you try to use the Database Wizard to create an Access database, you may be greeted with a message telling you that the wizard hasn't been installed. If so, open the Add/Remove Programs item in the Windows Control Panel, select Microsoft Office 97, and click the Add/Remove button. Then add the Access wizards.

ACCESS DATABASES ARE IN ONE FILE

Access databases are somewhat different from most other types of databases. When you create an Access database everything is added to a single file. All of the tables, reports, forms, queries, and programming are contained in that one file, so it is much easier for you to keep all of the pieces of the database together.

DON'T CLICK "EXIT THIS DATABASE"

Don't click the Exit this database button on the Main Switchboard form — this closes the entire database. Close the form by clicking the Close button in the upper-right corner of the Main Switchboard form. This allows the database to remain open so you can examine or modify the database structure. You may also need to click the Restore button on the database title bar to actually see the database components.

Continued

CROSS-REFERENCE

See Chapter 24 for more information on working with Access forms and reports.

FIND IT ONLINE

Visit **http://www.microsoft.com/access/ enhancements/address.asp** to download an Access personal address database.

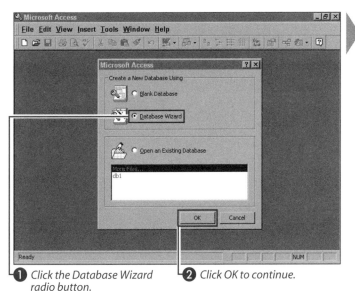

1 Click the Database Wizard radio button.

2 Click OK to continue.

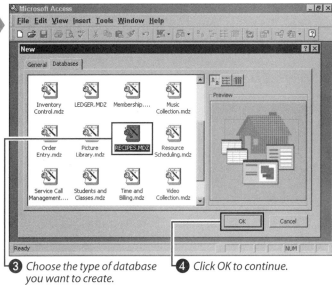

3 Choose the type of database you want to create.

4 Click OK to continue.

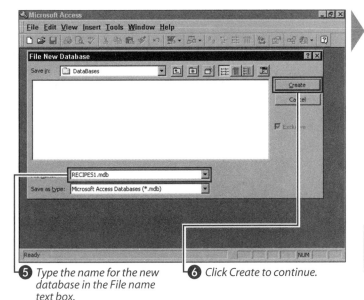

5 Type the name for the new database in the File name text box.

6 Click Create to continue.

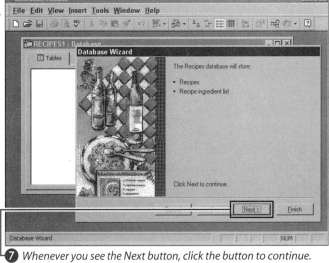

7 Whenever you see the Next button, click the button to continue.

Creating a Database
Continued

Databases vary in terms of the components that make up the database. The figures on the facing page show the steps required to create the sample recipes database. In this database four different related tables are used to hold all of the recipe information. Other databases may have more or fewer tables, depending on the type of information that they are storing.

You can add additional fields by placing a check in the checkbox in the fields list. You can also remove some of the existing fields if you know you will never have a use for them, but some of the fields are required. In the first figure on the facing page, for example, the Recipe ID is a required field because it is used in several tables to create the relationship between the tables. See the Take Note section for more information.

The Database Wizard also gives you the opportunity to select a number of nonessential database features such as the style used for various forms and reports. The styles you choose don't have any effect on how well your database functions, but they do affect the appearance. You may wish to experiment with the available options to see which styles you prefer. You can even choose to include a graphic on all of your reports. You might, for example, wish to incorporate a company logo on your reports. Access can include many types of image file formats on reports. The exact types available may depend on which graphics filters you installed when you

installed Office. It's usually a good idea to make certain that any picture you choose to include on your report is fairly simple — complex images may not reproduce very well if the report is sent to someone via fax.

TAKE NOTE

COMMON FIELDS ARE NEEDED FOR RELATIONSHIPS

Common fields are necessary to create relationships between database tables. The fields don't always need to have the same name, but they must hold the same type of data so that Access can determine which records in two or more tables are related. In the recipes database, the Recipe ID field shows which records in the Recipes and Recipe Ingredients tables are related. Additional common fields establish the remaining relationships between the other tables in the database.

DON'T REMOVE EXTRA FIELDS

When you're creating a database using the Access Database Wizard, you probably won't know why some of the fields appear in the database. This may tempt you into deleting fields whose purpose you don't understand. Resist the temptation to remove fields unless you're absolutely certain they won't serve a useful purpose. If you remove a field and later discover that it really is important you have to add the field manually, which is a lot more work than having the database wizard create it in the first place!

CROSS-REFERENCE
See Chapter 2 for more information on using Office wizards.

FIND IT ONLINE
Visit **http://www.microsoft.com/office/enhAccess.asp** to find additional Access enhancements.

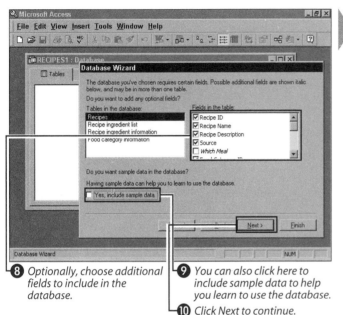

8 Optionally, choose additional fields to include in the database.

9 You can also click here to include sample data to help you learn to use the database.

10 Click Next to continue.

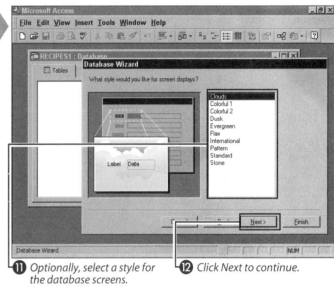

11 Optionally, select a style for the database screens.

12 Click Next to continue.

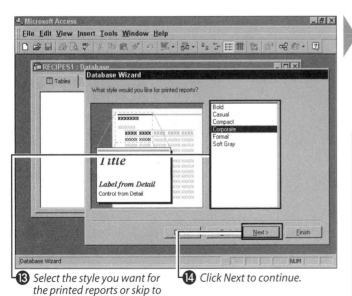

13 Select the style you want for the printed reports or skip to the next step.

14 Click Next to continue.

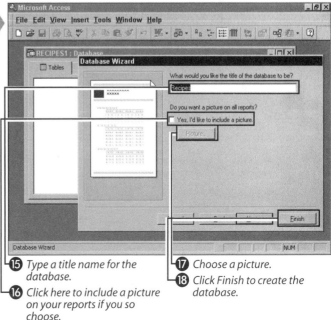

15 Type a title name for the database.

16 Click here to include a picture on your reports if you so choose.

17 Choose a picture.

18 Click Finish to create the database.

361

Modifying the Database Structure

I t's pretty unlikely that your first attempt at creating a database will produce perfect results. One of the most common problems new database developers face, is discovering that the database simply doesn't track all of the information that it should. Fortunately, that's a problem you can solve without too much trouble.

You can make room for data you forgot to include in an Access database table in two ways. You might be able to use one of the existing, unused fields, or you can add a new field to the table. It's probably safer to add a new field because you might find that an existing field has a purpose you hadn't considered.

When you add a field to an Access table you must enter a name for the field and choose the type of data the field will hold. Access automatically selects default settings for the field size, format, and several other options. You can change any of the default settings as necessary, to better control how Access stores your data.

Adding a field to a table doesn't automatically add that field to any existing input forms or to any existing reports. You can add information to the field in the table without having the new field referenced in any forms or reports, but you'll probably find that you want to make things a little more convenient. In the next chapter you learn how to modify forms and reports.

TAKE NOTE

GET HELP MODIFYING FIELDS

Access has a large range of options you can select while you're defining a field. If you're not certain how to specify one of the options, select the option (such as Field Size or Format) and press F1 to see the Access help screens that provide information about the selected option. Not only can you read a description of the option, but in many cases you are able to examine an example. You can also select Options ⇨ Print topic to print out a copy of the help screen.

SAVE YOUR MODIFICATIONS

Access automatically saves data you add to a database, but changes you make to the database structure aren't saved automatically. Be sure you select File ⇨ Save if you want to keep your changes. Access reminds you to save your changes before closing the database if you forget.

WATCH FOR THE DROP-DOWN LIST

Many field properties — such as the data type — have a limited set of options. When you select one of these properties Access displays a down arrow at the right edge of the list box. Click this arrow to drop-down the list box so you can select your choice from the available options.

CROSS-REFERENCE

See Chapter 24 for more information on using Access forms and reports.

FIND IT ONLINE

Visit **http://www.microsoft.com/access/ enhancements/Ac9701hlp.asp** to find additional Access help online.

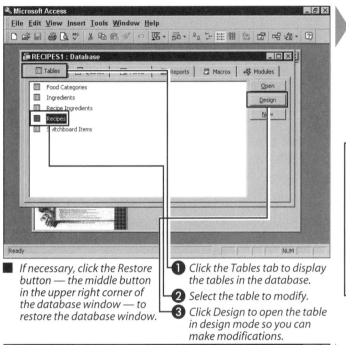

■ If necessary, click the Restore
button — the middle button
in the upper right corner of
the database window — to
restore the database window.

❶ Click the Tables tab to display
the tables in the database.

❷ Select the table to modify.

❸ Click Design to open the table
in design mode so you can
make modifications.

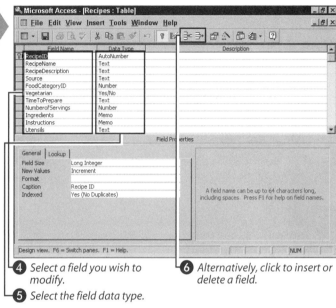

❹ Select a field you wish to
modify.

❺ Select the field data type.

❻ Alternatively, click to insert or
delete a field.

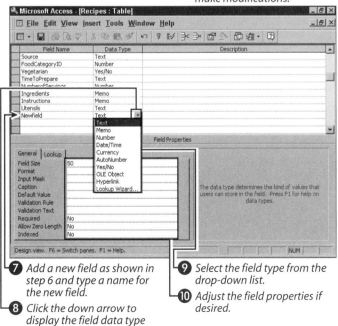

❼ Add a new field as shown in
step 6 and type a name for
the new field.

❽ Click the down arrow to
display the field data type
list box.

❾ Select the field type from the
drop-down list.

❿ Adjust the field properties if
desired.

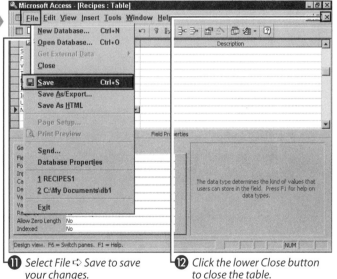

⓫ Select File ⇨ Save to save
your changes.

⓬ Click the lower Close button
to close the table.

Adding Records to a Table

A database really only becomes valuable when it contains data. The data you add to a database is in the form of records — groups of related information that describe a single database entry. A record may include one (and only one) entry in each field, but in some cases it may not be necessary to make an entry in every field for each record. For example, in an address table some records might include an entry in the middle name field, but you probably wouldn't have this information for every record.

When you use the Database Wizard to create a database, one of the types of objects the wizard creates is an input form. An input form is simply a tool that enables you to look at your database one record at a time. But there's no rule that says you must have data entry forms — you can also access your tables directly to view, modify, or add data. Working directly with your data in a table may, at times, even be more convenient than using a form. Working with the records in a table certainly provides a clearer picture of how Access stores your data.

The Access table view that displays the data in a spreadsheet-like format is called a Datasheet view. In this view your data is shown in rows and columns that look quite similar to an Excel worksheet. Each row in the table is one record, and each column is one field. Unlike an Excel worksheet, though, your

Access database automatically saves new or modified information as soon as you move to a new record (or if you close the database). As a result you don't have to worry about losing your data because you forgot to save your work when you closed Access.

Multiple table Access databases have relationships between the tables. It may not always be obvious where you can safely edit data because you must be careful not to disrupt the relationships. As the final figure on the facing page shows, you can view these relationships to see which fields connect the tables. The lines between the tables show how the tables are related. As a general rule you shouldn't delete any records in a table where the connecting line shows a 1 just above the line.

TAKE NOTE

▶ SOME FIELDS CANNOT BE MODIFIED

Access tables often include special fields you cannot modify directly. In the figures on the facing page the first field, Recipe ID, is an AutoNumber field — a numeric field that is automatically incremented as new records are added. AutoNumber fields are used to create unique record identifiers so that no two records use the same value in the field. Access won't allow you to change the value in an AutoNumber field.

SHORTCUT
Press Ctrl+F to locate specific values in a field.

FIND IT ONLINE
Visit **http://www.microsoft.com/accessdev/ Freestuff/printwiz/** to download a tool that prints Access relationships.

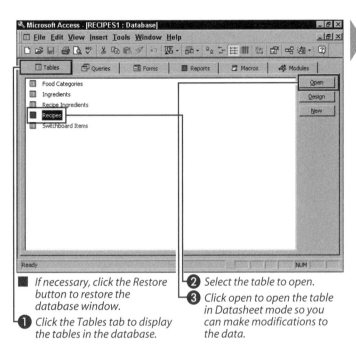

■ If necessary, click the Restore button to restore the database window.

❶ Click the Tables tab to display the tables in the database.

❷ Select the table to open.

❸ Click open to open the table in Datasheet mode so you can make modifications to the data.

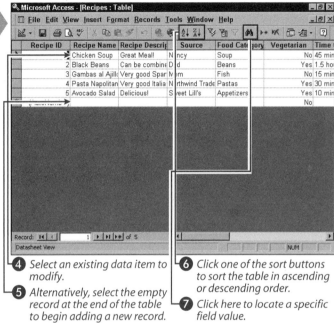

❹ Select an existing data item to modify.

❺ Alternatively, select the empty record at the end of the table to begin adding a new record.

❻ Click one of the sort buttons to sort the table in ascending or descending order.

❼ Click here to locate a specific field value.

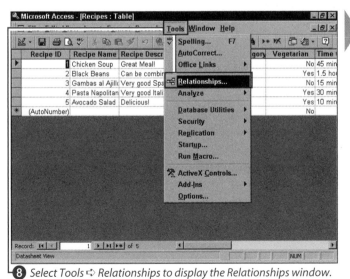

❽ Select Tools ➪ Relationships to display the Relationships window.

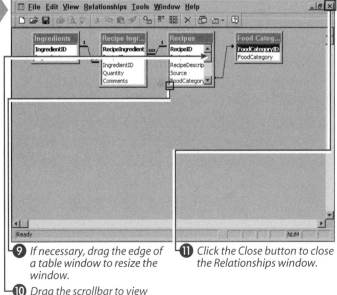

❾ If necessary, drag the edge of a table window to resize the window.

❿ Drag the scrollbar to view additional fields.

⓫ Click the Close button to close the Relationships window.

Personal Workbook

Q&A

1 Which Access database component holds your data?

_____

_____

_____

_____

_____

2 What do you call the view that shows your Access data in a spreadsheet-like format?

_____

_____

_____

_____

3 What are the two types of databases?

_____

_____

_____

_____

4 What type of Access database field automatically increments when you add a new record?

_____

_____

_____

_____

5 What one thing do you need in order to create a relationship between two tables?

_____

_____

_____

_____

6 What two things must you enter to add a new field to an Access database table?

_____

_____

_____

_____

_____

ANSWERS: PAGE 418

EXTRA PRACTICE

1 Use the Database Wizard to create a new Access database to organize your book collection.

2 Use the Datasheet view to add *Teach Yourself Office 97* to your new database.

3 Add a new field to one of the tables in the book collection database.

4 View the relationships between the tables in the book collection database.

5 Add a picture to a report.

6 Sort a table in descending order.

REAL-WORLD APPLICATIONS

✔ If you volunteer your time keeping track of contributions club members make towards a charitable project, you may want to use the Access Database Wizard to create a database to track those contributions for tax purposes.

✔ If you use the Access Household Inventory database to track your possessions for insurance purposes, you may need to modify the database to track items you loan out to your local art museum.

✔ If you discover that one of your favorite computer book authors has suddenly become a cult hero, you may want to search your book collection database to locate any books authored or coauthored by that author. This way, you can make certain you don't accidentally sell those books at your mother's garage sale.

Visual Quiz

What is the purpose of this dialog box? How can you display this dialog box?

_____

_____

_____

_____

_____

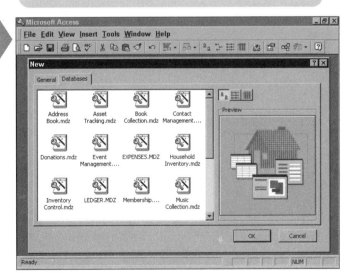

CHAPTER **24**

MASTER
THESE
SKILLS

▶ **Working with Access Forms**

▶ **Creating Reports**

▶ **Sorting Reports**

▶ **Adding Titles to Your Reports**

Creating Forms and Reports

An Access database table is a useful tool, but you can make your data more accessible through *forms* and *reports*. Forms provide a more convenient way to work with your data when compared to using a table. Generally forms concentrate all of the information for one record into a single window. It's usually easier to input or edit data in a form than directly in a table since all of the record's fields are visible at one time.

Reports make it much easier to understand your data. Reports not only show the raw data in a database, but they can also organize information so that you can actually use it. Rather than simply dumping unrelated information in your lap the way a database table does, a database report sorts and summarizes the information.

When you use the Access Database Wizard to create a database, the wizard generally creates tables, forms, reports, and possibly a few other database components as well. You may never need anything other than the forms and reports that are created automatically. Even so, understanding a bit about the design process of these two features is still important. If you understand how to create a form or report manually, you can also modify existing forms and reports to better suit your needs. This also enables you to have more control over your entire Access database. If you add or remove a field in a table, you need to do the same in forms and reports.

There's really very little difference between creating a new form or report, and modifying an existing form or report. Starting from scratch is a little more involved than working with a form or report you already have. In most cases it's faster to modify a form or report created with the Database Wizard. If you're worried about making a mistake, just make a copy before you start tinkering. Even though working on an existing form or report may be easier, in this chapter we show you how to create forms and reports from scratch. This way you learn some important points that you might otherwise miss. We use the recipes database shown in Chapter 23 as the basis for the new forms and reports.

Working with Access Forms

Access forms and the Datasheet view provide two different views of your data. In a form you generally see all of one record at a time rather than part of a number of records (although you should check out the Take Note section to learn about a special case). You can use forms for entering or editing information in your database.

The Database Wizard automatically creates forms when you create a new database. You can use these forms as is, modify them to suit your special needs, or create your own new forms. One advantage of starting with one of the Database Wizard forms is that much of the legwork has been done for you. But this can also be a disadvantage if you really want to understand how to create your own unique forms. In these next few pages you learn how to add a new form to your database from scratch. The results may not be pretty, but you can always clean up your form and get fancy later.

If you don't want to do it all yourself, open a form you wish to modify and choose View ⇨ Design View to place the form into design view. This view enables you to make most of the modifications you can make when creating a new form. Don't change the table associated with the form unless you're really sure of what you're doing. Changing the table — also known as the *data* or *record source* — breaks the associations between the existing form fields and the table.

Continued

TAKE NOTE

▶ FORMS CAN SHOW MULTIPLE RECORDS

Even though the most common forms you'll encounter only show one record at a time, it is possible to create a form that shows multiple records. The catch is that this only works if you have a form that shows information from two tables at a time. One of the tables must be a *master* table, and the other table must be a *detail* table. One record from the master table and multiple records from the detail table can be shown on a form. A typical application for this is an order form that uses a customer table as a master table, and a stock item table as the detail table.

▶ DON'T FORGET TO PICK A TABLE

One of the easiest mistakes you can make in creating database forms from scratch is to forget to choose the database table. Until you select a table, Access has no way to provide you with a list of fields to place on your form. If Access won't show you the field name list, you forgot to choose the data source. Select View ⇨ Properties and choose the table in the Record Source list box.

CROSS-REFERENCE
See Chapter 23 for more information on using the Database Wizard.

FIND IT ONLINE
For an online tutorial covering everything from basic to advanced forms and subforms, check out http://mis.commerce.ubc.ca/~brydon/MSAccess/tutorials.

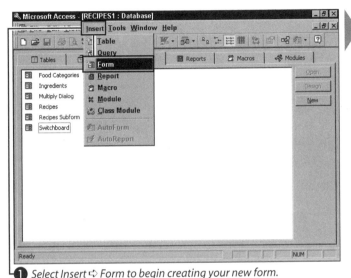

1 Select Insert ➪ Form to begin creating your new form.

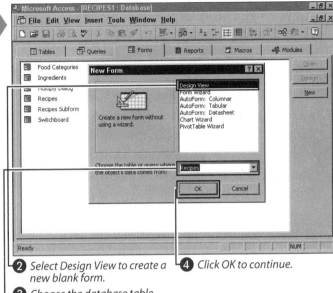

2 Select Design View to create a new blank form.

3 Choose the database table you want to use as the data source.

4 Click OK to continue.

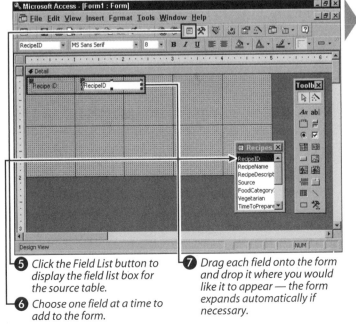

5 Click the Field List button to display the field list box for the source table.

6 Choose one field at a time to add to the form.

7 Drag each field onto the form and drop it where you would like it to appear — the form expands automatically if necessary.

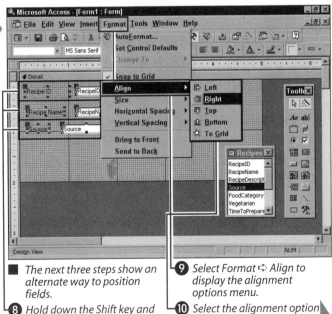

■ The next three steps show an alternate way to position fields.

8 Hold down the Shift key and click each field you want to align.

9 Select Format ➪ Align to display the alignment options menu.

10 Select the alignment option to make the selected fields move into alignment.

371

Working with Access Forms
Continued

Forms don't have to include all of the fields from their associated table. A good example of this might be a database that included sensitive information, such as employee payroll data as well as more general information such as telephone extensions. You might want to create a form that shows the general information but not the more sensitive information to prevent casual users from browsing where they shouldn't be. You can use the Tools ➪ Security commands to control who can use various forms.

Your forms can include more types of objects than simply database fields. The floating Toolbox provides you with many different options. You might wish to include text to provide users with onscreen help, or possibly a graphical image to create a uniform appearance in all the forms you create for a specific application.

All of the objects on a form (and indeed the form itself) have properties you can set to control both their appearance and functionality. The second figure on the facing page shows the properties box for the form. You can select from a broad range of properties, such as how the form will be used. If you were to select Yes for the Allow Additions property, but you selected No for the Allow Deletions property, a user would be able to add new records to the database but wouldn't be able to remove any records. You can view the properties dialog box for the selected object by selecting View ➪ Properties or — for most objects — by right-clicking the object and choosing Properties.

Unlike changes to your data, Access does not automatically save changes you make to the structure of your database. A warning message appears if you forget to save your work, but it's still a good idea to save your work regularly. That way you won't lose a lot of time if your computer is accidentally shut down or if you click the wrong button in error.

TAKE NOTE

▶ USE THE OBJECTS LIST TO SELECT OBJECTS

Before you select View ➪ Properties, make certain the Objects list box (at the left side of the Formatting toolbar) shows the correct object. To view or change the form properties, make sure that Form appears in the list box.

▶ USE TABS FOR ORGANIZATION

If you are creating a complex form, make it easier for users by adding tabs to the form. Click the Tab Control button on the Toolbox to create a tabbed multiple-page form. Then add the fields to the separate tabbed pages keeping related fields together. Your users may find this type of form easier to use and understand than placing a large number of fields together on one huge form page.

CROSS-REFERENCE

See Chapter 25 for information on using filters to limit what records your forms display.

FIND IT ONLINE

For a complete list of Access forms and examples of their uses, check out the Total Access SourceBook Procedure Reference at **http://www.fmsinc.com**.

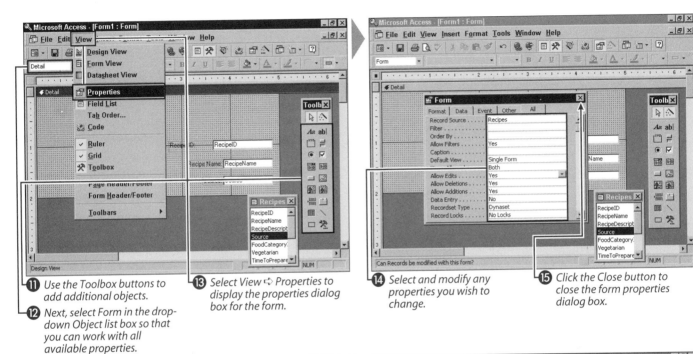

⓫ Use the Toolbox buttons to add additional objects.

⓬ Next, select Form in the drop-down Object list box so that you can work with all available properties.

⓭ Select View ➪ Properties to display the properties dialog box for the form.

⓮ Select and modify any properties you wish to change.

⓯ Click the Close button to close the form properties dialog box.

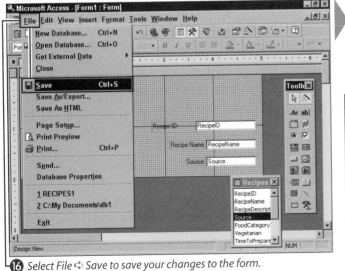

⓰ Select File ➪ Save to save your changes to the form.

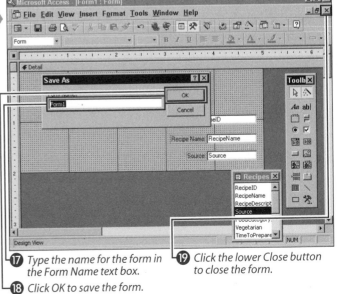

⓱ Type the name for the form in the Form Name text box.

⓲ Click OK to save the form.

⓳ Click the lower Close button to close the form.

Creating Reports

You may be both surprised and pleased to learn that creating Access reports is quite similar to creating Access forms. If you consider that both forms and reports are alternative methods of viewing database information, it's easier to understand how the two tasks might be similar.

In spite of the fact that creating forms and creating reports are similar tasks, there are some important differences between forms and reports. It is most likely that you will create forms for viewing on your screen, and lay them out with data entry as a top priority. Reports, on the other hand, work well if you intend to produce printed copies, laying them out with data analysis as the priority. These differences aside, what you've learned about forms will help you learn about reports.

When you're designing a report, it's good to think about the purpose of your report. If you want a short report that provides basic information, there's probably no reason to include all of the fields in the database. Just create a short summary report that includes only the necessary information. Not only will you use less paper, your short report will be much easier to use because you won't have to wade through information you don't need.

As you add fields to your new report, you can greatly improve the appearance by using the Format ⇨ Align options just as you did when you created a new form. Nothing spoils the appearance of a report more than fields that don't line up — especially fields that are in the same row. To select several fields and field labels at the same time, drag a selection box across all of them using the mouse. Once you've selected two or more fields you can choose the alignment options that look the best for your report. Be careful not to select fields that are in different rows when you specify vertical alignment options, or in different columns when you specify horizontal alignment options. If you make a mistake, select Edit ⇨ Undo immediately to return the objects to their previous positions.

Continued

TAKE NOTE

▶ USE LESS PAPER

When you're designing a report, remember that each record uses the amount of space you've allocated in the detail area of the report. To reduce wasted paper, keep the fields near the top of the detail area, and drag the separator between the detail and page footer areas up to reduce the size of the detail area.

▶ USE THE RIGHT ORIENTATION

If you need to include quite a bit of information about each record, you may want to consider using landscape rather than portrait orientation. Select File ⇨ Page Setup and click the Page tab to select the page orientation.

CROSS-REFERENCE

See "Sorting Reports" later in this chapter.

FIND IT ONLINE

For a complete listing of Access reports and examples of their uses, check out the Total Access SourceBook Procedure Reference at **http://www.fmsinc.com**.

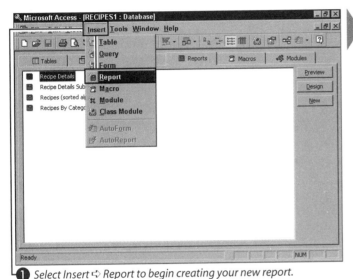

❶ Select Insert ➪ Report to begin creating your new report.

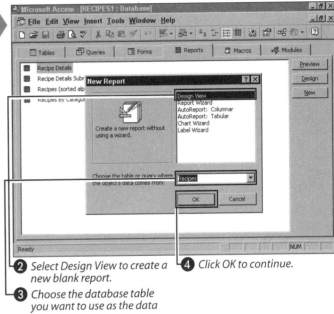

❷ Select Design View to create a new blank report.

❸ Choose the database table you want to use as the data source.

❹ Click OK to continue.

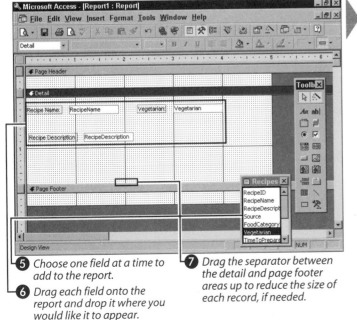

❺ Choose one field at a time to add to the report.

❻ Drag each field onto the report and drop it where you would like it to appear.

❼ Drag the separator between the detail and page footer areas up to reduce the size of each record, if needed.

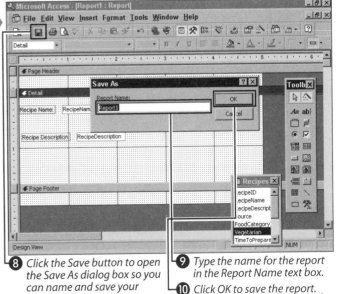

❽ Click the Save button to open the Save As dialog box so you can name and save your report.

❾ Type the name for the report in the Report Name text box.

❿ Click OK to save the report.

Once you've laid out the basic report you will probably want to make some improvements. You may wish to consider quite a few changes in your search for the best report layout. Some of these changes will be fairly general, while others will be changes you make to individual fields on the report.

One example of a change you probably want to consider on a field-by-field basis is whether you need the field labels. Field labels help you determine just which information is being displayed, but in many cases you can eliminate the field labels without adversely affecting the report. Eliminating the redundant field labels gives you the opportunity to pack the fields in a bit tighter and further reduce the size of the printed report. You may even make the report somewhat easier to read by eliminating some useless clutter.

Not all report fields should be unlabeled, of course. The recipes database contains an example of a field that really must be labeled to be understandable. The "Vegetarian" field is a *Boolean* field — a field that can only contain the values Yes or No (these could also be True and False). Someone looking at a report about your recipes would have a hard time understanding what this field represented if the field wasn't labeled — especially if the database contained more than one Boolean field.

Rather than wasting a lot of paper testing your report layout, use the Print Preview button to display an onscreen representation of the printed report as shown in the third figure on the facing page. If you're doing the layout work you should preview your report often, that way you won't be surprised by the final report appearance. Remember, objects that appear in Design View may not necessarily appear in the printed report — especially if you've changed their visible property to No.

TAKE NOTE

▶ WATCH OUT FOR MEMO FIELDS

Access databases often contain *memo fields* that can hold essentially unlimited amounts of data. When you place a memo field on a report you need to consider how much data you're likely to place in that field and adjust the size of the report field appropriately. If possible you may want to place memo fields in a row by themselves, and adjust their size to fit the full width of the report page. You may also wish to adjust their Can Grow and Can Shrink properties as shown in the final figure on the facing page.

▶ USE THE PROPERTIES DIALOG BOXES

As you work on refining your report, remember to use the Properties dialog boxes. Right-click any report object and select Properties to see which properties you can adjust.

CROSS-REFERENCE

See "Adding Titles to Your Reports" later in this chapter.

SHORTCUT

Delete unneeded field labels by selecting them and pressing Delete.

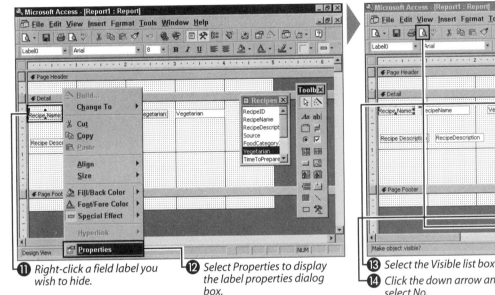

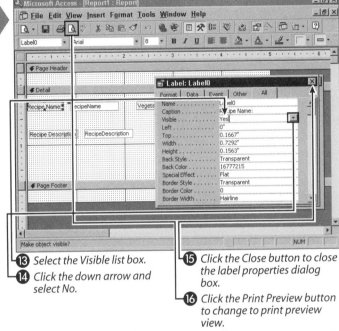

⓫ *Right-click a field label you wish to hide.*

⓬ *Select Properties to display the label properties dialog box.*

⓭ *Select the Visible list box.*

⓮ *Click the down arrow and select No.*

⓯ *Click the Close button to close the label properties dialog box.*

⓰ *Click the Print Preview button to change to print preview view.*

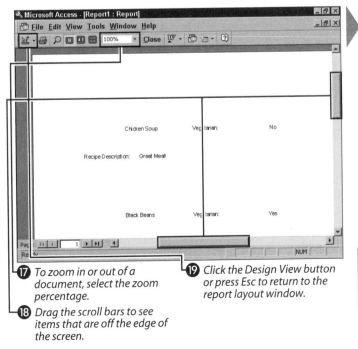

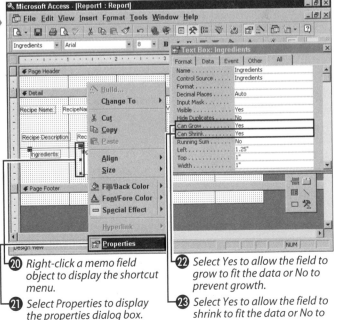

⓱ *To zoom in or out of a document, select the zoom percentage.*

⓲ *Drag the scroll bars to see items that are off the edge of the screen.*

⓳ *Click the Design View button or press Esc to return to the report layout window.*

⓴ *Right-click a memo field object to display the shortcut menu.*

㉑ *Select Properties to display the properties dialog box.*

㉒ *Select Yes to allow the field to grow to fit the data or No to prevent growth.*

㉓ *Select Yes to allow the field to shrink to fit the data or No to prevent shrinkage.*

Sorting Reports

You may not realize it while you're working with small sample databases, but virtually all reports should be sorted if they're going to be of any use. Imagine how difficult the largest database report most people ever use — a telephone book — would be to use if the listings weren't sorted in alphabetical order. Finding someone's phone number would be a nightmare!

As useful as it is to have your telephone book sorted alphabetically by name, wouldn't it be pretty handy to be able to sort those listings other ways? Imagine how useful it might be to be able to sort your telephone book by address or by phone number. When you create an Access report you can do just that. With only a few minor exceptions you can sort your reports using any of the fields to control the sort. You can't use certain special types of fields — memos, hyperlinks, or OLE objects — to sort the records since these types of sorts would be meaningless.

Your telephone book illustrates another important idea about sorting database records. Not only are the phone records sorted by last name, but they are also sorted by first name and then by address. If you happen to be looking for someone named Paul Johnson, you'd first look for Johnson, and then for Paul, within the Johnsons. If there were several Paul Johnsons, you'd look at the addresses to locate the correct listing. Since the last name is the most important, all records are sorted first according to the last name

field values. Any ties that result are then sorted according to the next most important field — first name. You can specify as many sort levels as necessary for your Access reports, but in most cases the lower-level sort keys won't have much effect unless you have a huge database. As the final figure on the facing page shows, it's always a good idea to preview your report to make certain the sort worked as you planned.

TAKE NOTE

▶ YOUR REPORTS MAY ALREADY BE SORTED

Even if you don't specify a sort order for your reports you may find they're already sorted. By default Access reports use the sort order of the underlying database table, so you may not need to do anything special to sort your reports. However, it's still a good idea to explicitly specify a sort order.

▶ WATCH OUT FOR BLANK ENTRIES

If your database table includes any records that don't contain a value in a field you're sorting, those records appear first when you sort in ascending order. Either add values to those records or specify a second sort field to make your report more useful.

CROSS-REFERENCE

See Chapter 25 for more information on sorting tables.

FIND IT ONLINE

Download Pennsylvania State Univeristy's tutorial for help with organizing reports: **http://www.psu.edu/ dept/cac/ets/projects/modules**.

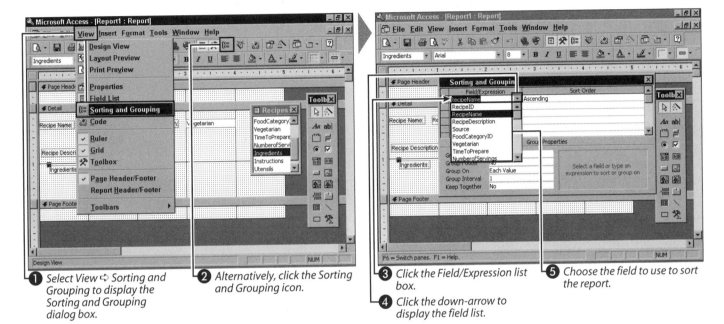

1 Select View ⇨ Sorting and Grouping to display the Sorting and Grouping dialog box.

2 Alternatively, click the Sorting and Grouping icon.

3 Click the Field/Expression list box.

4 Click the down-arrow to display the field list.

5 Choose the field to use to sort the report.

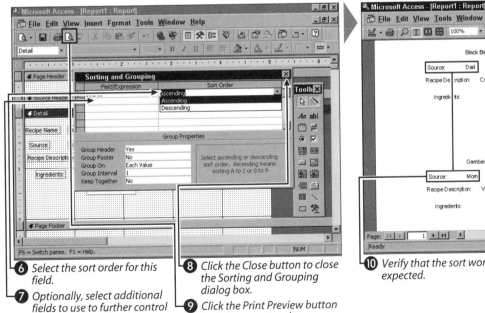

6 Select the sort order for this field.

7 Optionally, select additional fields to use to further control the sort.

8 Click the Close button to close the Sorting and Grouping dialog box.

9 Click the Print Preview button to test your sort order.

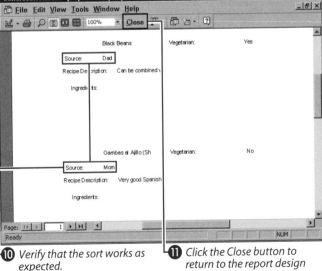

10 Verify that the sort works as expected.

11 Click the Close button to return to the report design view.

Adding Titles to Your Reports

Would you like a quick way to make your reports look a lot more professional? Of course you do! Adding titles, as well as page numbers or other document information is a great way to improve a report's appearance in addition to making it a lot more useful.

You use *headers* and *footers* to add most of this type of information to a report. Headers appear at the top of a page, and footers appear at the bottom. In most instances you will probably just use page headers and footers — these appear on each page of the report. If you want a special header or footer that only appears once — either at the beginning of the report for a header or at the end for a footer — you can select View ⇨ Report Header/Footer and follow essentially the same steps you use to create page headers and footers.

You can add text or graphics to headers or footers using either the Insert menu or the Toolbox options. Don't worry if the default header or footer seems to be the wrong size, you can resize the header or footer area by dragging the lower edge of either area. Also, if you add an object that is larger than the existing area, Access automatically resizes the area for you. You may still want to fine-tune the sizes of the report sections for maximum efficiency once you've added everything you want.

If you add page numbers or dates to a report, Access must figure out the correct information to print at the time when the report is printed. That's why you use special dialog boxes to add these features, as shown on the facing page. What Access actually adds to the report layout is a special field that is updated at run time.

TAKE NOTE

WATCH WHERE YOU PUT THINGS

Report design view can be a little confusing at first. It's hard to know just where to place objects that you want on your report, but if you place them in the wrong section they won't print where you expect to see them. Make certain you place objects you only want to see once per-page — such as page numbers — in the page header or page footer section. Objects you only want once per-report belong in the report header or footer.

PREVENT RECORDS FROM BREAKING

If you want to make certain that all of the information in a record remains in one piece rather than breaking across pages, make certain the Keep Together property for the detail section is set to Yes. You can find this property on the All tab of the Detail Property dialog box which appears when you right-click the detail section and select Properties.

CROSS-REFERENCE

See Chapter 9 for information on adding WordArt images to documents.

FIND IT ONLINE

Learn tips on using Access features at
http://odeyssey.apana.org.au/~abrowne/
xbase-05.html.

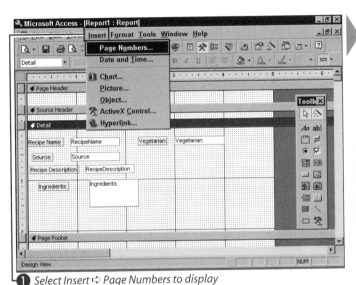

1 Select Insert ➪ Page Numbers to display the Page Numbers dialog box.

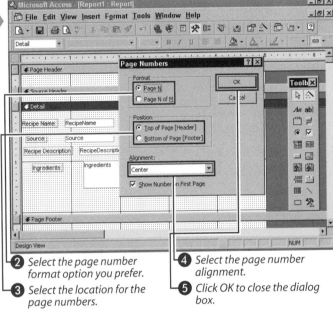

2 Select the page number format option you prefer.

3 Select the location for the page numbers.

4 Select the page number alignment.

5 Click OK to close the dialog box.

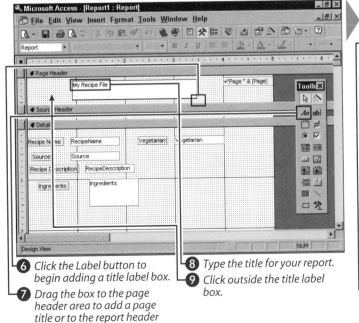

6 Click the Label button to begin adding a title label box.

7 Drag the box to the page header area to add a page title or to the report header area to add a report title.

8 Type the title for your report.

9 Click outside the title label box.

10 Click the title label box once to select the box.

11 Choose the title formatting options you prefer.

12 Click the Save button to save your work.

Personal Workbook

Q&A

1 How is the view of your data different in a form than in a table?

_____

_____

2 Is it possible for a form to show multiple records?

_____

_____

3 What important step is necessary before Access will show you a list of fields you can use on a form?

_____

_____

_____

4 How many of a table's fields must you include on a form?

_____

_____

_____

5 What can you do if your report won't fit the width of your paper?

_____

_____

6 What happens if you don't specify a sort order for your reports?

_____

_____

_____

7 What happens if you specify a sort on a field where some records are blank?

_____

_____

_____

8 What property do you have to set to prevent a record from starting on one page and finishing on the next?

_____

_____

_____

ANSWERS: PAGE 419

EXTRA PRACTICE

1. Create a new form for the recipes database that is based on the recipe ingredients table.

2. Create a new report based on the recipe ingredients table.

3. Sort your new report using the IngredientID field.

4. Add a report title to the new report.

5. Add page numbers to the bottom of each page of the report.

6. Add the date to the bottom of the last page of the report.

REAL-WORLD APPLICATIONS

✔ If you volunteer to maintain the membership database for an organization, you might need to prepare a form to make it easy to sign in the members at an annual dinner meeting.

✔ If you become the organization's treasurer, you might need to produce a report that shows when each club member's dues are due.

✔ If you are asked to produce a report on your company's sales, you might need to be able to sort the report in several different ways to please each of the company directors.

Visual Quiz

What is the purpose of the dialog box titled Toolbox? How can you display this dialog box? What do you need to do to make the associated report area appear in the design window?

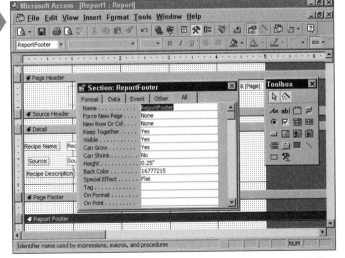

CHAPTER **25**

MASTER
THESE
SKILLS

▶ **Using Filters**

▶ **Creating Queries**

▶ **Using Query Wizards**

▶ **Sorting Records**

Working with Records

The most complete database in the world wouldn't be of much value if it didn't have a good way to find and sort information. You need methods of locating *subsets* of the data — the records that meet criteria that you specify. That way you are able to make use of the data. You might, for example, want to find out which of your customers live in California so you can send them an announcement about the stores you're opening in that state. Or, you might wish to only view your vegetarian recipes for houseguests who don't eat meat.

Access provides two methods of locating specific records — *filters* and *queries*. In some cases, you have the option of using either one to find the information you need. However, if you need to do some complex record selection, you generally need to use a query rather than a filter.

Filters are easier to create than queries, but queries are more powerful. If you want to view a subset of the records, you can quickly filter the records to see only those that you want. If you only want to see some of the fields in the record, wish to perform calculations on selected record values, or need to use additional tables in choosing the information you want to see, you need to create a query.

Filters and queries work much the same way. You specify either an exact value or wildcards (keyboard characters that can be used to represent other characters) that will match a desired set of values for one or more of the fields. Access then searches through the database and shows you which records match the sample values.

Sometimes even the best filter or query doesn't quite solve your needs. It's not always possible to determine just what information you need without looking at the complete set of data in an organized fashion. That's when it's handy to control how your data is sorted. Often it's possible to see new and useful patterns in a database simply by sorting the information differently. You might find that sorting orders by the day of the week shows which days are most profitable, or you might discover that sorting orders based on the day of the month uncovers that most purchases are made right after payday. Sort your customer table by address and you may find you can cut delivery expenses simply by better planning.

Using Filters

Access database filters work very much like a window screen. Because the holes in a window screen are too small for most insects to pass through, the bugs are filtered out and only fresh air comes through the screen. Make the holes a little larger and some of the smaller insects will be able to pass through, but the larger ones are still prevented from coming through. Thus the size of the holes in the window screen is the criteria that selects what can pass through the screen.

Database filters are quite a bit more sophisticated that the holes in a window screen. Rather than simply opening up a wider hole, when you specify a filter, you are creating something that's more like a missing piece of a jigsaw puzzle. Only those pieces of data that actually fit the filter pattern are allowed through. If you create your filter carefully enough, you can end up with just the records you need without having to look at any you don't.

Access has several different types of filters, but to understand how filters work it's best to start with the simplest option. Access calls this option *Filter By Selection*. To use the Filter By Selection option, you choose the first field value you wish to use as a filter. If you wish to narrow the selection further, you choose a filter value in another field. Each time you add another criteria to your filter, fewer and fewer records are likely to meet all the criteria.

Before you can apply a filter, you must open an Access database table. The figures on the facing page start with the Recipes1 database already open. In addition, some extra records were added to the Recipes table so you can get a better idea of how filters work. Be sure to add some additional records to your sample data before you follow along.

Continued

TAKE NOTE

▶ YOU CAN'T CREATE FILTERS IN REPORTS

You can create a filter for a table, a query, or a form, but not for a report. This doesn't mean you can't use filters to control what is shown in a report, however. As long as a report is based on a table that has been filtered, the report uses the same subset of database records that the filter produced in the filtered table.

▶ DON'T LET BOOLEAN FIELDS CONFUSE YOU

Boolean fields — ones that accept only Yes or No (or True or False) answers — may show values you might not expect. When you select a Boolean field, Access may show Yes or True as -1, and No or False as 0. Actually, though, any non-zero numeric value is the same as Yes, and No is always zero.

CROSS-REFERENCE
See "Creating Tables" in Chapter 23 for more information on using fields.

SHORTCUT
Double-click a table to quickly open it.

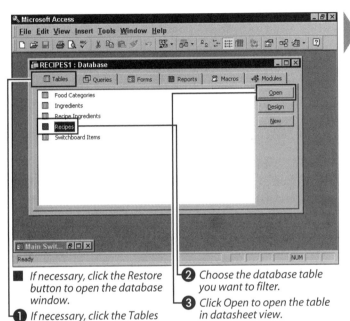

■ If necessary, click the Restore button to open the database window.

❶ If necessary, click the Tables tab.

❷ Choose the database table you want to filter.

❸ Click Open to open the table in datasheet view.

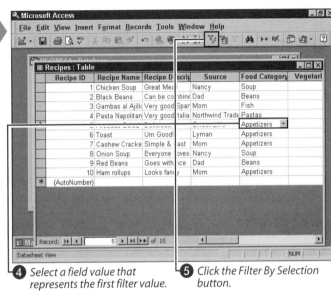

❹ Select a field value that represents the first filter value.

❺ Click the Filter By Selection button.

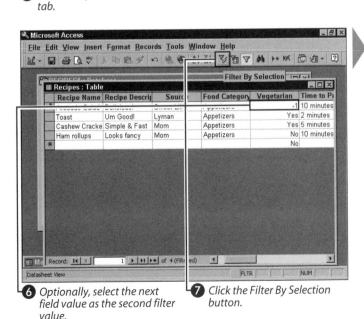

❻ Optionally, select the next field value as the second filter value.

■ Boolean fields show numeric values when selected.

❼ Click the Filter By Selection button.

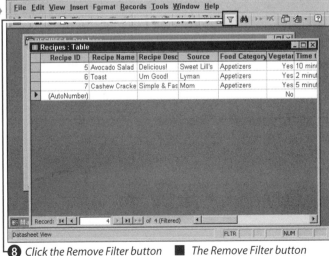

❽ Click the Remove Filter button to again display all the records.

■ The Remove Filter button removes all filters — not just the most recently applied filter.

387

Using Filters
Continued

Narrowing the set of records that is displayed by using the Filter By Selection button has one large obvious drawback — you can only specify the selection criteria one field at a time. While this might not be too difficult in a very small database such as the sample used in this chapter, imagine how much work would be involved if you were selecting records from a very large database which contained thousands of records and hundreds of fields. You could end up making dozens of individual selections, building your filter piece by piece.

What may not be such an obvious drawback to using the Filter By Selection option is that this option creates a very restrictive filter. Only those records that meet all of the selection criteria will be displayed. But what if you'd like to choose all of the records that met one criteria or another — such as all recipes that were for appetizers or that were for beans? The Filter By Selection option cannot give you these results.

One very good solution to this problem is to use the Filter By Form option to build your filter. Not only can you use this option to build an entire filter in one operation, but you also have the option of specifying alternate selection criteria so that selected records must pass one set of filters or the other.

Filter By Form displays a list of the database table fields in a single row. To create a complete filter, you add the filter values to each of the fields you want to use to filter the table. A record must match all of the filter values to pass through the completed filter. To specify alternate filters, click the Or tab at the bottom of the Filter By Form window and build the new filter on the new tab. A record only needs to meet the criteria of one of the Or filters to pass through the filters. You can create as many Or filters as necessary.

TAKE NOTE

▶ CREATING OR FILTERS

When you create alternate filters using the Or tab as shown in the second figure on the facing page, remember that each filter must be complete on its own. If you want to only select vegetarian recipes in either the beans or appetizers categories, make certain you select the vegetarian option in both of the filter tabs.

▶ DON'T LOSE ALL YOUR FILTERS!

Watch out for the Clear Grid button on the Filter/Sort toolbar. If you click this button your entire filter will be removed — not just the selections you've made on the active tab. If you want to remove one selection criteria from a single tab, select that criteria and choose Edit ⇨ Cut.

CROSS-REFERENCE
See "Creating Queries" next in this chapter for an alternate way to select records.

SHORTCUT
Remove a filter criteria by selecting it and pressing Delete.

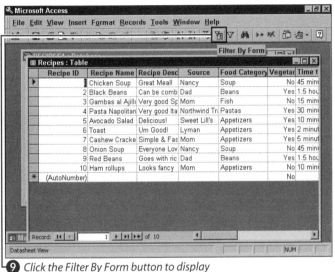

9 Click the Filter By Form button to display the Filter By Form window.

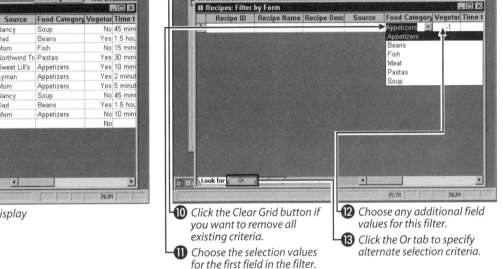

10 Click the Clear Grid button if you want to remove all existing criteria.

11 Choose the selection values for the first field in the filter.

12 Choose any additional field values for this filter.

13 Click the Or tab to specify alternate selection criteria.

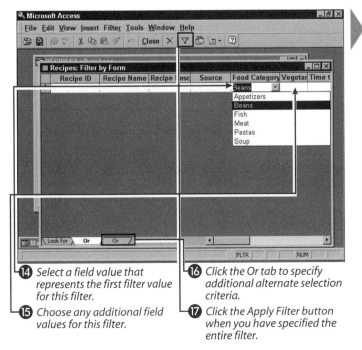

14 Select a field value that represents the first filter value for this filter.

15 Choose any additional field values for this filter.

16 Click the Or tab to specify additional alternate selection criteria.

17 Click the Apply Filter button when you have specified the entire filter.

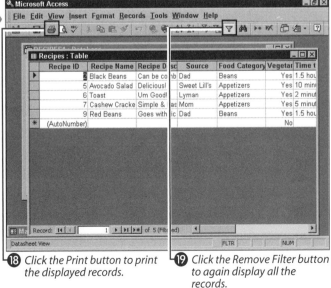

18 Click the Print button to print the displayed records.

19 Click the Remove Filter button to again display all the records.

Creating Queries

Like filters, queries also enable you to select and display a subset of the records in a database. However, queries are much more powerful. You can create queries that display related information from several different data sources, such as from two or more tables in the database. An example of this might be to use a query to create a shopping list of the ingredients for all of your vegetarian recipes before your sister, the vegetarian, came for a visit.

You can create Access queries in several different ways. You can save one of your filters as a query, you can build a query from scratch as demonstrated in this section, or you can use a query wizard to automate the process as you learn in the next section. Building a query from scratch involves the most work, but you learn more about how queries work by trying this method first.

A complex query may use several *joined* database tables to produce the desired results. Joined tables are simply database tables that are related, such as the Recipes, the Recipe Ingredients, and the Ingredients tables in the sample recipes database. See the Take Note section for more information on joins. Each recipe may have several ingredients, and you want to be able to determine which ingredients are used in vegetarian recipes.

When you create a query, you can tell Access to display fields from one or more of the tables used in the query. You don't have to show information from every table. This is true even if you've used values from the records in a table to select the records to show from another table. The figures on the facing page, and the following pages, demonstrate this idea by showing that you can use the Vegetarian field in the Recipes table to determine which ingredients to display from the Ingredients table. You don't have to display the contents of the Vegetarian field from the Recipes table, and indeed, probably wouldn't want to. But you would want to make certain that your shopping list was only made up of ingredients that were used in vegetarian recipes.

Continued

TAKE NOTE

CREATING JOINS

You must have join lines between all of the tables included in a query. Normally the tables you add to a query already have the join lines in place from when the database was first created. If the lines are missing, simply drag the join field from one table to the related field in the other table and Access adds the join line.

INCLUDE ALL THE FIELDS YOU WANT TO SEE

Unlike filter results, query results only show the fields you add to the query. Make certain you add every field you want in the result to your query.

CROSS-REFERENCE
See "Sorting Records" later in this chapter for information on sorting the query results.

SHORTCUT
If you forget to add a table, click the Show Table button.

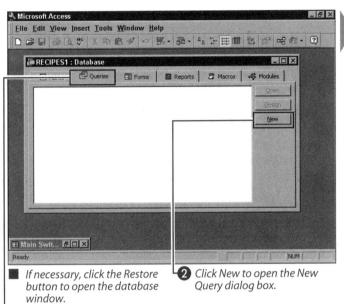

■ If necessary, click the Restore button to open the database window.

1 If necessary, click the Queries tab.

2 Click New to open the New Query dialog box.

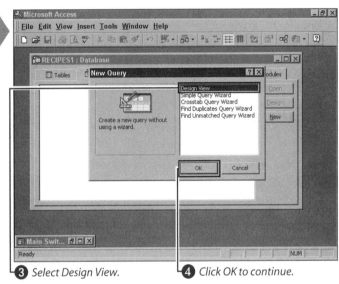

3 Select Design View.

4 Click OK to continue.

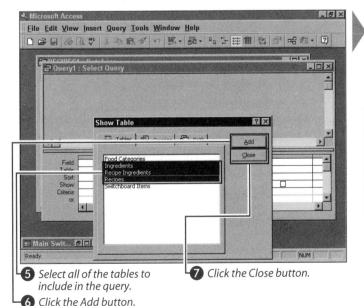

5 Select all of the tables to include in the query.

6 Click the Add button.

7 Click the Close button.

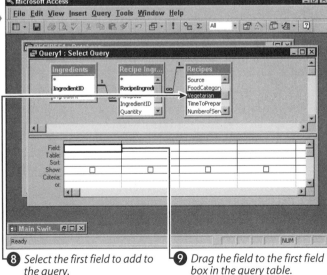

8 Select the first field to add to the query.

9 Drag the field to the first field box in the query table.

Creating Queries

Continued

Just as when creating filters, you use some of the fields you add to a query to select which information to show in the results. In the following example you use the Vegetarian field from the Recipes table to choose ingredients that belong in vegetarian recipes. Unlike creating a filter, you cannot simply select a field value from the table to use as the selection criteria. In a query you must create a simple formula that specifies how the records are to be selected. In the first figure on the facing page the formula =*yes* has been added to the Criteria box for the Vegetarian field.

Each field in the query table includes a Show box. If this box is checked the field will be shown in the results when you run the query. Normally, you want to remove the check if you specify only one criteria for the field, since showing the same value for each record would be redundant. If you specify more than one criteria using the "Or" boxes, you may want to leave the Show box checked.

If you include entries in the Criteria box for more than one field, only those records that match all of the criteria will be displayed. For example, if you included the Source field from the Recipes table and specified = "*Mom*" as the selection criteria for this field, and you left the =*yes* criteria for the Vegetarian field, the only records that would be displayed would be those which were vegetarian recipes that had come from Mom.

Notice that even though the Recipes and Ingredients tables aren't directly joined, you can use results from the Recipes table to select records from the Ingredients table. Both of these tables are joined to the Recipe Ingredients table, and that table provides the links you need to make your query work.

TAKE NOTE

BOOLEAN FIELDS AREN'T TEXT FIELDS

If you want to use a Boolean field like the Vegetarian field to specify selection criteria, you must remember that Boolean fields aren't text fields, even though they display values like Yes or No. When you specify text field values in the Criteria box, you must include the text in quotation marks, but if you do this with a Boolean field, Access displays an error message when you try to run the query. Boolean values must be used without quotation marks.

BE CAREFUL OF COMPLEX QUERIES

If you build queries that include selection criteria in several fields, be sure to test your query to make certain it works correctly. It's very easy to build a query that cannot be satisfied because the criteria are mutually exclusive. Always think through your query to make certain it makes sense.

CROSS-REFERENCE

See "Using Query Wizards" next in this chapter for information on another method of creating a query.

SHORTCUT

Click one of the Sort buttons to sort the results.

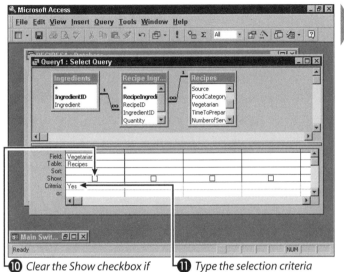

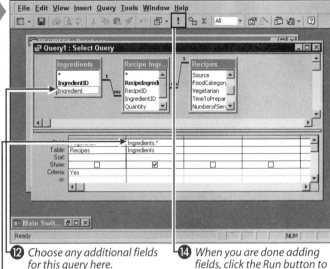

10 Clear the Show checkbox if you wish to remove this field from the results.

11 Type the selection criteria formula in the Criteria box.

12 Choose any additional fields for this query here.

13 Drag (or double-click) the additional field to the next available Field box.

14 When you are done adding fields, click the Run button to run the query.

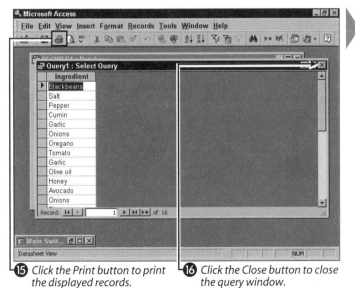

15 Click the Print button to print the displayed records.

16 Click the Close button to close the query window.

17 Click Yes to save the query design.

■ Once you click Yes, enter a name for the query and click Save to save the query.

Using Query Wizards

You don't have to create queries completely from scratch — you can also use query wizards to help you build a query. Query wizards can speed the process somewhat, especially if you want to create a more complicated query. In this case, we demonstrate how the Simple Query Wizard handles a query similar to the one you created in the last section.

As you use query wizards you'll soon discover that knowing how to create and modify queries manually is very helpful. Even though query wizards make creating a simple query pretty easy, you will probably need to tune up the query yourself to get just the results you seek. That's one reason this chapter shows you how to create your own query from scratch — so you can modify the query easily.

When you use query wizards to create a query you're given the option to select fields from any of the tables or queries that already exist in the database. At first you may be a little confused by the option to base a query on another query, but once you understand the reason for this option you will appreciate the flexibility it provides. When you run a query, the result is a table that contains the most current results from the query. You could, for example, create a very simple query (Query A) on the Recipes table that selected just the vegetarian recipes. Later you could use this query as one of the items for the

basis of a new query (Query B) that extracted a shopping list. If you later decided you wanted to switch to a nonvegetarian diet, all you'd have to do would be to modify Query A. Any other queries (Query B, Query C, and so on) that used Query A would automatically show the new results the next time they were run. This modular approach makes it much easier to maintain your database since you only need to make one small change to update all of the queries that use the same selections.

TAKE NOTE

▶ ADD YOUR OWN CRITERIA

Once you create a query using a query wizard, you'll probably notice that the results are somewhat different from what you expected. One reason for this is the way query wizards work. When you select a field to include in a query wizard query, the field is shown in the results, and no selection formula is generated in the criteria box. You need to add your own criteria, such as =*yes* to refine the selection process.

▶ CREATE SIMPLE QUERIES FIRST

If you decide to create a simple query that will serve as the basis for additional queries, remember to create the simple query first. You can only base new queries on existing tables and queries.

CROSS-REFERENCE
See "Creating Queries" earlier in this chapter for information on modifying a query.

SHORTCUT
Click the New Object button to create a new object, such as a query.

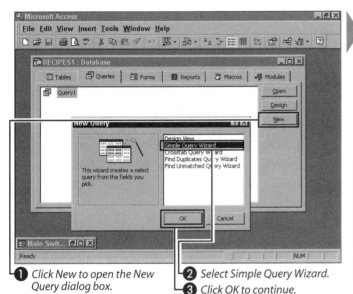

1 Click New to open the New Query dialog box.

2 Select Simple Query Wizard.

3 Click OK to continue.

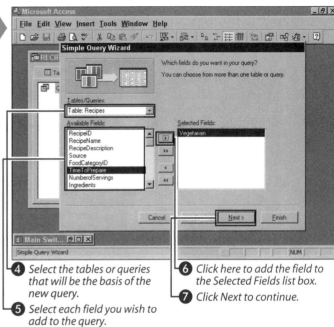

4 Select the tables or queries that will be the basis of the new query.

5 Select each field you wish to add to the query.

6 Click here to add the field to the Selected Fields list box.

7 Click Next to continue.

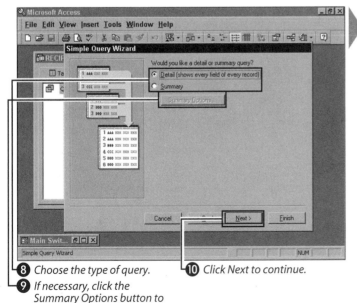

8 Choose the type of query.

9 If necessary, click the Summary Options button to choose the type of summary you want.

10 Click Next to continue.

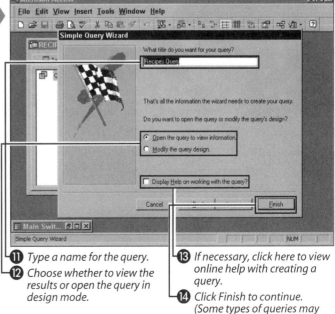

11 Type a name for the query.

12 Choose whether to view the results or open the query in design mode.

13 If necessary, click here to view online help with creating a query.

14 Click Finish to continue. (Some types of queries may require additional steps.)

Sorting Records

If you already have an idea of just what information you're trying to get from your database, a query or a filter may be just what you need. Sometimes, though, you may not really be able to define just what you want to know. You may know that the information you need is in the database, but you may not be able to create a useful filter or query.

When a filter or a query won't do the job, sorting the database table may do the trick. With a sort, you have the flexibility of sorting the data in many different ways. You could, for example, sort your address list by name, but you could also sort it by telephone number or by city and address. Each of these types of sorting offers the possibility of discovering quite useful information that you might never notice any other way.

Access offers two slightly different sort options. If you choose Records ⇨ Sort or click one of the Sort buttons on the toolbar, Access sorts the table using a simple sort that sorts the table according to the values in a single field. This simple sort may be all you need in many cases, but it falls far short of adequate in others. For example, a simple one-field sort really wouldn't be too useful for sorting an address list with thousands of entries. For a task like this you need a sorting method that has the capability to sort the data based on values in several fields — such as last name, first name, and then address.

Creating an advanced sort is very similar to creating an advanced filter or a query. In fact, you may be surprised to find that the advanced sorting options fall under the filter options rather than the sort options on the Record menu.

Be sure to add the fields to the Filter dialog box in the correct order. Since Access sorts the records according to the position of the fields in the Filter dialog box field list, you must place more important sort fields to the left of less important sort fields. You can, however, place fields in the list without sorting on those fields.

TAKE NOTE

▶ QUERIES CAN SORT, TOO

When you create a query you can produce sorted output by choosing an option in the Sort box for each field in the query. Remember, though, that the sort will be based on the order of the fields in the query. Fields that appear further to the left in the query dialog box have precedence over fields to their right.

▶ SORTS ARE SAVED WITH THE DATABASE

If you create an advanced sort for a table, Access saves the sort order and applies it when the table is opened in the future.

CROSS-REFERENCE
See "Sorting Reports" in Chapter 24 for more information on sorting database information.

SHORTCUT
Click the down arrow next to a field in the Filter dialog box to choose a different field.

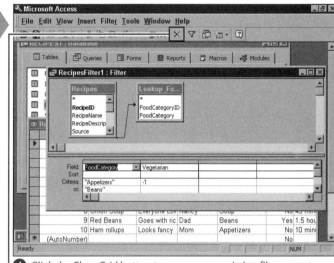

① Select the database table for the advanced sort.

② Click Open to open the table in datasheet view.

③ Select Records ➪ Filter ➪ Advanced Filter/Sort.

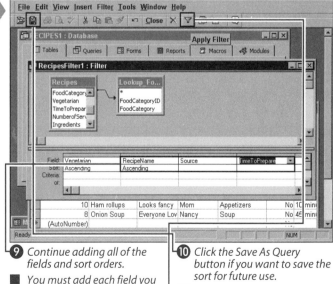

④ Click the Clear Grid button to remove any existing filter or sort.

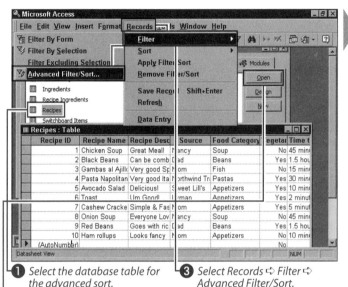

⑤ Double-click a field to add it to the next Field box.

⑥ Click the Sort box.

⑦ Click the down-arrow to display the drop-down list.

⑧ Choose the type of sort.

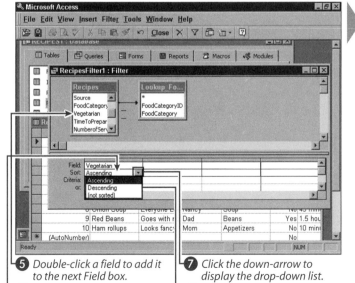

⑨ Continue adding all of the fields and sort orders.

■ You must add each field you want in the sorted table even if you do not sort on the field.

⑩ Click the Save As Query button if you want to save the sort for future use.

⑪ Click the Apply Filter button to view the sorted records.

Personal Workbook

Q&A

1 How many database fields can you use to select records when you use the Filter By Selection option?

_____

_____

2 What do you need to remember when you specify criteria for selecting a Boolean field?

_____

_____

3 How can you further narrow the subset of records after you've used the Filter By Selection option?

_____

_____

4 What are joined tables?

_____

_____

5 What is the one thing you must do before you can show data from more than one table in query results?

_____

_____

6 How can you use a field to select records in a query without showing that field's values in the results?

_____

_____

_____

7 What method can you use to create multiple queries that you can update by changing one formula?

_____

_____

_____

8 How do you control the order of precedence when you use multiple fields to sort your data?

_____

_____

9 How can you make fields appear earlier in the query results without affecting the sort order?

_____

_____

_____

ANSWERS: PAGE 419

EXTRA PRACTICE

① Create a new filter for the Recipes table choosing vegetarian appetizers.

② Sort the Recipes table by source.

③ Create an advanced sort that shows the nonvegetarian appetizer ingredient list.

④ Use the Simple Query Wizard to create a query that summarizes the ingredients for the soup recipes.

⑤ Create a query that shows the recipes names and preparation times sorted by the amount of time required to prepare each recipe.

REAL-WORLD APPLICATIONS

✓ If you have a large customer database, you may need to produce a list of the customers in an area before your boss travels to the area so he can write off the trip as a business expense.

✓ If your publisher suddenly shows an interest in that all-meat cookbook you've been mentioning, you might need to filter your recipe list to eliminate all of the vegetarian items.

✓ If you are placed in charge of a last-minute meeting intended to determine why sales have been off by 50 percent in some areas, you might need to create an advanced sort to show that all of your ice cream stores in cold regions of the country do poorly during the winter months.

Visual Quiz

What is the purpose of this dialog box? How can you display this dialog box? What do you need to do to add additional tables to the view?

_____

_____

_____

_____

_____

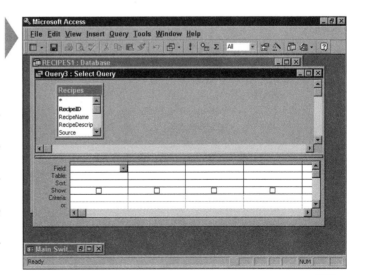

Personal Workbook
Answers

Chapter 1

see page 4

1 **What are two different ways to open an Office 97 program?**

A: Office programs can be launched either by opening a shortcut menu on the desktop, or by clicking Start ⇨ Programs and selecting a program from the menu.

2 **How can you close a program without using the window's close (X) button?**

A: Besides using the window's close (X) button, you can close a program by choosing File ⇨ Exit from the menu bar.

3 **What is the quickest way to reject changes you make in a dialog box?**

A: Close a dialog box and reject the changes you made by pressing Esc on your keyboard, or click Cancel in the dialog box.

4 **What does an ellipses (...) next to a menu item mean?**

A: Menu items that have an ellipsis (...) next to them lead to dialog boxes.

5 **How do you know if a menu item contains a submenu?**

A: Submenus are indicated by right-facing arrows next to menu items.

6 **How do you open a context menu?**

A: A context menu can be opened by right-clicking an item or selection.

7 **Which Office 97 programs have toolbars?**

A: All Office 97 programs have toolbars. Toolbars vary depending on the program in question, and there are usually many different toolbars to choose from.

8 **Where can you find the dialog box that enables you to customize your toolbars?**

A: You can customize your toolbars by clicking View ⇨ Toolbars ⇨ Customize.

9 **What does the Page Layout view represent?**

A: Page Layout view shows more accurately what a document will look like once it is printed on paper.

Visual Quiz

Q: **How do you open the program shown here? How do you show the Drawing toolbar as displayed here? How can you display the dialog box needed to make these changes? How can you switch to Page Layout view?**

A: Word is opened by clicking Start ⇨ Programs ⇨ Microsoft Word, or by opening the desktop icon for Word. Additional toolbars can be displayed from the Customize dialog box, opened by clicking View ⇨ Toolbars ⇨ Customize. To view this document in Page Layout view, click View ⇨ Page Layout on the menu bar.

Personal Workbook Answers

Chapter 2

see page 20

❶ What does the Office Assistant usually show when you start an Office 97 program?

A: When you first start an Office 97 program, the Office Assistant displays a Tip of the Day.

❷ How can you search for help using the Office Assistant?

A: Click the Office Assistant and type a question in the text box that appears. Click Search to search help using the Office Assistant.

❸ What key can you press to quickly open the Office Assistant?

A: Press F1 to quickly launch the Office Assistant.

❹ What's the quickest way to create a professional-looking fax cover sheet?

A: You can create a fax cover sheet quickly using Word's Fax Wizard.

❺ How do you open the Office Help System?

A: Open Office Help by clicking Help ⇨ Contents and Index.

❻ Which tab in the Office Help System lets you search for a keyword or phrase?

A: The Find tab of the Office Help System helps you search Help for keywords or phrases.

❼ How do you print a help topic?

A: To print a help topic, click Options ⇨ Print topic from within the topic window.

❽ Give two examples of software you can download from Microsoft to augment Office programs.

A: Microsoft offers a wide selection of software you can download, including patches, templates, special plug-ins, wizards, Office Assistants, and more.

Visual Quiz

Q: How do you find the help topic shown here? How do you print a copy of it? What part of this topic links to another help topic?

A: Help topics can be accessed by searching with the Office Assistant, or you can open the help system by clicking Help ⇨ Microsoft Word Help and browsing the index. To print the topic, click the Options button near the top of the window and choose Print Topic. Underlined items link to other help topics.

Chapter 3

see page 36

❶ How can you save an Office document?

A: Save an Office document by clicking File ⇨ Save on the menu bar. You can also click the Save button on the toolbar, or press Ctrl+S.

❷ How can you save a copy of an Office document with a new name?

A: To save a document with a new name, click File ⇨ Save As on the menu bar and type a new name for the document.

❸ Should you always wait until you are finished to save your work?

A: It is a good idea to save your work periodically to ensure it is not accidentally lost.

④ How do you open an Office document without first opening an Office program?

A: You can open Office documents without first opening their programs by opening a document icon from within Windows Explorer or My Computer. You can also click Start ➪ Documents and choose a document you have worked on recently.

⑤ What dialog box should you open if you want to rename an existing file from within an Office program?

A: To rename an existing file, open the Save As dialog box, right-click the filename, and choose Rename.

⑥ How long can a filename be?

A: Windows 95 and NT 4.0 allow filenames that are up to 256 characters long.

⑦ What are two ways to delete a file?

A: You can delete a file by right-clicking it in the Save As dialog box and choosing Delete. You can also delete files from within Windows Explorer or My Computer.

⑧ How do you create a new folder from within an Office program?

A: In the Save or Save As dialog box, click the New Folder button to create a new folder. Don't forget to name it!

⑨ What is the quickest way to combine the text of two separate documents?

A: You can quickly combine the text of two separate documents by inserting one file into the other.

Visual Quiz

Q: How do you create the Articles folder that this file is saved in? How do you change the name of one of the other files in this folder? How do you save the article as a text-only file? What does the icon which reads "In the Hall of the Mountain King" represent? How did it get there?

A: New folders can be easily created from within the Save As dialog by clicking the New Folder button. If you want to rename a file shown in this dialog box, right-click it and choose Rename from the context menu. If you want to save a file in another format, click the drop-down arrow next to Save as Type and choose another format. In the document shown, the "In the Hall of the Mountain King" icon is a sound object that has been inserted.

Chapter 4

see page 54

❶ What is the quickest way to print a document?

A: The quickest way to print a document is to click the Print button on the toolbar.

❷ How do you select a range of pages to print?

A: Select a range of pages to print by selecting the Pages radio button in the Print dialog box and typing a range in the text box.

❸ What are two ways of opening the Print dialog box?

A: You can open the Print dialog by clicking File ➪ Print on the menu bar, or just press Ctrl+P.

❹ Why is it a good idea to use Print Preview before printing your work?

A: Print Preview can save you time, paper, and printer ink by showing you what the document will look like on paper *before* you actually print it there.

Personal Workbook Answers

5 **What are two ways of closing Print Preview without printing?**

A: You can close Print Preview without printing by clicking Close on the toolbar, or press Esc on your keyboard.

6 **How do you print multiple copies of a document?**

A: You can print multiple copies of a document by changing the number next to "Number of copies" in the Print dialog box.

7 **Can you print to a printer that is not connected to your computer?**

A: You can print to a printer that is connected to another printer by first printing the document to a print file.

8 **Can you print to a printer if its driver is not installed on your computer?**

A: You must have the printer driver installed for any printer you print to, even if it is not actually connected to your computer.

9 **How long should the filename of a print file be?**

A: You should not give a print file a name that is longer than eight characters.

Visual Quiz

Q: **How do you open this dialog box? Where do you click to select a different printer? How do you select only certain pages to print? Where can you increase the number of copies to be printed? What does the Collate option do?**

A: Open the Print dialog by clicking File ⇨ Print on the menu bar, or press Ctrl+P on your keyboard. If you want to choose a different printer, click the drop-down arrow next to Printer Name and choose another entry. You can print only specific pages by choosing options in the Page Range area, and you can click spinner box arrows next to Number of Copies to print additional copies of a document. Collated documents are printed all at once, while noncollated documents print all copies of the first page, then all copies of the second, and so on.

Chapter 5

see page 66

1 **How can you select a whole paragraph without dragging the mouse pointer over the whole thing?**

A: You can quickly select a whole paragraph by triple-clicking it.

2 **How do you select an object using only the keyboard?**

A: To select something with the keyboard, first position the cursor at the beginning of the selection. Hold the Shift key and run the arrow keys across the area you want to select.

3 **How do you select a graphic?**

A: You can select a graphic by clicking it once.

4 **How do you select a graphic that is also a hyperlink?**

A: If you need to select a graphic that is also a hyperlink, place the cursor before the graphic, hold the Shift key, and use the arrow keys to select the graphic.

5 **How do you know if something like a MIDI sound object is selected?**

A: Any nontext object that is selected will have manipulation handles around the border.

6 **What is the difference between cut and copy?**

A: When you cut an object you remove it from its original location, presumably to place it in a new location. Copying an object means that it stays in the original location, but you can place copies of it elsewhere.

7 **When you cut or copy an object, where does it go?**

A: Objects that are cut or copied are placed on the Windows Clipboard.

8 **How do you paste an object using only the keyboard?**

A: To paste something from the Clipboard using the keyboard, press Ctrl+V.

Visual Quiz

Q: How can you move the picture of the motorcycle to the bottom of the screen? Can it be moved to a different program altogether? How? Why do you suppose the same MIDI sound object appears at both the top and bottom of the page? Can you reproduce that action without the mouse? How?

A: Objects such as pictures can be moved around by copying or cutting and then pasting them to a new location. Objects can also be moved or copied to other programs using the same methods. The MIDI object shown here has been copied to both the top and bottom of the document. To copy an object without the mouse, press Ctrl+C. You can then paste it using Ctrl+V.

Chapter 6

see page 80

1 **How do you create a Web document using Word?**

A: You can turn a Word document into a Web document by saving it as an HTML file.

2 **Can you publish documents you create in Word on the Internet?**

A: Any HTML files you create in Word can be published on the Internet.

3 **How should you name files to be used on the Internet?**

A: If you plan to publish your HTML files on the Internet, keep the filenames less than eight characters.

4 **What is the easiest way to align text alongside an image rather than under it?**

A: You can align text alongside an image in a Web document by using a table to control the layout.

5 **What is a hyperlink?**

A: A hyperlink is a piece of text or other object that, when clicked with a mouse pointer, links the reader to a new file or location.

6 **How do you create a hyperlink?**

A: You can create a hyperlink by selecting some text or a picture to serve as the link, and then clicking the Insert Hyperlink toolbar button.

7 **What kind of graphic files may be used on the Internet?**

A: Graphics that are used on the Internet must be JPEG or GIF format files.

8 **What is a thumbnail?**

A: A thumbnail is a small version of a larger image. Usually, a thumbnail serves as a hyperlink to the larger image.

9 **Do you have to have a Web browser program to view Web documents?**

A: If you do not have a Web browser, you can view Web documents using Word and the Web toolbar.

PERSONAL WORKBOOK ANSWERS

Visual Quiz

Q: How was this Word document turned into a Web document? Can it be published on the Internet? How could the image be aligned alongside the text rather than above it? What does the underlined text mean?

A: Word documents can be converted to Web documents by simply saving them as HTML or Web documents. Any HTML document can be published on the Internet. If you want to align text and images alongside each other in Web documents, one way is to use cells of a table. Underlined text indicates a hyperlink. Click a hyperlink to see where it leads.

Chapter 7

see page 96

❶ What are document templates?

A: Document templates are special Word files that you use as the basis for creating new documents.

❷ If you don't select a template, which template does Word use?

A: If you don't select a template, Word uses Normal.dot.

❸ What does a wavy red underline under a word mean?

A: A wavy red underline means that the word is misspelled.

❹ What does a wavy green underline under a phrase mean?

A: A wavy green underline means that Word has detected a grammatical error.

❺ When using Find and Replace, when should you use the Find Next button rather than the Replace all button?

A: Use the Find Next button rather than the Replace all button if the word or phrase you are replacing is an actual word that may be used correctly somewhere in the document.

❻ How can you replace the same words in more than one document without retyping the Find what and Replace with phrases?

A: You can replace the same words in more than one document without retyping the Find what and Replace with phrases by not closing Word between opening each document.

❼ What is likely to happen if you replace all the paragraph marks in your document with spaces?

A: If you replace all the paragraph marks in your document with spaces the entire document will be collapsed into a single paragraph.

❽ How can you see the paragraph marks in a document?

A: You can see the paragraph marks in a document by clicking the Show/Hide button on the toolbar.

❾ How can you create a different first page footer?

A: You can create a different first page footer by clicking the Different first page checkbox in the Page Setup dialog box.

Visual Quiz

Q: How do you display the dialog box shown here? What do you need to do to display the advanced options shown at the bottom of the dialog box? How can you reuse a search phrase you used earlier?

A: To display the dialog box select Edit ➪ Replace. Click the More button to display the advanced options or the Less button to hide them. Click the down arrow next to the Find what or Replace with list box to select a phrase you used earlier.

Chapter 8

see page 112

❶ What is the difference between character and paragraph formatting?

A: Character formatting affects individual letters and words; paragraph formatting affects entire paragraphs.

❷ What is the unit of measurement used to measure font size?

A: Font size is measured in points.

❸ What are the four kinds of paragraph alignment that Word supports?

A: Word supports the following paragraph alignments: Left, Right, Center, and Justify.

❹ At what interval are the default tab stops spaced?

A: By default, tabs are spaced every one-half inch.

❺ What are the four kinds of tab stops you can set on the ruler? (Bonus: What is the fifth kind of tab stop, available only from the Tabs dialog box?)

A: Left, Right, Center, and Decimal are the four kinds of tab stops you can set on the ruler. The fifth kind is Bar.

❻ What are the default margins on a new, blank document in Word?

A: The default margins on a new, blank document are 1" at top and bottom; 1.25" at left and right.

❼ How can you have more than one set of margin settings in a single document?

A: To use more than one set of margins in the same document, create a section break.

❽ What's the difference between a margin and an indent?

A: A margin applies to the entire document; an indent applies only to a specific paragraph.

❾ What's the easiest way to create a new style?

A: To create a new style, format some text the way you want the style to be, and then type a style name in the Style box on the toolbar and press Enter.

Visual Quiz

Q: How do you display the dialog box shown here? Which controls in it are also available from the toolbar?

A: Choose Format ➪ Font to display the box. The controls that are also available from the toolbar are Font, Font Style, Size, Color, and Underline (single only).

Chapter 9

see page 128

❶ How would you change the wording of your WordArt?

A: To change the WordArt text, click the Edit Text button.

❷ Besides clip art, what three types of files does the Clip Gallery allow you to manage?

A: The Clip Gallery manages Pictures, Videos, and Sounds, in addition to clip art.

❸ Name two sources of additional clip art besides the clip art that is installed on your hard drive in Office 97.

A: The Office 97 CD and the Microsoft Web site are two additional sources of clip art.

Personal Workbook Answers

4 **What does it mean if your Insert ⇨ Picture menu doesn't have the From Scanner command on it?**

A: If you don't have an Insert ⇨ Picture ⇨ From Scanner command, it means you do not have a TWAIN-compatible scanner installed.

5 **Which of the following is not a valid image type that Word accepts: BMP, QIR, or JPG?**

A: QIR is not a valid image format. BMP and JPG both are valid.

6 **How would you reset a picture that you had tried to edit but made mistakes with?**

A: Click the Reset Picture button on the toolbar to reset a picture that you have edited.

7 **What would be the advantage of editing a picture through the Format Picture dialog box rather than from the Picture toolbar?**

A: The advantage of using the Format Picture dialog box is that it has some exclusive controls. You can also specify precise measurements for commands such as cropping and resizing.

Visual Quiz

Q: **What is wrong with this WordArt, and how would you fix it?**

A: This WordArt is on top of the regular text. It needs to be dragged up above the text, so it will modify it, rather than obscuring it.

Chapter 10

see page 142

1 **If you want Word to create a bulleted list automatically, what symbol should you type in front of each paragraph?**

A: To create bullets automatically, place an asterisk (*) before each paragraph.

2 **How would you turn off AutoFormatting, so Word did not create automatic bulleted and numbered lists?**

A: To turn off AutoFormatting as you type, choose Tools ⇨ AutoCorrect and click the AutoFormat As You Type tab. Deselect checkboxes for the features to turn off.

3 **Name two fonts whose characters can be used for bullets.**

A: All fonts can be used for bullets — it was a trick question. But two common ones are Wingdings and Webdings.

4 **Name two ways to create a table in Word.**

A: To create a table in Word, choose Table ⇨ Insert Table, or click the Table button on the toolbar, or draw a table with Table ⇨ Draw Table.

5 **What effect does holding down the Shift key have when dragging a table column to resize it?**

A: Holding down the Shift key as you resize a table column changes the overall size of the table.

6 **How do you get a vertical line to appear between your columns when using multiple columns in a document?**

A: To place a line between columns, click the Line Between checkbox in the Columns dialog box.

7 **What happens if you change the number of columns in a document and you don't select any text first? What happens if you do select text first?**

A: If you change the number of columns without selecting text, the entire section is affected. (If there are no section breaks, the entire document is affected.) If you select text first, Word inserts section breaks before and after the selected text.

Visual Quiz

Q: What is wrong with this numbered list? How would you fix it?

A: The numbered list should continue after the note, not begin again. To fix it, right-click the second #1 paragraph and choose Bullets and Numbering. Click Continue Previous List, and then click OK.

Chapter 11

see page 160

1 **Which of the following cannot be used directly for a merge data source: Word documents, Outlook address book, Excel worksheet, or Access database?**

A: An Access database cannot directly be used for a data source. However, you can export one of its tables to Word or Excel and use it there.

2 **True or false: When you create a new data source with the Mail Merge Helper, the data becomes a saved part of the mail merge file, rather than being saved in a separate document.**

A: False. A new data source created by Mail Merge Helper becomes a separate, autonomous Word file.

3 **What is the difference between a Mail Merge main document and a normal Word document?**

A: A Mail Merge main document displays the Mail Merge toolbar and is connected (via the Mail Merge Helper) to a data file.

4 **True or false: It is okay to type the field names into the main document, instead of selecting them from the drop-down list on the Mail Merge toolbar.**

A: False. Mail merge will not work if you type the field names. You must insert them from the toolbar.

5 **True or false: If you click the Merge to Printer button, Word prints all the merged letters immediately, without creating a new Word file containing them.**

A: True. The Merge to Printer button bypasses creating a document.

6 **True or false: You should place your envelope in the printer in whatever way is shown on the Feed button in the Envelopes and Labels dialog box.**

A: False. The Feed button merely shows a picture of whatever setting is currently chosen. It may not be the right setting for your printer.

7 **Where do the addresses that appear when you click the Address Book button in the Envelopes and Labels dialog box come from?**

A: They come from your Outlook address book.

8 **What must you do to save the envelope's information with the letter?**

A: Click the Add to Document button to add an envelope to a letter's Word file.

Personal Workbook Answers

Visual Quiz

Q: What is wrong with the merge fields in this letter, and how would you fix them?

A: There are no spaces between the fields, so the data will print all smashed together like this: JohnSmith 123ValleyRoad IndianapolisIN46240. Click to place the insertion point between two fields, and press the space bar to insert space between them.

Chapter 12

see page 176

❶ Which Word views can you use to create outlines in?

A: You can create an outline in any view, but you have access to the Outlining toolbar only in Outline view, so that's the preferred view to use.

❷ What key(s) do you press to demote an outline item?

A: Press Tab to demote an outline item.

❸ What keys(s) do you press to promote an item?

A: Press Shift+Tab to promote an outline item.

❹ How would you change the numbering format used on your outline, if you did not like the default?

A: To change the numbering format, choose Format ⇨ Bullets and Numbering and make your change on the Outline Numbered tab.

❺ The Heading 3 style on the Styles drop-down list corresponds to which outline level?

A: Heading 3 style corresponds to outline level 3.

❻ How would you change the formatting of all first-level outline lines?

A: To change the formatting of all your first-level outline items, change the Heading 1 style.

❼ True or false: A plus sign next to an outline item means that there are subordinate headings beneath it that you cannot see right now because they are collapsed.

A: False. A plus sign means that there are subordinate headings beneath, but not necessarily that they are hidden.

❽ True or false: When you're ready to type the body text under your headings, you should change to Normal or Page Layout view.

A: True. You should do your regular typing and editing in Normal or Page Layout view, not Outline view.

Visual Quiz

Q: Based on what you can see in this figure, at least how many levels does this outline have?

A: This is a tricky question. There are three outline levels visible, but several of the third-level items have plus signs next to them, indicating that there is at least one hidden level. So there are at least four levels to this outline.

Chapter 13

see page 188

❶ What does it mean when a word has a green wavy underline?

A: A green wavy underline points to a possible grammar error.

❷ What's the easiest way to look up the correct spelling for a single word that has a red underline?

A: The easiest way to look up and correct a single word's spelling is to right-click it.

3 **What is a custom dictionary and how is it different from Word's main dictionary?**

A: A custom dictionary is one that holds the spelling additions you supply when you click the Add button during a spell check. In contrast, the Main dictionary is the unchangeable one that comes with Word.

4 **What is the difference between Ignore and Ignore All when checking spelling and grammar?**

A: Ignore bypasses a single instance; Ignore All bypasses all other instances for the current Word session.

5 **True or false: Word's grammar suggestions are almost always worth taking.**

A: False; do not rely on Word's grammar checker for sound grammar advice. It is wrong as often as it is correct.

6 **How do you prevent Word from showing red wavy underlines as you type?**

A: To turn off red wavy underlined, choose Tools ⇨ Options and click the Spelling and Grammar tab. Deselect the Check spelling as you type checkbox. Or, to turn them off for the current document only, select Hide spelling errors in this document.

7 **True or false: When using revision marks, added text appears in bold.**

A: False. When using revision marks, added text appears underlined, and a different color.

Visual Quiz

Q: **What command would you use to display this dialog box?**

A: To display this dialog box, click the Options button when spell-checking and then click the Settings button in the dialog box that appears.

Chapter 14

see page 206

1 **What kind of data can you enter in a cell?**

A: Text, numbers, images, and almost any other kind of data can be entered into cells.

2 **Should you use a specific format when you enter a date into a cell?**

A: When you enter a date, use a format that is standard in your geographic location.

3 **How can you quickly enter the current date in a cell?**

A: Press Ctrl+; to quickly enter the current date into a cell.

4 **Where is the Fill Handle located?**

A: The Fill Handle is a little square located in the lower right-hand corner of a selection.

5 **What happens if you select a cell with a date in it and then drag the Fill Handle down several rows?**

A: If you select a cell with a date in it and then drag the fill handle down several rows, dates will automatically be filled into the selected rows in ascending order.

6 **How do you specify a series to increase by an increment of 5?**

A: You can fill cells by a specific increment by choosing Series from the Fill context menu. Choose Trend to set the increment options.

7 **What is the quickest way to move back to the top of a worksheet?**

A: You can move back to the top of a worksheet instantly by clicking Ctrl+Home.

PERSONAL WORKBOOK ANSWERS

8 **How do you move to another worksheet within a workbook?**

A: Switch between worksheets in the workbook by clicking the appropriate worksheet tab at the bottom of the window.

9 **Can you select nonadjacent cells in a range? How?**

A: Select nonadjacent cells in a range by holding the Ctrl key as you click each one.

10 **If you want to refer to cells A1 through B7 in Sheet3, how should the reference look?**

A: A reference to cells A1 through B7 in Sheet3 would look like: Sheet3!A1:B7.

11 **How do you delete an entire row in a worksheet?**

A: To delete an entire row, right-click the row number and choose Delete.

Visual Quiz

Q: Cell C2 displays only a month and year, but in the formula bar a day is also given. Why is the day not displayed on the actual worksheet? How can this be changed? How was the series of dates created? What is the easiest way to create the series of numbers in column A?

A: The date formats for the cells in column C have been set to display only the month and year, even though the full date is recorded by Excel. You can change this using the Format menu. The easiest way to create a series, be it consecutive or not, is to drag the fill handle at the bottom right corner of selections. Columns and rows can be deleted by right-clicking the heading and choosing a delete option from the context menu. A cell reference to cells A2 through A11 would be A2:A11.

Chapter 15

see page 226

1 **Which character must precede any formula?**

A: The equal sign (=) should precede all formulas.

2 **In a formula, what is the order of arithmetic calculations?**

A: Excel calculates arithmetic functions from left to right, with multiplication and division performed before addition and subtraction.

3 **Do ranges used in formulas have to contain adjacent cells?**

A: A range used in a formula does not have to have adjacent cells.

4 **What is the quickest way to find the total of a column of numbers?**

A: You can quickly total a column of numbers using AutoSum.

5 **What does a dollar sign ($) in front of a column reference mean?**

A: A dollar sign in front of a reference indicates that it is absolute, and will not change even if the formula is copied to other cells.

6 **Do formulas change if you copy them to different cells?**

A: Relative formulas automatically change if they are copied to different cells.

7 **What is a function?**

A: A Function is a short keyword that tells Excel to perform a series of predetermined calculations.

8 What function lets you perform a logical test on a piece of data?

A: You can perform a logical test on data by using the IF function.

Visual Quiz

Q: What is the quickest way to display the column totals shown near the bottom? In the formula shown in the formula bar, what does the asterisk (*) mean? What does IF mean in that formula? Based on the information displayed in cell E4, is the result true or false?

A: The quickest way to total data in columns and rows is with AutoSum. In a formula, an asterisk takes the place of a times sign for multiplication. The IF function tests the data for certain criteria; based on what is shown here, it appears that the result was false.

Chapter 16

see page 246

1 How do you format a number so that it displays as currency?

A: Select the cell, right-click it and choose Format Cells. On the Numbers tab choose Currency.

2 Can you apply special formatting to text in worksheet cells?

A: You can apply almost any special formatting you want to text used in cells.

3 How do you align text so that it reads vertically in a cell rather than horizontally?

A: You can adjust the alignment of text in cells on the Alignment tab of the Format Cells dialog box.

4 What is the quickest way to change the width of a column?

A: You can quickly adjust the width of a column by clicking and dragging its border at the column heading.

5 Can you change the width of only one cell in a column?

A: If you adjust the size of a cell in a column, all other cells in that column must also change.

6 How is row height measured?

A: Row height is measured in Points. Standard cells are 12.75 points high.

7 What is a frozen pane?

A: A frozen pane is an area of cells that remain in view as you scroll around the worksheet.

8 How do you automatically apply formatting to a range of cells in a worksheet?

A: Select the cells you want to format and choose AutoFormat from the Format menu.

Visual Quiz

Q: How do you make the text in the heading appear as it does here? How do you make the numbers appear as dollar values? Why are rows 2 through 6 not shown? How was row 1 kept in view? Some AutoFormatting was applied to this worksheet; was the special formatting of the labels created before or after the AutoFormat feature was used?

A: Text can be made to appear like this by adjusting the Alignment settings in the Format Cells dialog box. Numbers will be shown as dollar values if they are formatted to display as currency. Rows 2 through 6 are out of view because row 1 was frozen. Special formatting in this worksheet had to be applied after AutoFormatting.

Personal Workbook Answers

Chapter 17

see page 262

❶ What must you do before starting the Chart Wizard?

A: Before starting the Chart Wizard, make sure you have selected a range of data you want to chart.

❷ What kind of data works best with a pie chart?

A: Data that is best expressed in percentages — such as budgets — are best illustrated with a pie chart.

❸ Why would a month-by-month record of expenses not work very well with a pie chart?

A: Pie charts don't work well with monthly expense reports because the actual percentages in that example are not very important. Data that suggests a trend in expenses is better expressed with a line chart.

❹ What will happen to your chart if you update the data on the worksheet?

A: Charts are automatically updated when you modify the data.

❺ How do you change the text of a chart title?

A: You can change a chart title by clicking it and typing new text.

❻ Can you use an Excel chart in a Word document? How?

A: You can use an Excel chart in Word by copying, linking, or embedding it.

❼ How do you move chart objects around on your worksheet?

A: To move a chart object, click it once and hold the left mouse button. When the pointer changes to four arrows, click and drag the chart.

❽ Can the size of a chart be modified?

A: You can modify the size of a chart with the manipulation handles, just as you would a graphic object.

Visual Quiz

Q: What kind of chart is the round one? What do the different colored areas represent? How do you move a chart like this so that it's not in the way? How do you change the style of chart being used? Can you change the data labels on the round chart? How?

A: The round chart shown here is a pie chart. Different colored areas in the pie chart indicate different pieces of data. Charts can be moved and resized like other graphics objects by using the manipulation handles on the sides of the object. You can change a chart type by choosing Chart Type from the context menu after right-clicking the chart. Labels and legends can also be modified through the use of context menu items.

Chapter 18

see page 280

❶ What are the two kinds of templates you can use to create a presentation and how are they different?

A: The two kinds of templates are Presentation templates, which include both sample text and formatting, and Presentation Design templates, which include only formatting.

❷ Once you've started a presentation in a particular template, how do you pick up a design (colors, background, and so on) from a different template?

A: To copy a design from another template, use Format ➪ Apply Design.

PERSONAL WORKBOOK ANSWERS

3 After you close the PowerPoint dialog box that appears when you start the program, how do you open it again?

A: The only way to reopen the PowerPoint dialog box that appears when you start the program is to close and reopen the program.

4 Which view is best for editing slide text?

A: Outline view is best for editing text.

5 There are three ways to place a graph on a slide. Name two of them.

A: The three ways to place a graph on a slide are: 1) to use a layout that includes a placeholder for a graph, 2) to place a graph with Insert ⇨ Chart command, or 3) to copy and paste one from an Excel workbook.

6 True or false: To move a picture, drag one of its selection handles.

A: False. Dragging selection handles resizes an object; dragging it by any other area moves it.

7 True or false: The New button on the toolbar inserts a new slide in your presentation.

A: False. The New button on the toolbar starts a whole new presentation file.

8 What is the difference between a layout and a design?

A: A design picks up a formatting scheme from another template and applies it to all slides in the presntation; a layout rearranges placeholder frames on a single slide.

Visual Quiz

Q: This slide uses a very dark color scheme. What kinds of presentations would it be good for? What would it not be appropriate for?

A: A dark color scheme like this would be appropriate for an onscreen show or a 35mm slide show. It would not be appropriate for use as an overhead transparency or as a printout.

Chapter 19

see page 294

1 Why would you want to edit the Slide Master?

A: If you want to make a change that affects every slide in the presentation, edit the Slide Master.

2 How do you get out of the Slide Master and back to your regular presentation editing?

A: To exit the Slide Master, click the floating Close button.

3 Name two ways to delete a slide from a presentation.

A: To delete a slide, select it in Slide Sorter view and press the Delete key, or in any view select it and choose Edit ⇨ Delete Slide.

4 What is the difference between transitions and animations?

A: Transitions affect entire slides, while animations affect objects on slides.

5 True or false: You can animate only bulleted text with preset animations.

A: True: Preset animations are only for bulleted text. To animate other objects, use Custom Animation.

6 True or false: To associate a sound with a transition, use the Insert ⇨ Movies and Sounds command.

A False: To associate a sound with a transition, choose a sound from the Slide Transition dialog box.

7 How do you jump to a specific slide during a presentation?

A: Right-click and choose Go To to jump to a specific slide.

Personal Workbook Answers

Visual Quiz

Q: What are two ways you could run your slide show from here?

A: Any of these: Choose Slide Show ⇨ View Show; choose View ⇨ Slide Show, or click the Slide Show View icon.

Chapter 20

see page 312

❶ Describe two ways of opening a window and creating a new message?

A: You can begin creating a new message by clicking the New Message button on the toolbar, or press Ctrl+N.

❷ Can you apply special formatting to text in a message?

A: You can apply some special formatting to message text, such as boldface and coloring.

❸ Will all message recipients be able to see that formatting?

A: Many message recipients will not be able to read special formatting in an e-mail message.

❹ Where does the address for the primary recipient go?

A: The address for the primary recipient goes in the To: field.

❺ How do you send a copy of the message to additional recipients?

A: You can copy a message to someone by including them in the Cc: field.

❻ How do you send a "secret" copy to another recipient?

A: Secret copies can be sent by using the Bcc: field.

❼ What kind of files can be attached to an e-mail?

A: You can attach almost any kind of file you want to an e-mail message.

❽ How do you unsend a message?

A: Once you have sent a message, it cannot be "unsent."

❾ How do you check for new messages?

A: Check for new messages by clicking Tools ⇨ Check for New Mail on the menu bar.

❿ How do you know if a message in your Inbox is new?

A: New messages are listed in boldface in your Inbox.

Visual Quiz

Q: How do you open a window to create this message? How were the addresses entered in the To:, Cc:, and Bcc: fields? What does Bcc: mean? What does the icon at the bottom of the page called "SHistory.rtf" represent? How did it get there? How can you send this message?

A: Click the New Message button in Outlook to open a new message window. Addresses can be entered in several ways, but the easiest is to click the To:, Cc:, and Bcc: buttons and choose people from your address book. Bcc: stands for "Blind Carbon Copy" and means that other recipients will not know about that person receiving it. The message shown here has an attached file, evidenced by the Shistory.rtf icon near the bottom of the window. Send this message by simply clicking Send on the toolbar.

PERSONAL WORKBOOK ANSWERS

Chapter 21

see page 326

1 **What kind of information is stored in Contacts?**

A: Contacts stores addresses and phone numbers for the people and businesses you need to keep in touch with.

2 **How can categories help you better organize your contacts?**

A: Categories can help you better organize your Contacts because they enable you to sort into logical groups.

3 **What is one way to change the view of the Contact list?**

A: You can modify the Contact List view by changing which fields are displayed. You can also have them displayed by category, or in a more basic list format.

4 **How do you add an event to your calendar?**

A: Add an event to your calendar by clicking a time slot and typing an entry.

5 **Other than placing a note in your calendar, what can the Meeting Planner do for you?**

A: The Meeting Planner places a note in your calendar, and can also send notification messages to attendees and give you a reminder just beforehand.

6 **How do you add something to your task list?**

A: You can create a new task by clicking the New Task button on the toolbar, or by pressing Ctrl+Shift+K.

7 **What should you do when a task has been completed?**

A: You should place a checkmark next to all tasks that have been completed.

8 **What kind of things are recorded in the Outlook journal automatically?**

A: The Outlook journal tracks Outlook usage along with other Office programs. It tells you who used what, when they used it, and for how long.

Visual Quiz

Q: **How do you open the section of Outlook shown here? Why are there seven days shown in the middle instead of just one? How do you get four months to display in the upper right frame rather than just two? What do the bold numbers on the calendar indicate? What does the check mark next to the last task indicate? How do you schedule a meeting from this window?**

A: You can open the Calendar by clicking Calendar on the Outlook bar on the left side of the window. The middle of the calendar can be set to show just one day, seven, or more. To view more months of the calendar here, drag the border for the month area to provide more space. Bold numbers on the calendar indicate an appointment on that day. Tasks with a check mark have been completed. To schedule a new meeting, click the drop-down arrow on the far left of the toolbar and choose New Meeting.

Chapter 22

see page 342

1 **How do you delete a message in Outlook?**

A: You can delete a message by selecting it in the Inbox and pressing Delete on the toolbar.

2 **How do you delete a Contact card?**

A: Delete an old contact by selecting it and clicking Delete on the toolbar.

PERSONAL WORKBOOK ANSWERS

3 **How do you create a new folder in Outlook?**

A: To create a folder in Outlook, right-click a folder in the Inbox and choose Create Subfolder from the context menu.

4 **Where should you create new folders for your Outlook messages?**

A: Subfolders for Outlook messages should be created within the Inbox itself.

5 **How do you move a message into another folder?**

A: You can move a message to a new folder by right-clicking it in the Inbox and choosing Move from the context menu.

6 **When should you create a new folder?**

A: You should create a new folder whenever you want a group of e-mails to be in a separate folder. You can create as many folders as you need.

7 **Can you move appointments from your Calendar into a different folder?**

A: Calendar items and tasks cannot be moved within Outlook.

8 **How do you send a fax?**

A: You send a fax by selecting Actions ⇨ Send New Fax, filling in the address, subject, and message, and then clicking Send.

Visual Quiz

Q: This message is currently stored in a folder called Office 97 stuff. How was this folder created? How did the message get here? How can the message be deleted? Can it be restored? How?

A: You can create new folders for mail by clicking File ⇨ New ⇨ Folder within the correct folder. To move a message in Outlook, right-click it and choose Move from the context menu. You will then see a brief dialog box listing folders that you can choose from. To delete a message, select it and click Delete on the Outlook toolbar. To restore it, visit the Deleted Items folder and move the item back to the folder where you want it.

Chapter 23

see page 356

1 **Which Access database component holds your data?**

A: The Access database component that holds your data is called a table.

2 **What do you call the view that shows your Access data in a spreadsheet-like format?**

A: The view that shows your Access data in a spreadsheet-like format is called the Datasheet view.

3 **What are the two types of databases?**

A: The two types of databases are known as flat-file and relational databases.

4 **What type of Access database field automatically increments when you add a new record?**

A: The Access AutoNumber database field type automatically increments when you add a new record.

5 **What one thing do you need in order to create a relationship between two tables?**

A: You need a field that contains the same type of data in both tables in order to create a relationship between two tables.

6 **What two things must you enter to add a new field to an Access database table?**

A: You must enter both a field name and a data type to add a new field to an Access database table.

PERSONAL WORKBOOK ANSWERS

Visual Quiz

Q: What is the purpose of this dialog box? How can you display this dialog box?

A: The dialog box is used to select one of the database wizards. Select File ⇨ New Database to display the dialog box.

Chapter 24

see page 368

① How is the view of your data different in a form than in a table?

A: The view of your data is different in a form than in a table because a form typically shows one complete record rather than several partial records.

② Is it possible for a form to show multiple records?

A: A form can show multiple records from a detail table if the form is based on a master table.

③ What important step is necessary before Access will show you a list of fields you can use on a form?

A: Before Access will show you a list of fields you can use on a form you must choose the table that will be the data source.

④ How many of a table's fields must you include on a form?

A: You only need to include one field on a form no matter how many fields there are in the underlying table. You don't need to include all of the fields in the table.

⑤ What can you do if your report won't fit the width of your paper?

A: If your report won't fit the width of your paper you may be able to make it fit by changing to landscape orientation, by adjusting the margins, by rearranging the field layout, or by eliminating fields you don't really need.

⑥ What happens if you don't specify a sort order for your reports?

A: If you don't specify a sort order for your reports, the printed report will use the same sort order as the table upon which the report is based.

⑦ What happens if you specify a sort on a field where some records are blank?

A: If you specify a sort on a field where some records are blank, those records will appear at the beginning of the sort if you choose ascending sort order, or at the end of the list if you choose descending sort order.

⑧ What property do you have to set to prevent a record from starting on one page and finishing on the next?

A: You have to set the detail section Keep Together property to prevent a record from starting on one page and finishing on the next.

Visual Quiz

Q: What is the purpose of the dialog box titled Toolbox? How can you display this dialog box? What do you need to do to make the associated report area appear in the design window?

A: The dialog box enables you to set the properties for the report footer. Select View ⇨ Report Header/Footer to display the footer and then right-click the footer and select Properties to display the dialog box.

Chapter 25

see page 384

① How many database fields can you use to select records when you use the Filter By Selection option?

A: You can only use the database field to select records when you use the Filter By Selection option.

PERSONAL WORKBOOK ANSWERS

② **What do you need to remember when you specify criteria for selecting a Boolean field?**

A: When you specify criteria for selecting a Boolean field you need to remember that Boolean fields do not contain text values, so your selection formula should not use quotation marks.

③ **How can you further narrow the subset of records after you've used the Filter By Selection option?**

A: You can further narrow the subset of records after you've used the Filter By Selection option by selecting another field to select records.

④ **What are joined tables?**

A: Joined tables are database tables that are related by having a field that holds the same type of data.

⑤ **What is the one thing you must do before you can show data from more than one table in query results?**

A: Before you can show data from more than one table in query results you must make certain the tables are joined.

⑥ **How can you use a field to select records in a query without showing that field's values in the results?**

A: You can use a field to select records in a query without showing that field's values in the results by making certain the Show checkbox for the field is not checked.

⑦ **What method can you use to create multiple queries that you can update by changing one formula?**

A: You can create multiple queries that you can update by changing one formula by basing each of the queries in part on a simple query that selects the field value you want to use when updating the queries.

⑧ **How do you control the order of precedence when you use multiple fields to sort your data?**

A: You control the order of precedence when you use multiple fields to sort your data by placing the most important sort fields to the left of the less important sort fields.

⑨ **How can you make fields appear earlier in the query results without affecting the sort order?**

A: You can make fields appear earlier in the query results without affecting the sort order by not sorting on those fields.

Visual Quiz

Q: **What is the purpose of this dialog box? How can you display this dialog box? What do you need to do to add additional tables to the view?**

A: This dialog box enables you to create a new query so you can select specific records. Click the New button on the Query tab to display the dialog box. Select Query ➪ Show Table to add a new table to the query.

Index

Symbols

! (exclamation mark), 220
$ (dollar sign), 234
% (percent sign), 228
* (asterisk), 228
<= (less than or equal to sign), 236, 242
+ (plus sign), 228
- (minus sign), 228
/ (slash), 228
= (equal sign), 228, 230, 240
>= (greater than or equal to sign), 236, 242
<> (not equal to sign), 236, 242
@ (at symbol), 318
^ (caret), 228
> (greater than sign), 236, 242
... (ellipsis), 8

A

Access, *See also* databases; forms; reports
    enhancements for, 360
    files in, 358
    online help for, 362
Accounting Advisers, 272
Action Settings dialog box, 304
add-ins
    for Excel, 242, 250
    for Office, 28
    for Outlook, 344, 350
addition, AutoSum and, 230
addition operator (+), 228

address books, *See also* Contact list
    accessing for merges, 172, 173
    adding names to, 318, 319
    addressing e-mail messages using, 318–319
    as mail merge data sources, 164, 165
    importing and exporting address files and, 318
addresses
    e-mail, 318–319
    Internet, 90
alignment
    converting documents to HTML and, 116
    for reports, 374
    of paragraphs, 116, 117
    of text and numbers in worksheets, 250–251
animation
    in presentations, 302–303
    of numbers in numbered lists, 148–149
annotating, of Help System, 28
Apply Design command, 282
Apply Design dialog box, 290, 291
Appointment dialog box, 334
appointments, scheduling, *See* Calendar
archiving files, on diskettes, 44
arithmetic operators, 228
Arrow and Pen command, 306
ASCII text, 50
at symbol (@), in e-mail addresses, 318
attachments, to e-mail messages, 320–321
attributes, of text, 114, 115
AutoContent Wizard, 282
AutoCorrect, 106–107
    creating entries for, 106
    spell checking and, 192
AutoCorrect dialog box, 106, 107
AutoFormat
    for tables, 152
    in Excel, 258–259
    in Word, 122–123

Index

continued

Index

Index

Index

INDEX

INDEX